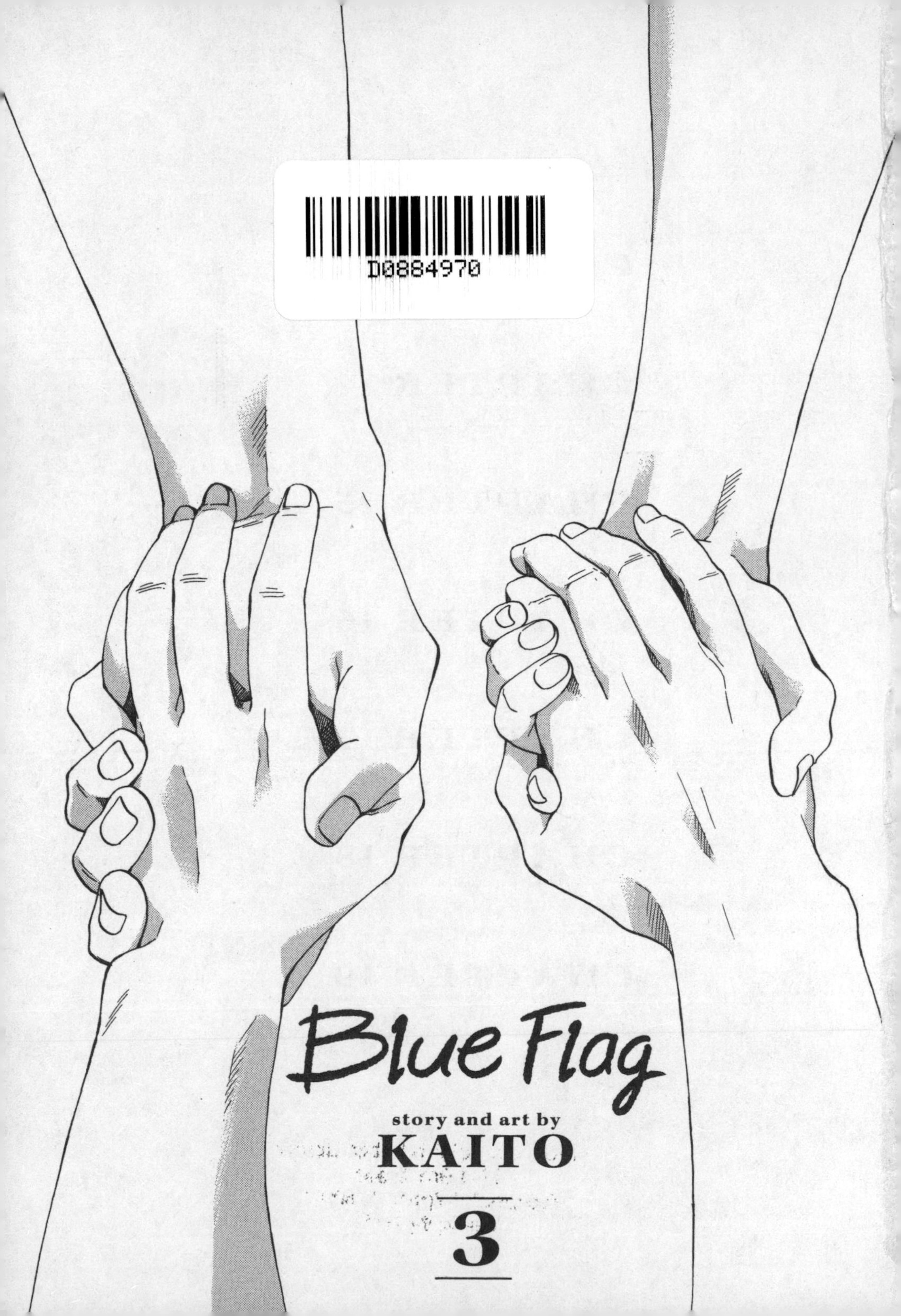

Blue Flag

story and art by

KAITO

3

CHAPTER 13

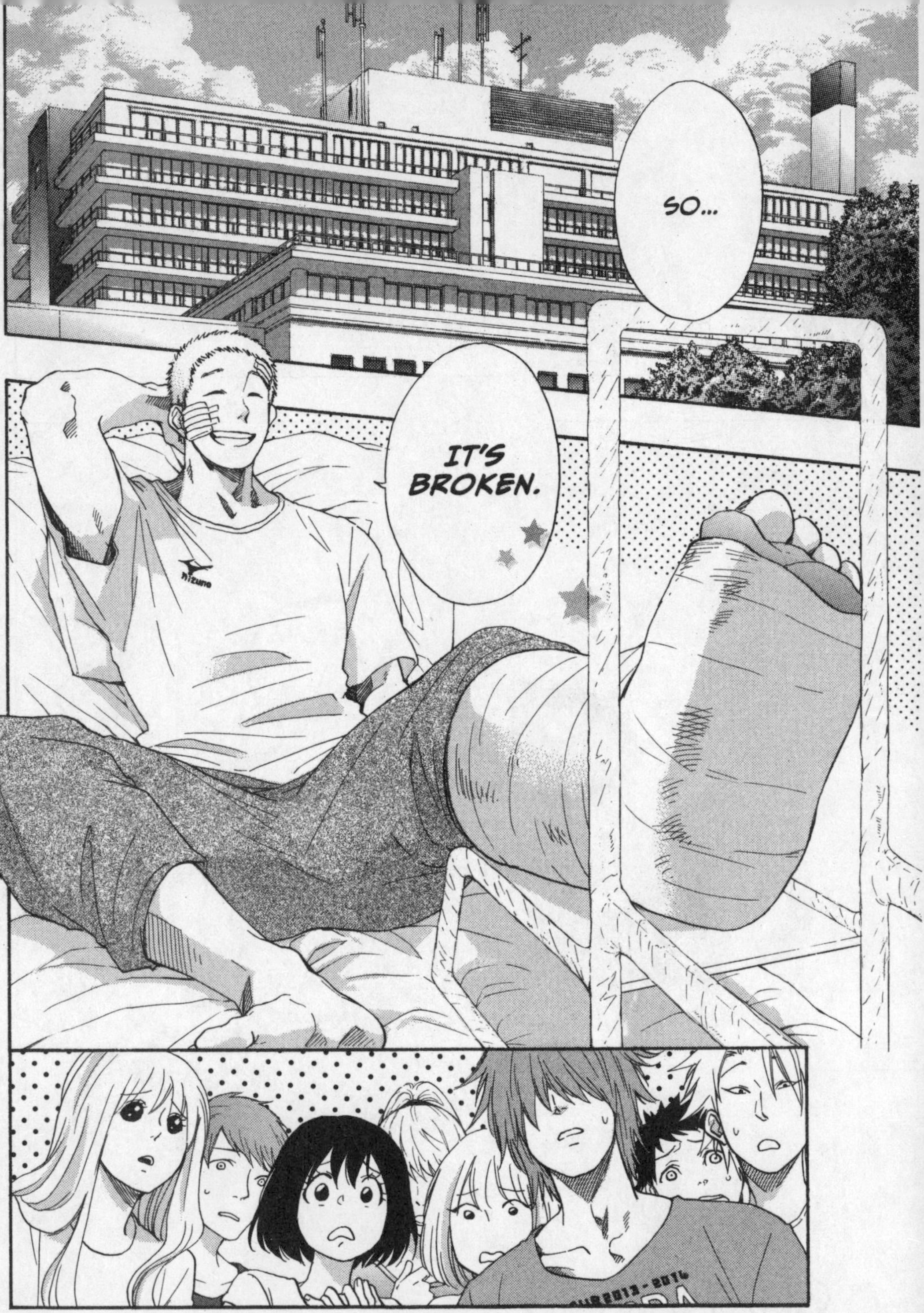
SO...
IT'S BROKEN.

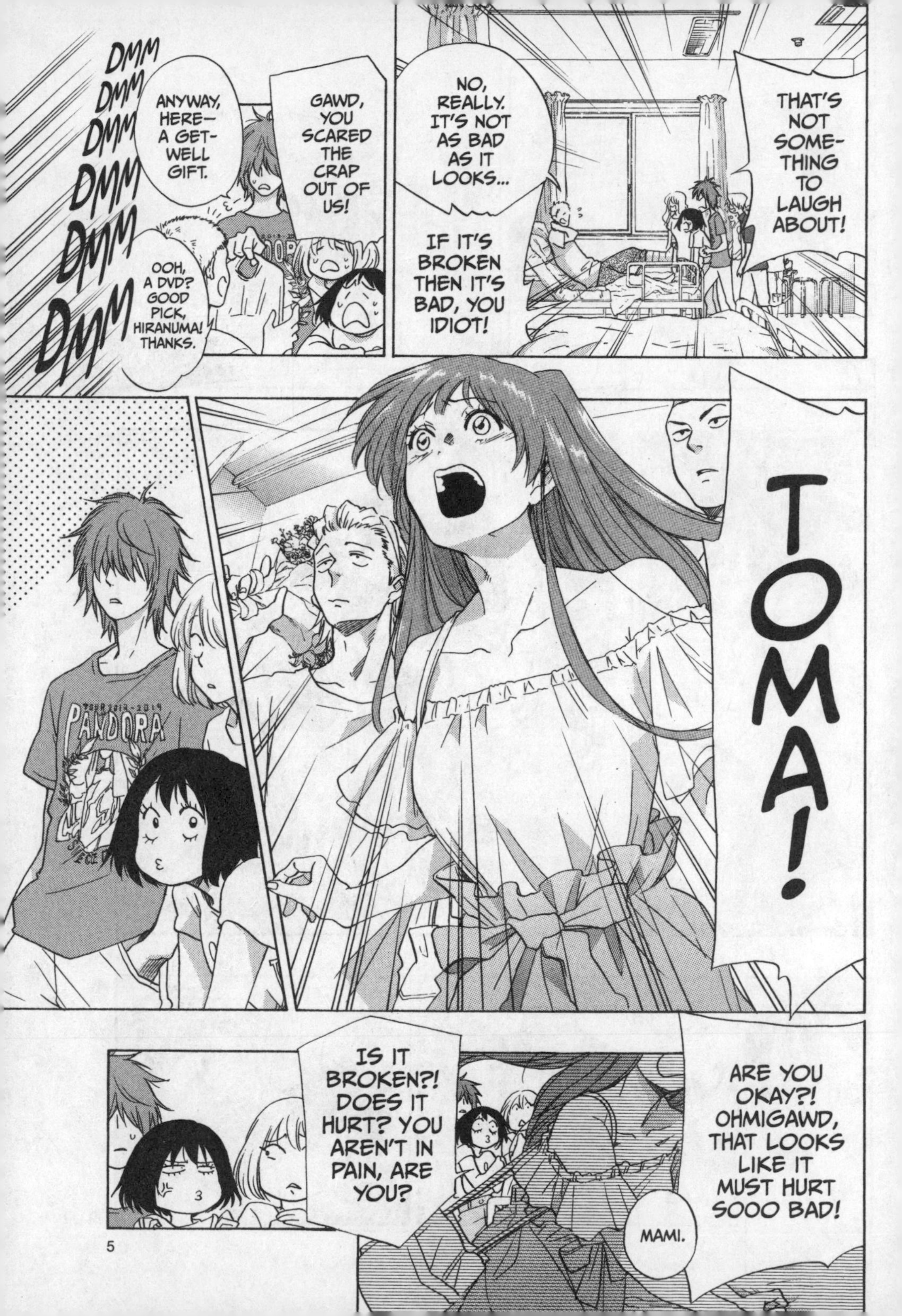
THAT'S NOT SOMETHING TO LAUGH ABOUT!
NO, REALLY. IT'S NOT AS BAD AS IT LOOKS...
IF IT'S BROKEN THEN IT'S BAD, YOU IDIOT!
GAWD, YOU SCARED THE CRAP OUT OF US!
ANYWAY, HERE— A GET-WELL GIFT.
OOH, A DVD? GOOD PICK, HIRANUMA! THANKS.
DMM DMM DMM DMM DMM DMM
TOMA!
PANDORA
ARE YOU OKAY?! OHMIGAWD, THAT LOOKS LIKE IT MUST HURT SOOO BAD!
MAMI.
IS IT BROKEN?! DOES IT HURT? YOU AREN'T IN PAIN, ARE YOU?

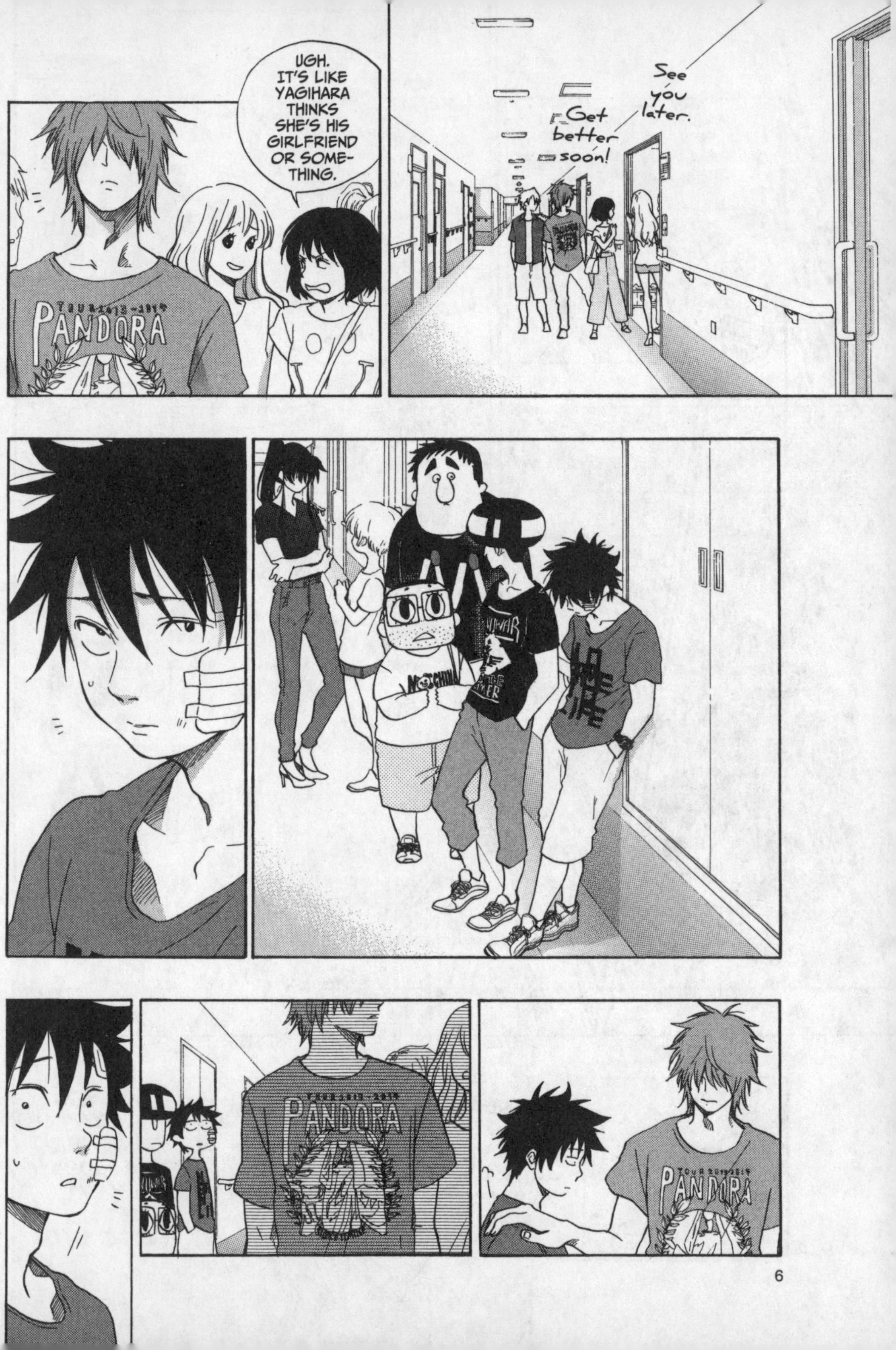

See you later.
Get better soon!
UGH. IT'S LIKE YAGIHARA THINKS SHE'S HIS GIRLFRIEND OR SOME-THING.

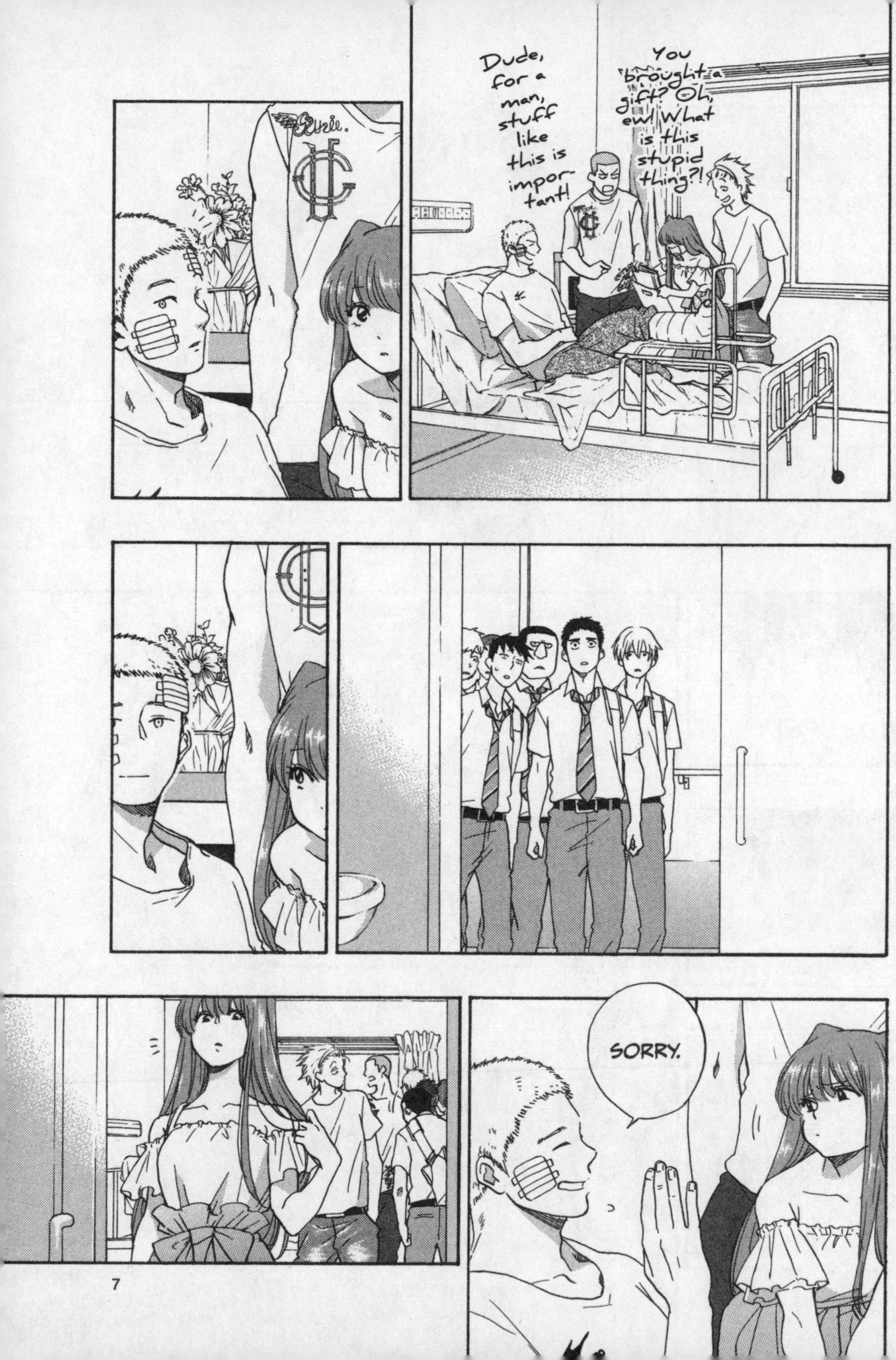
You brought a gift? Oh, ew! What is this stupid thing?!
Dude, for a man, stuff like this is important!
SORRY.

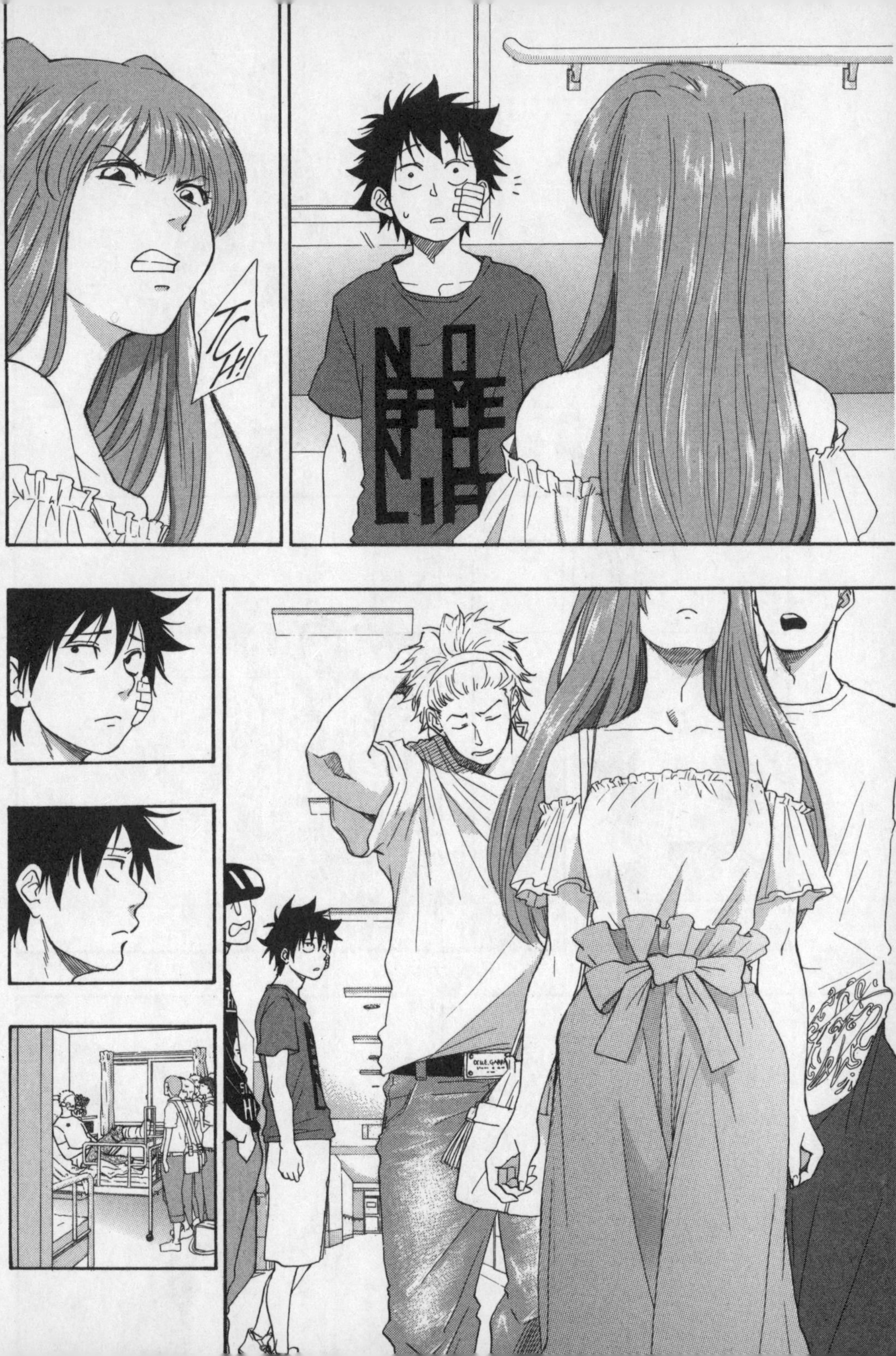
TCH!

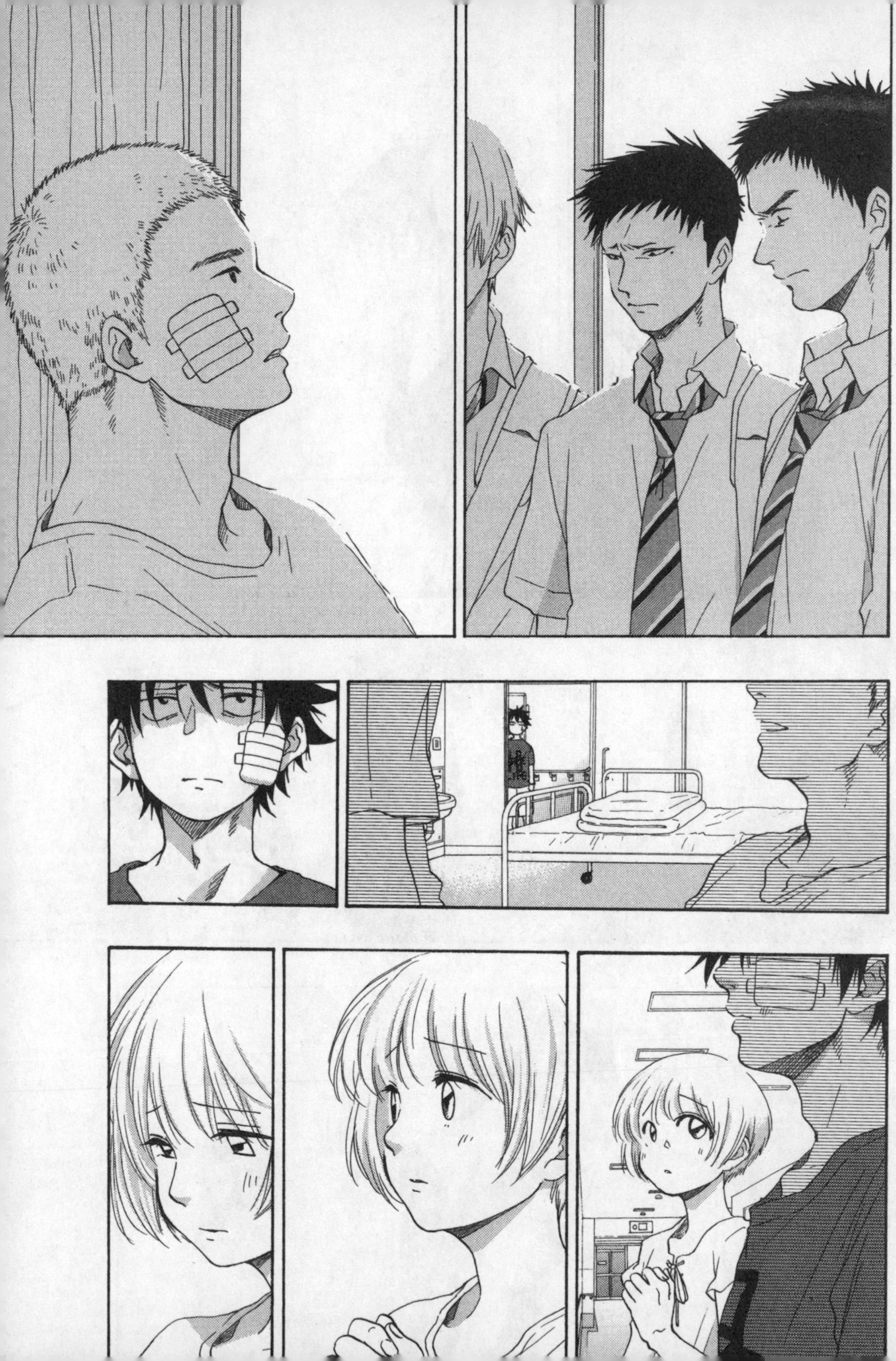

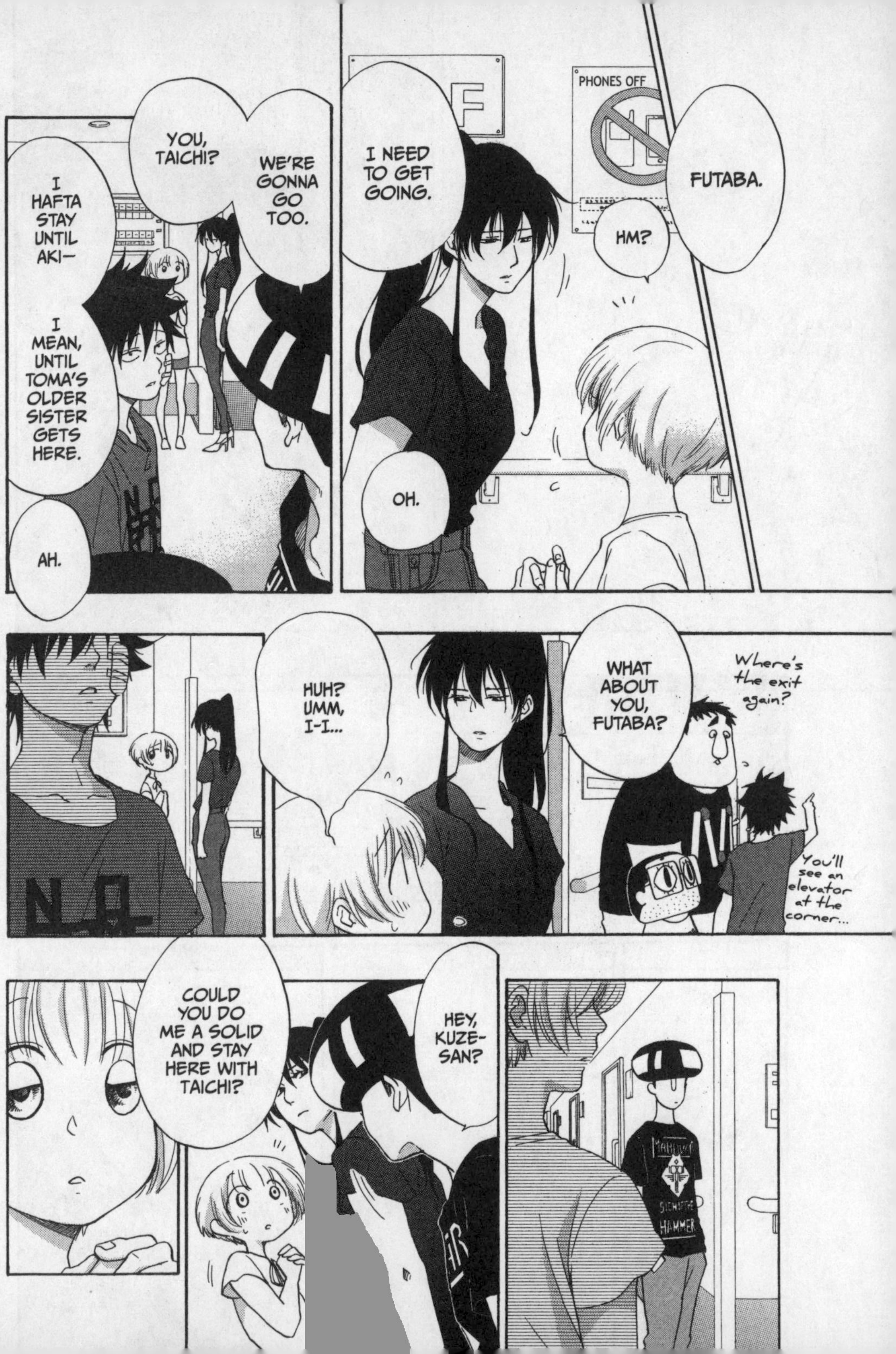
PHONES OFF
FUTABA.
HM?
I NEED TO GET GOING.
OH.
WE'RE GONNA GO TOO.
YOU, TAICHI?
I HAFTA STAY UNTIL AKI—
I MEAN, UNTIL TOMA'S OLDER SISTER GETS HERE.
AH.
Where's the exit again?
You'll see an elevator at the corner...
WHAT ABOUT YOU, FUTABA?
HUH? UMM, I-I...
HEY, KUZE-SAN?
COULD YOU DO ME A SOLID AND STAY HERE WITH TAICHI?

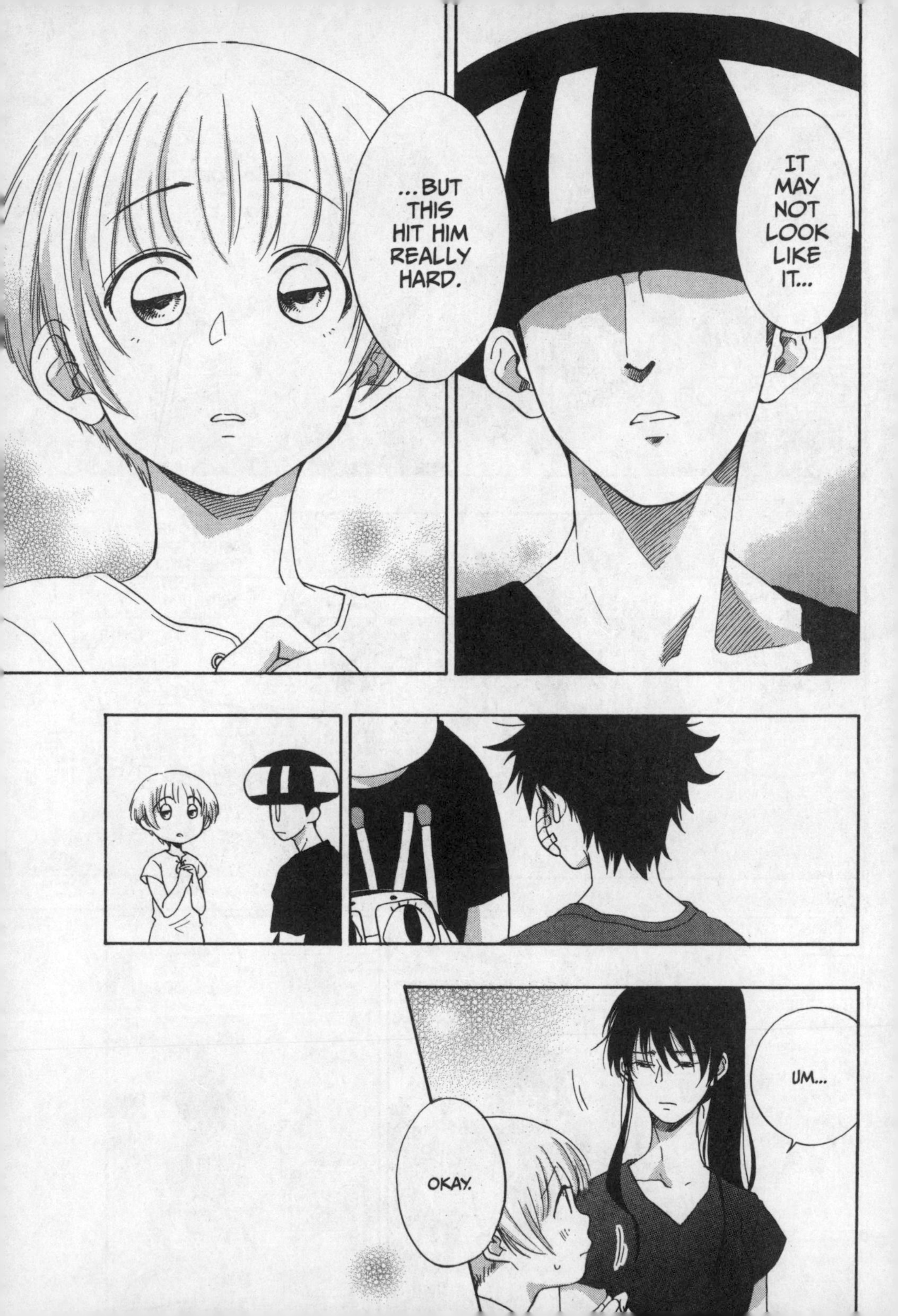
IT MAY NOT LOOK LIKE IT...
...BUT THIS HIT HIM REALLY HARD.
UM...
OKAY.

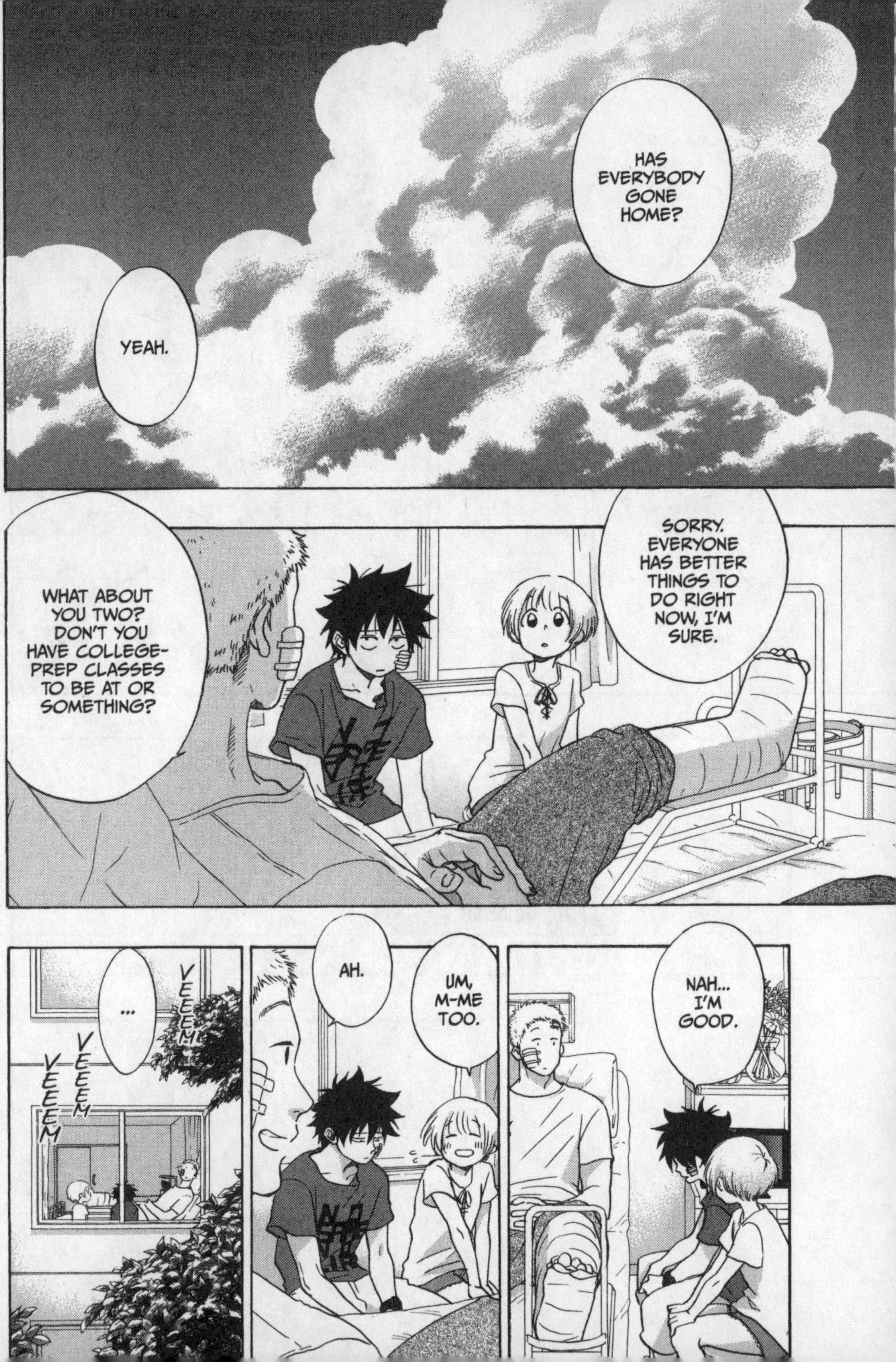
HAS EVERYBODY GONE HOME?
YEAH.
SORRY. EVERYONE HAS BETTER THINGS TO DO RIGHT NOW, I'M SURE.
WHAT ABOUT YOU TWO? DON'T YOU HAVE COLLEGE-PREP CLASSES TO BE AT OR SOMETHING?
NAH... I'M GOOD.
UM, M-ME TOO.
AH.
VEEEEM
...
VEEEM
VEEEEM

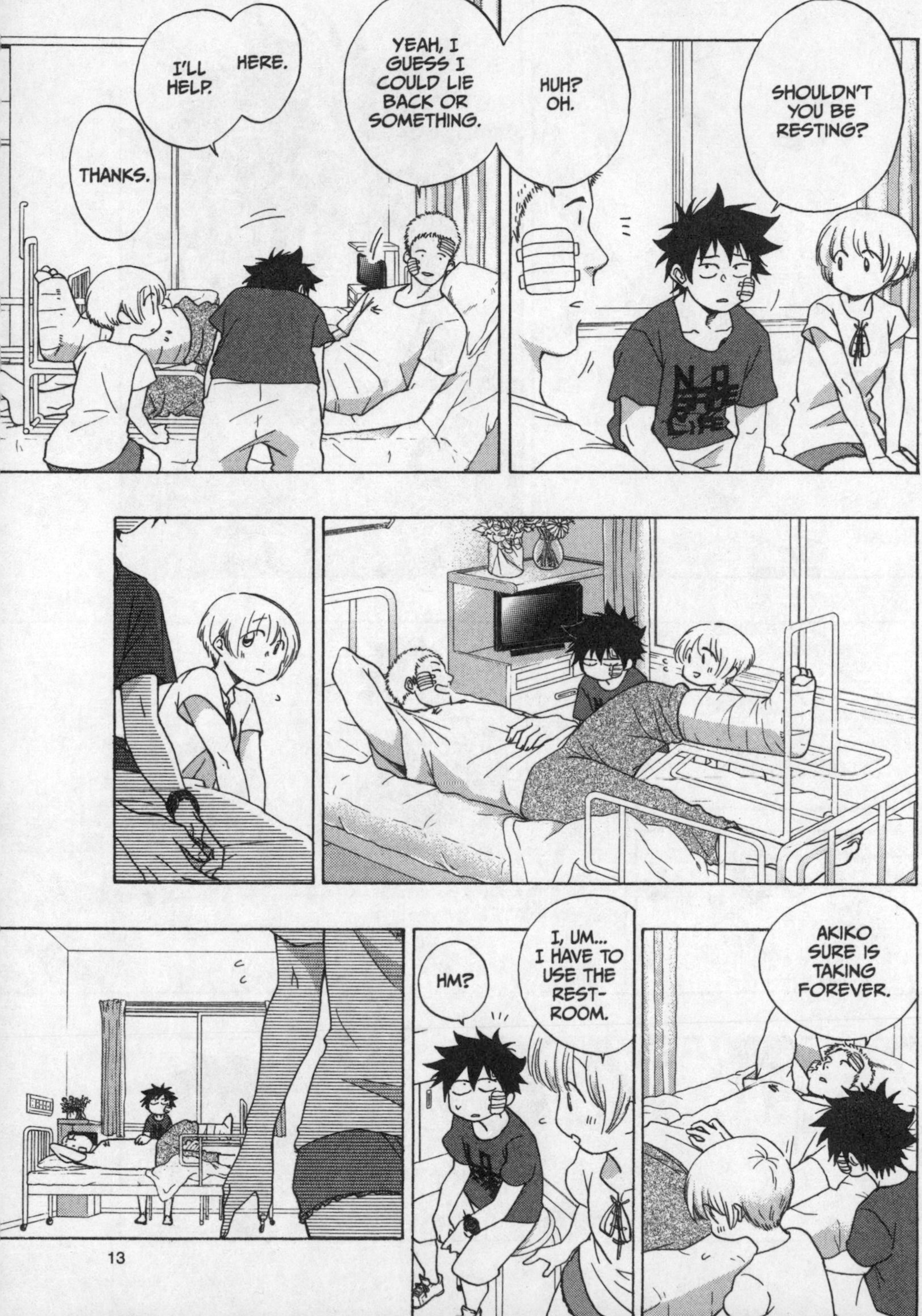
SHOULDN'T YOU BE RESTING?
HUH? OH.
YEAH, I GUESS I COULD LIE BACK OR SOMETHING.
HERE.
I'LL HELP.
THANKS.
AKIKO SURE IS TAKING FOREVER.
I, UM... I HAVE TO USE THE REST-ROOM.
HM?

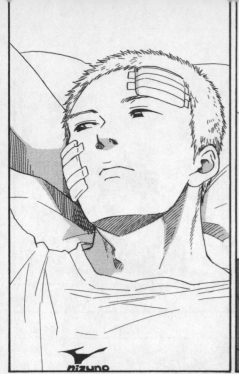

...

YOUR FACE.

TAI-CHAN.

SORRY.

THIS LITTLE THING? IT'S—

YOU OKAY?

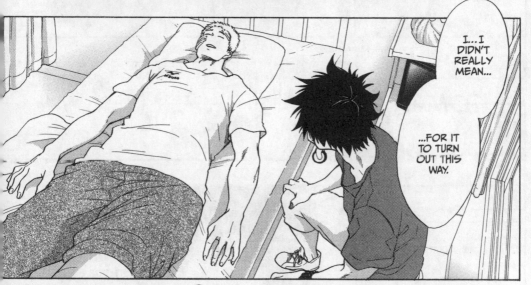

I...I DIDN'T REALLY MEAN...

...FOR IT TO TURN OUT THIS WAY.

WHAT?

WHY ARE YOU APOLOGIZ-ING?

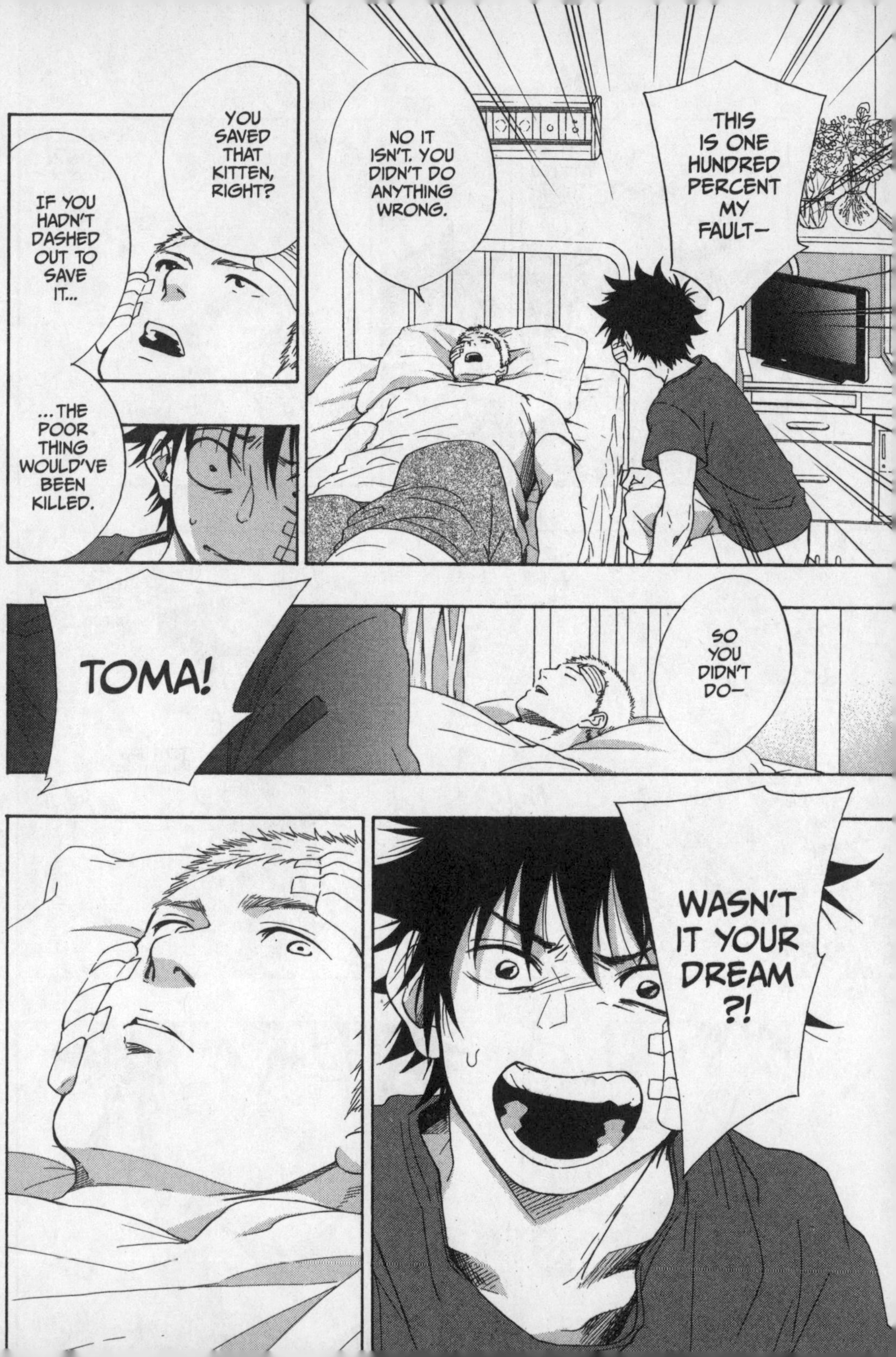
THIS IS ONE HUNDRED PERCENT MY FAULT—
NO IT ISN'T. YOU DIDN'T DO ANYTHING WRONG.
YOU SAVED THAT KITTEN, RIGHT?
IF YOU HADN'T DASHED OUT TO SAVE IT...
...THE POOR THING WOULD'VE BEEN KILLED.
SO YOU DIDN'T DO—
TOMA!
WASN'T IT YOUR DREAM ?!

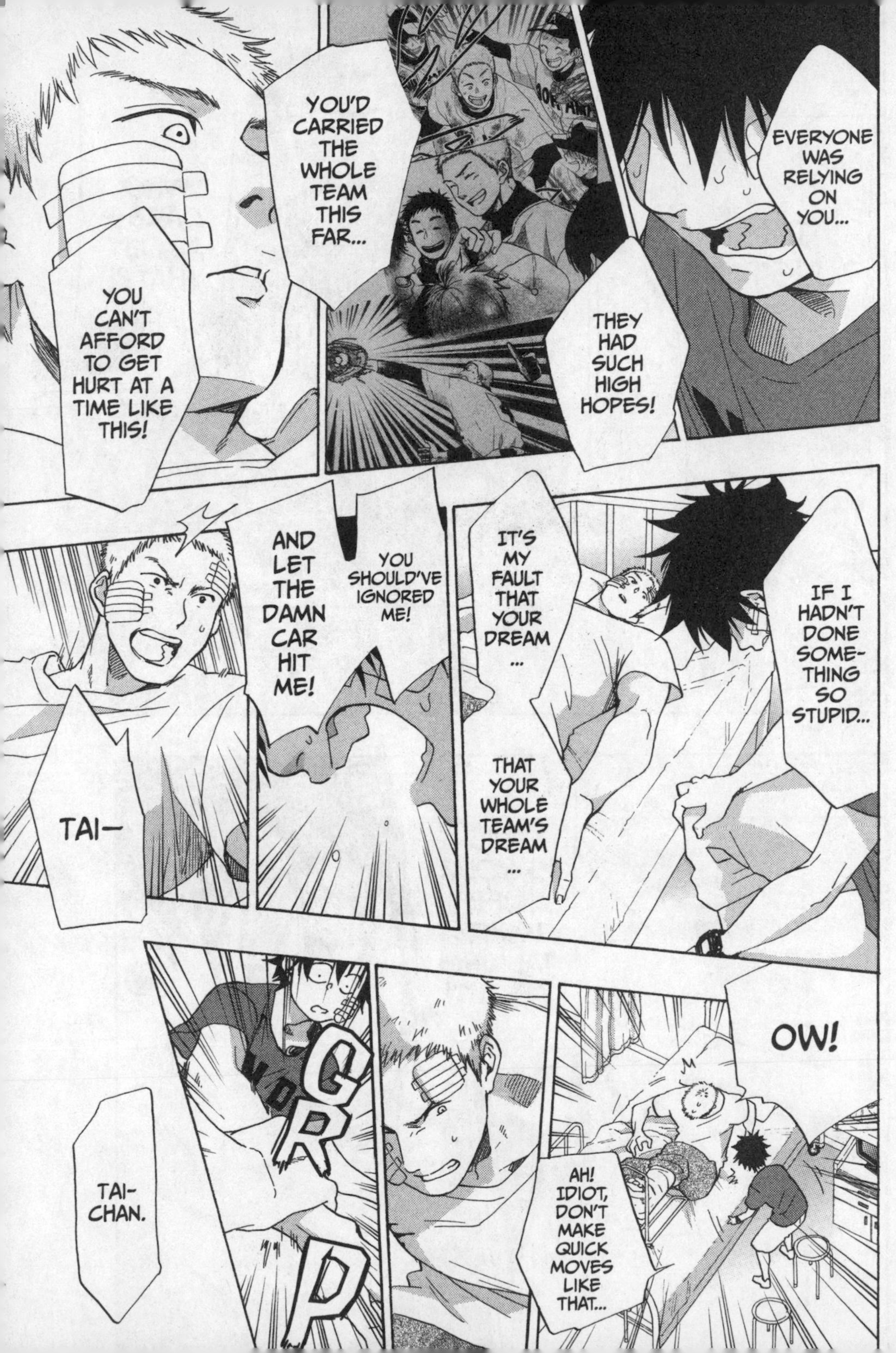
EVERYONE WAS RELYING ON YOU...
THEY HAD SUCH HIGH HOPES!
YOU'D CARRIED THE WHOLE TEAM THIS FAR...
YOU CAN'T AFFORD TO GET HURT AT A TIME LIKE THIS!
IF I HADN'T DONE SOMETHING SO STUPID...
IT'S MY FAULT THAT YOUR DREAM ...
THAT YOUR WHOLE TEAM'S DREAM ...
YOU SHOULD'VE IGNORED ME!
AND LET THE DAMN CAR HIT ME!
TAI—
OW!
AH! IDIOT, DON'T MAKE QUICK MOVES LIKE THAT...
GRP
TAI-CHAN.

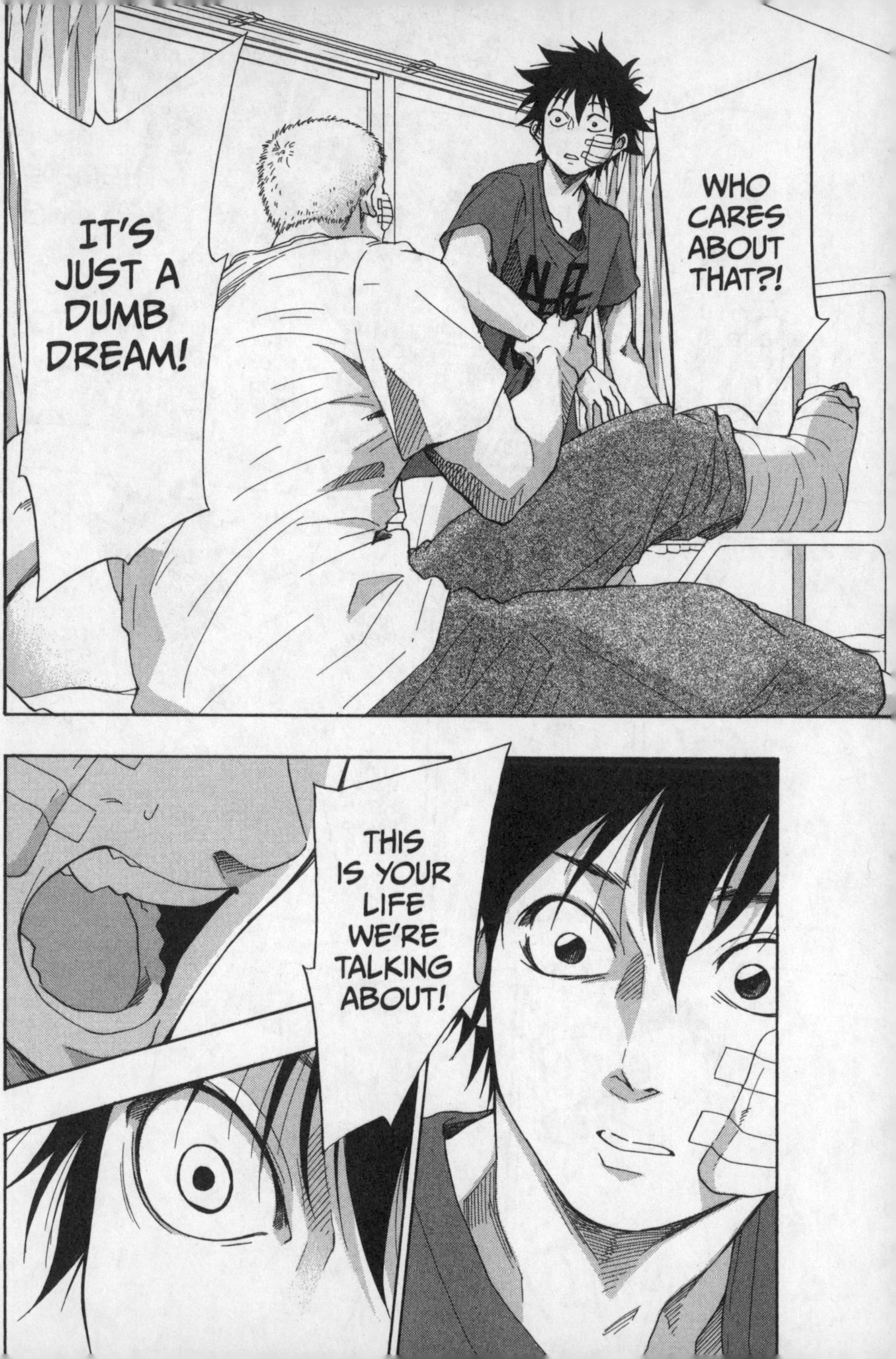
WHO CARES ABOUT THAT?!
IT'S JUST A DUMB DREAM!
THIS IS YOUR LIFE WE'RE TALKING ABOUT!

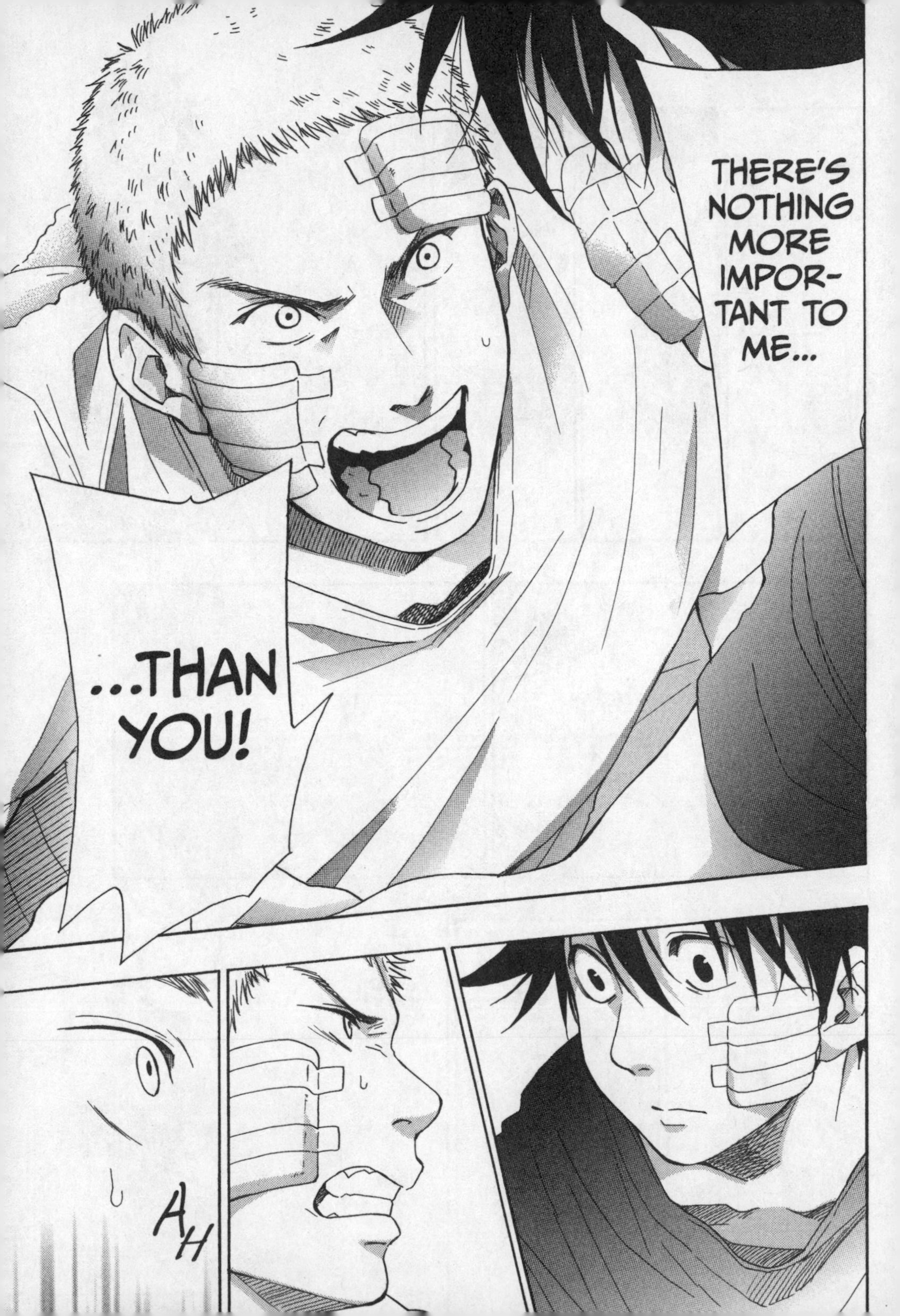
THERE'S NOTHING MORE IMPOR-TANT TO ME...
...THAN YOU!
AH

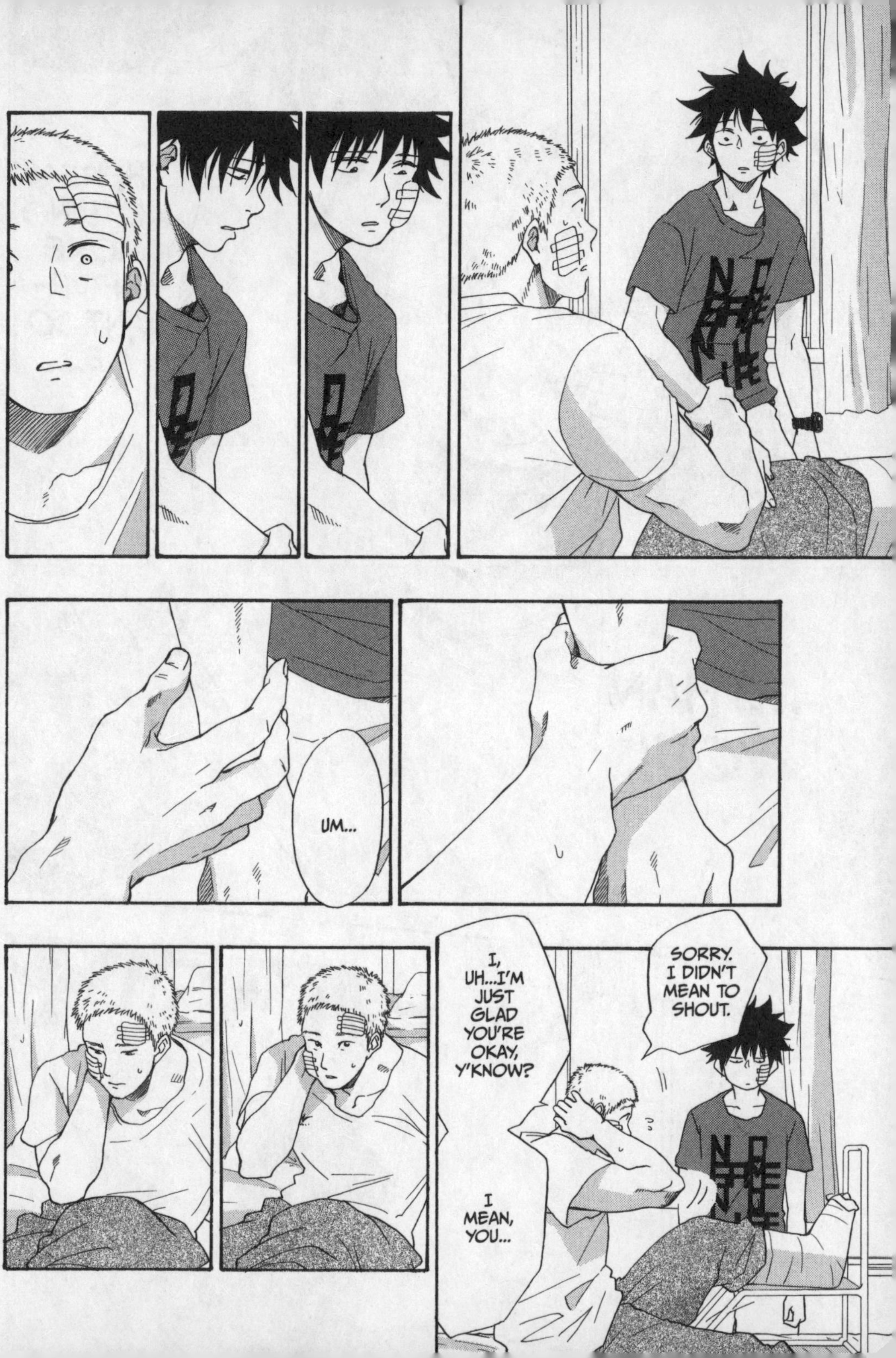
UM...
SORRY. I DIDN'T MEAN TO SHOUT.
I, UH...I'M JUST GLAD YOU'RE OKAY, Y'KNOW?
I MEAN, YOU...

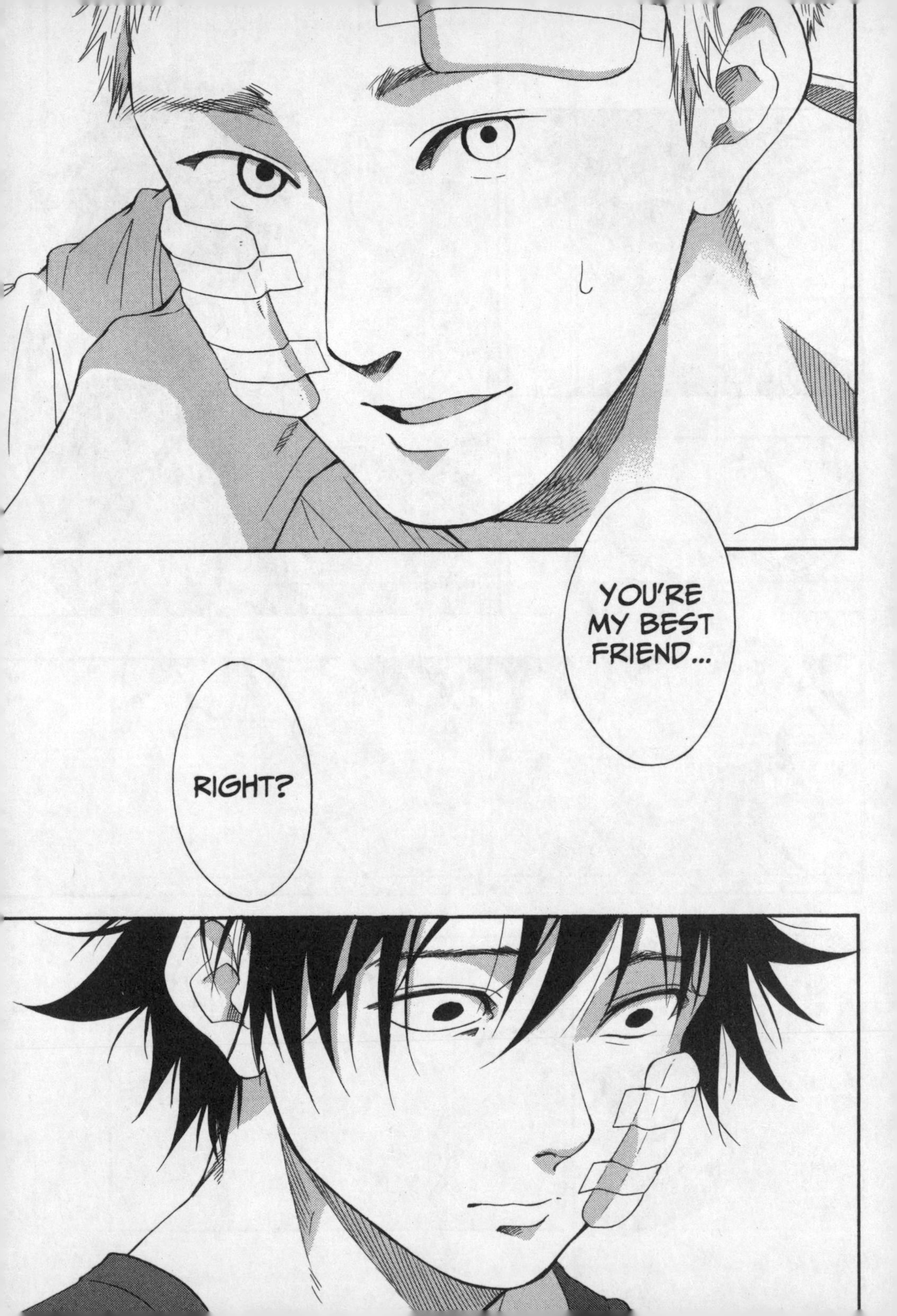
YOU'RE MY BEST FRIEND...
RIGHT?

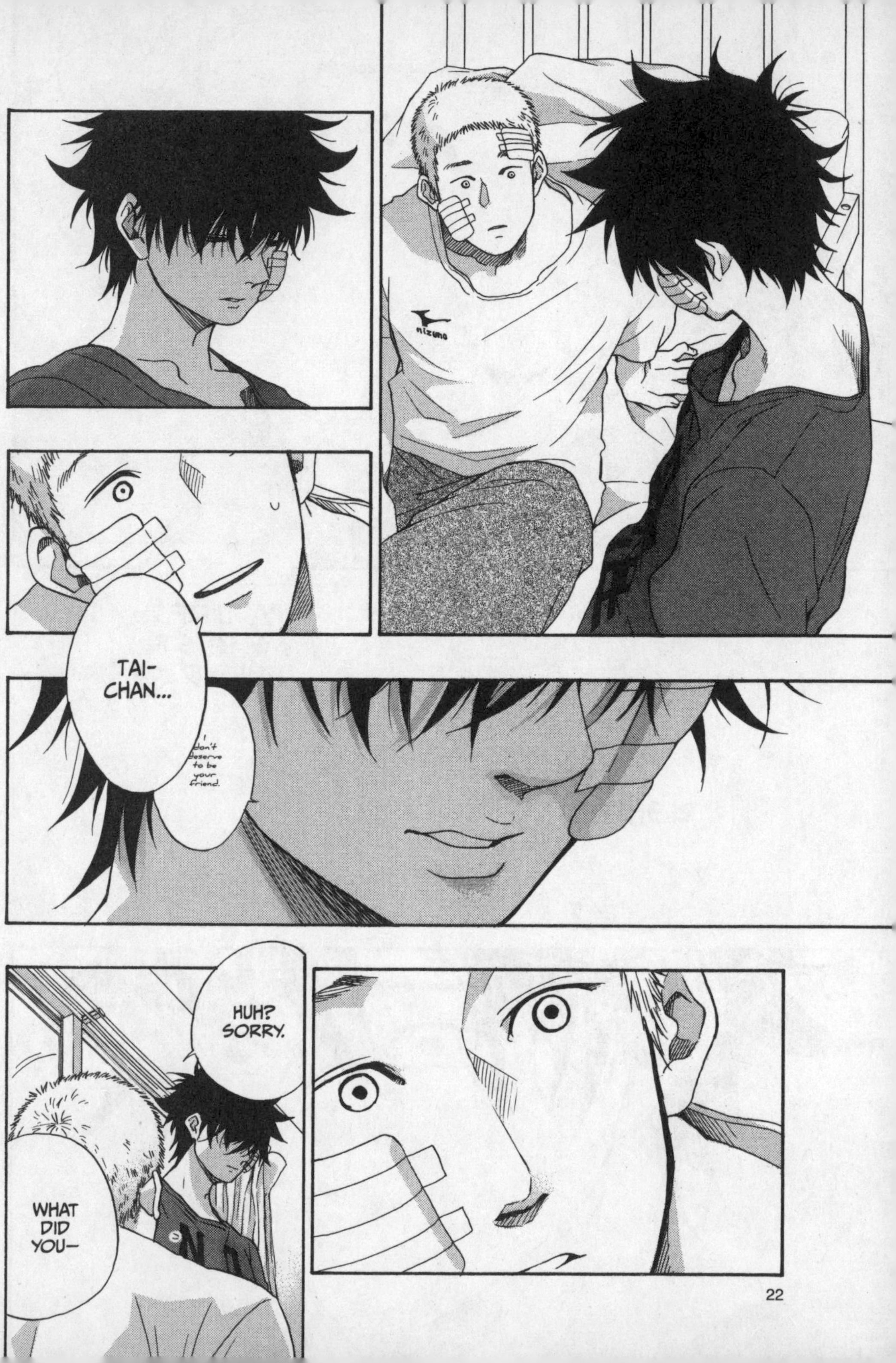
TAI-CHAN...
I don't deserve to be your friend.
HUH? SORRY.
WHAT DID YOU—

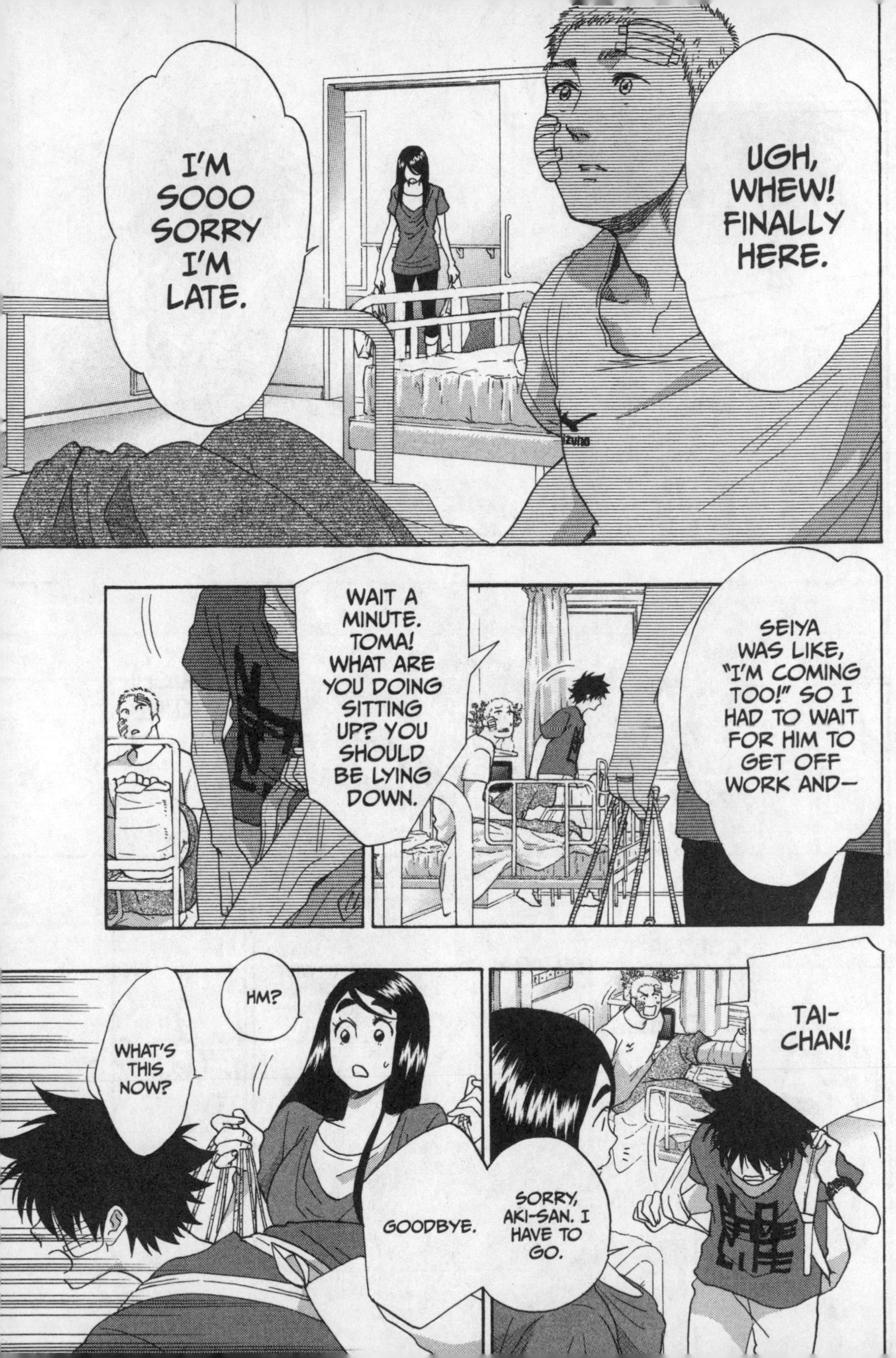

UGH, WHEW! FINALLY HERE.
I'M SOOO SORRY I'M LATE.
SEIYA WAS LIKE, "I'M COMING TOO!" SO I HAD TO WAIT FOR HIM TO GET OFF WORK AND—
WAIT A MINUTE. TOMA! WHAT ARE YOU DOING SITTING UP? YOU SHOULD BE LYING DOWN.
TAI-CHAN!
SORRY, AKI-SAN. I HAVE TO GO.
GOODBYE.
HM?
WHAT'S THIS NOW?

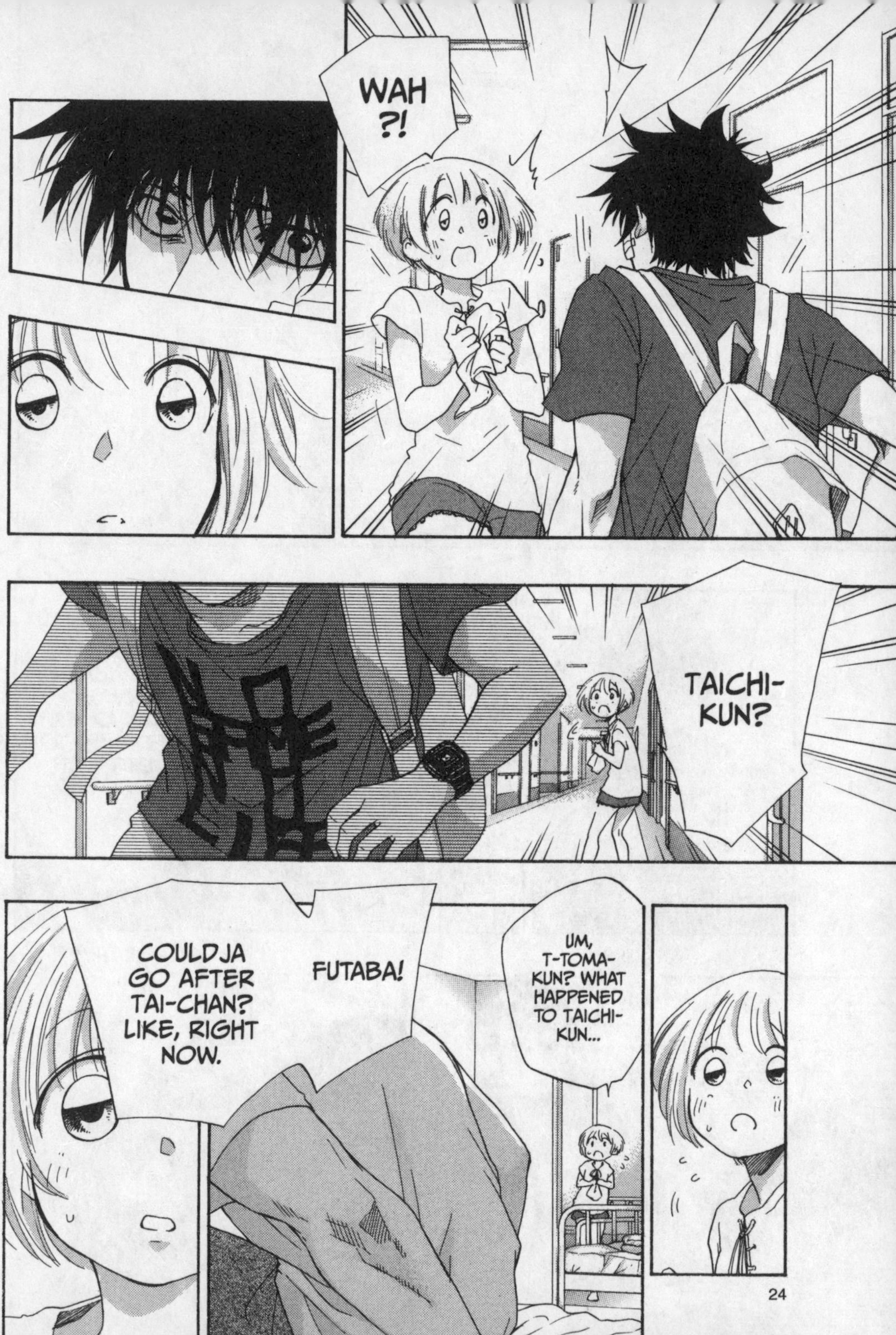
WAH ?!
TAICHI-KUN?
UM, T-TOMA-KUN? WHAT HAPPENED TO TAICHI-KUN...
FUTABA!
COULDJA GO AFTER TAI-CHAN? LIKE, RIGHT NOW.

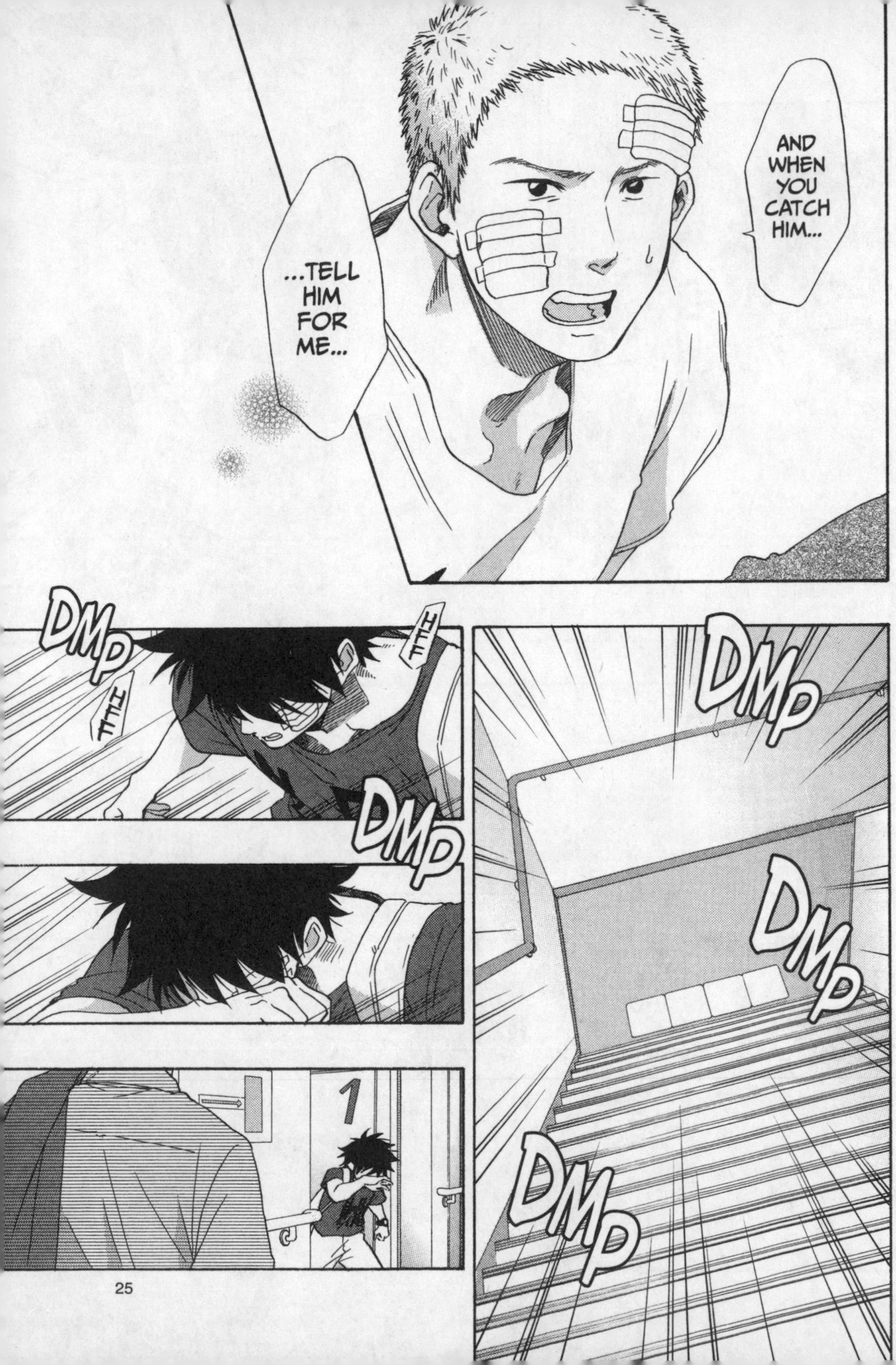
AND WHEN YOU CATCH HIM...
...TELL HIM FOR ME...
DMP
HFF
HFF
DMP
DMP
DMP
DMP
1

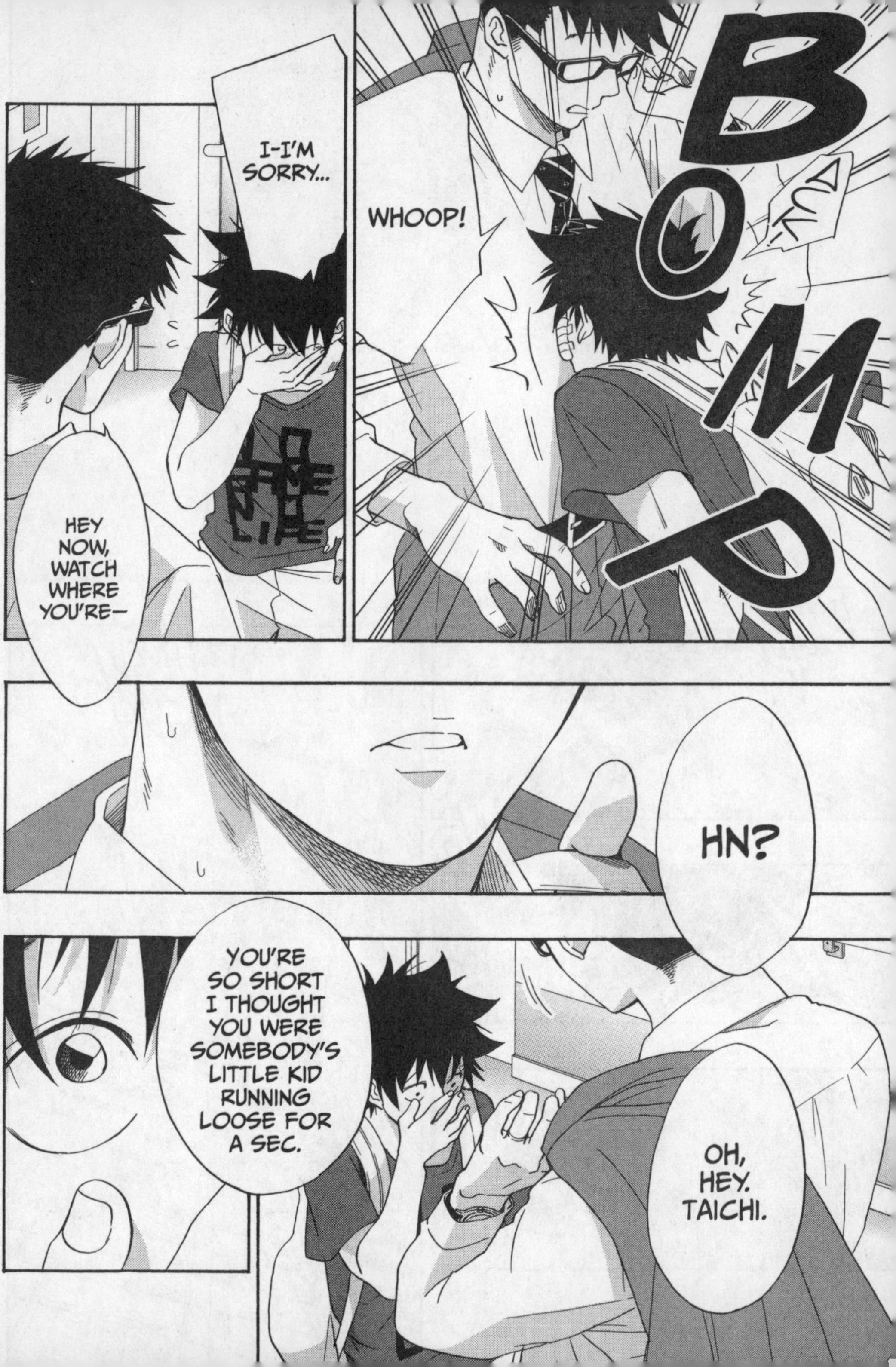
BOMP
ACK!
WHOOP!
I-I'M SORRY...
HEY NOW, WATCH WHERE YOU'RE—
HN?
OH, HEY. TAICHI.
YOU'RE SO SHORT I THOUGHT YOU WERE SOMEBODY'S LITTLE KID RUNNING LOOSE FOR A SEC.

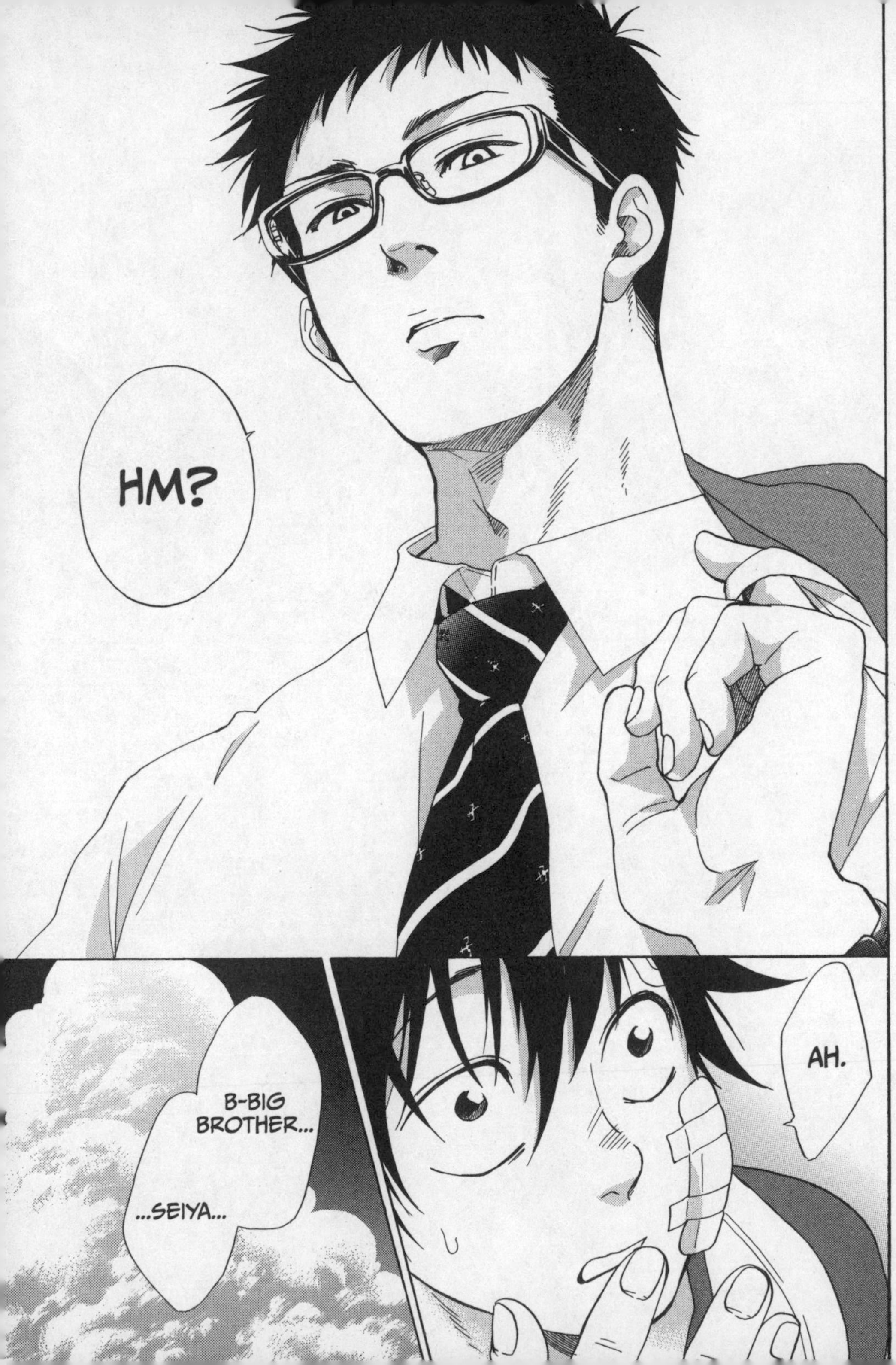
HM?
AH.
B-BIG BROTHER...
...SEIYA...

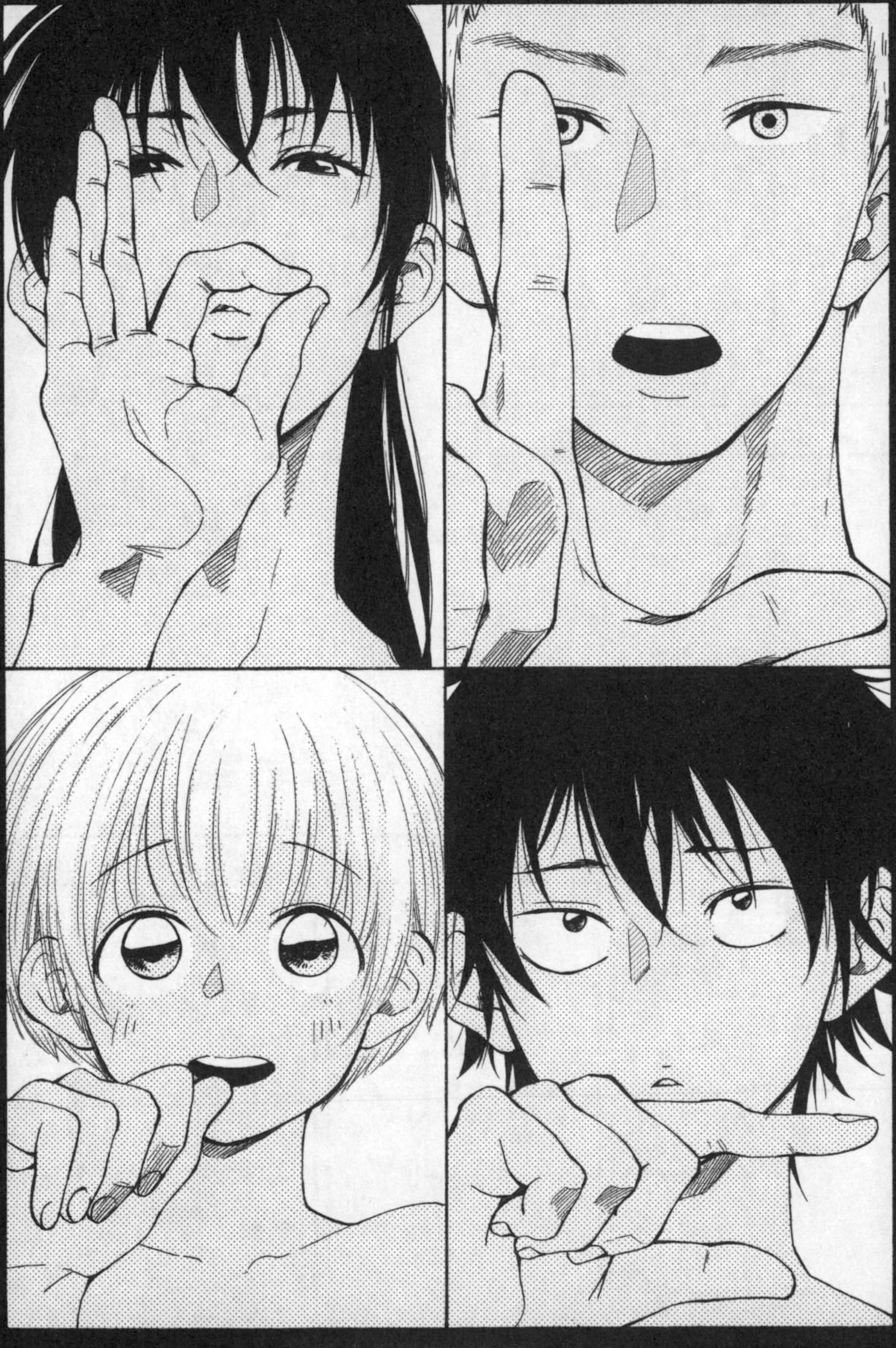

CHAPTER 14

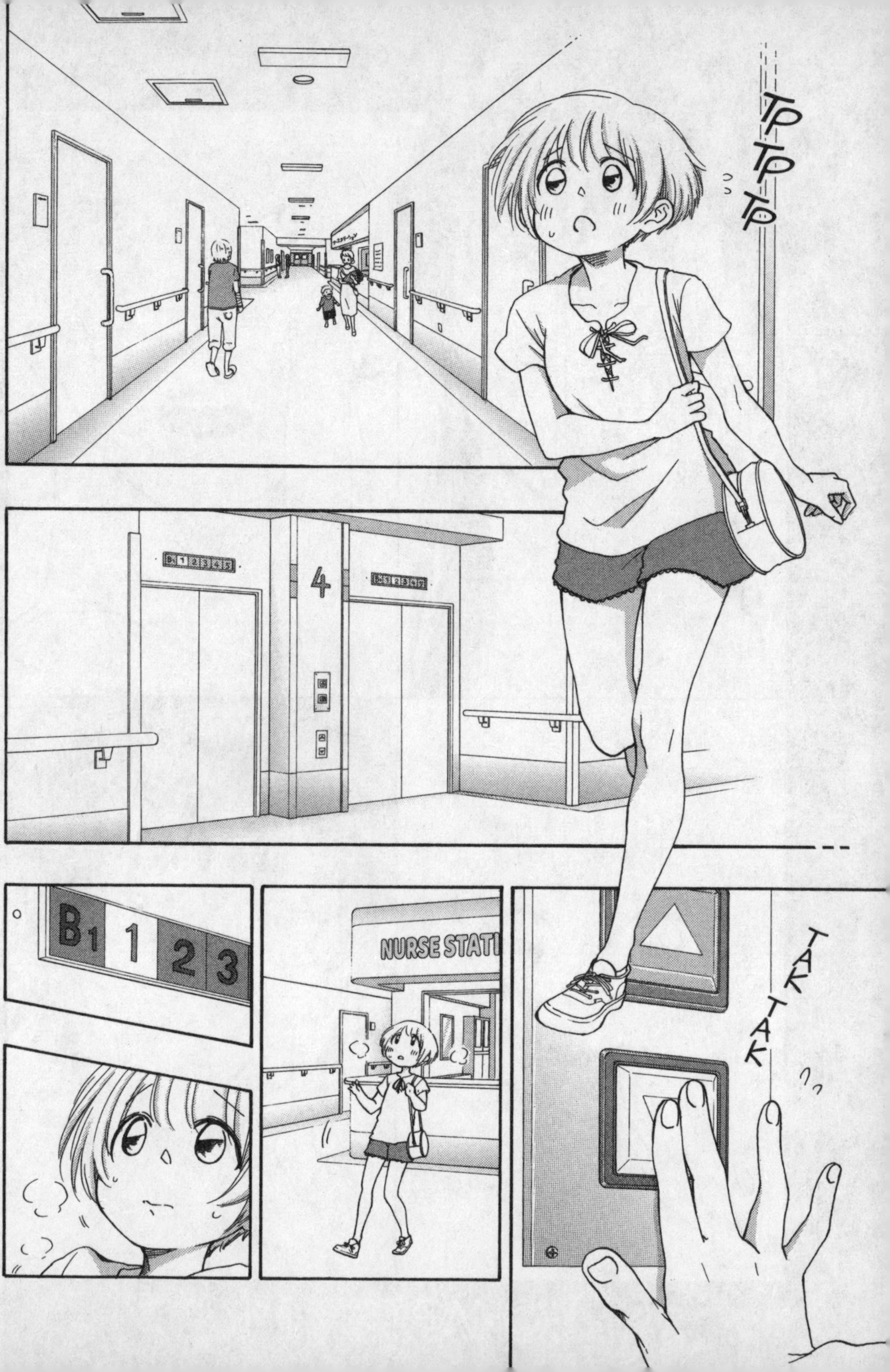

TP TP TP
B1 1 2 3
NURSE STATI
TAK TAK

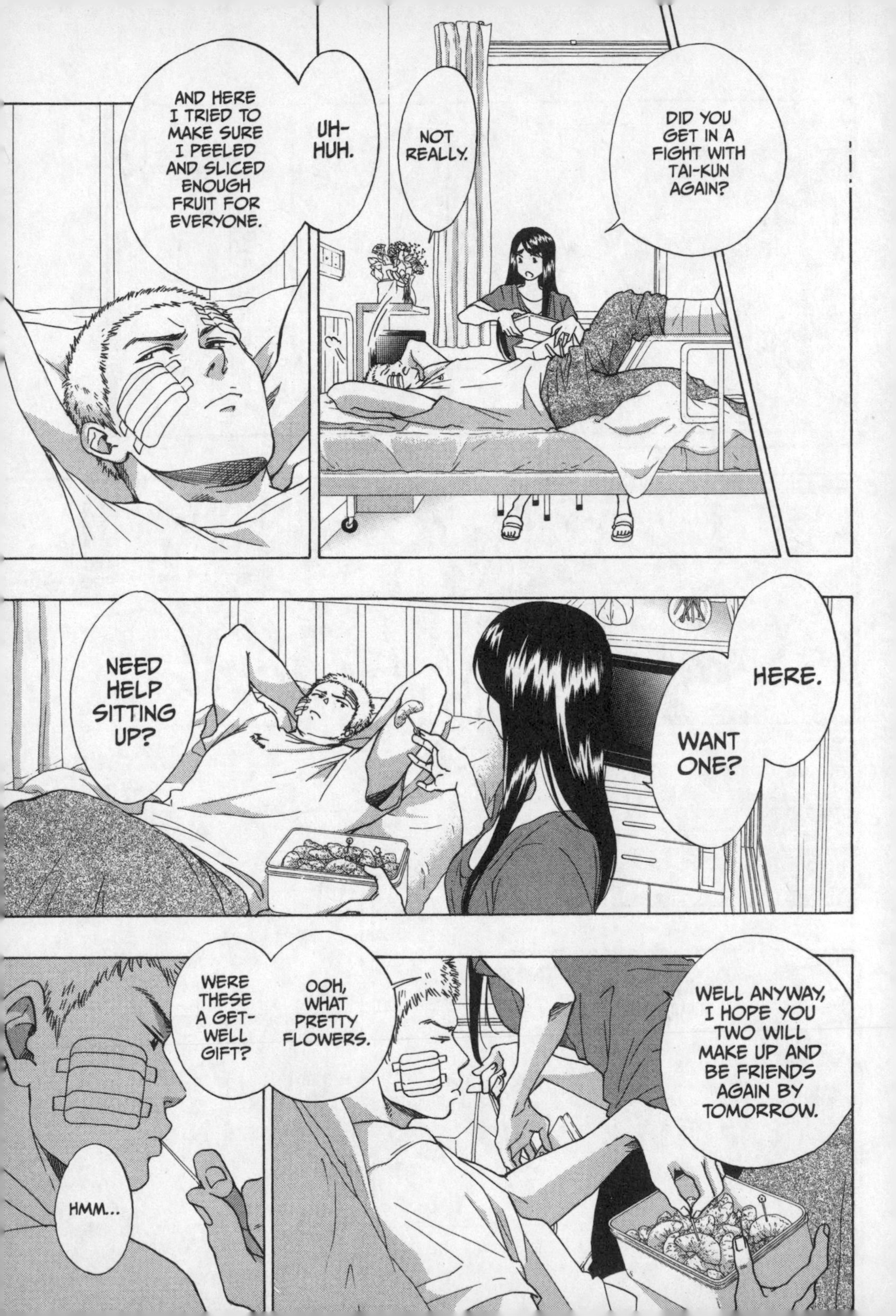

DID YOU GET IN A FIGHT WITH TAI-KUN AGAIN?
NOT REALLY.
UH-HUH.
AND HERE I TRIED TO MAKE SURE I PEELED AND SLICED ENOUGH FRUIT FOR EVERYONE.
HERE.
WANT ONE?
NEED HELP SITTING UP?
WELL ANYWAY, I HOPE YOU TWO WILL MAKE UP AND BE FRIENDS AGAIN BY TOMORROW.
OOH, WHAT PRETTY FLOWERS.
WERE THESE A GET-WELL GIFT?
HMM...

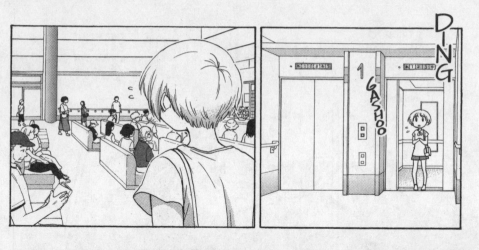

DING

GASHOO

TAICHI-KUN'S NOT HERE...

MAYBE HE LEFT ALREADY?

AH!

B/p

KAKLUNK

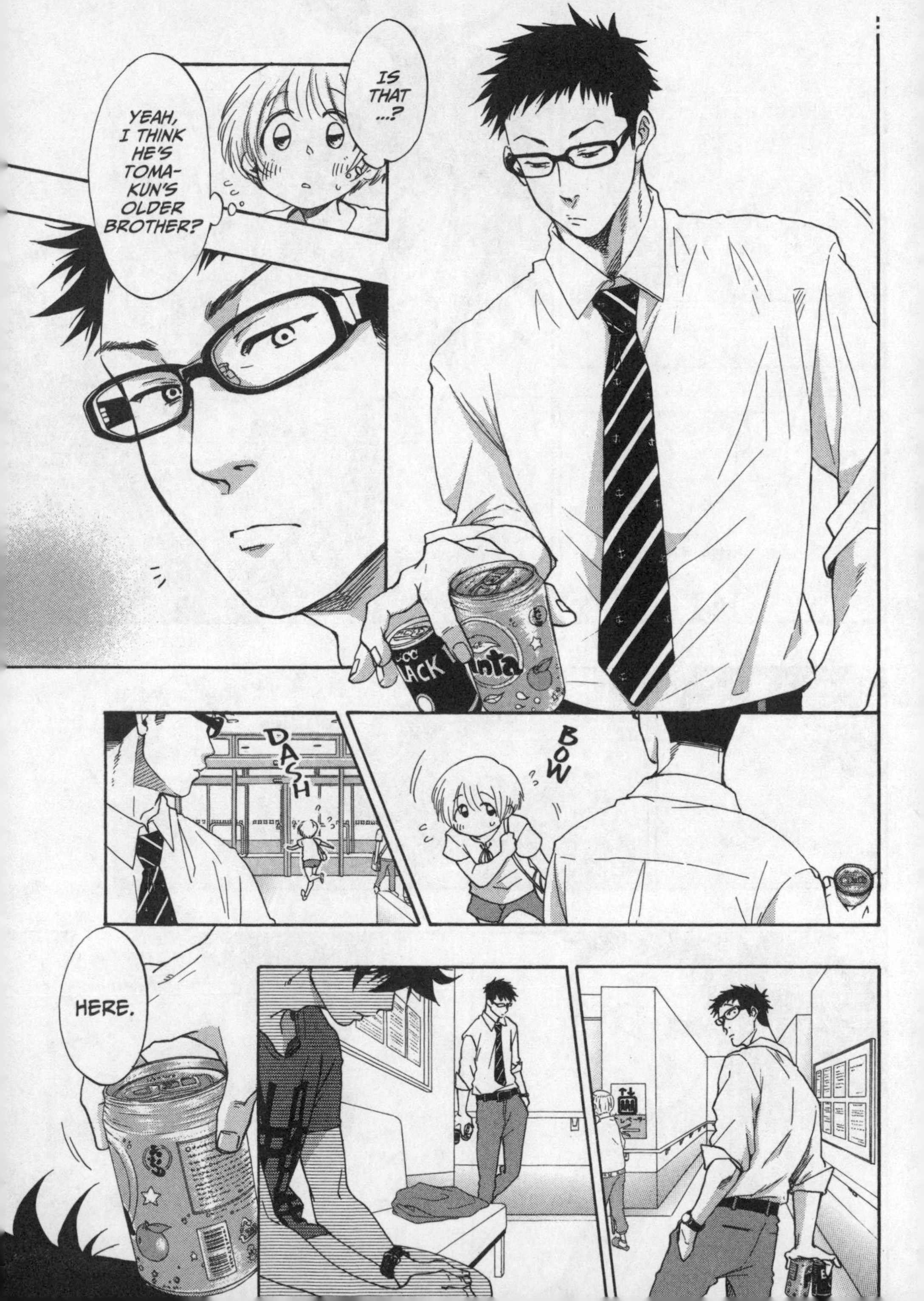
IS THAT ...?
YEAH, I THINK HE'S TOMA-KUN'S OLDER BROTHER?
BOW
DASH
HERE.

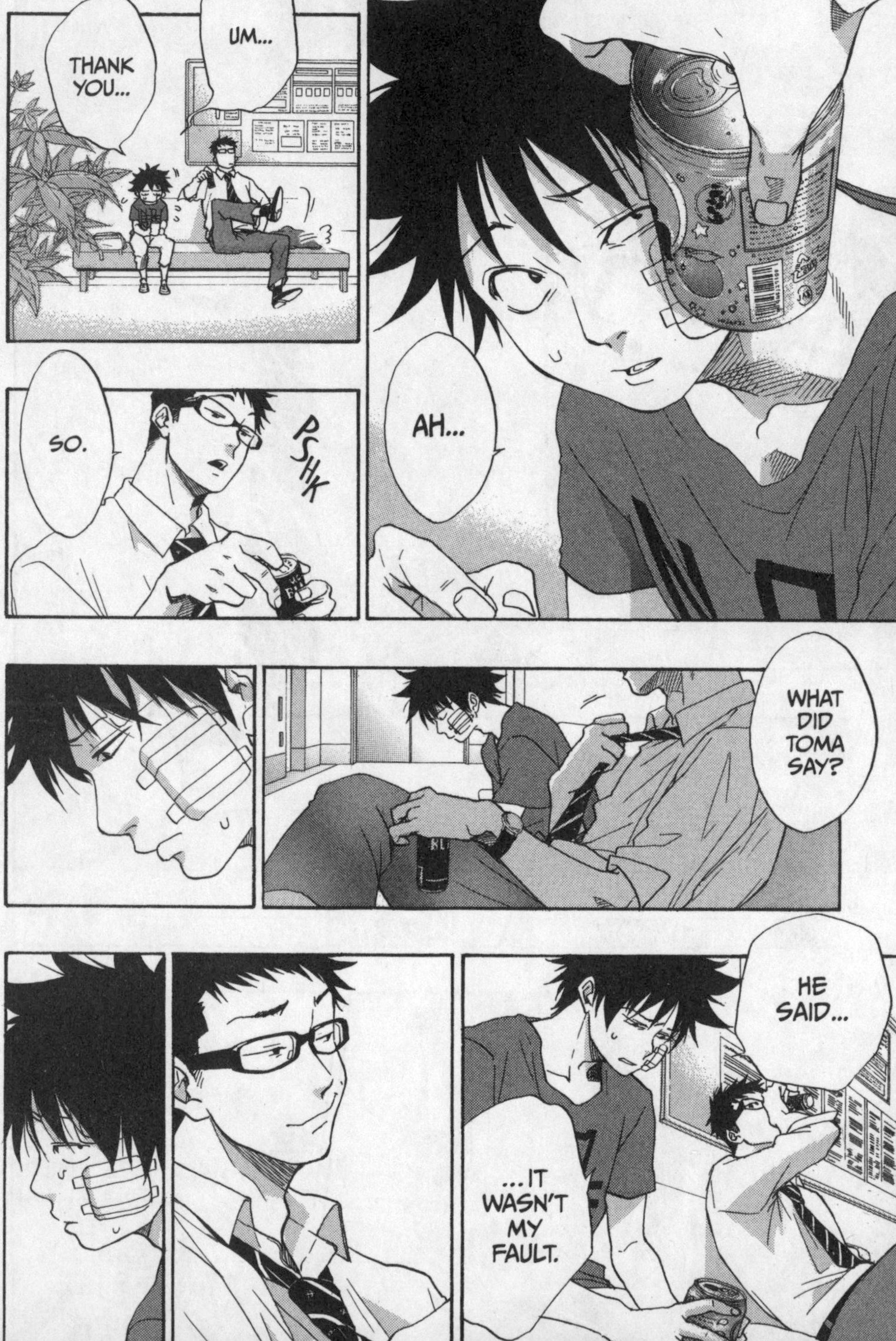
AH...
UM...
THANK YOU...
SO.
PSHK
WHAT DID TOMA SAY?
HE SAID...
...IT WASN'T MY FAULT.

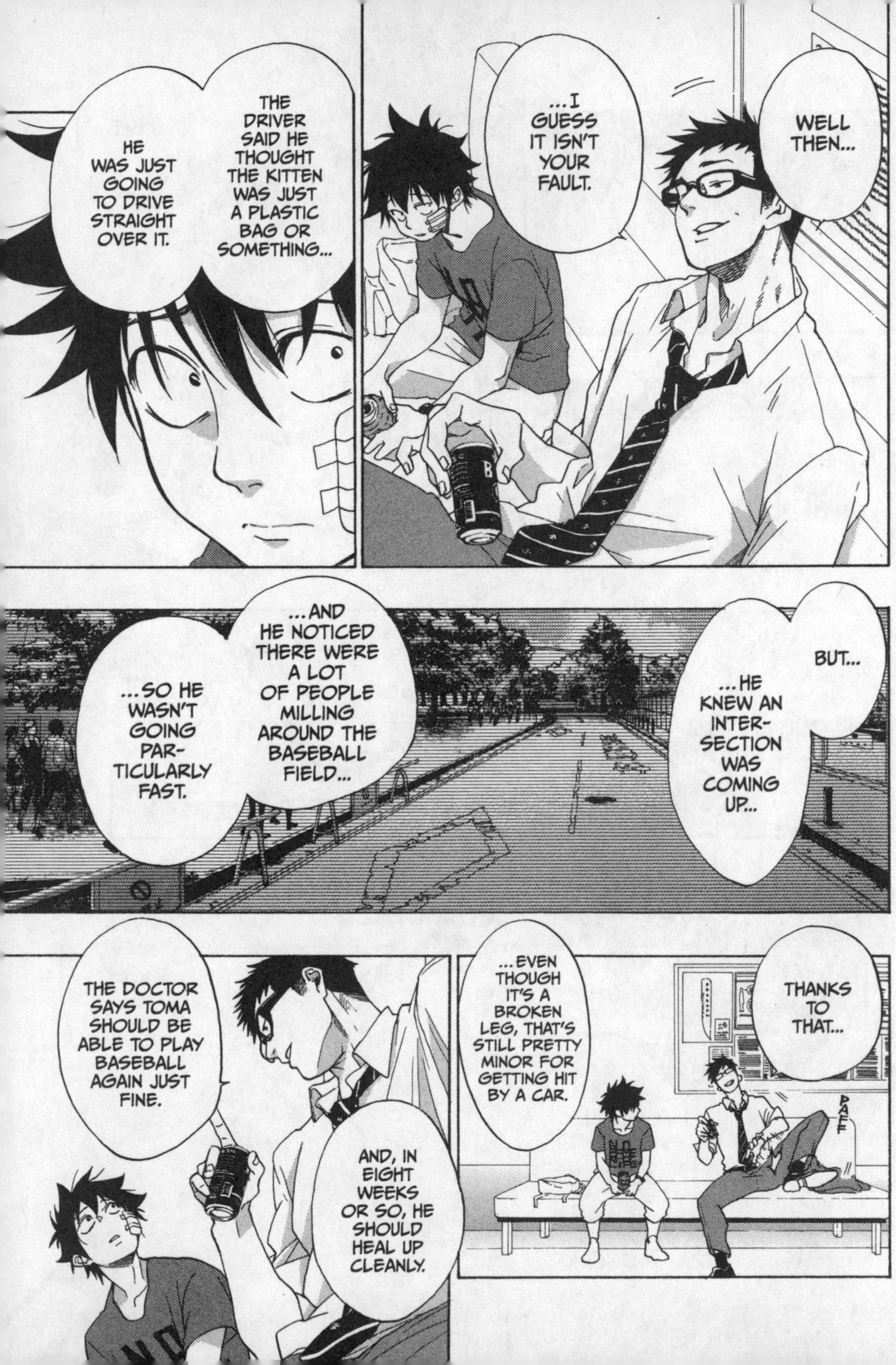
WELL THEN...
...I GUESS IT ISN'T YOUR FAULT.
THE DRIVER SAID HE THOUGHT THE KITTEN WAS JUST A PLASTIC BAG OR SOMETHING...
HE WAS JUST GOING TO DRIVE STRAIGHT OVER IT.
BUT...
...HE KNEW AN INTER-SECTION WAS COMING UP...
...AND HE NOTICED THERE WERE A LOT OF PEOPLE MILLING AROUND THE BASEBALL FIELD...
...SO HE WASN'T GOING PAR-TICULARLY FAST.
THANKS TO THAT...
...EVEN THOUGH IT'S A BROKEN LEG, THAT'S STILL PRETTY MINOR FOR GETTING HIT BY A CAR.
PAFF
THE DOCTOR SAYS TOMA SHOULD BE ABLE TO PLAY BASEBALL AGAIN JUST FINE.
AND, IN EIGHT WEEKS OR SO, HE SHOULD HEAL UP CLEANLY.

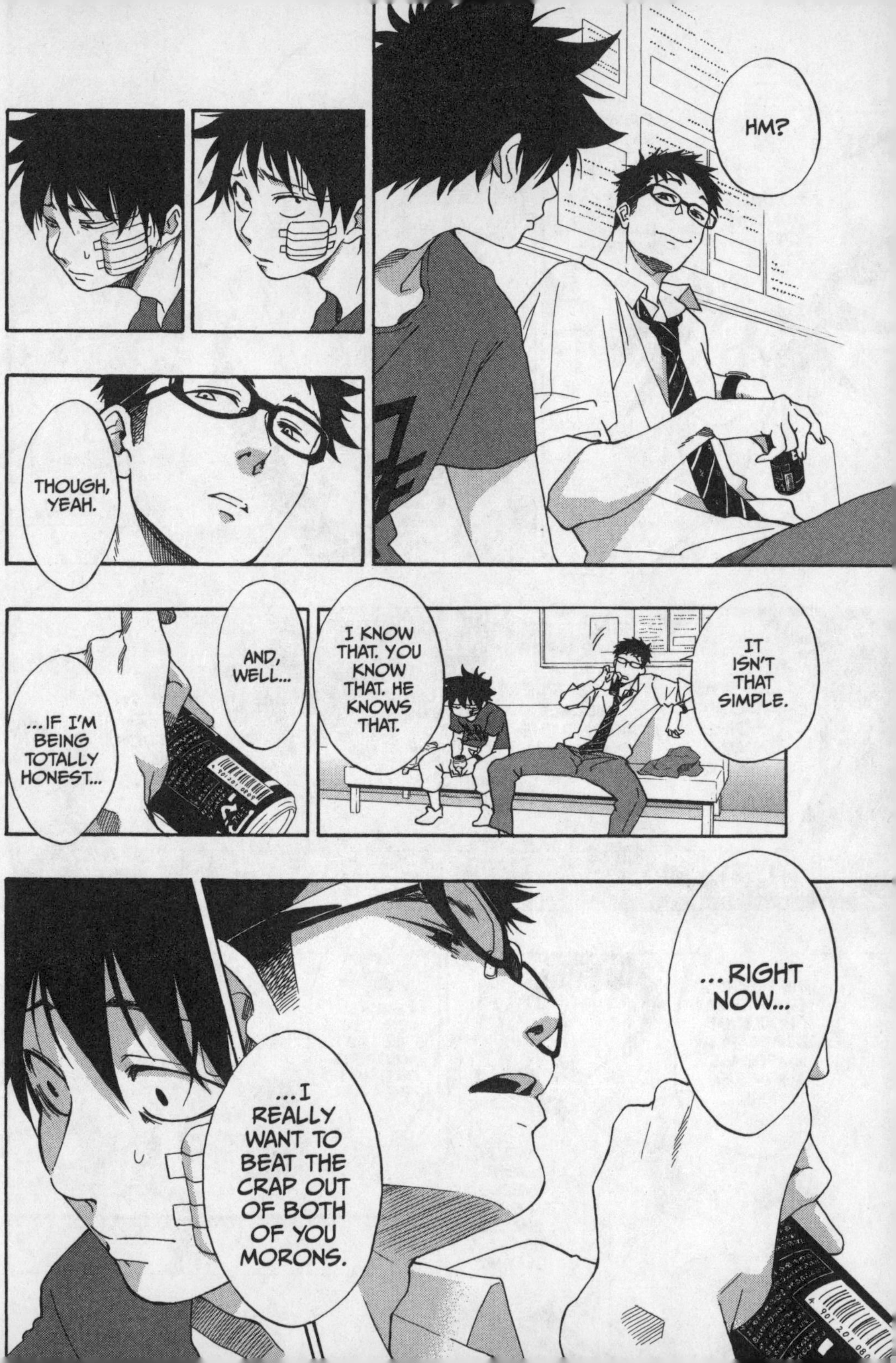
HM?
THOUGH, YEAH.
IT ISN'T THAT SIMPLE.
I KNOW THAT. YOU KNOW THAT. HE KNOWS THAT.
AND, WELL...
...IF I'M BEING TOTALLY HONEST...
...RIGHT NOW...
...I REALLY WANT TO BEAT THE CRAP OUT OF BOTH OF YOU MORONS.

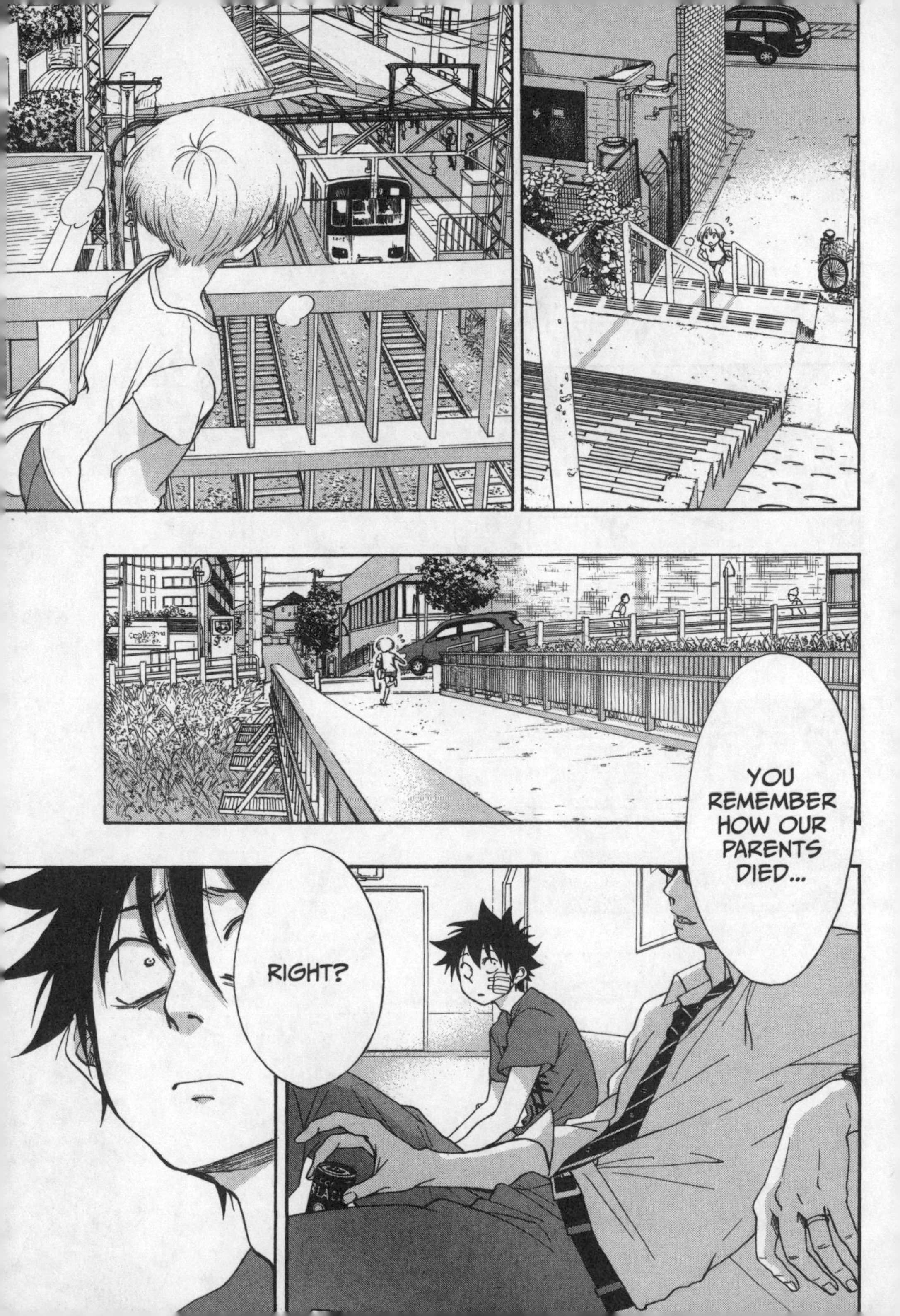
YOU REMEMBER HOW OUR PARENTS DIED...
RIGHT?

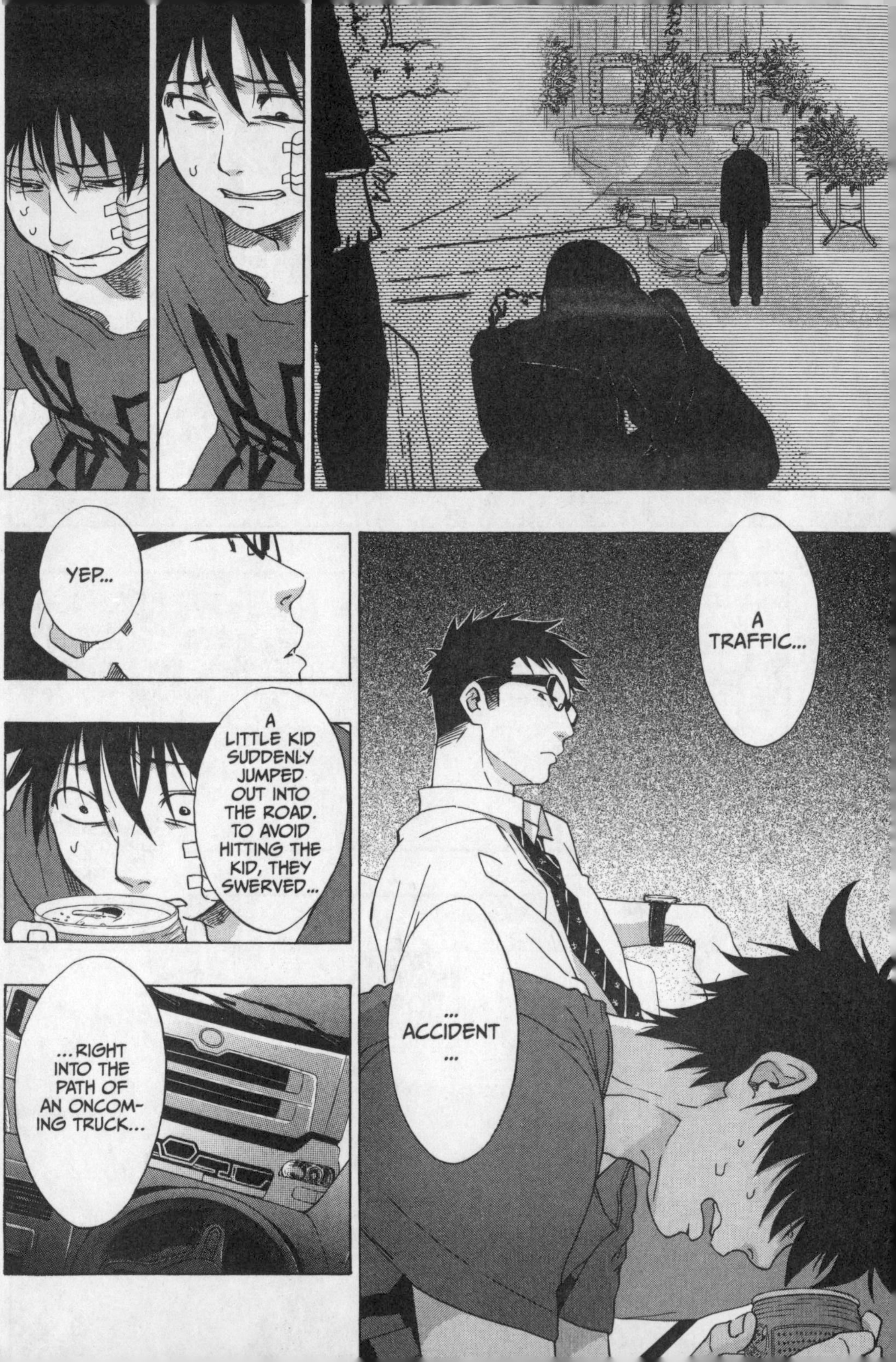
A TRAFFIC...
YEP...
... ACCIDENT ...
A LITTLE KID SUDDENLY JUMPED OUT INTO THE ROAD. TO AVOID HITTING THE KID, THEY SWERVED...
...RIGHT INTO THE PATH OF AN ONCOMING TRUCK...

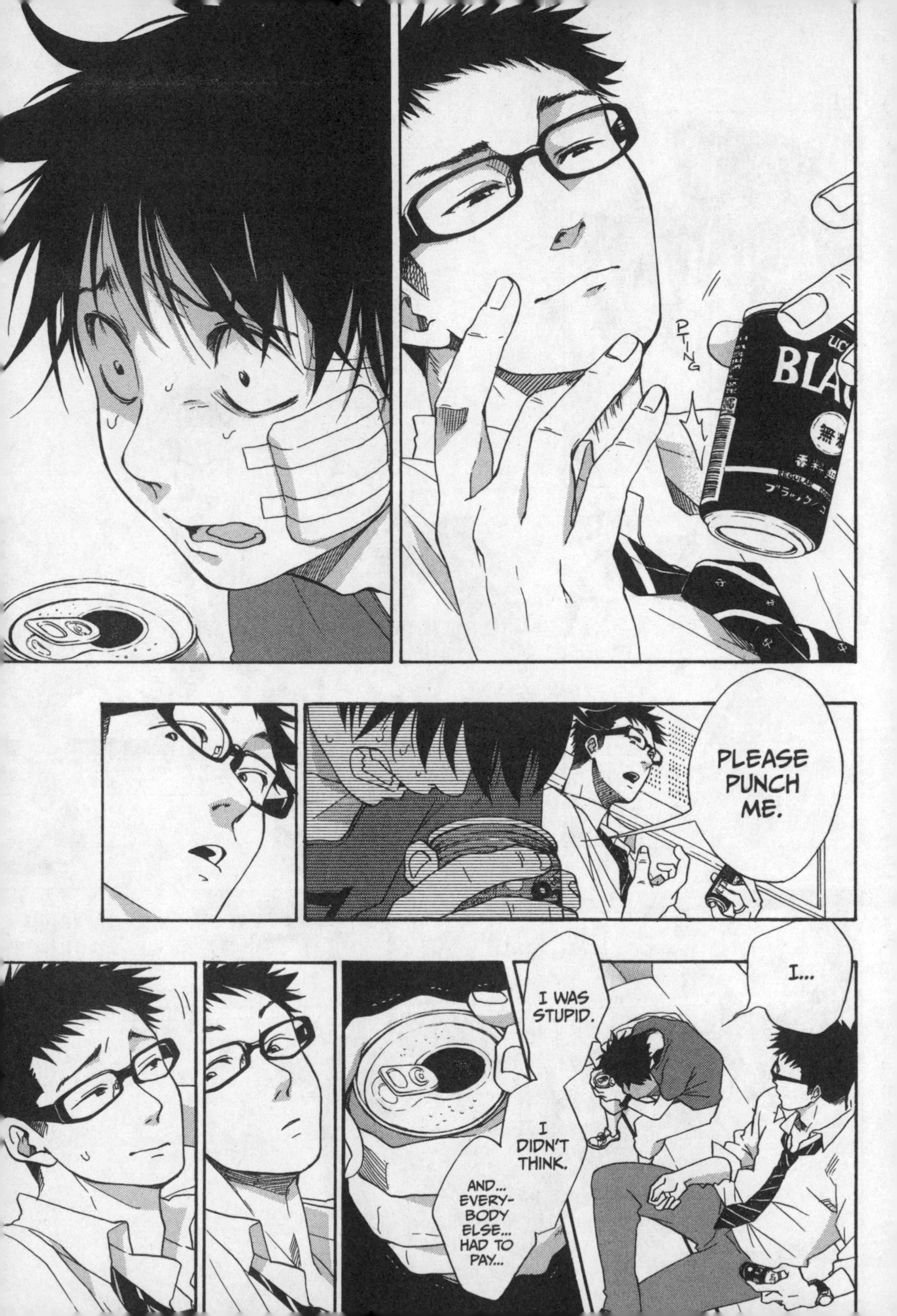

PTING
BLACK
PLEASE PUNCH ME.
I...
I WAS STUPID.
I DIDN'T THINK.
AND... EVERYBODY ELSE... HAD TO PAY...

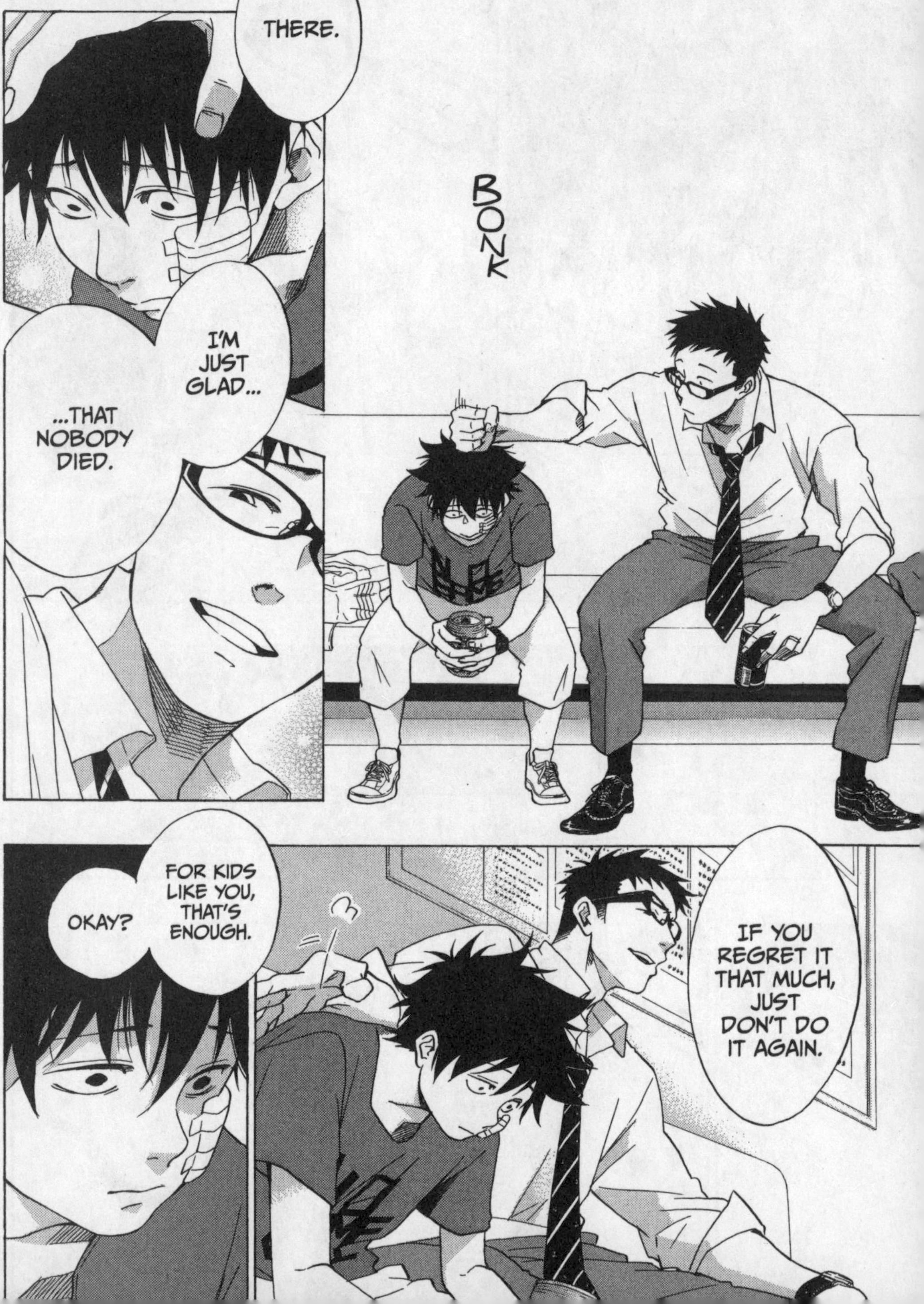
THERE.
BONK
I'M JUST GLAD...
...THAT NOBODY DIED.
IF YOU REGRET IT THAT MUCH, JUST DON'T DO IT AGAIN.
FOR KIDS LIKE YOU, THAT'S ENOUGH.
OKAY?

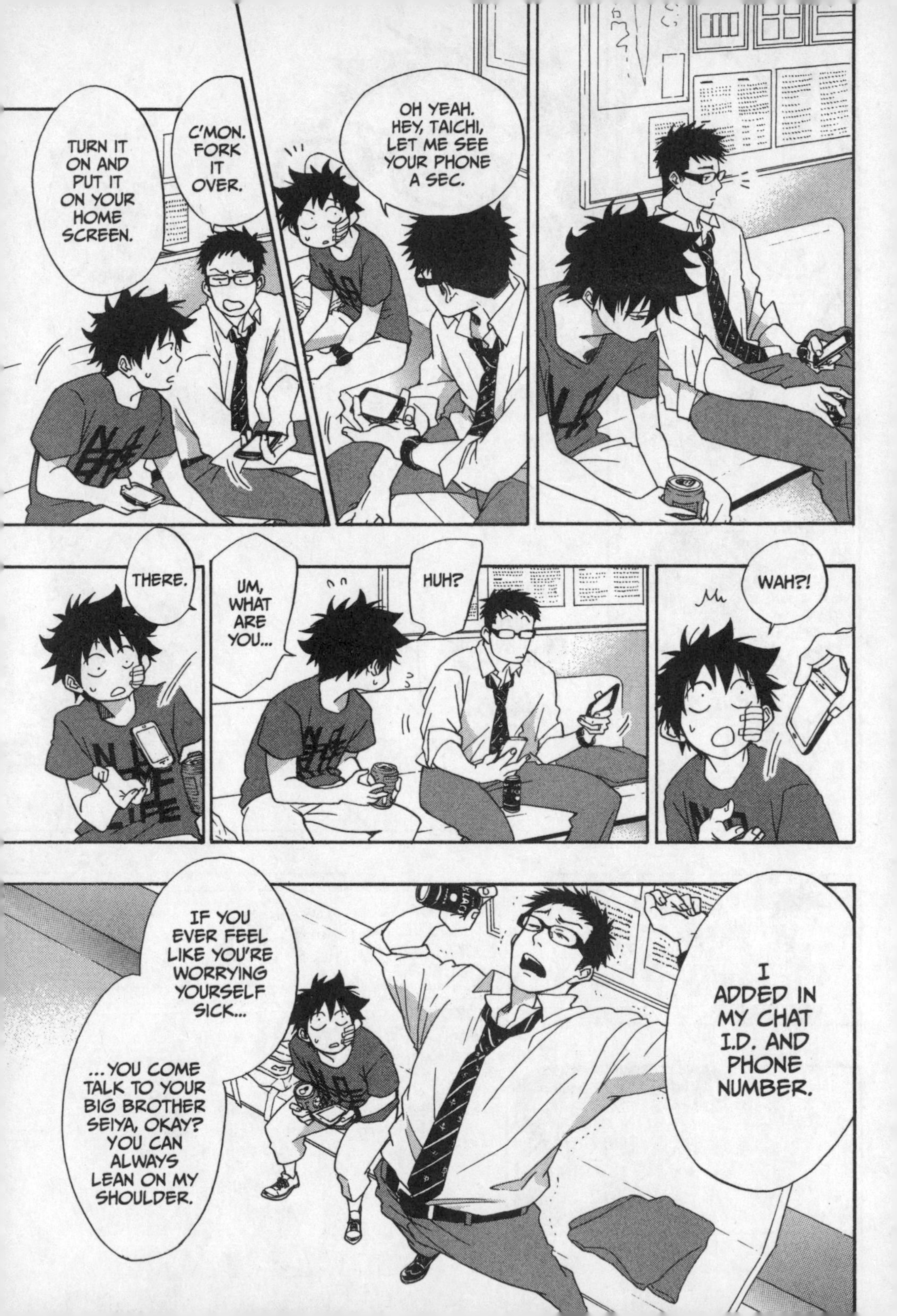
OH YEAH. HEY, TAICHI, LET ME SEE YOUR PHONE A SEC.
C'MON. FORK IT OVER.
TURN IT ON AND PUT IT ON YOUR HOME SCREEN.
WAH?!
HUH?
UM, WHAT ARE YOU...
THERE.
I ADDED IN MY CHAT I.D. AND PHONE NUMBER.
IF YOU EVER FEEL LIKE YOU'RE WORRYING YOURSELF SICK...
...YOU COME TALK TO YOUR BIG BROTHER SEIYA, OKAY? YOU CAN ALWAYS LEAN ON MY SHOULDER.

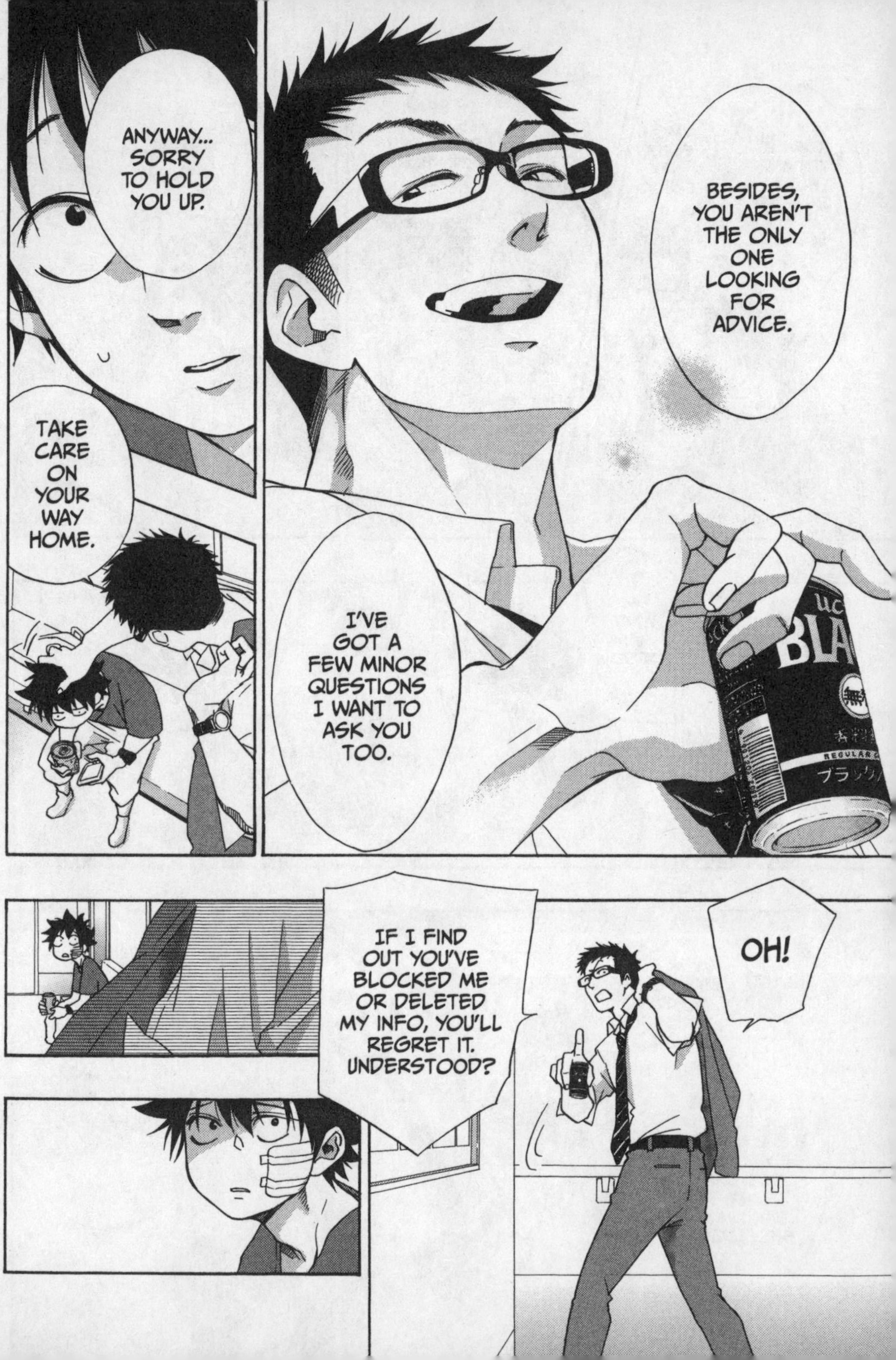
BESIDES, YOU AREN'T THE ONLY ONE LOOKING FOR ADVICE.
I'VE GOT A FEW MINOR QUESTIONS I WANT TO ASK YOU TOO.
ANYWAY... SORRY TO HOLD YOU UP.
TAKE CARE ON YOUR WAY HOME.
OH!
IF I FIND OUT YOU'VE BLOCKED ME OR DELETED MY INFO, YOU'LL REGRET IT. UNDERSTOOD?

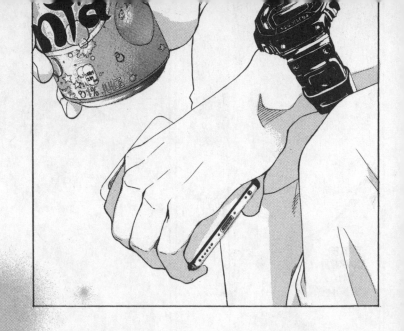

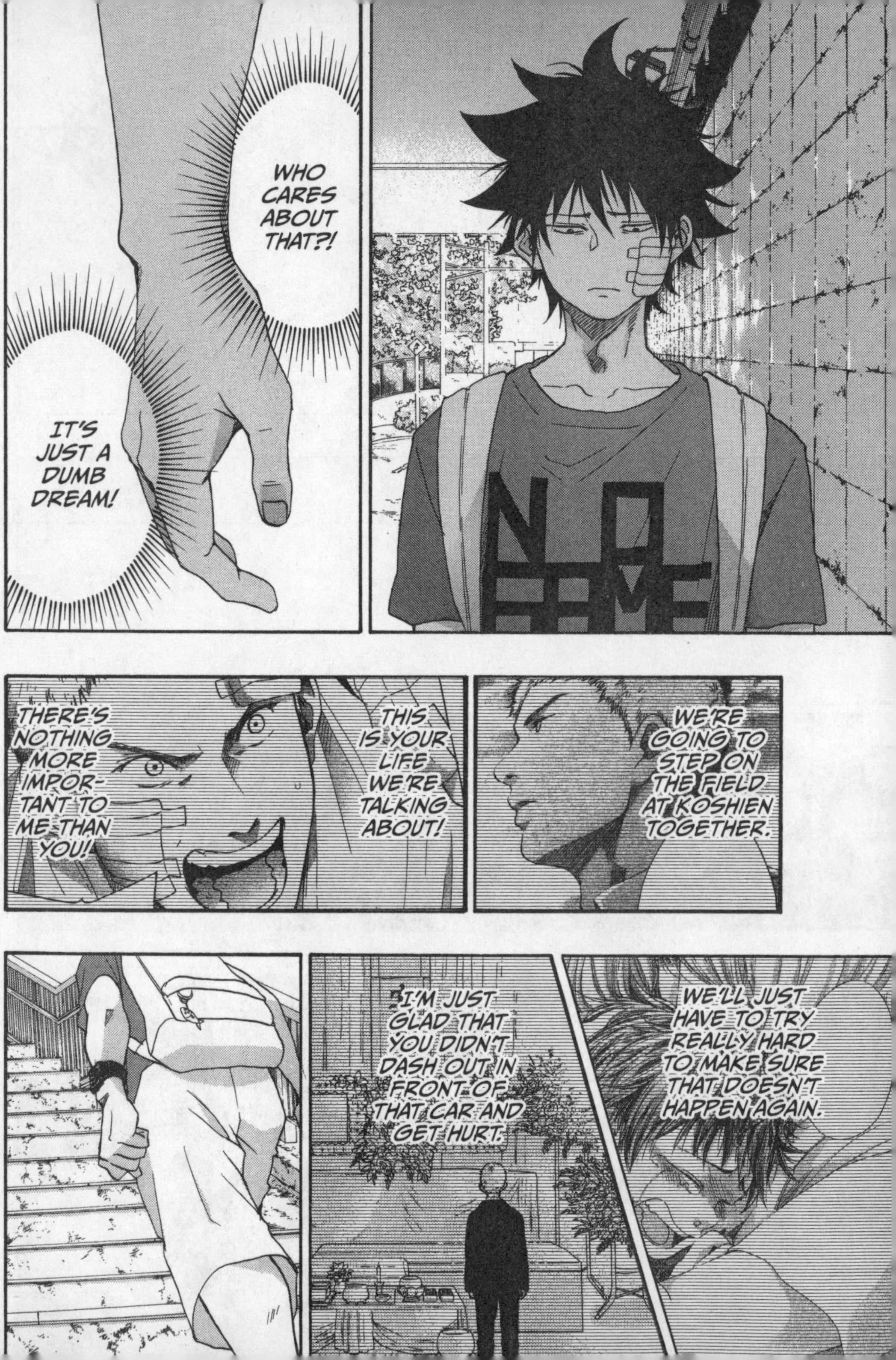
WHO CARES ABOUT THAT?!
IT'S JUST A DUMB DREAM!
WE'RE GOING TO STEP ON THE FIELD AT KOSHIEN TOGETHER.
THIS IS YOUR LIFE WE'RE TALKING ABOUT!
THERE'S NOTHING MORE IMPOR-TANT TO ME THAN YOU!
WE'LL JUST HAVE TO TRY REALLY HARD TO MAKE SURE THAT DOESN'T HAPPEN AGAIN.
I'M JUST GLAD THAT YOU DIDN'T DASH OUT IN FRONT OF THAT CAR AND GET HURT.

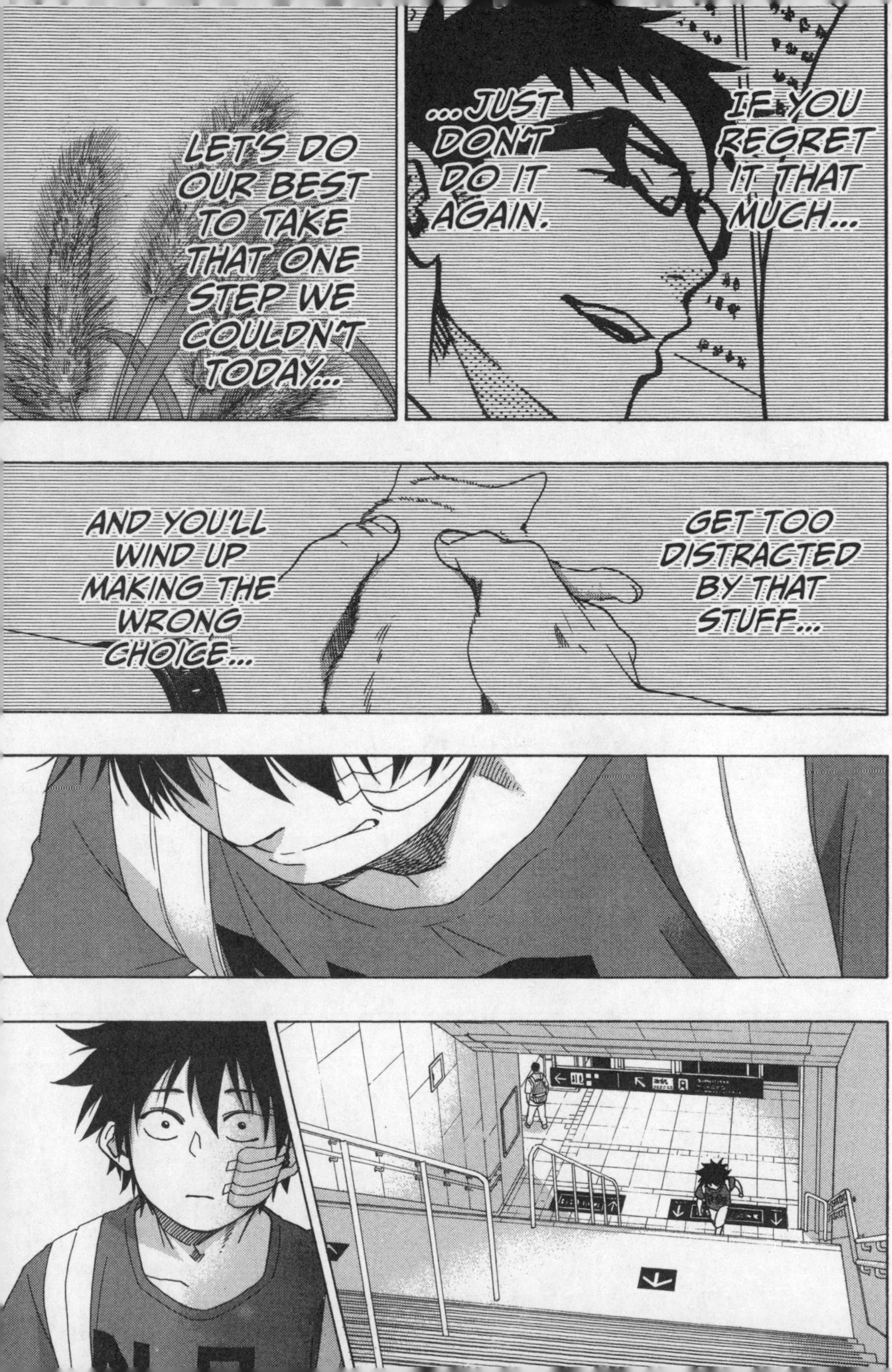
IF YOU REGRET IT THAT MUCH...
...JUST DON'T DO IT AGAIN.
LET'S DO OUR BEST TO TAKE THAT ONE STEP WE COULDN'T TODAY...
GET TOO DISTRACTED BY THAT STUFF...
AND YOU'LL WIND UP MAKING THE WRONG CHOICE...

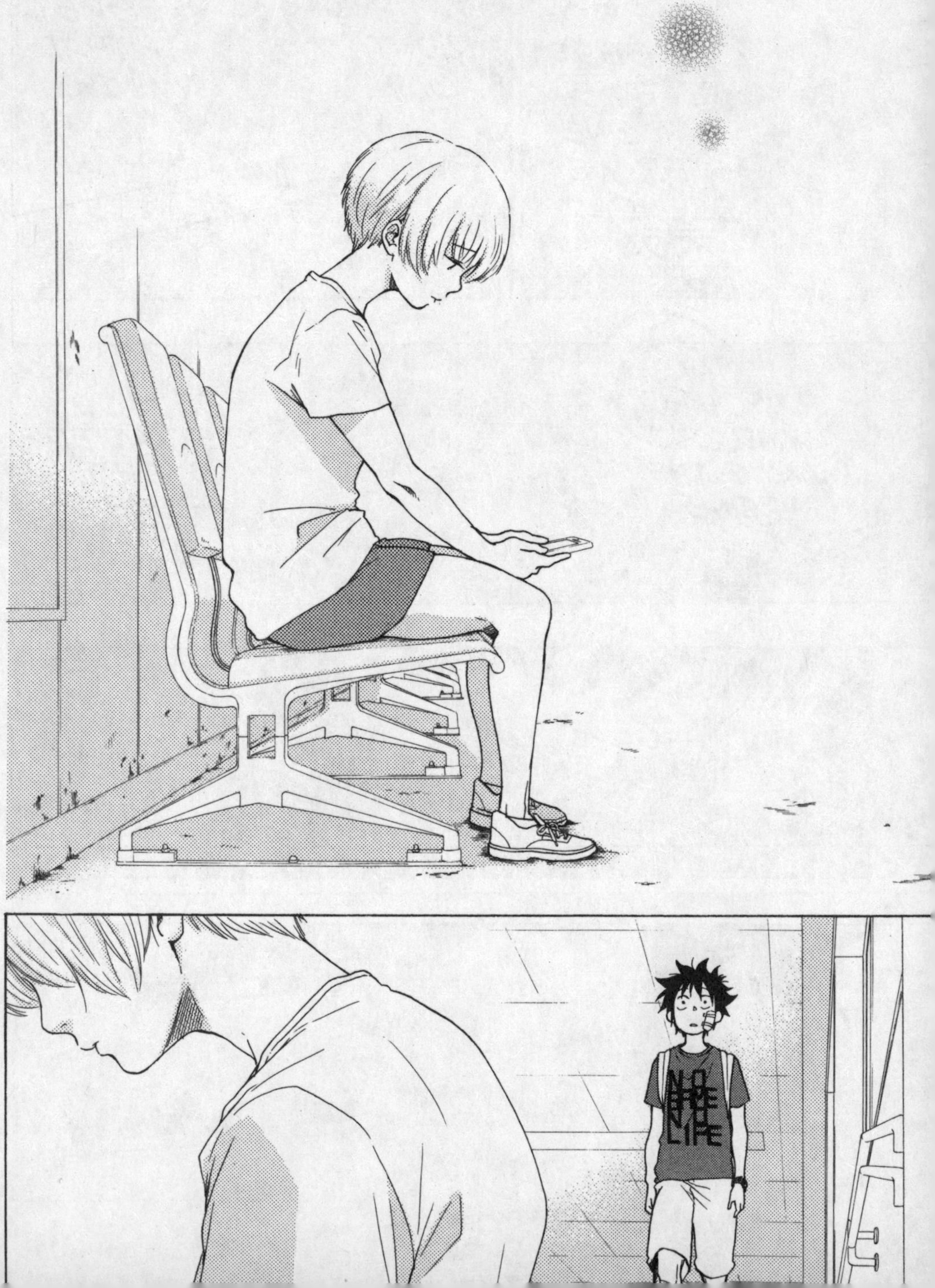

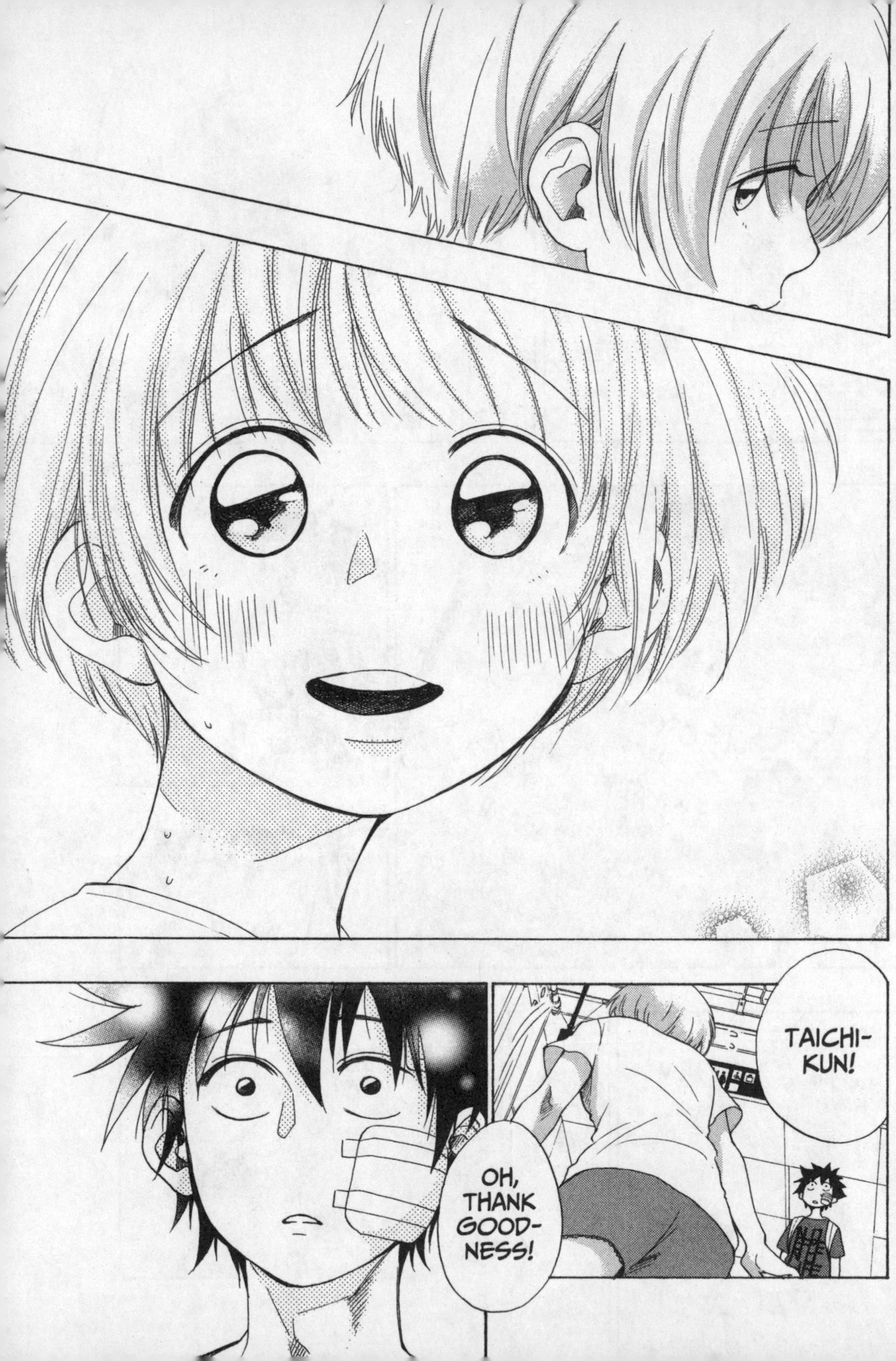
TAICHI-KUN!
OH, THANK GOODNESS!

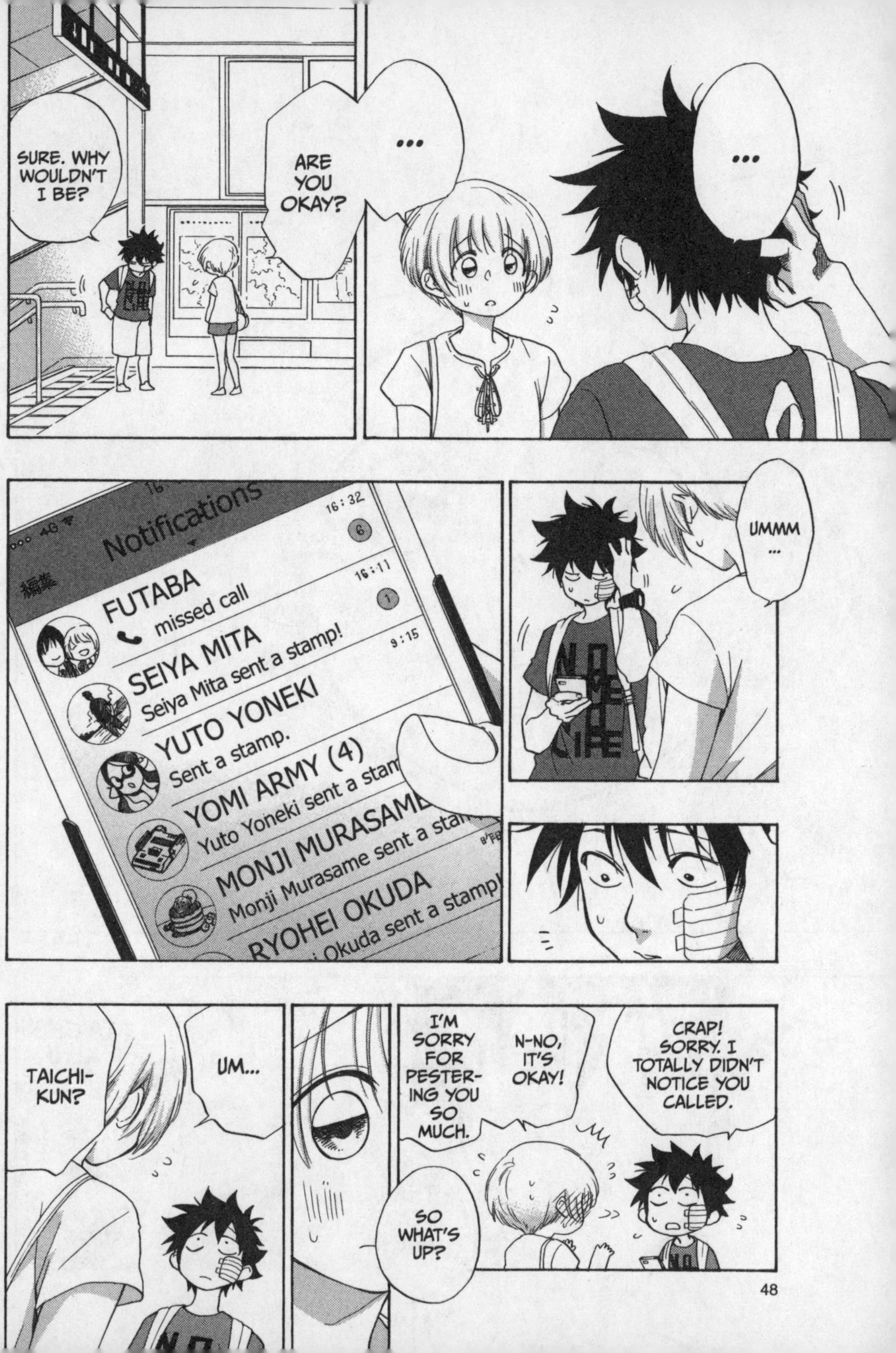
...
...
ARE YOU OKAY?
SURE. WHY WOULDN'T I BE?
UMMM ...
Notifications
16:32
FUTABA
missed call
16:11
SEIYA MITA
Seiya Mita sent a stamp!
9:15
YUTO YONEKI
Sent a stamp.
YOMI ARMY (4)
Yuto Yoneki sent a stam
MONJI MURASAME
Monji Murasame sent a stam
RYOHEI OKUDA
Okuda sent a stamp
CRAP! SORRY. I TOTALLY DIDN'T NOTICE YOU CALLED.
N-NO, IT'S OKAY!
I'M SORRY FOR PESTERING YOU SO MUCH.
SO WHAT'S UP?
UM...
TAICHI-KUN?

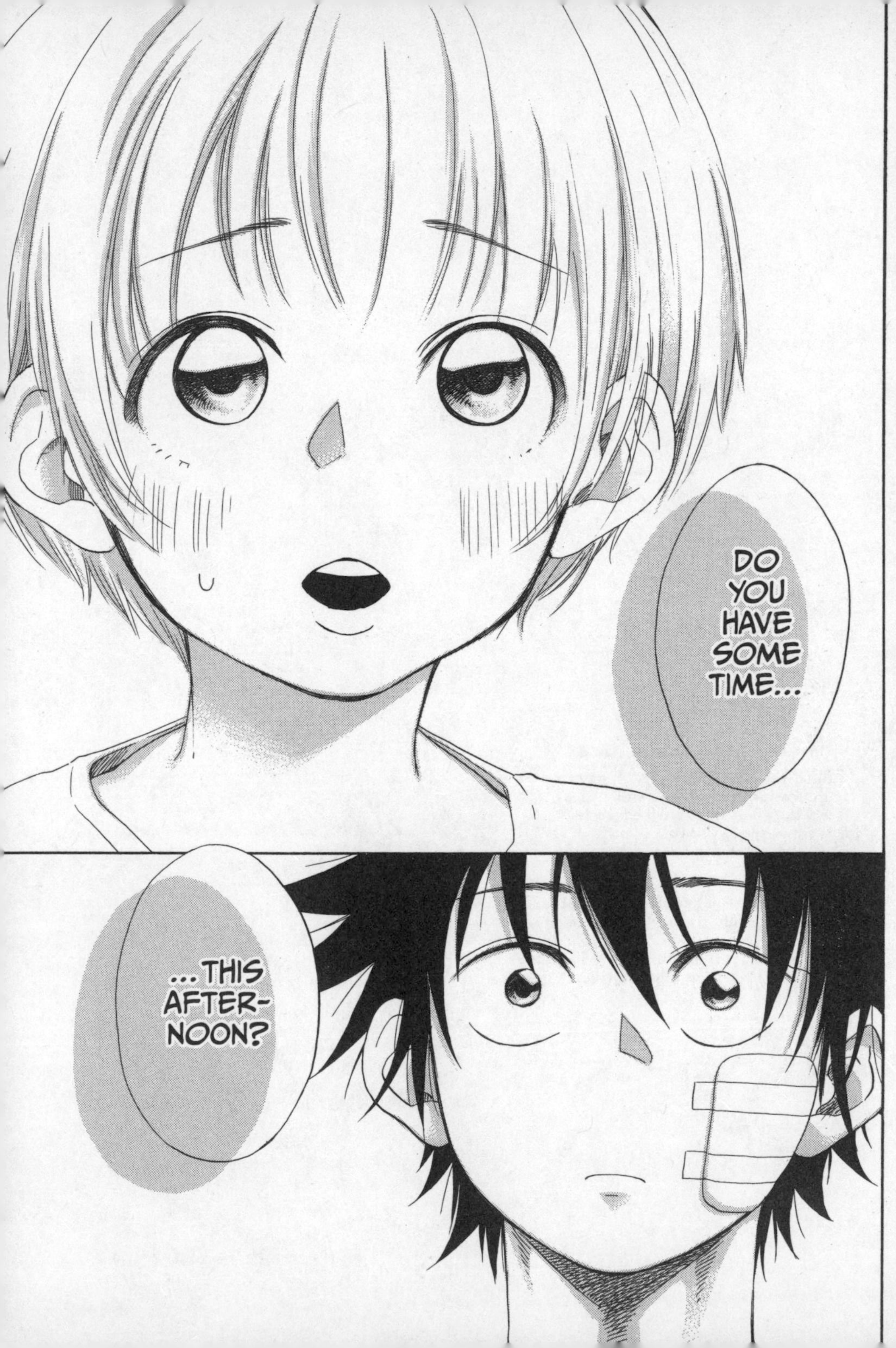
DO YOU HAVE SOME TIME...
... THIS AFTER-NOON?

The Characters as Animals, Part 4

Big brother Seiya immediately gave me the impression of a wolf, so a wolf he was. It wouldn't have been fun if I'd just left it like that, though, so I asked my staff for suggestions. But in the end, he stayed a wolf.

On the other hand, I couldn't think of anything for Aki-san at all. So I called upon the power of my wonderful staff, and they suggested a seal. The moment they said it, I realized just how obvious it was.

CHAPTER 15

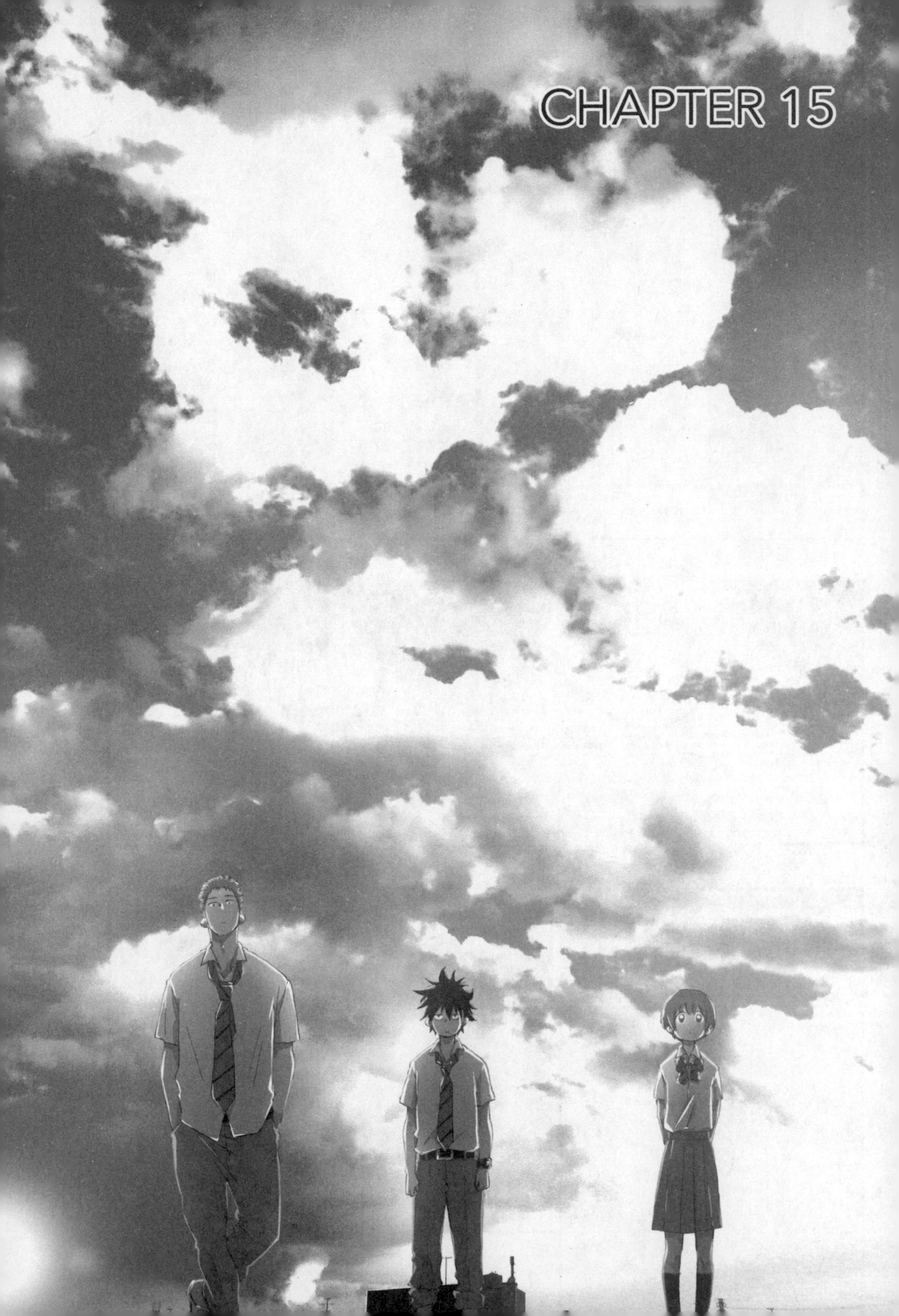

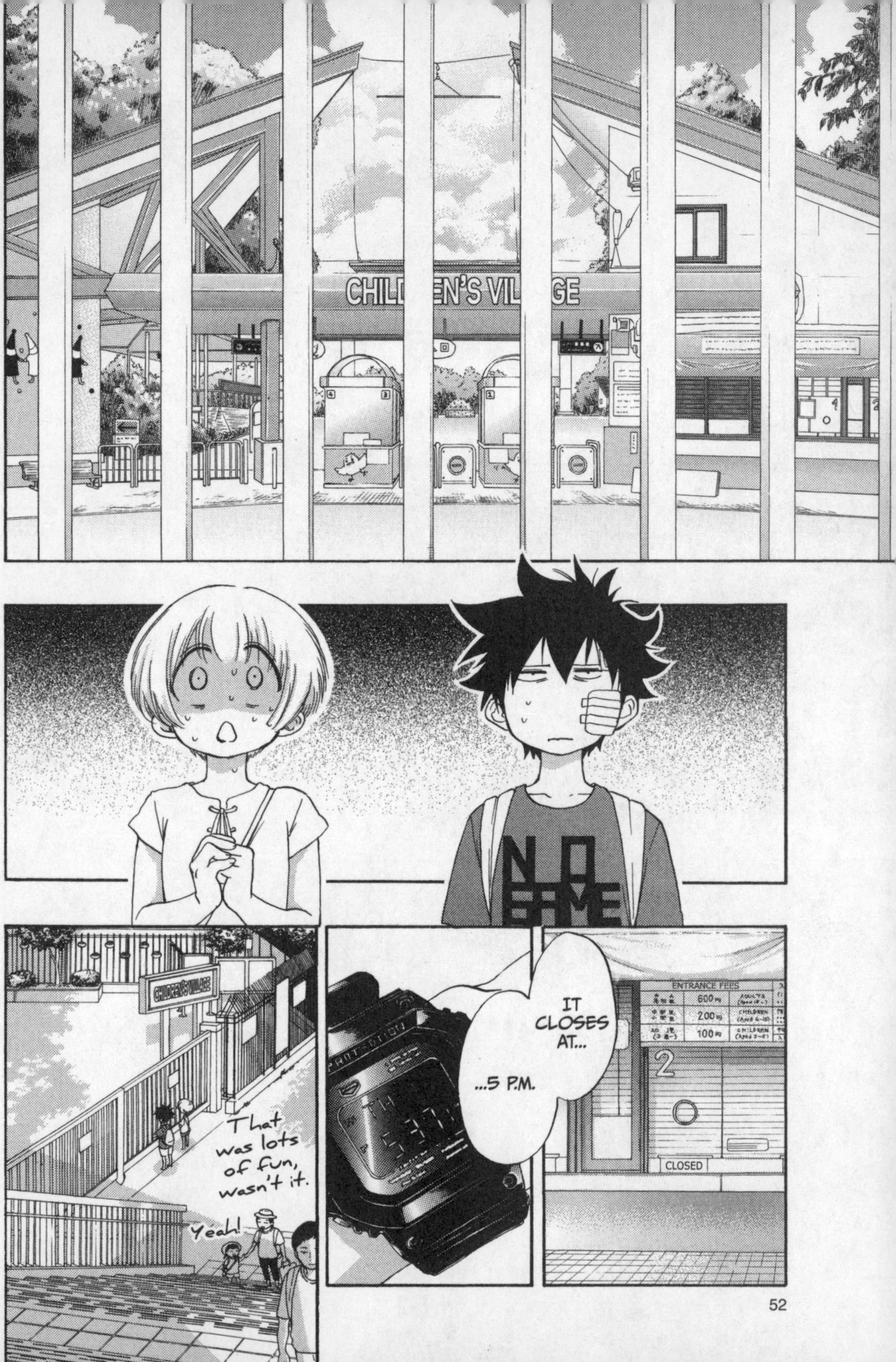

CHILDREN'S VILLAGE
ENTRANCE FEES
CLOSED
IT CLOSES AT...
...5 P.M.
That was lots of fun, wasn't it.
Yeah!

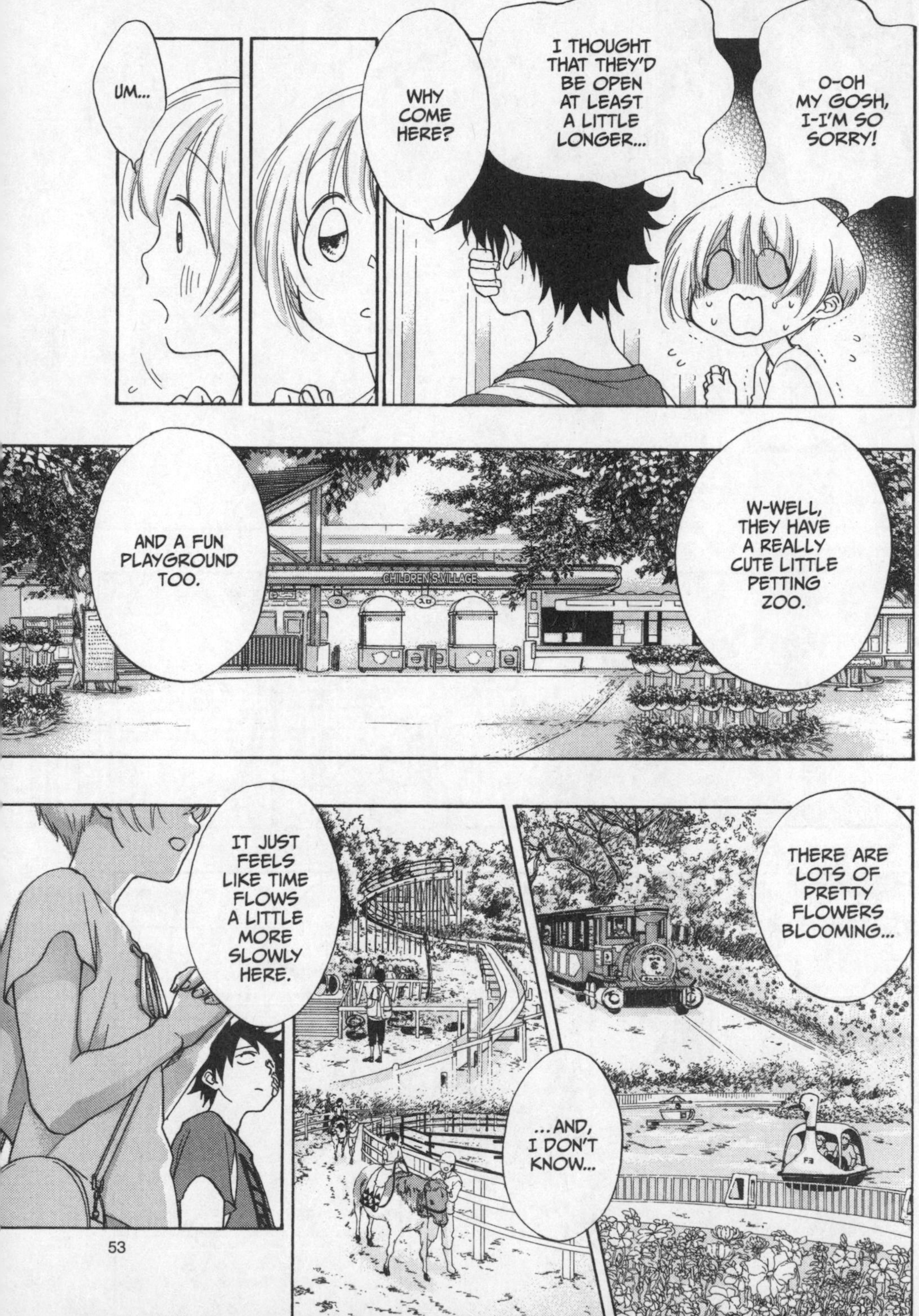
O-OH MY GOSH, I-I'M SO SORRY!
I THOUGHT THAT THEY'D BE OPEN AT LEAST A LITTLE LONGER...
WHY COME HERE?
UM...
W-WELL, THEY HAVE A REALLY CUTE LITTLE PETTING ZOO.
CHILDREN'S VILLAGE
AND A FUN PLAYGROUND TOO.
THERE ARE LOTS OF PRETTY FLOWERS BLOOMING...
...AND, I DON'T KNOW...
IT JUST FEELS LIKE TIME FLOWS A LITTLE MORE SLOWLY HERE.

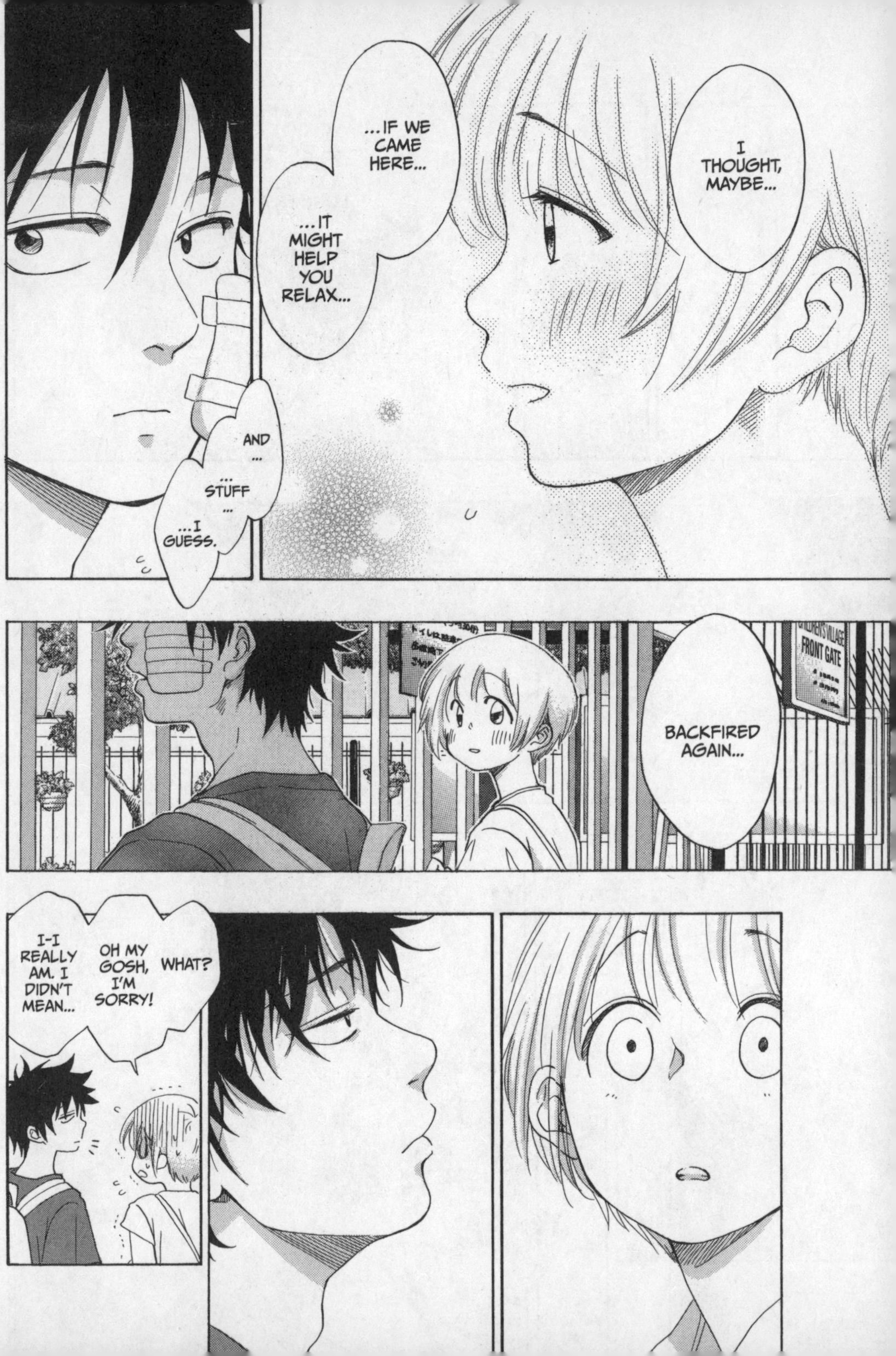
I THOUGHT, MAYBE...
...IF WE CAME HERE...
...IT MIGHT HELP YOU RELAX...
AND ... ... STUFF ... ...I GUESS.
CHILDREN'S VILLAGE FRONT GATE
BACKFIRED AGAIN...
WHAT?
OH MY GOSH, I'M SORRY!
I-I REALLY AM. I DIDN'T MEAN...

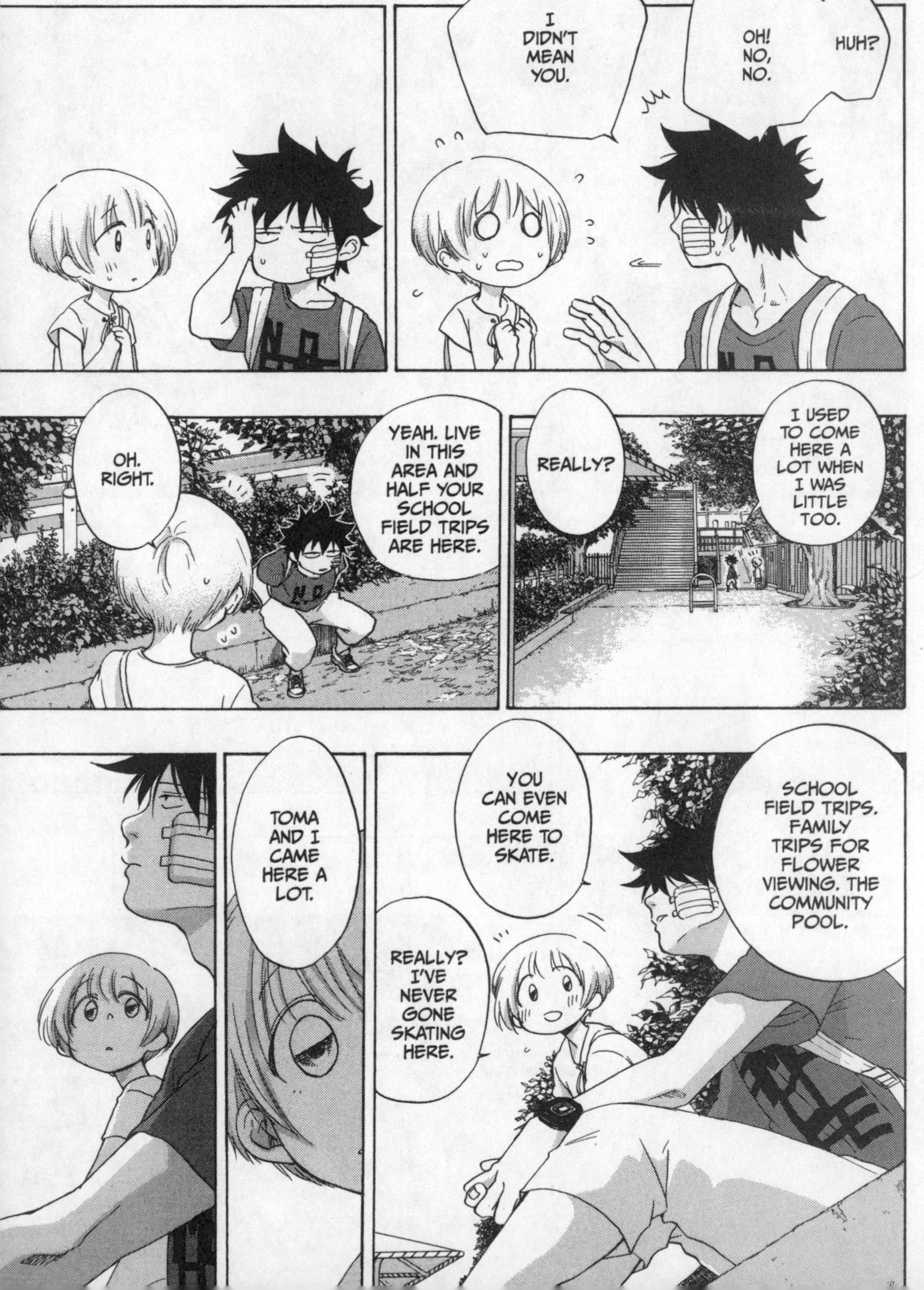
HUH?
OH! NO, NO.
I DIDN'T MEAN YOU.
I USED TO COME HERE A LOT WHEN I WAS LITTLE TOO.
REALLY?
YEAH. LIVE IN THIS AREA AND HALF YOUR SCHOOL FIELD TRIPS ARE HERE.
OH. RIGHT.
SCHOOL FIELD TRIPS. FAMILY TRIPS FOR FLOWER VIEWING. THE COMMUNITY POOL.
YOU CAN EVEN COME HERE TO SKATE.
REALLY? I'VE NEVER GONE SKATING HERE.
TOMA AND I CAME HERE A LOT.

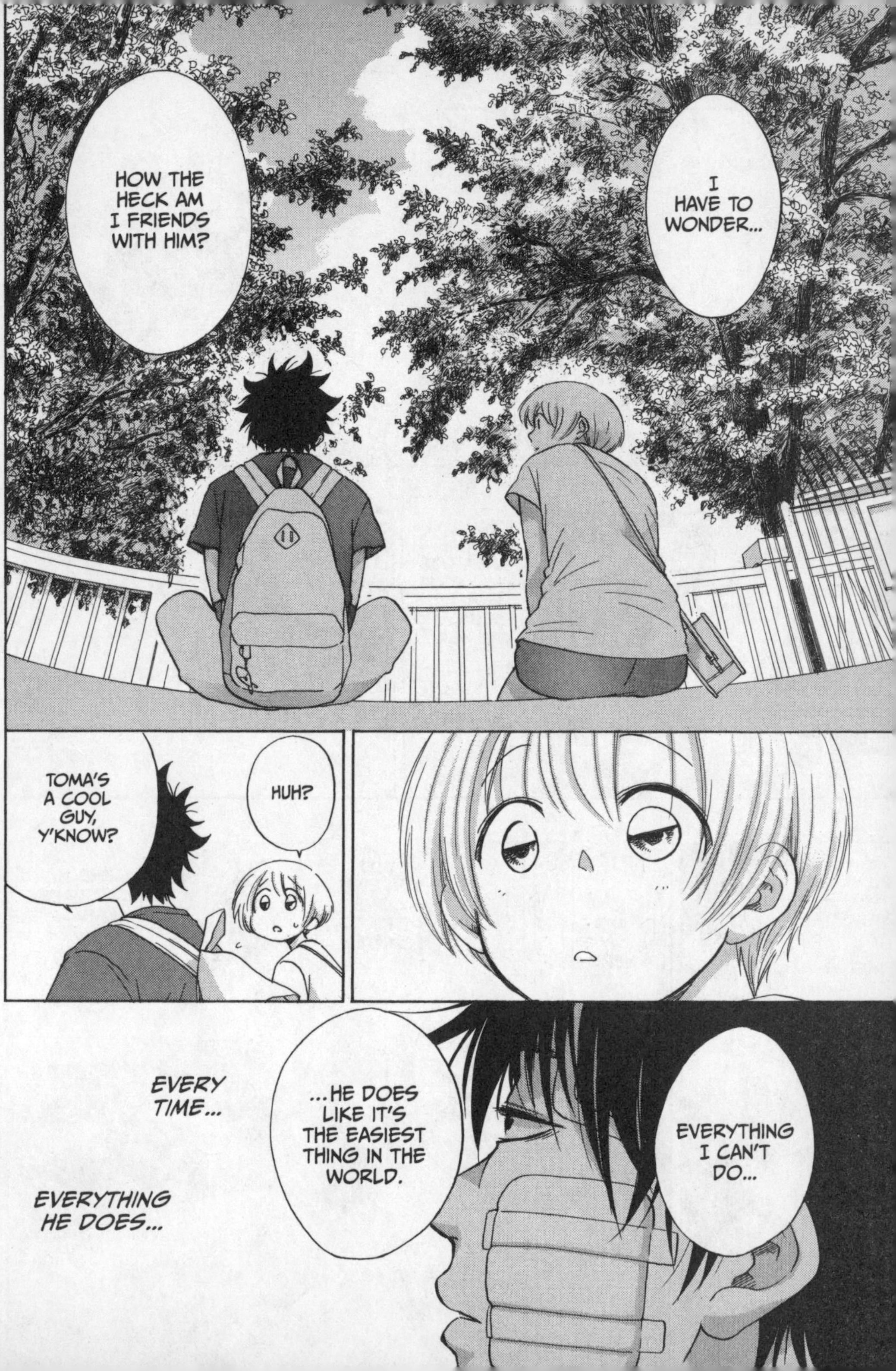
I HAVE TO WONDER...
HOW THE HECK AM I FRIENDS WITH HIM?
HUH?
TOMA'S A COOL GUY, Y'KNOW?
EVERYTHING I CAN'T DO...
...HE DOES LIKE IT'S THE EASIEST THING IN THE WORLD.
EVERY TIME...
EVERYTHING HE DOES...

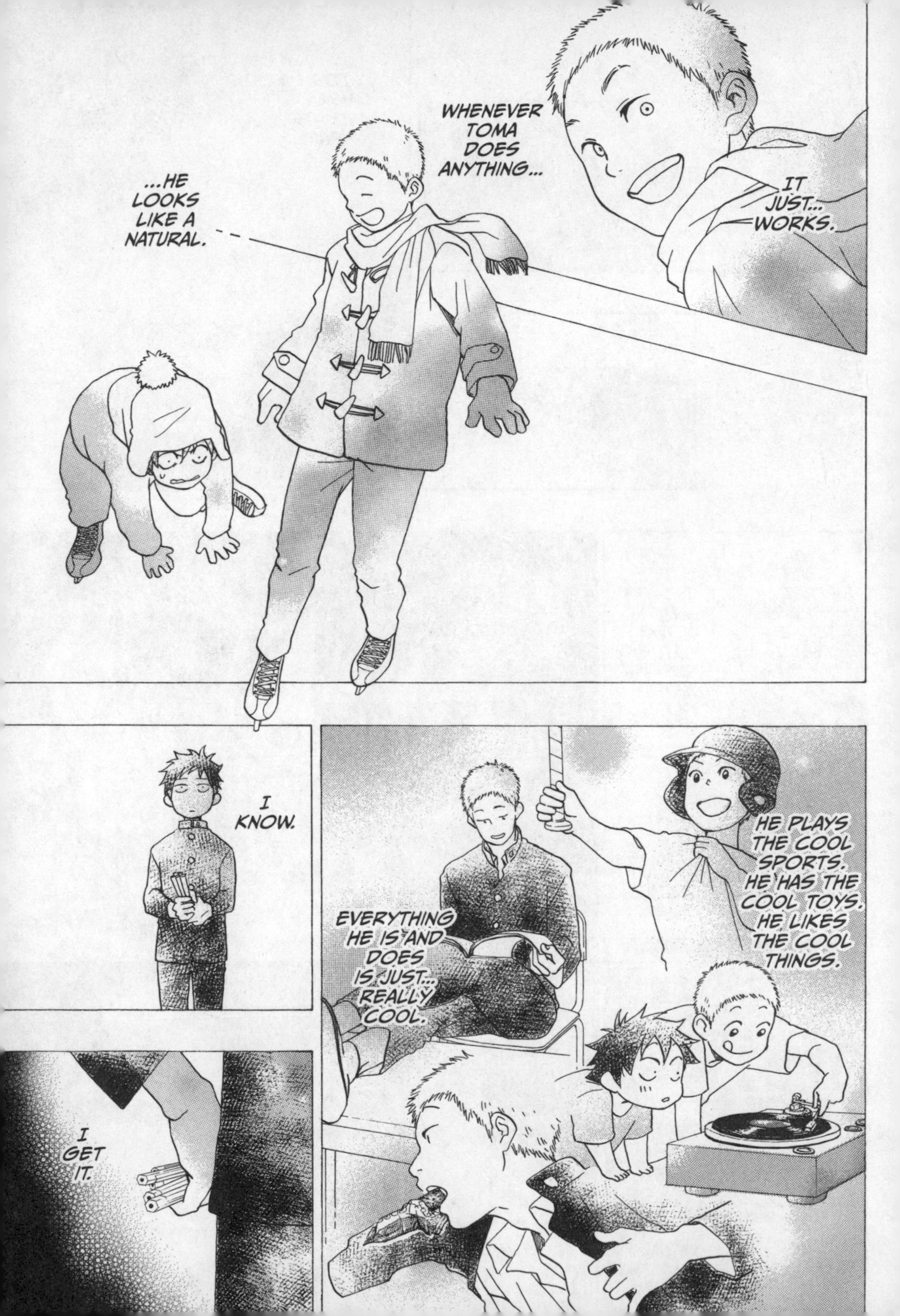
WHENEVER TOMA DOES ANYTHING...
IT JUST... WORKS.
...HE LOOKS LIKE A NATURAL.
HE PLAYS THE COOL SPORTS. HE HAS THE COOL TOYS. HE LIKES THE COOL THINGS.
EVERYTHING HE IS AND DOES IS JUST... REALLY COOL.
I KNOW.
I GET IT.

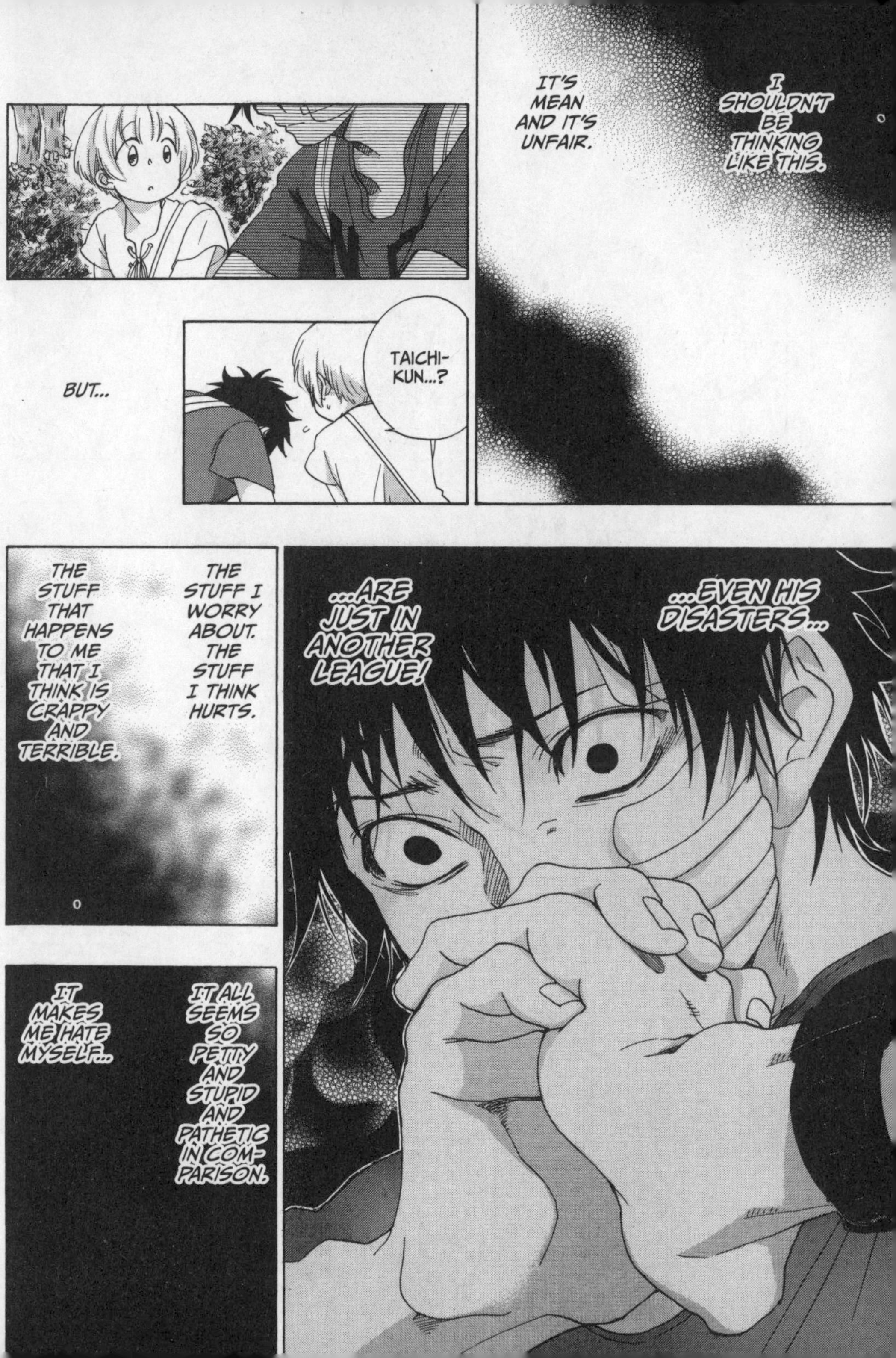
I SHOULDN'T BE THINKING LIKE THIS.
IT'S MEAN AND IT'S UNFAIR.
TAICHI-KUN...?
BUT...
...EVEN HIS DISASTERS...
...ARE JUST IN ANOTHER LEAGUE!
THE STUFF I WORRY ABOUT. THE STUFF I THINK HURTS.
THE STUFF THAT HAPPENS TO ME THAT I THINK IS CRAPPY AND TERRIBLE.
IT ALL SEEMS SO PETTY AND STUPID AND PATHETIC IN COMPARISON.
IT MAKES ME HATE MYSELF...

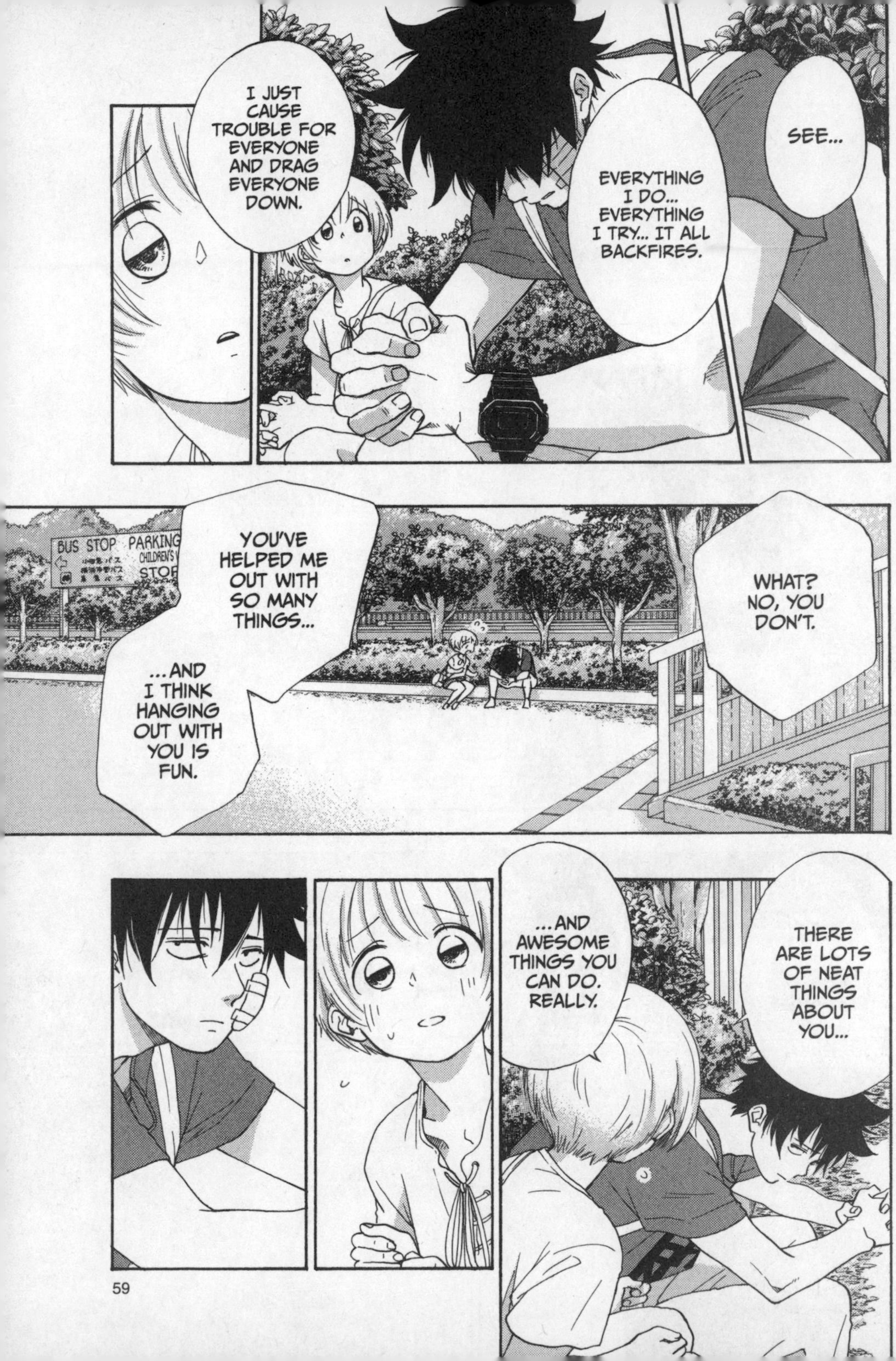
SEE...
EVERYTHING I DO... EVERYTHING I TRY... IT ALL BACKFIRES.
I JUST CAUSE TROUBLE FOR EVERYONE AND DRAG EVERYONE DOWN.
WHAT? NO, YOU DON'T.
YOU'VE HELPED ME OUT WITH SO MANY THINGS...
...AND I THINK HANGING OUT WITH YOU IS FUN.
BUS STOP
PARKING
THERE ARE LOTS OF NEAT THINGS ABOUT YOU...
...AND AWESOME THINGS YOU CAN DO. REALLY.

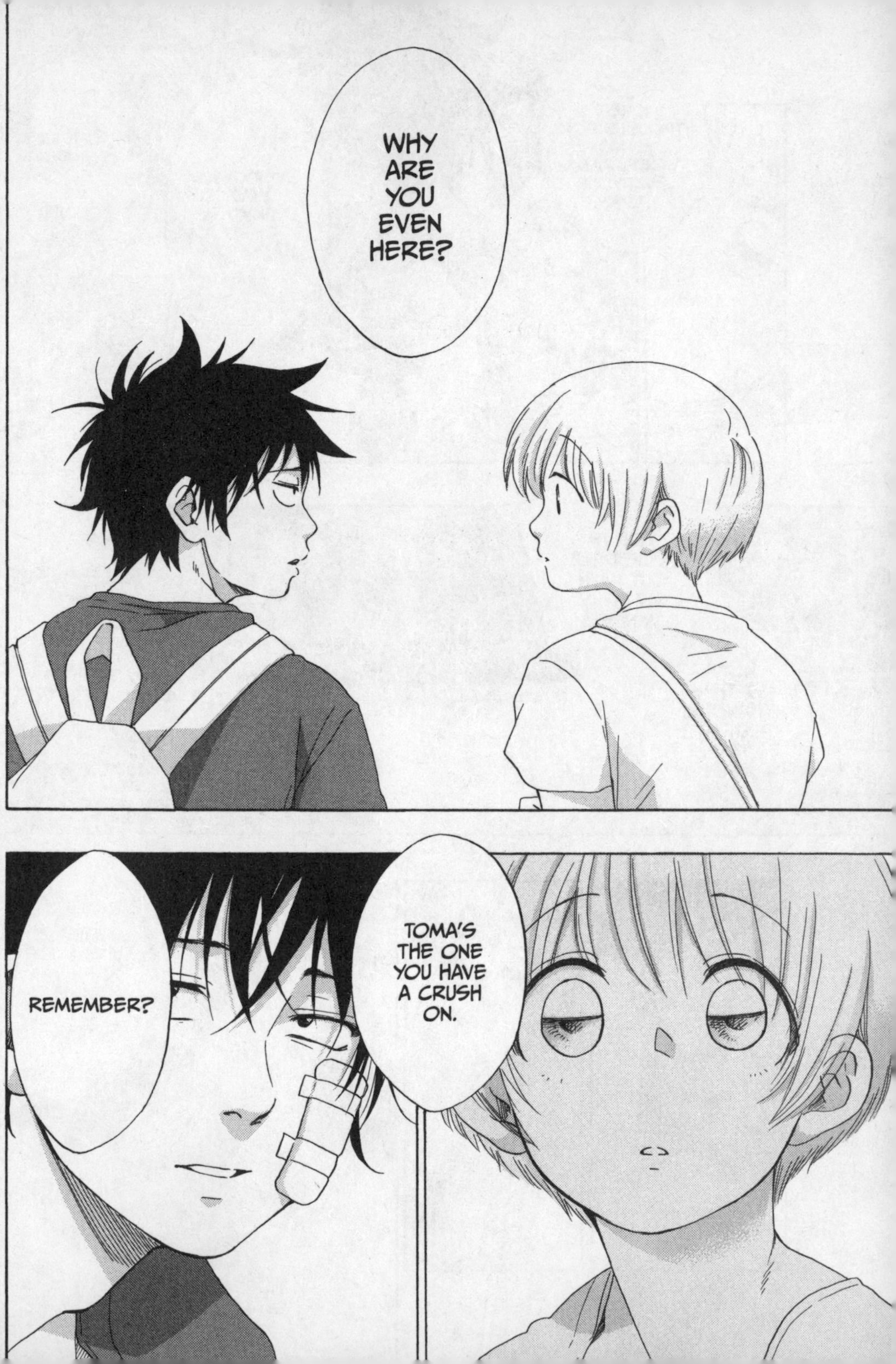
WHY ARE YOU EVEN HERE?
TOMA'S THE ONE YOU HAVE A CRUSH ON.
REMEMBER?

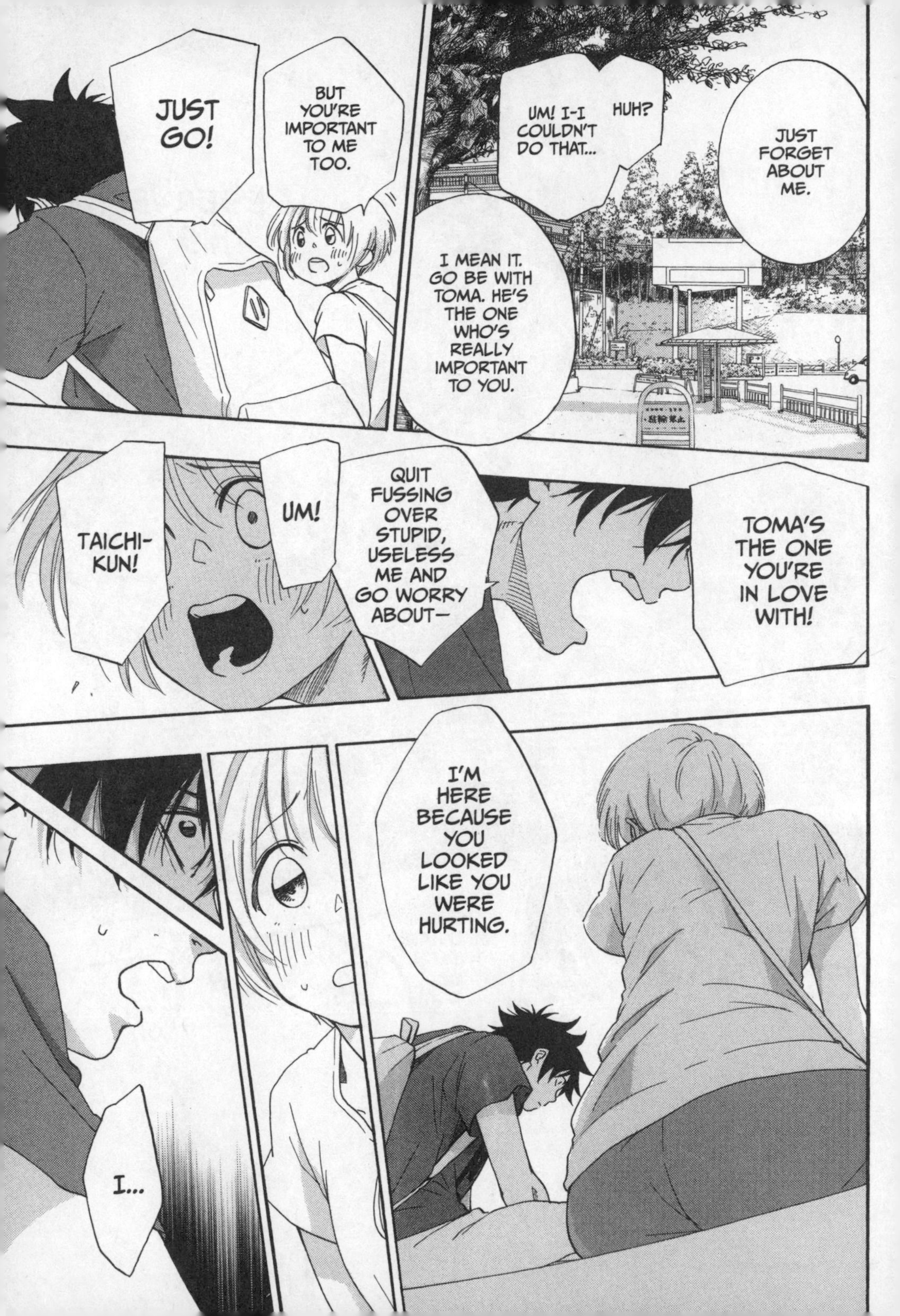
JUST FORGET ABOUT ME.
HUH?
UM! I-I COULDN'T DO THAT...
I MEAN IT. GO BE WITH TOMA. HE'S THE ONE WHO'S REALLY IMPORTANT TO YOU.
BUT YOU'RE IMPORTANT TO ME TOO.
JUST GO!
TOMA'S THE ONE YOU'RE IN LOVE WITH!
QUIT FUSSING OVER STUPID, USELESS ME AND GO WORRY ABOUT—
UM!
TAICHI-KUN!
I'M HERE BECAUSE YOU LOOKED LIKE YOU WERE HURTING.
I...

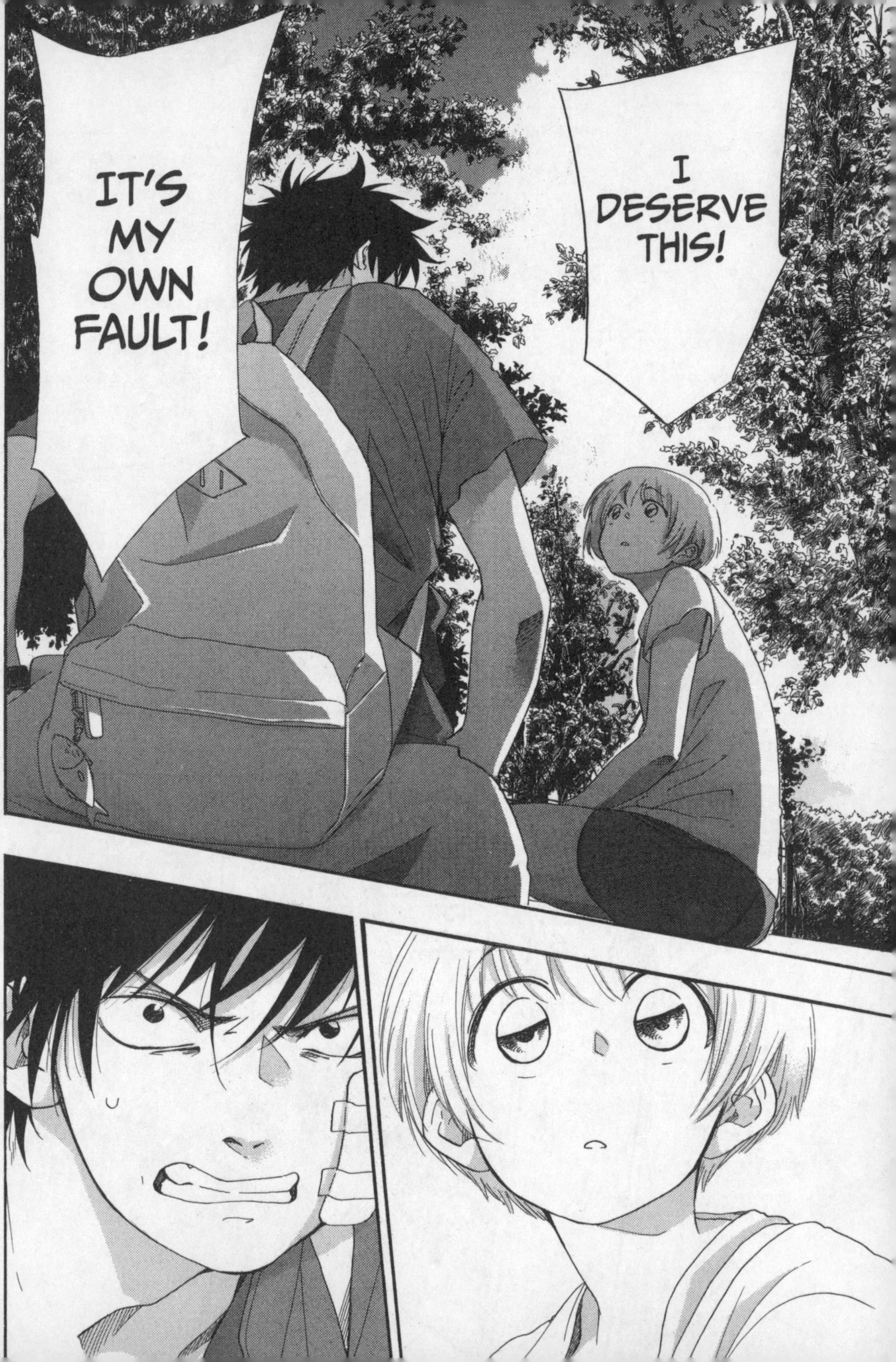
I DESERVE THIS!
IT'S MY OWN FAULT!

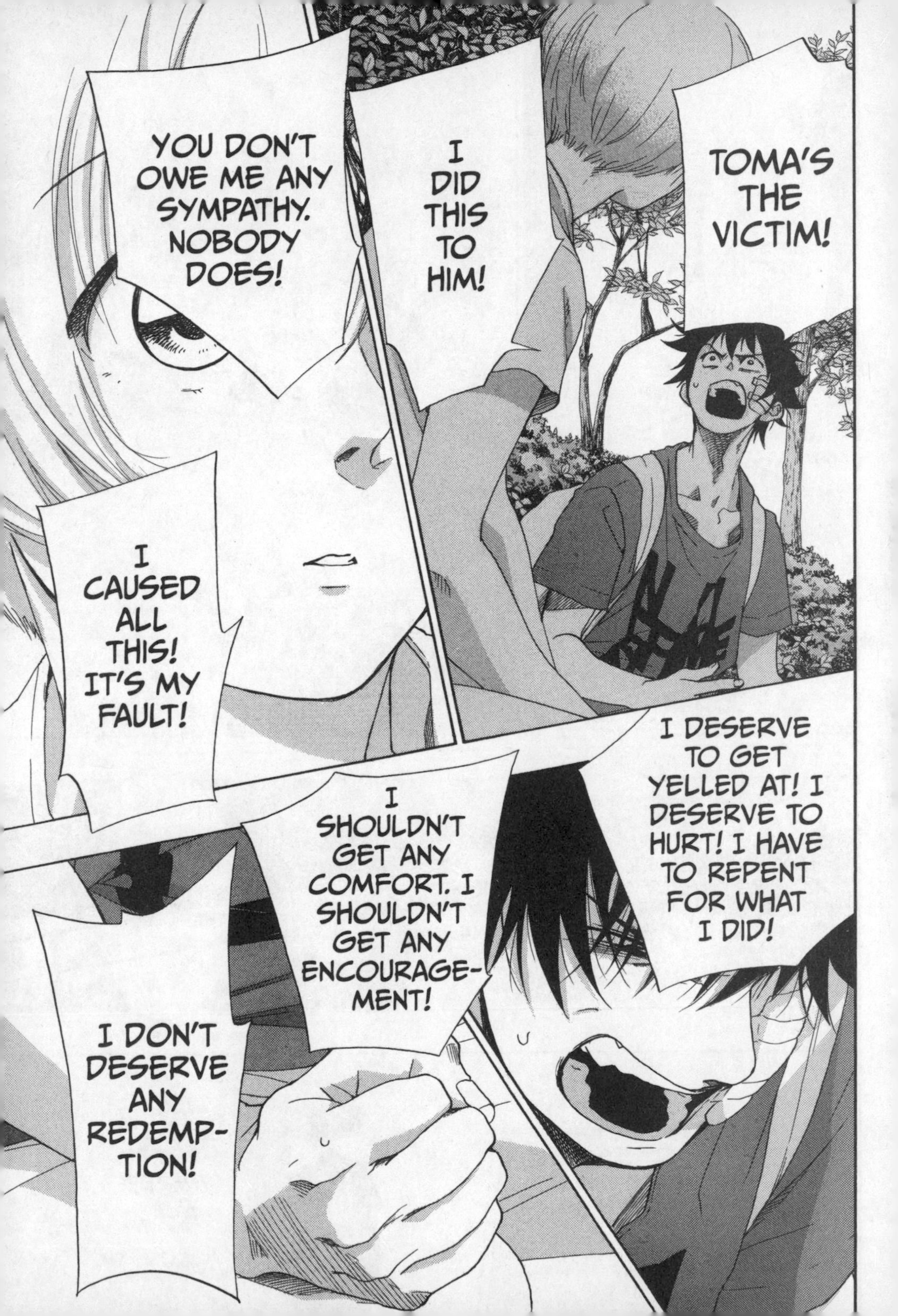
TOMA'S THE VICTIM!
I DID THIS TO HIM!
YOU DON'T OWE ME ANY SYMPATHY. NOBODY DOES!
I CAUSED ALL THIS! IT'S MY FAULT!
I DESERVE TO GET YELLED AT! I DESERVE TO HURT! I HAVE TO REPENT FOR WHAT I DID!
I SHOULDN'T GET ANY COMFORT. I SHOULDN'T GET ANY ENCOURAGE-MENT!
I DON'T DESERVE ANY REDEMP-TION!

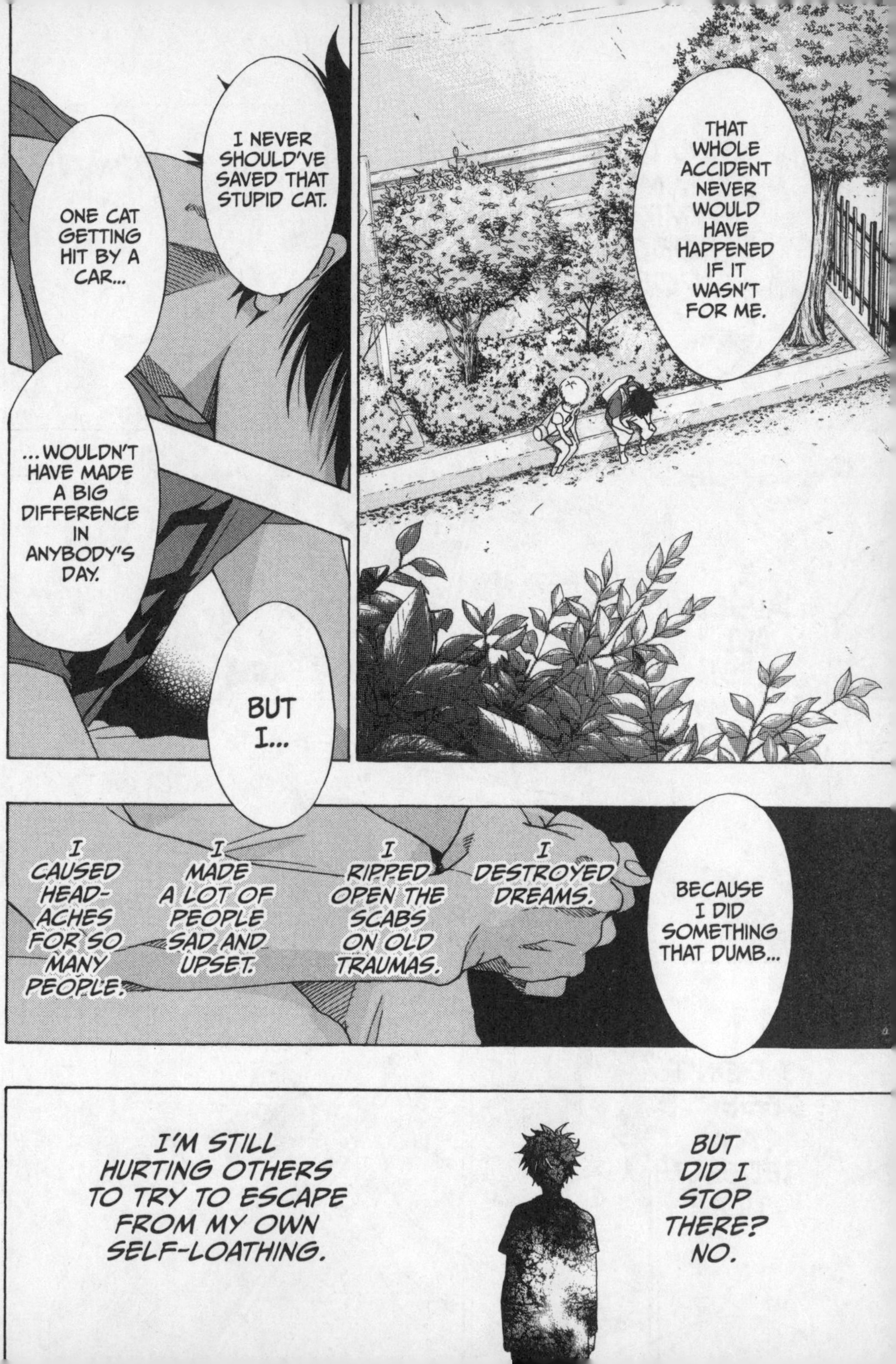
THAT WHOLE ACCIDENT NEVER WOULD HAVE HAPPENED IF IT WASN'T FOR ME.
I NEVER SHOULD'VE SAVED THAT STUPID CAT.
ONE CAT GETTING HIT BY A CAR...
...WOULDN'T HAVE MADE A BIG DIFFERENCE IN ANYBODY'S DAY.
BUT I...
BECAUSE I DID SOMETHING THAT DUMB...
I DESTROYED DREAMS.
I RIPPED OPEN THE SCABS ON OLD TRAUMAS.
I MADE A LOT OF PEOPLE SAD AND UPSET.
I CAUSED HEAD-ACHES FOR SO MANY PEOPLE.
BUT DID I STOP THERE? NO.
I'M STILL HURTING OTHERS TO TRY TO ESCAPE FROM MY OWN SELF-LOATHING.

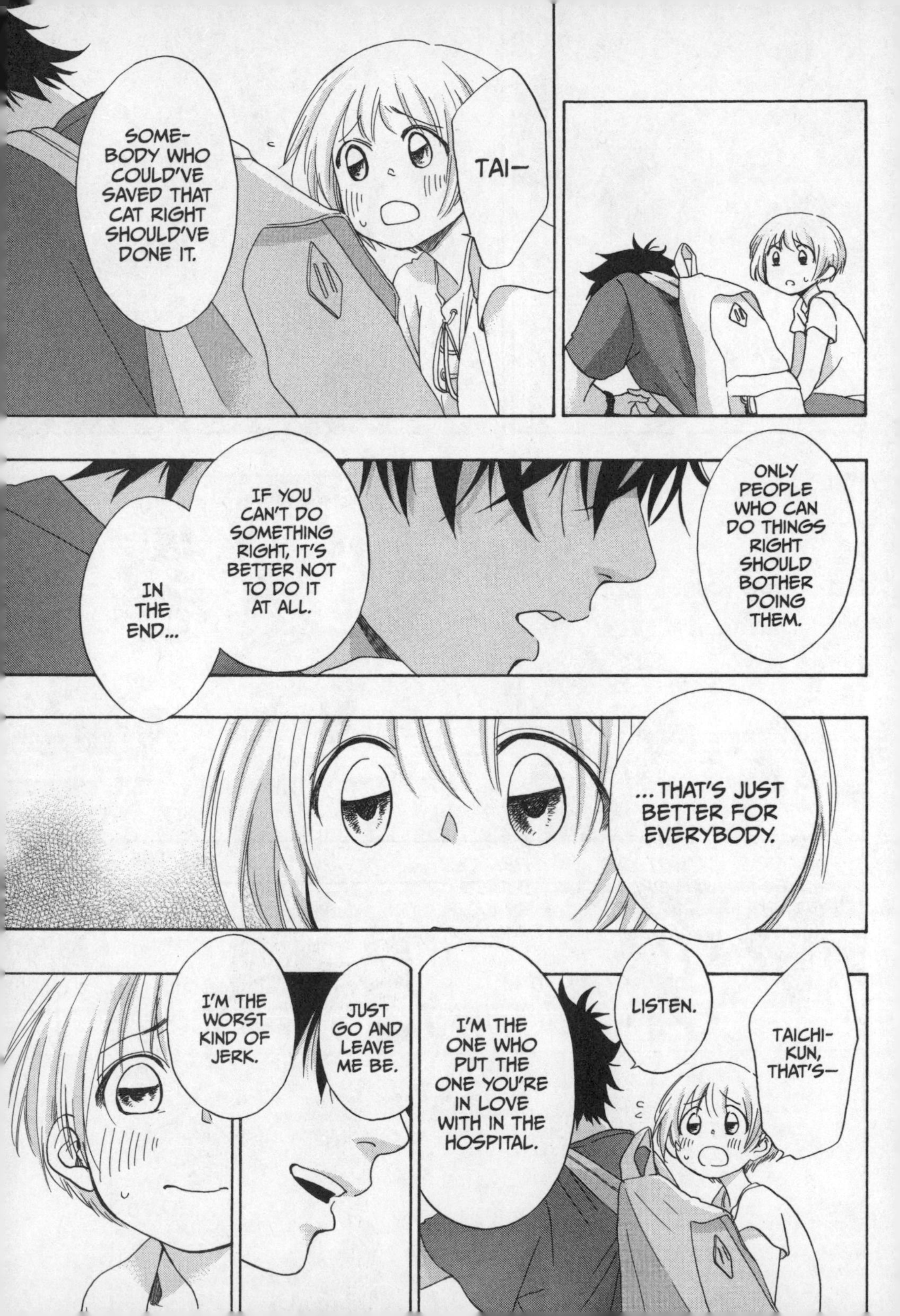
TAI—
SOME-BODY WHO COULD'VE SAVED THAT CAT RIGHT SHOULD'VE DONE IT.
ONLY PEOPLE WHO CAN DO THINGS RIGHT SHOULD BOTHER DOING THEM.
IF YOU CAN'T DO SOMETHING RIGHT, IT'S BETTER NOT TO DO IT AT ALL.
IN THE END...
...THAT'S JUST BETTER FOR EVERYBODY.
TAICHI-KUN, THAT'S—
LISTEN.
I'M THE ONE WHO PUT THE ONE YOU'RE IN LOVE WITH IN THE HOSPITAL.
JUST GO AND LEAVE ME BE.
I'M THE WORST KIND OF JERK.

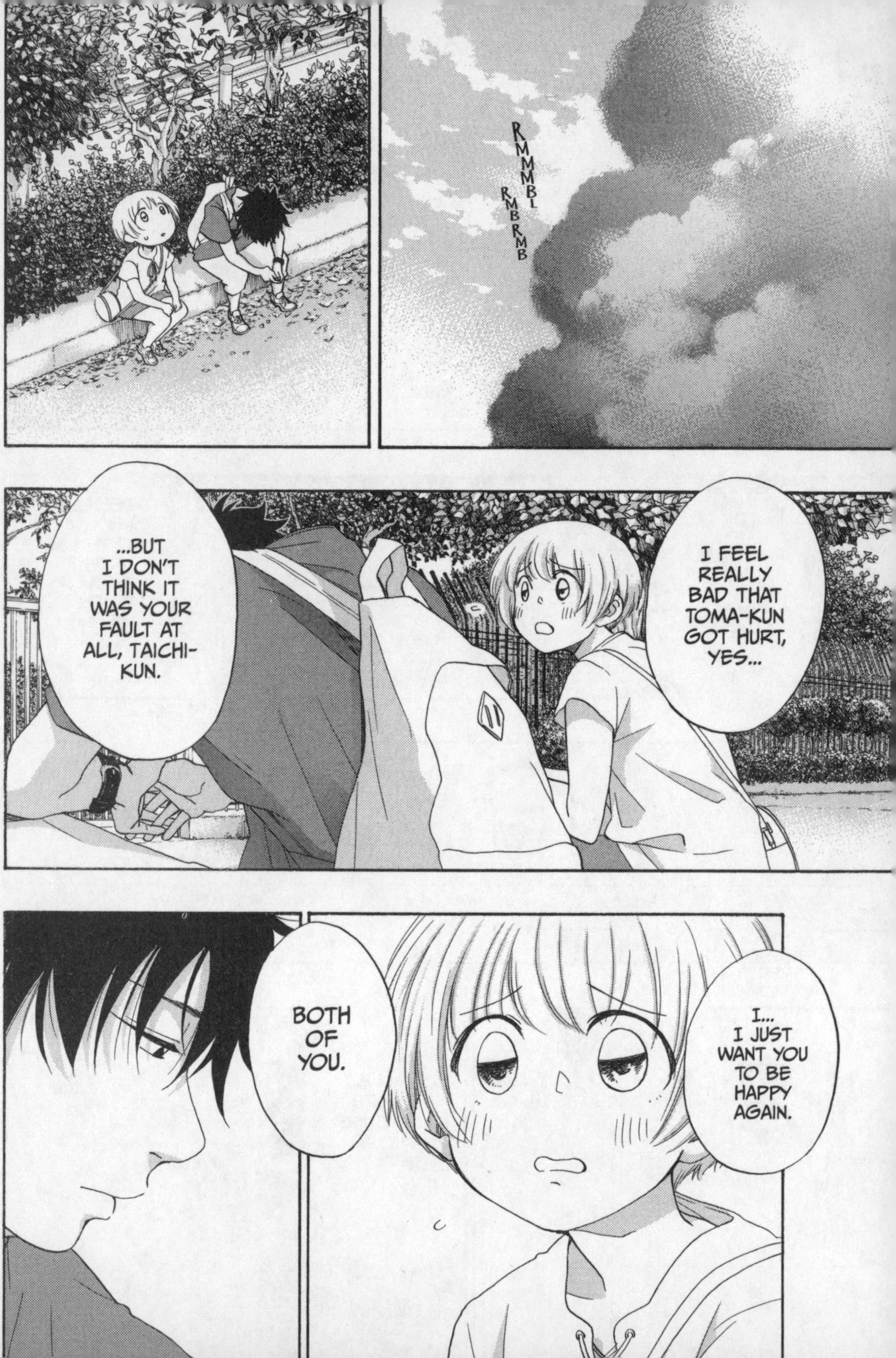
RMMMBL
RMBRMB
I FEEL REALLY BAD THAT TOMA-KUN GOT HURT, YES...
...BUT I DON'T THINK IT WAS YOUR FAULT AT ALL, TAICHI-KUN.
I... I JUST WANT YOU TO BE HAPPY AGAIN.
BOTH OF YOU.

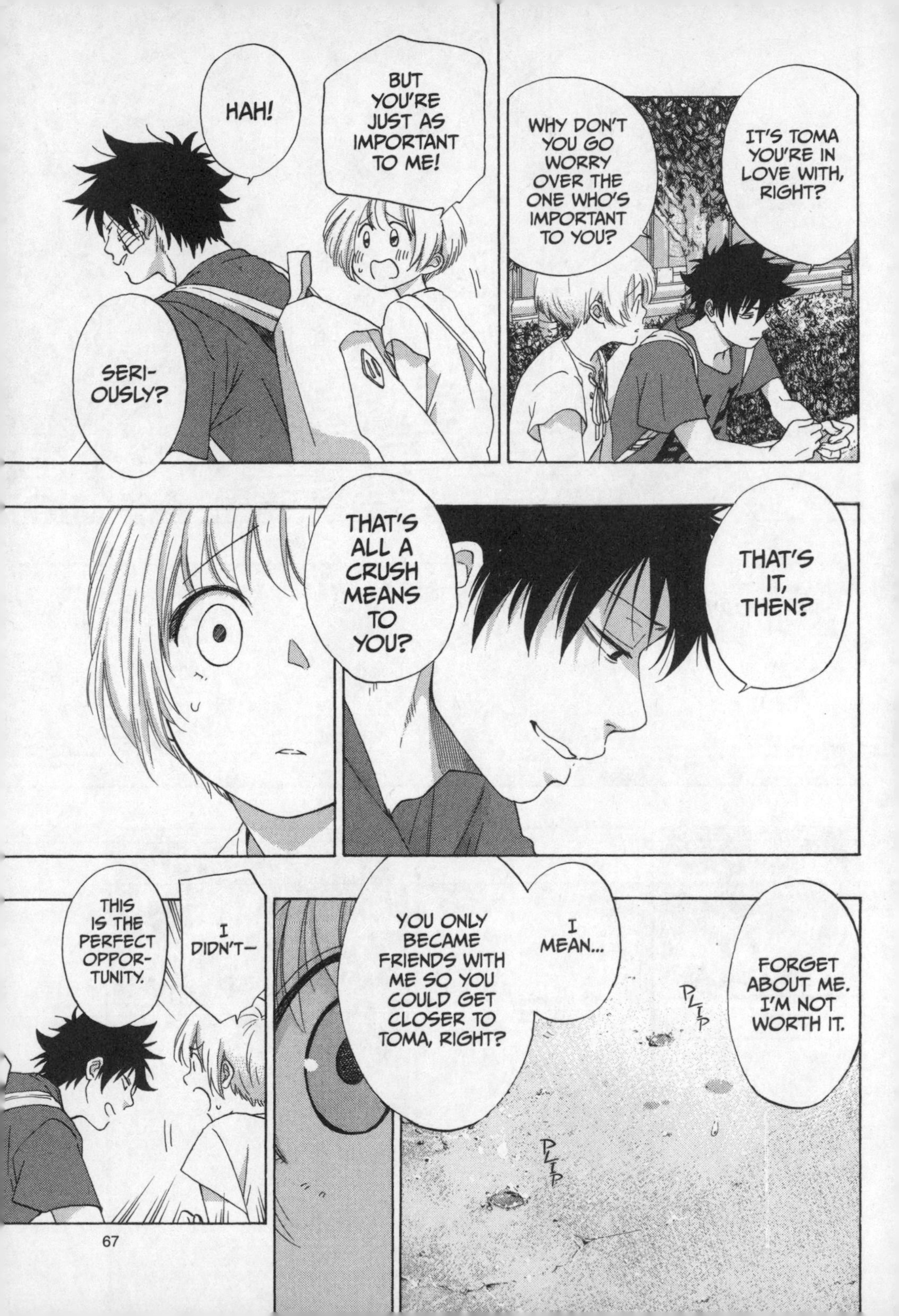
IT'S TOMA YOU'RE IN LOVE WITH, RIGHT?
WHY DON'T YOU GO WORRY OVER THE ONE WHO'S IMPORTANT TO YOU?
BUT YOU'RE JUST AS IMPORTANT TO ME!
HAH!
SERI-OUSLY?
THAT'S IT, THEN?
THAT'S ALL A CRUSH MEANS TO YOU?
FORGET ABOUT ME. I'M NOT WORTH IT.
PLIP
I MEAN...
YOU ONLY BECAME FRIENDS WITH ME SO YOU COULD GET CLOSER TO TOMA, RIGHT?
PLIP
I DIDN'T—
THIS IS THE PERFECT OPPOR-TUNITY.

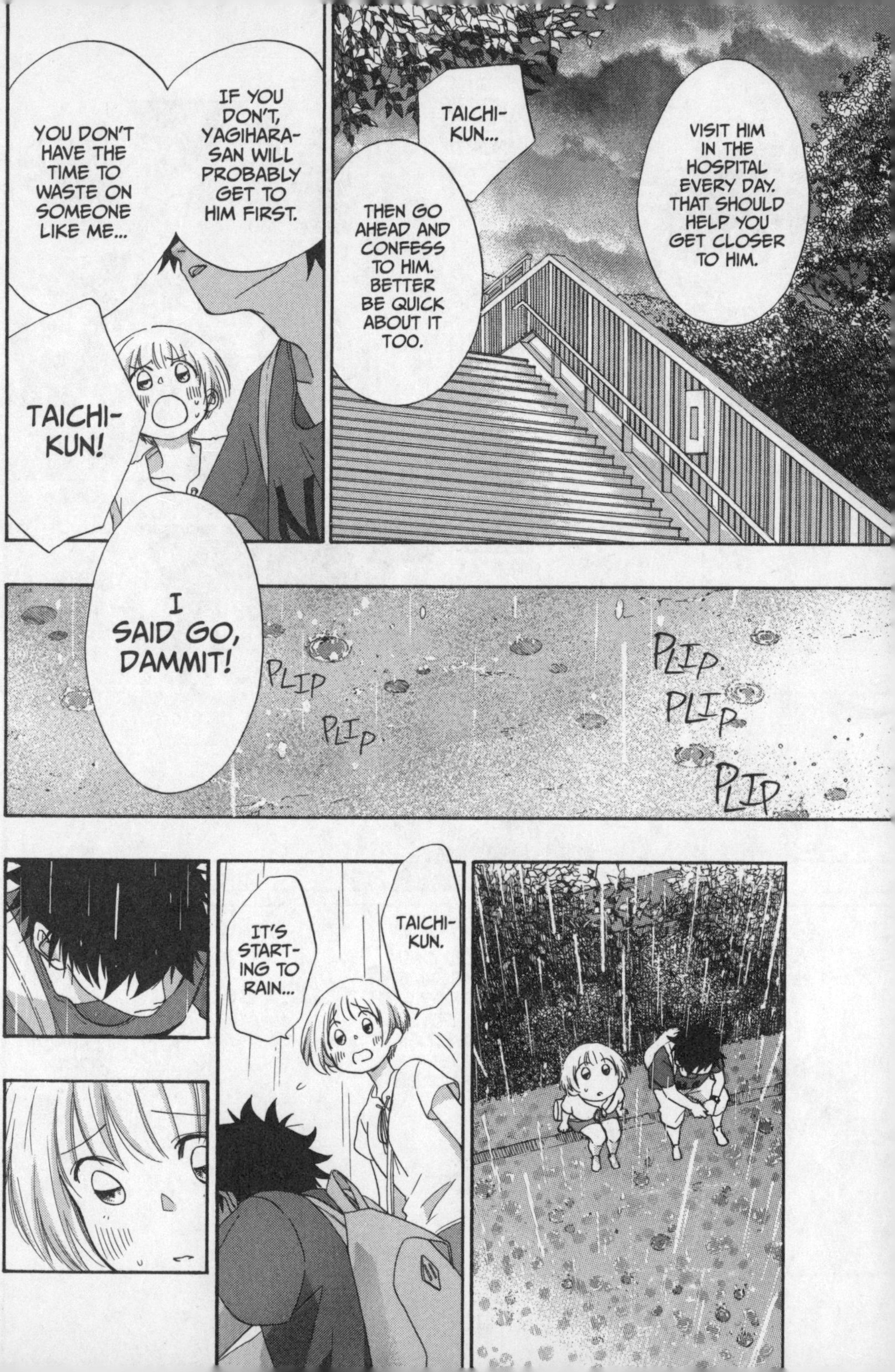

VISIT HIM IN THE HOSPITAL EVERY DAY. THAT SHOULD HELP YOU GET CLOSER TO HIM.
TAICHI-KUN...
THEN GO AHEAD AND CONFESS TO HIM. BETTER BE QUICK ABOUT IT TOO.
IF YOU DON'T, YAGIHARA-SAN WILL PROBABLY GET TO HIM FIRST.
YOU DON'T HAVE THE TIME TO WASTE ON SOMEONE LIKE ME...
TAICHI-KUN!
I SAID GO, DAMMIT!
PLIP
PLIP
PLIP
PLIP
PLIP
TAICHI-KUN.
IT'S STARTING TO RAIN...

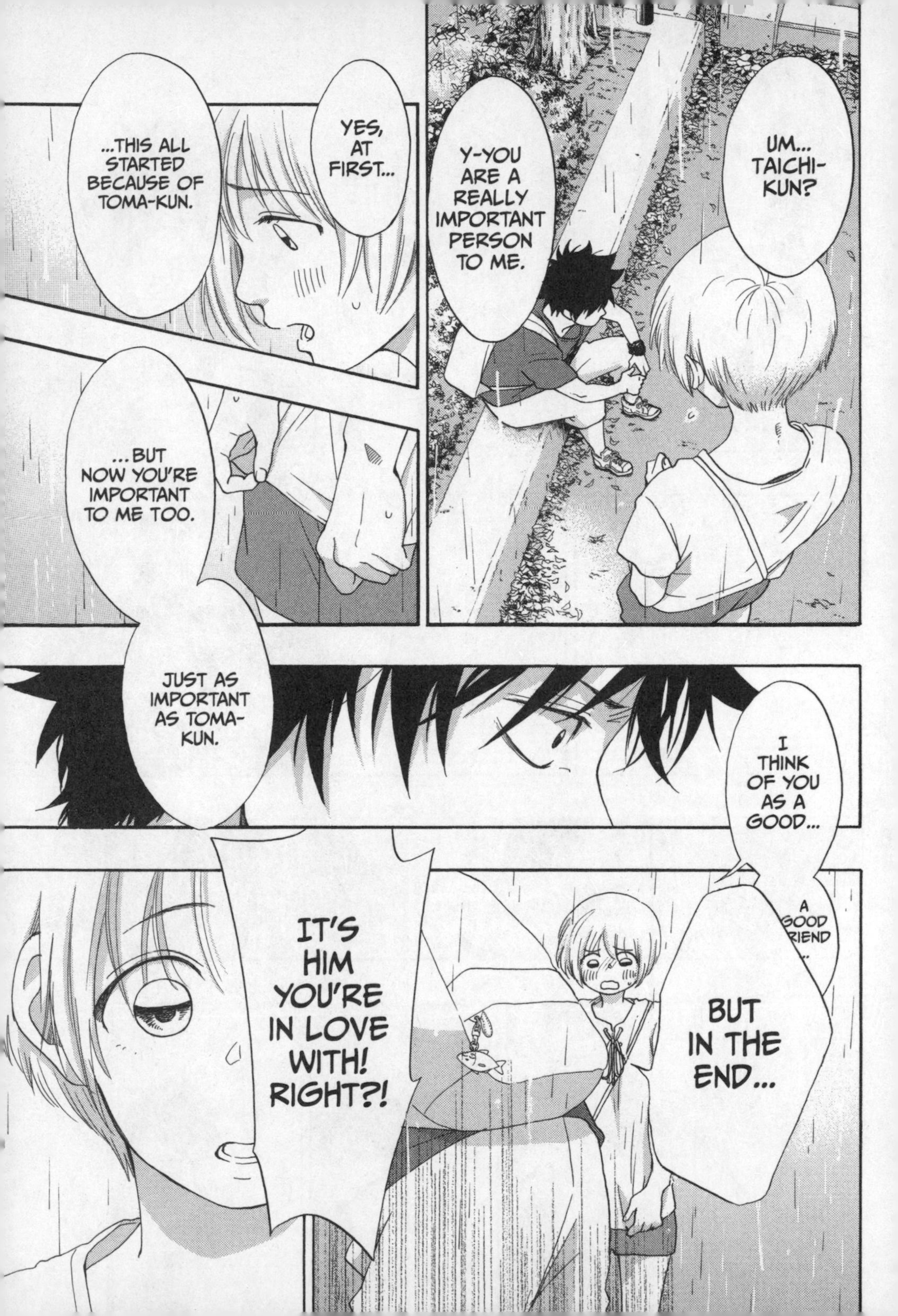
UM... TAICHI-KUN?
Y-YOU ARE A REALLY IMPORTANT PERSON TO ME.
YES, AT FIRST...
...THIS ALL STARTED BECAUSE OF TOMA-KUN.
...BUT NOW YOU'RE IMPORTANT TO ME TOO.
JUST AS IMPORTANT AS TOMA-KUN.
I THINK OF YOU AS A GOOD...
A GOOD
BUT IN THE END...
IT'S HIM YOU'RE IN LOVE WITH! RIGHT?!

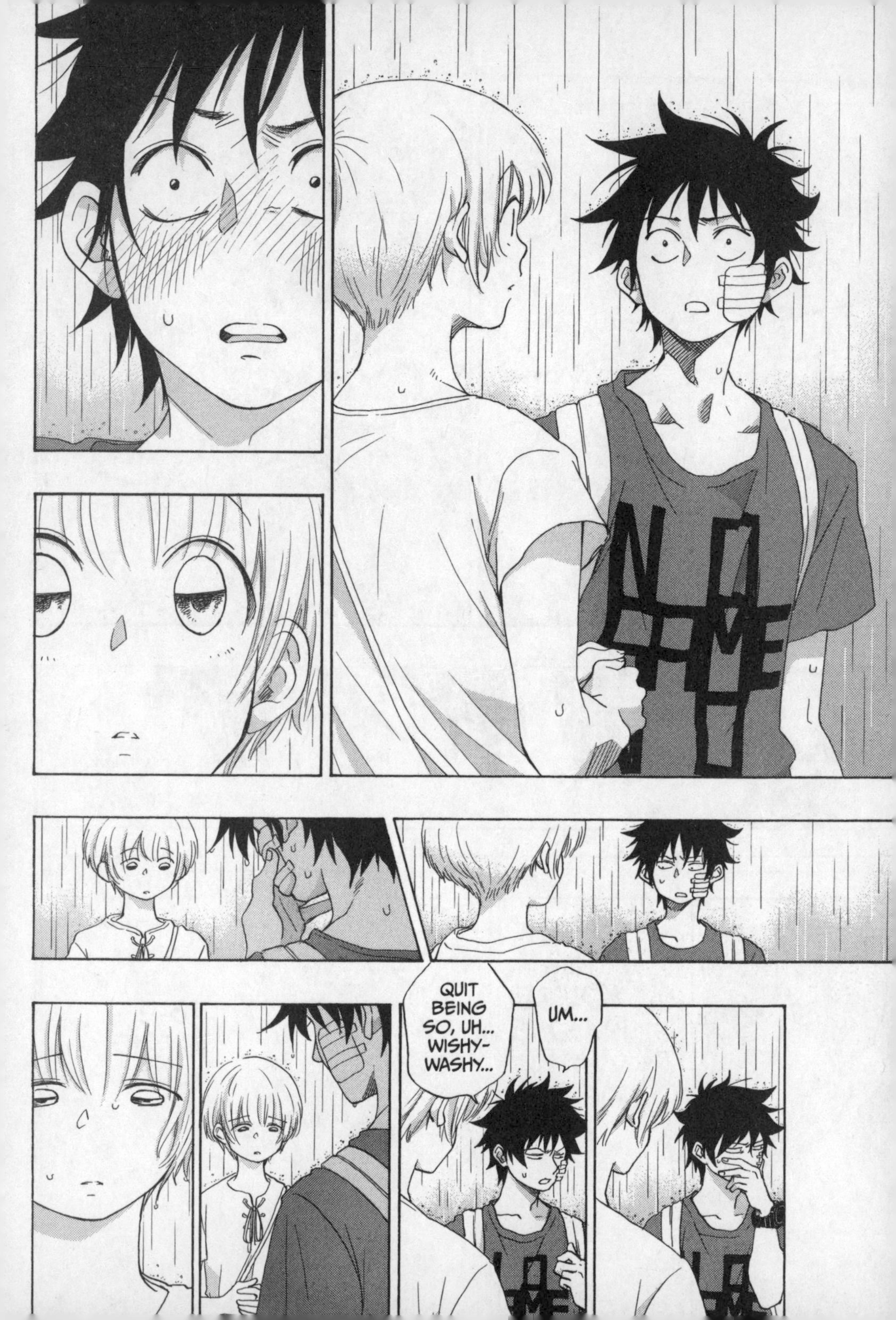
UM...
QUIT BEING SO, UH... WISHY-WASHY...

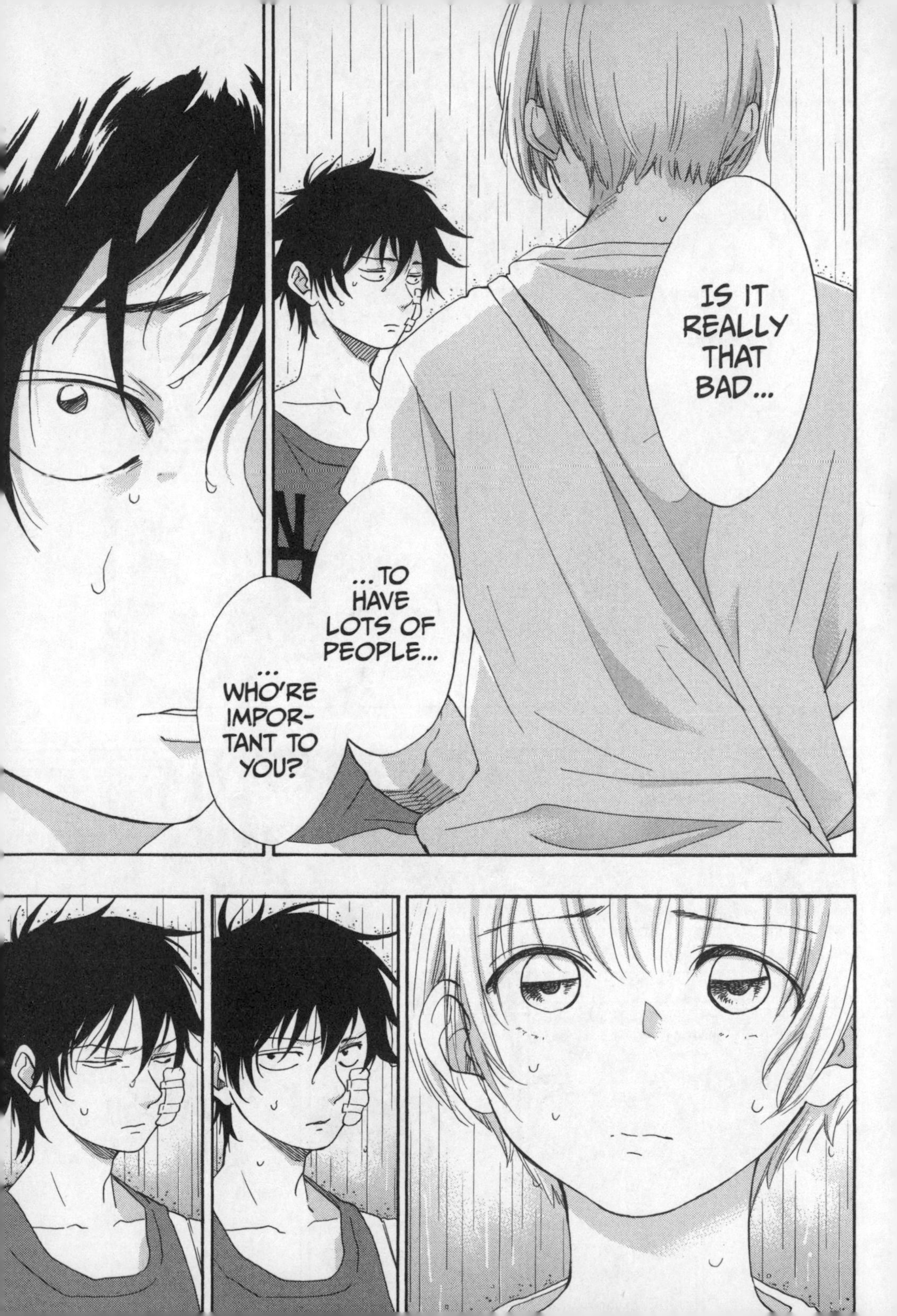
IS IT REALLY THAT BAD...
...TO HAVE LOTS OF PEOPLE...
...WHO'RE IMPORTANT TO YOU?

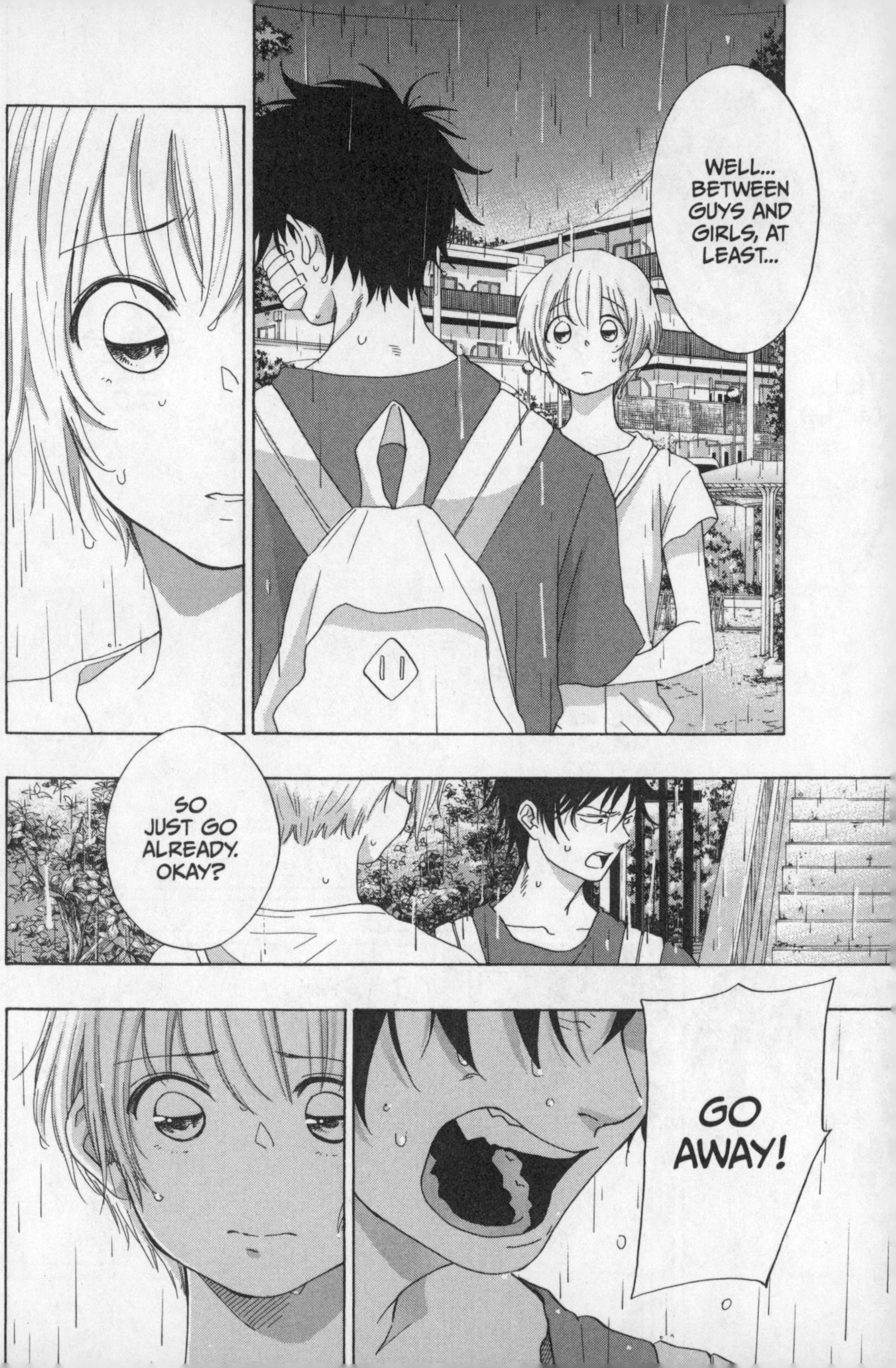
WELL... BETWEEN GUYS AND GIRLS, AT LEAST...
SO JUST GO ALREADY. OKAY?
GO AWAY!

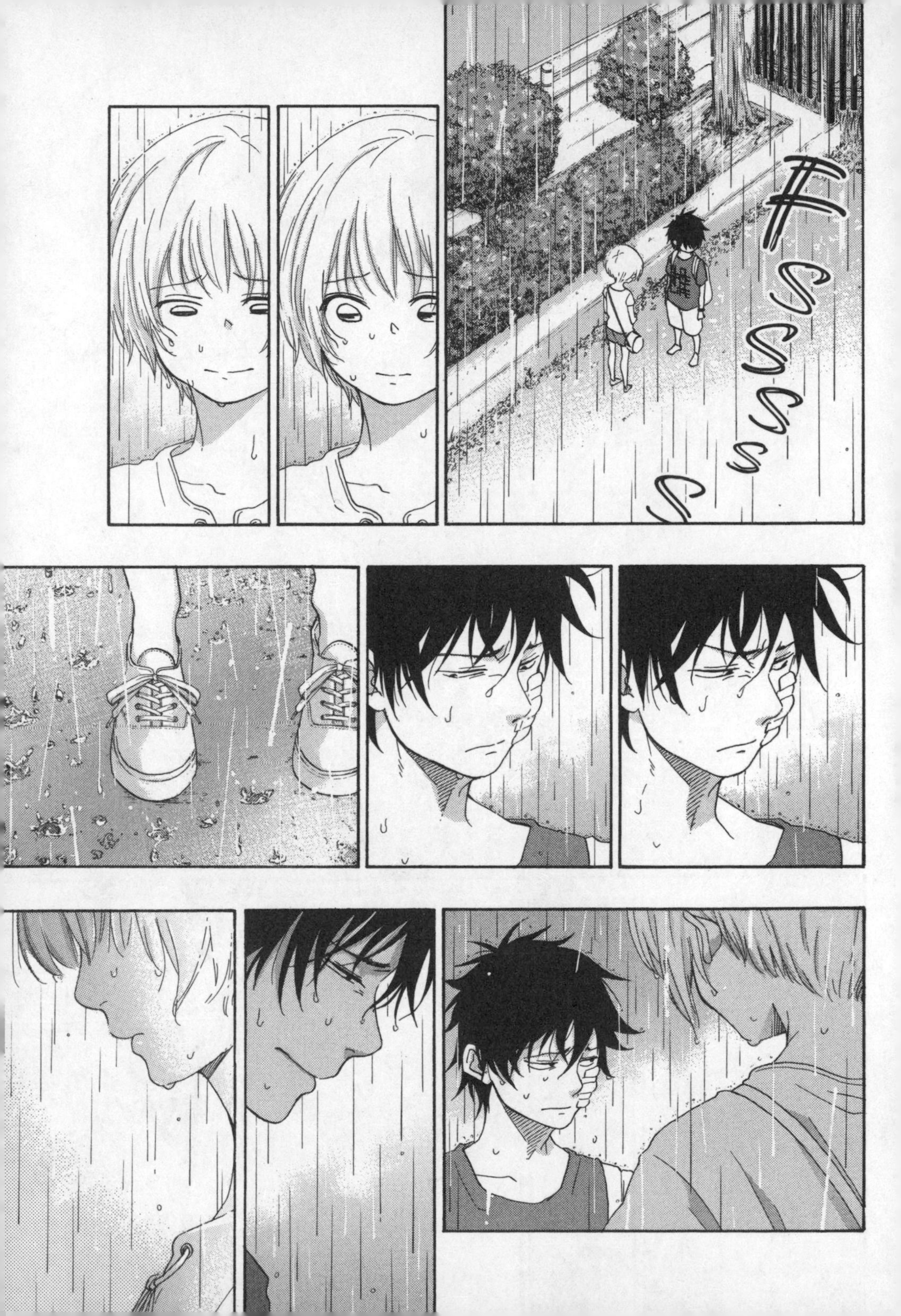
FSSSSSS

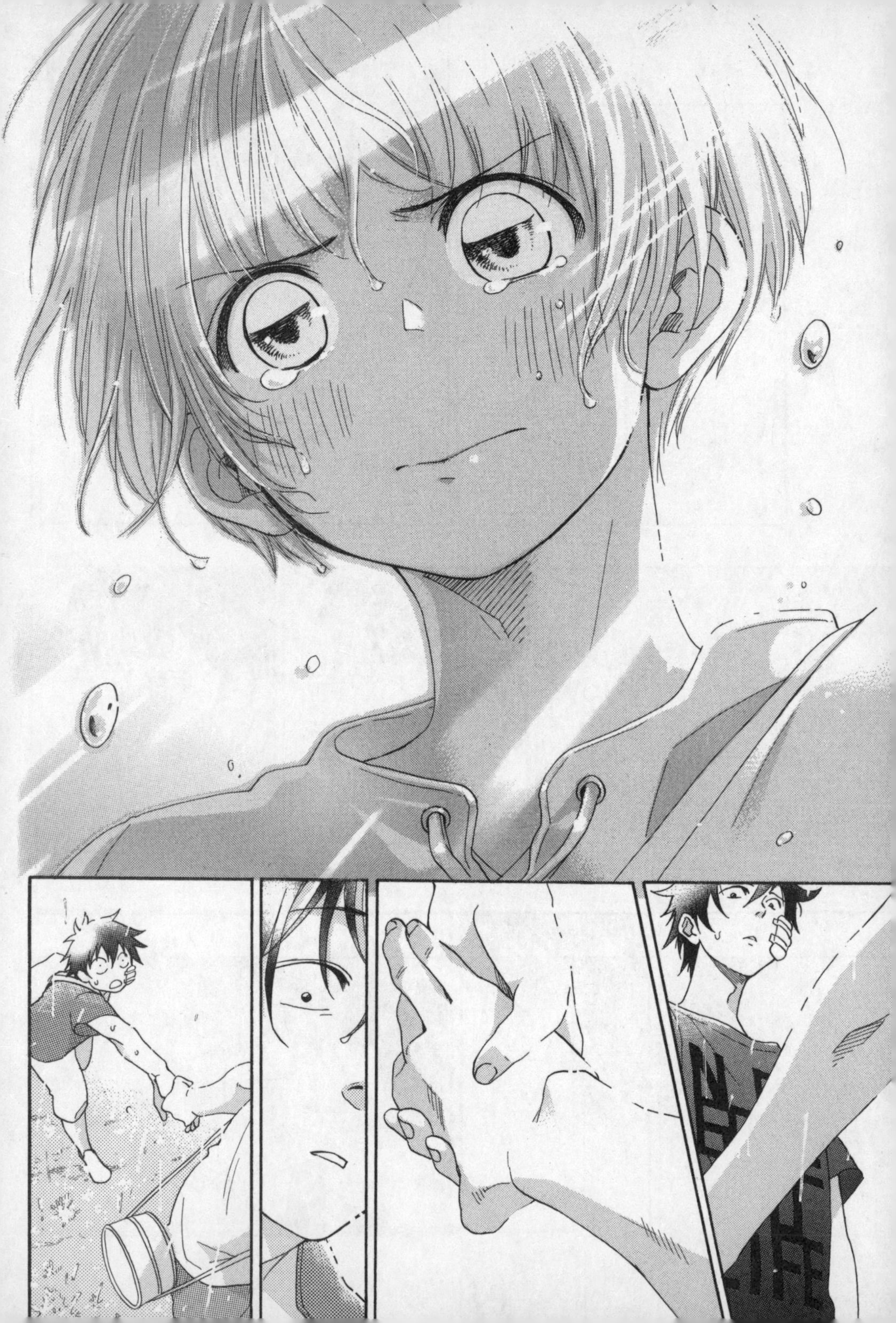

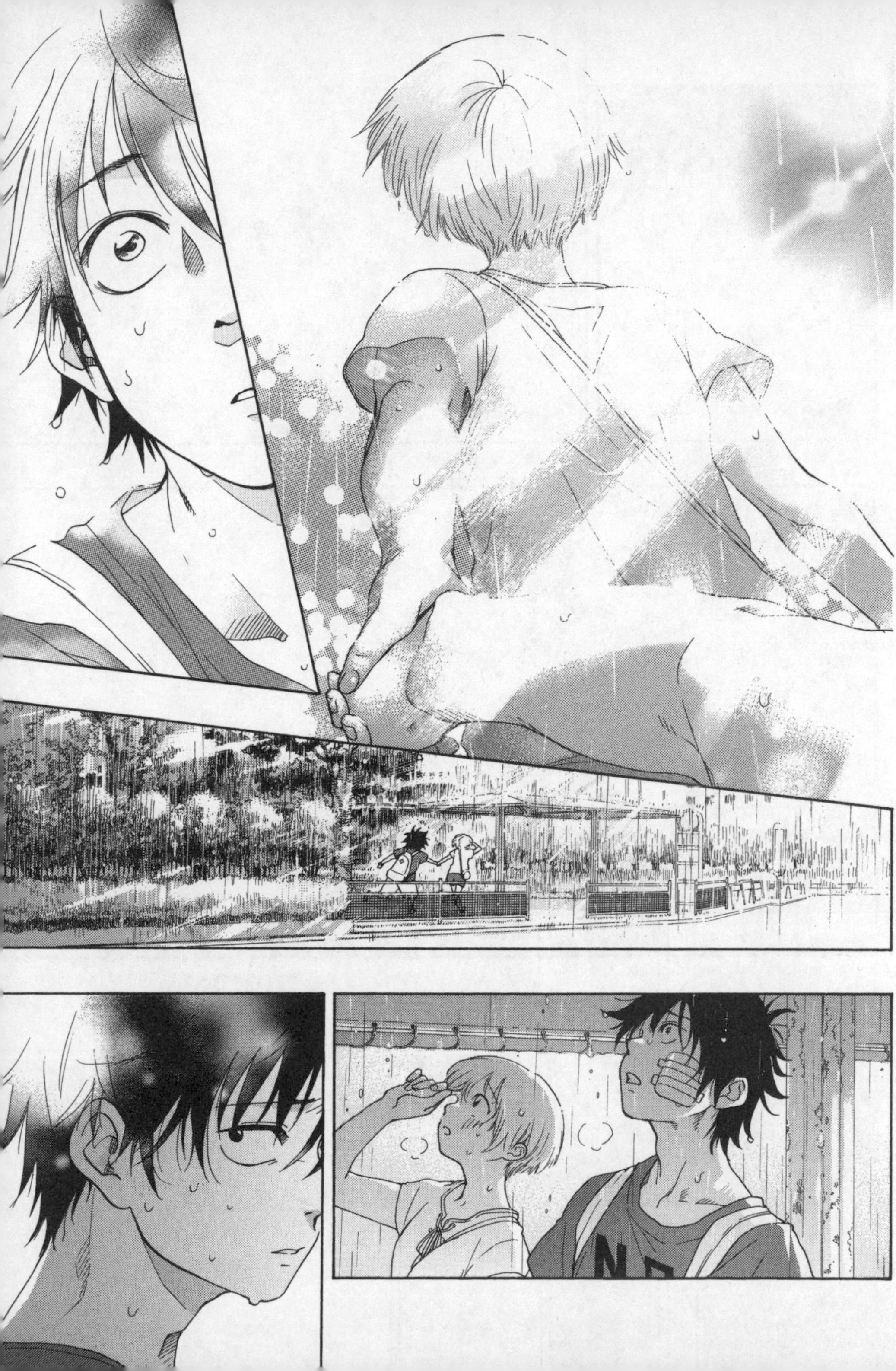

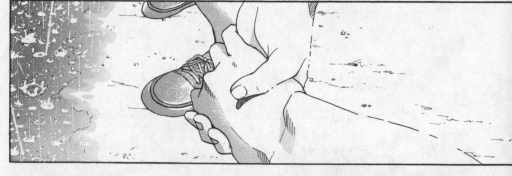

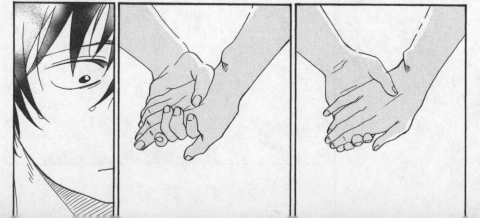

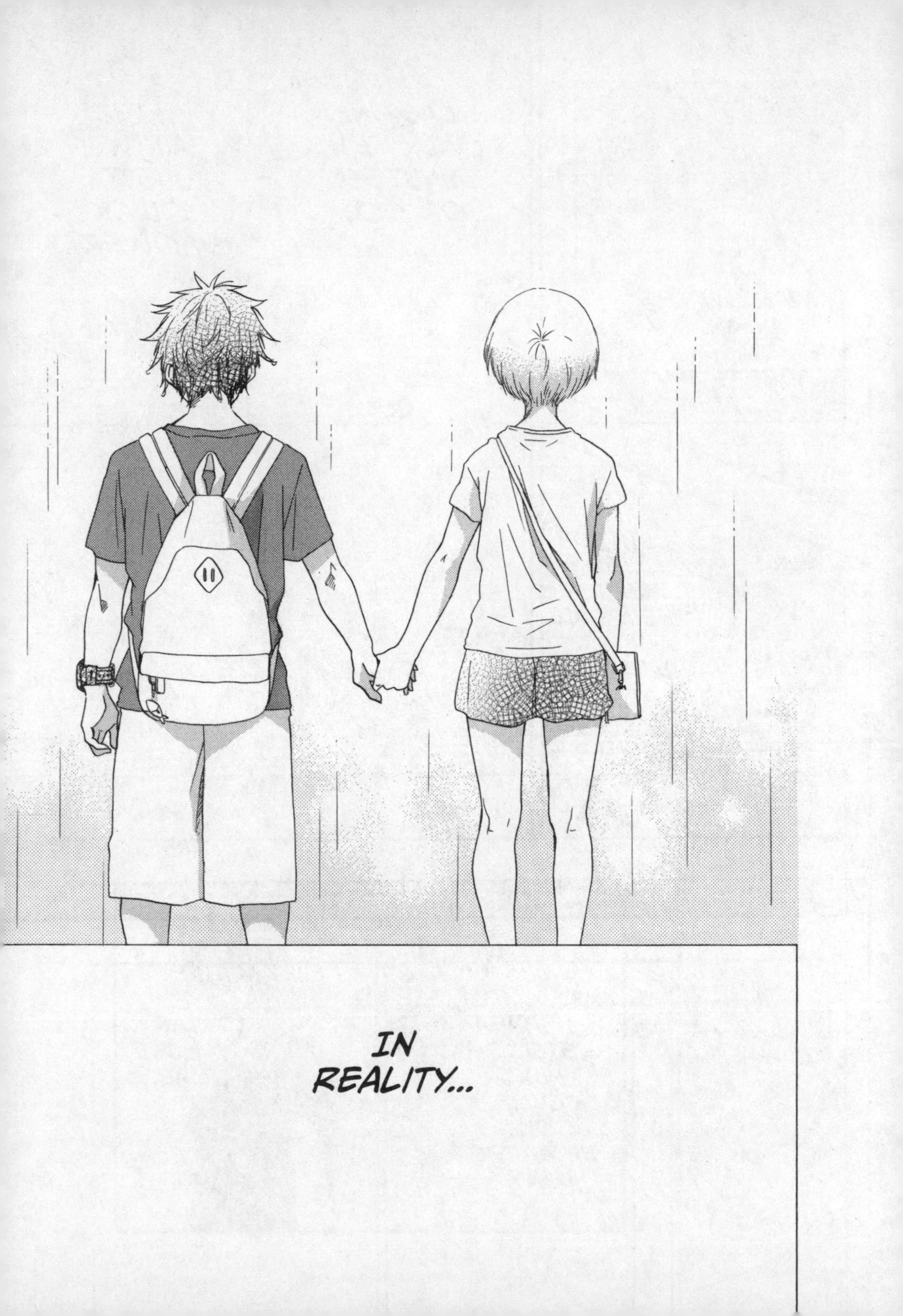
IN REALITY...

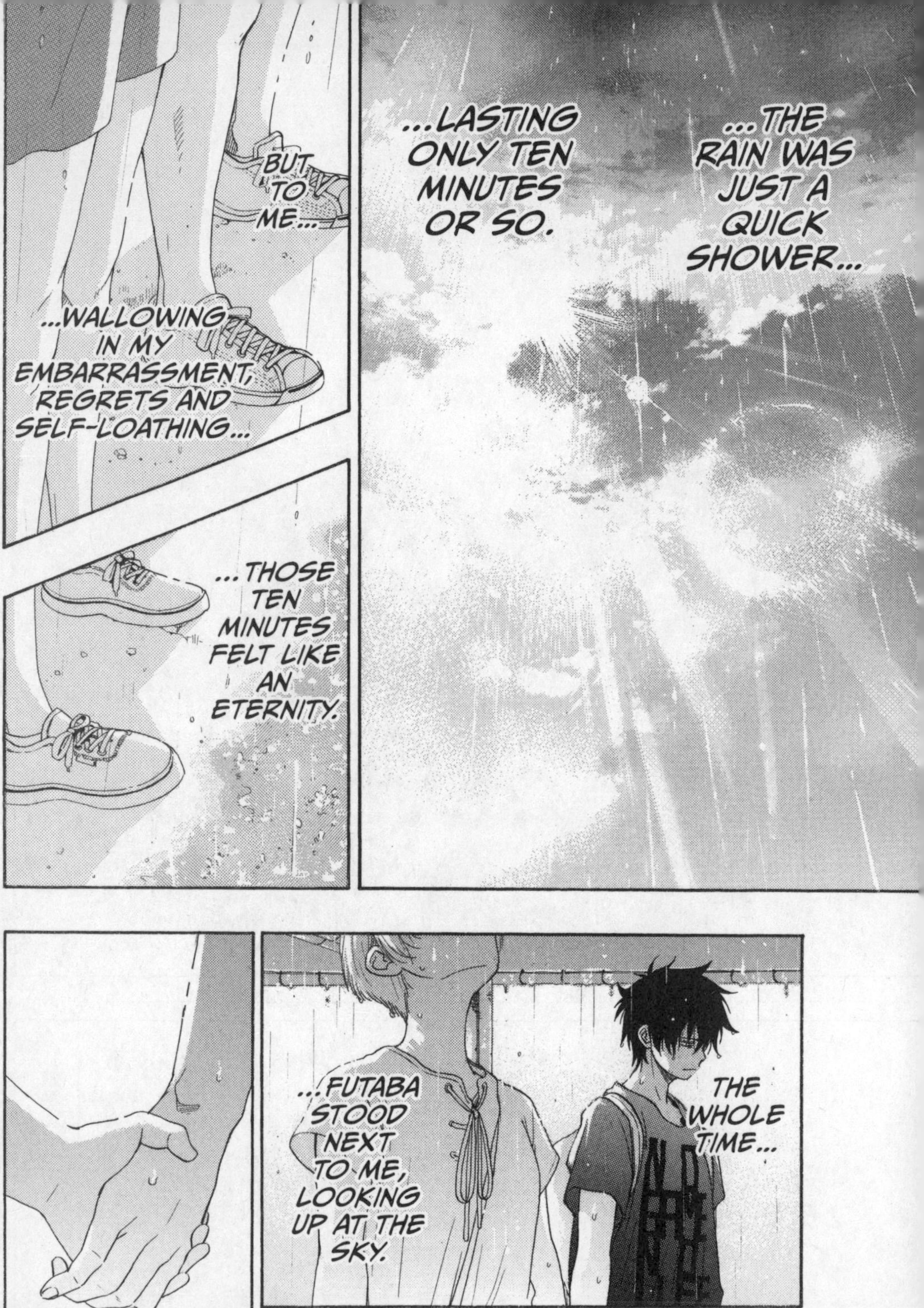
...THE RAIN WAS JUST A QUICK SHOWER...
...LASTING ONLY TEN MINUTES OR SO.
BUT TO ME...
...WALLOWING IN MY EMBARRASSMENT, REGRETS AND SELF-LOATHING...
...THOSE TEN MINUTES FELT LIKE AN ETERNITY.
THE WHOLE TIME...
...FUTABA STOOD NEXT TO ME, LOOKING UP AT THE SKY.

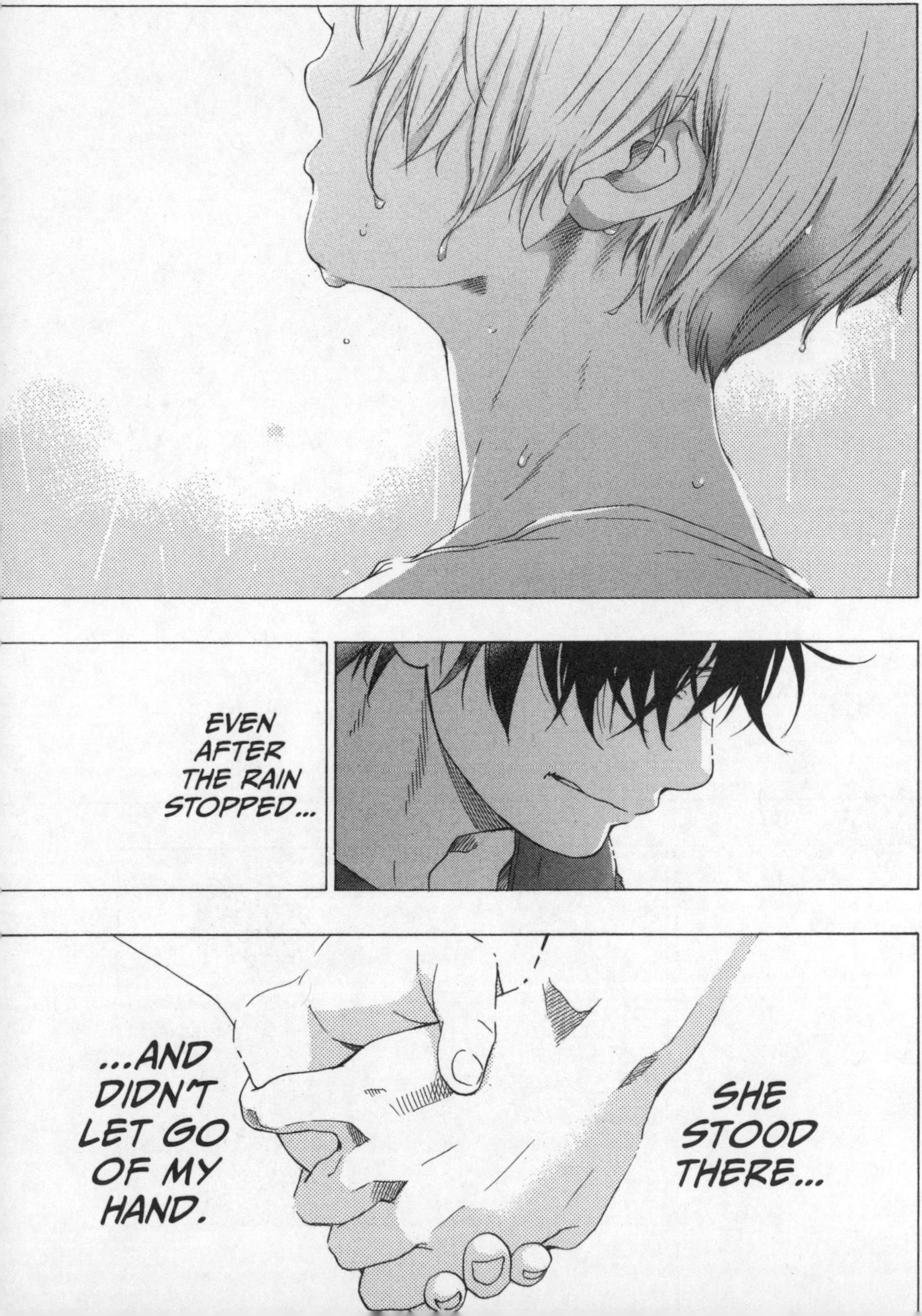
EVEN AFTER THE RAIN STOPPED...
SHE STOOD THERE...
...AND DIDN'T LET GO OF MY HAND.

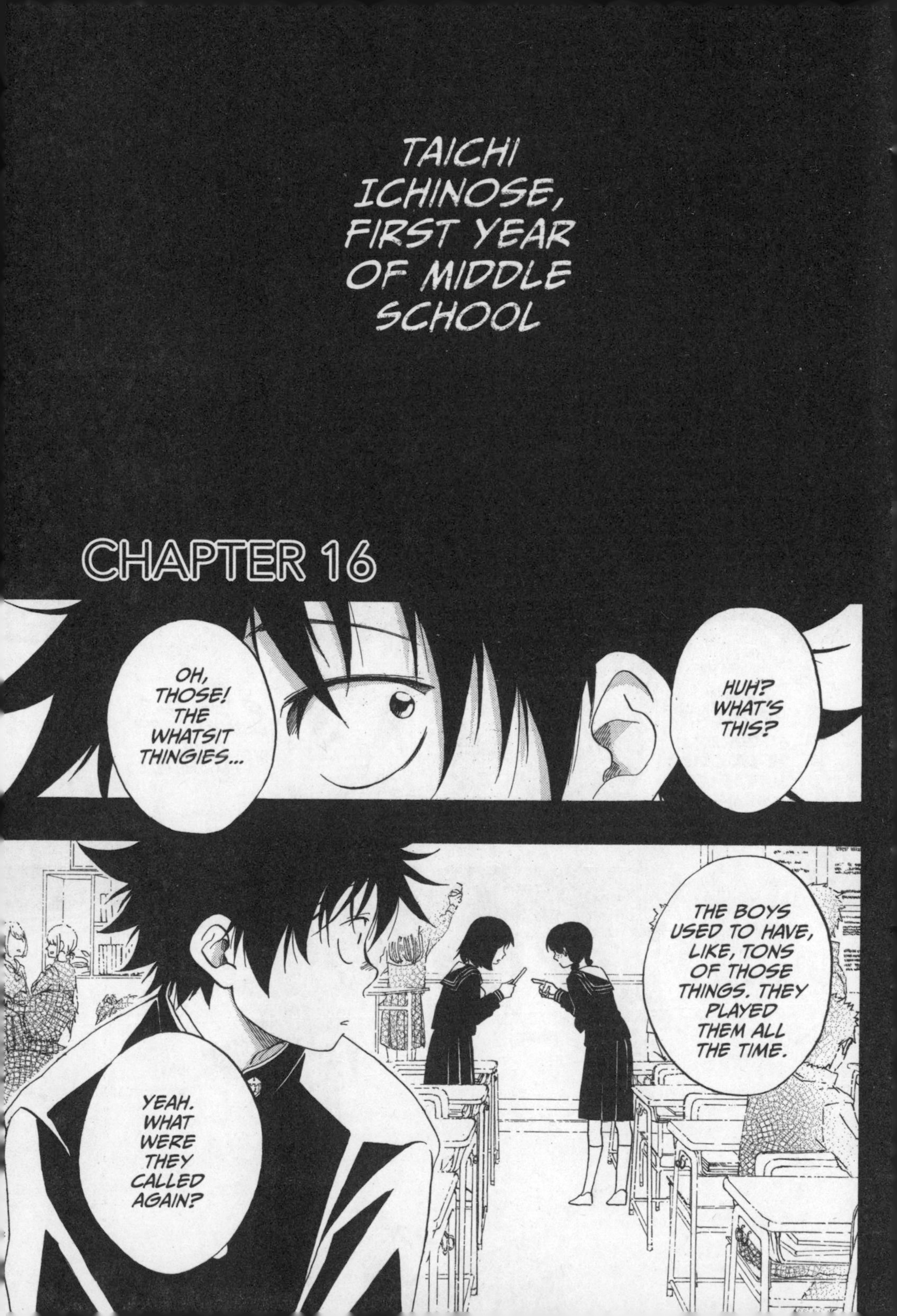
TAICHI ICHINOSE, FIRST YEAR OF MIDDLE SCHOOL
CHAPTER 16
HUH? WHAT'S THIS?
OH, THOSE! THE WHATSIT THINGIES...
THE BOYS USED TO HAVE, LIKE, TONS OF THOSE THINGS. THEY PLAYED THEM ALL THE TIME.
YEAH. WHAT WERE THEY CALLED AGAIN?

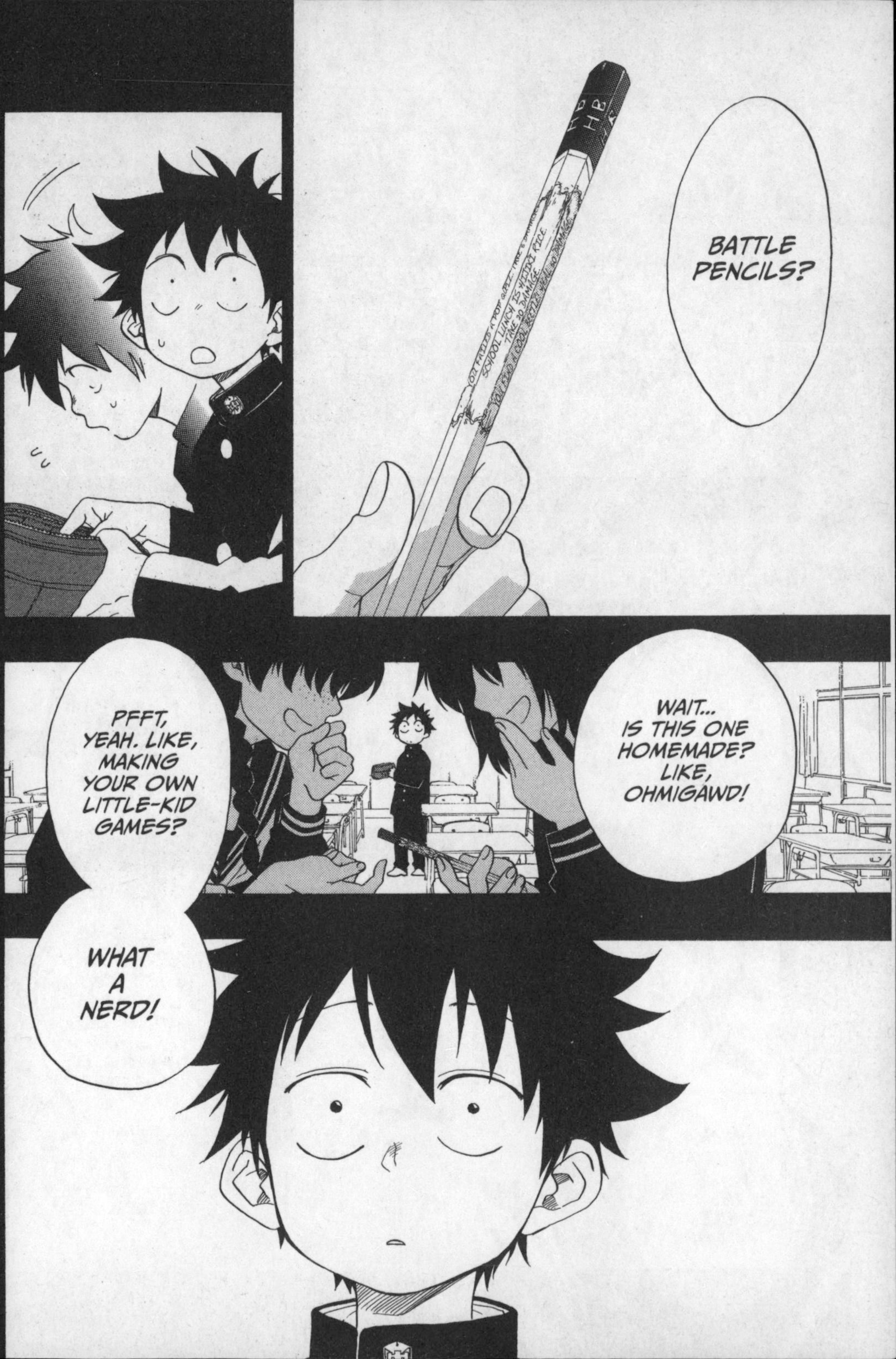
BATTLE PENCILS?
SCHOOL LUNCH IS HIJIKI RICE.
TAKE 30 DAMAGE.
WAIT... IS THIS ONE HOMEMADE? LIKE, OHMIGAWD!
PFFT, YEAH. LIKE, MAKING YOUR OWN LITTLE-KID GAMES?
WHAT A NERD!

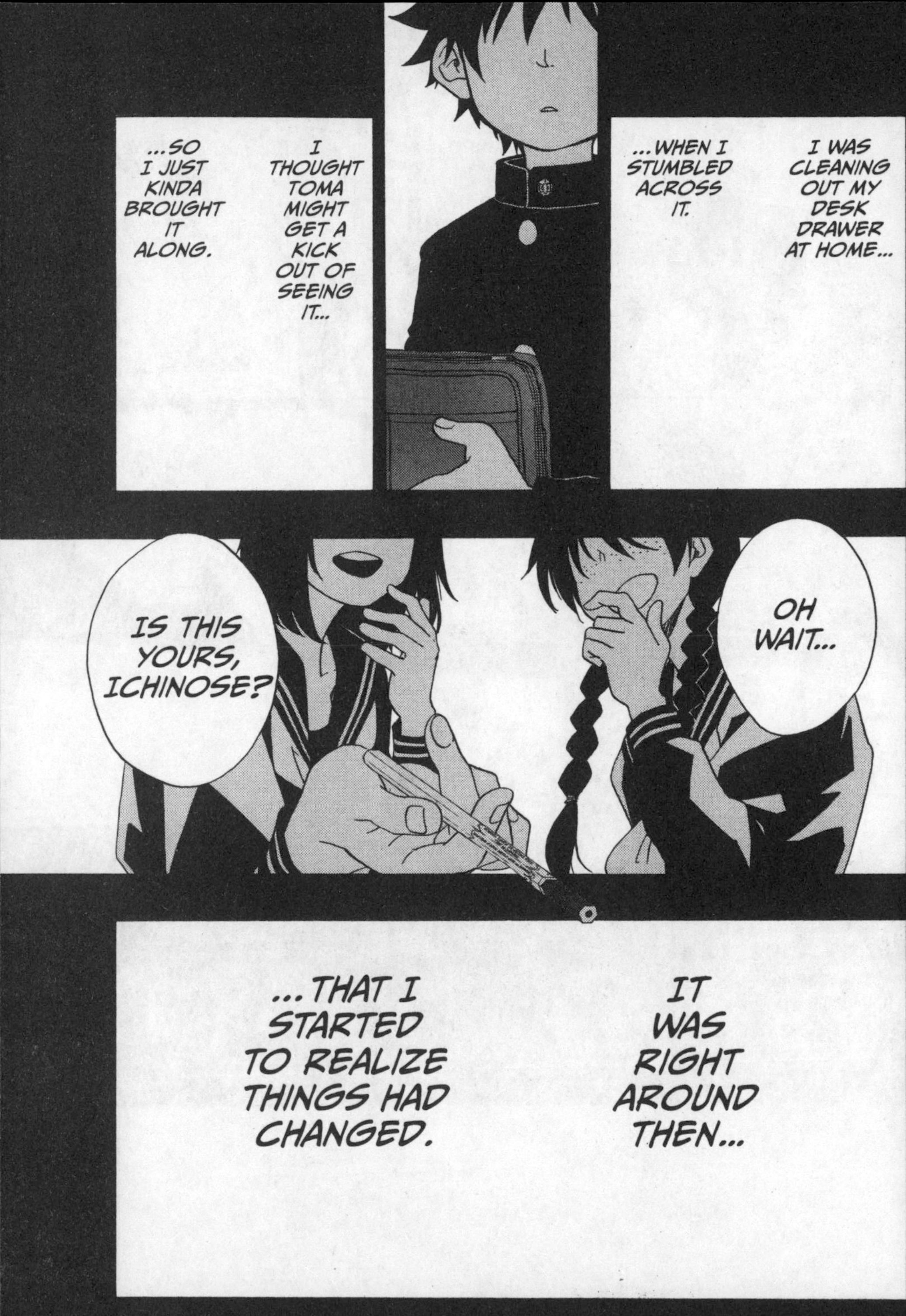
I WAS CLEANING OUT MY DESK DRAWER AT HOME...
...WHEN I STUMBLED ACROSS IT.
I THOUGHT TOMA MIGHT GET A KICK OUT OF SEEING IT...
...SO I JUST KINDA BROUGHT IT ALONG.
OH WAIT...
IS THIS YOURS, ICHINOSE?
IT WAS RIGHT AROUND THEN...
...THAT I STARTED TO REALIZE THINGS HAD CHANGED.

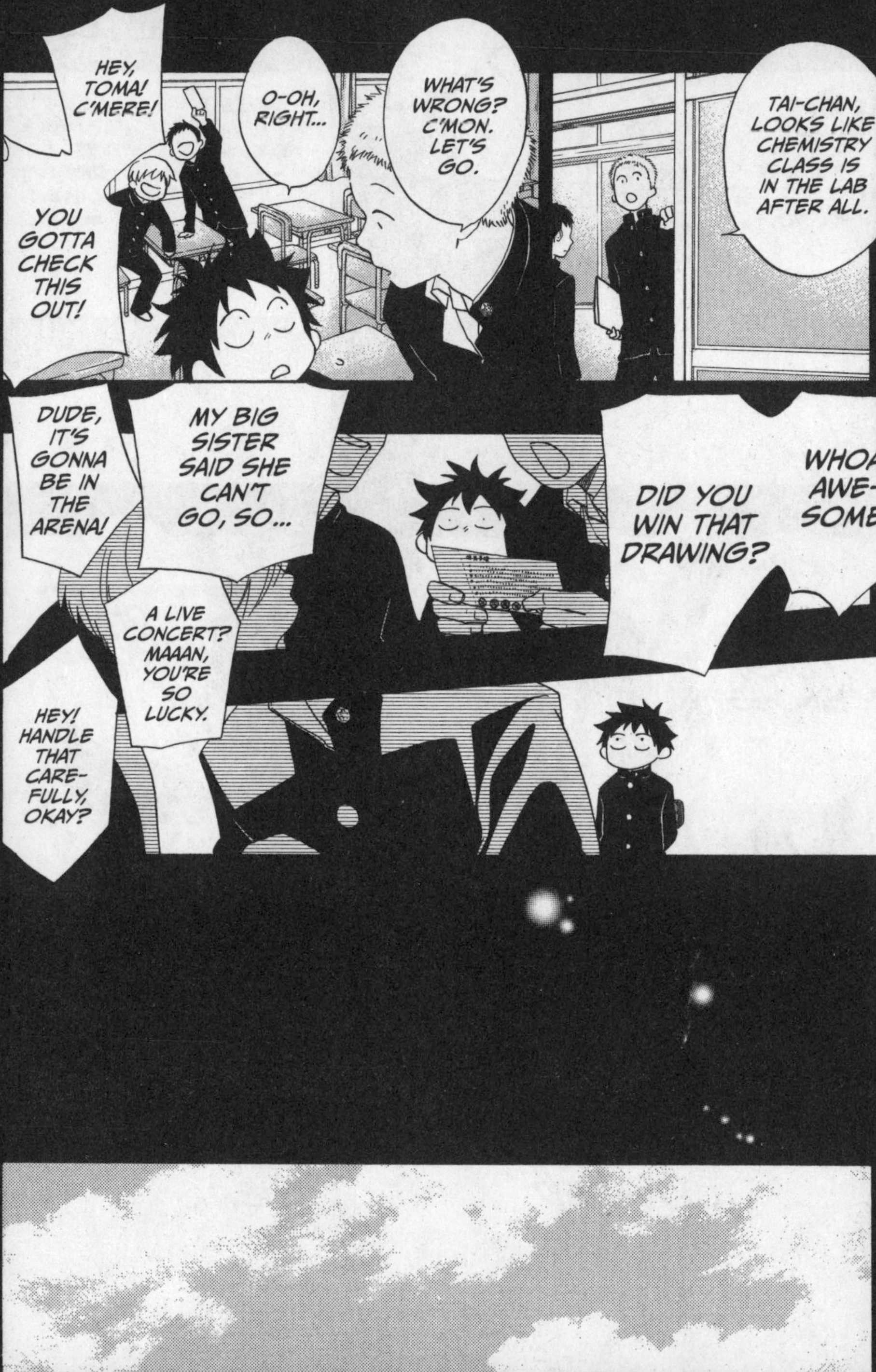
TAI-CHAN, LOOKS LIKE CHEMISTRY CLASS IS IN THE LAB AFTER ALL.
WHAT'S WRONG? C'MON. LET'S GO.
O-OH, RIGHT...
HEY, TOMA! C'MERE!
YOU GOTTA CHECK THIS OUT!
WHOA, AWE-SOME!
DID YOU WIN THAT DRAWING?
MY BIG SISTER SAID SHE CAN'T GO, SO...
DUDE, IT'S GONNA BE IN THE ARENA!
A LIVE CONCERT? MAAAN, YOU'RE SO LUCKY.
HEY! HANDLE THAT CARE-FULLY, OKAY?

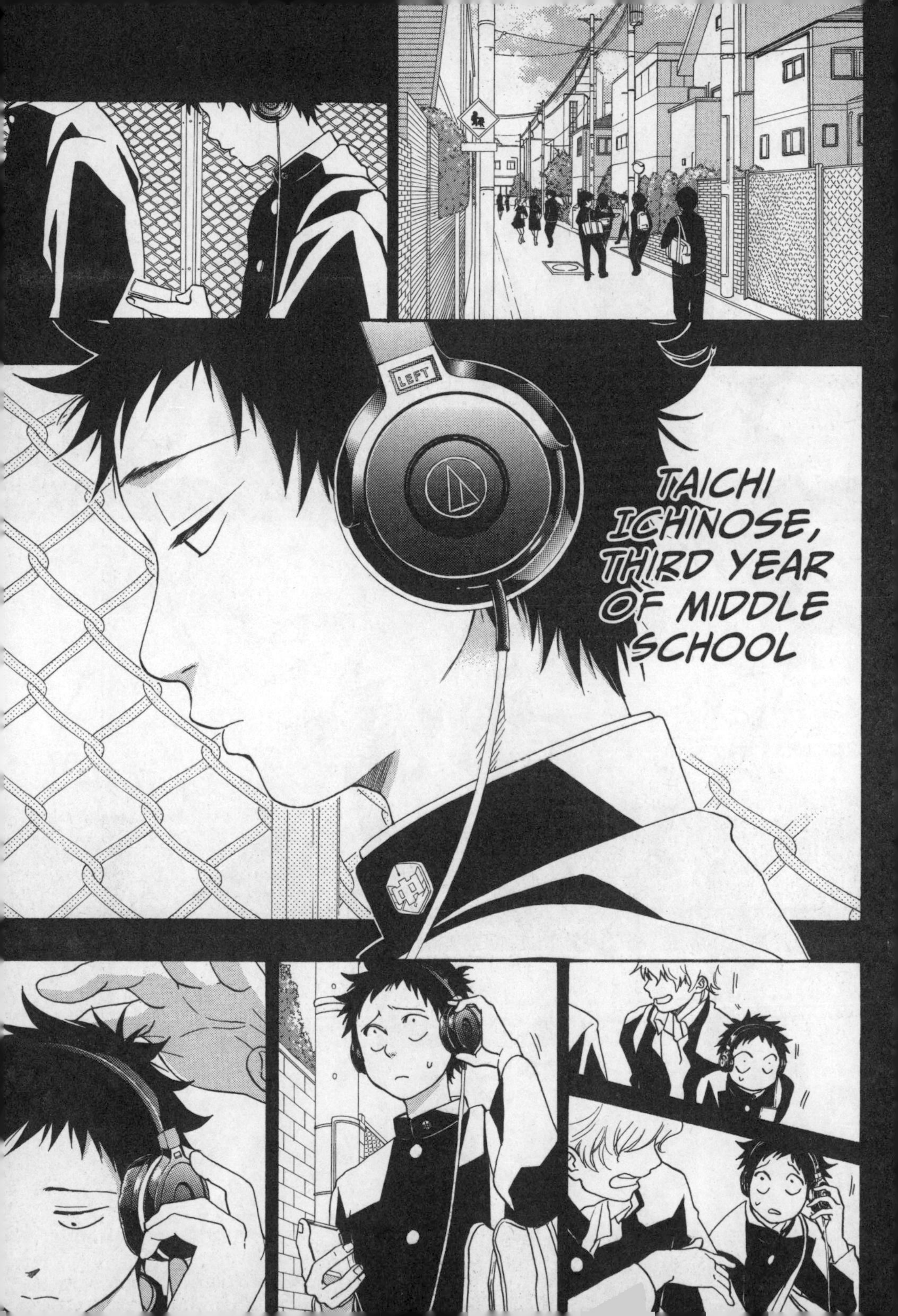

LEFT
TAICHI ICHINOSE, THIRD YEAR OF MIDDLE SCHOOL

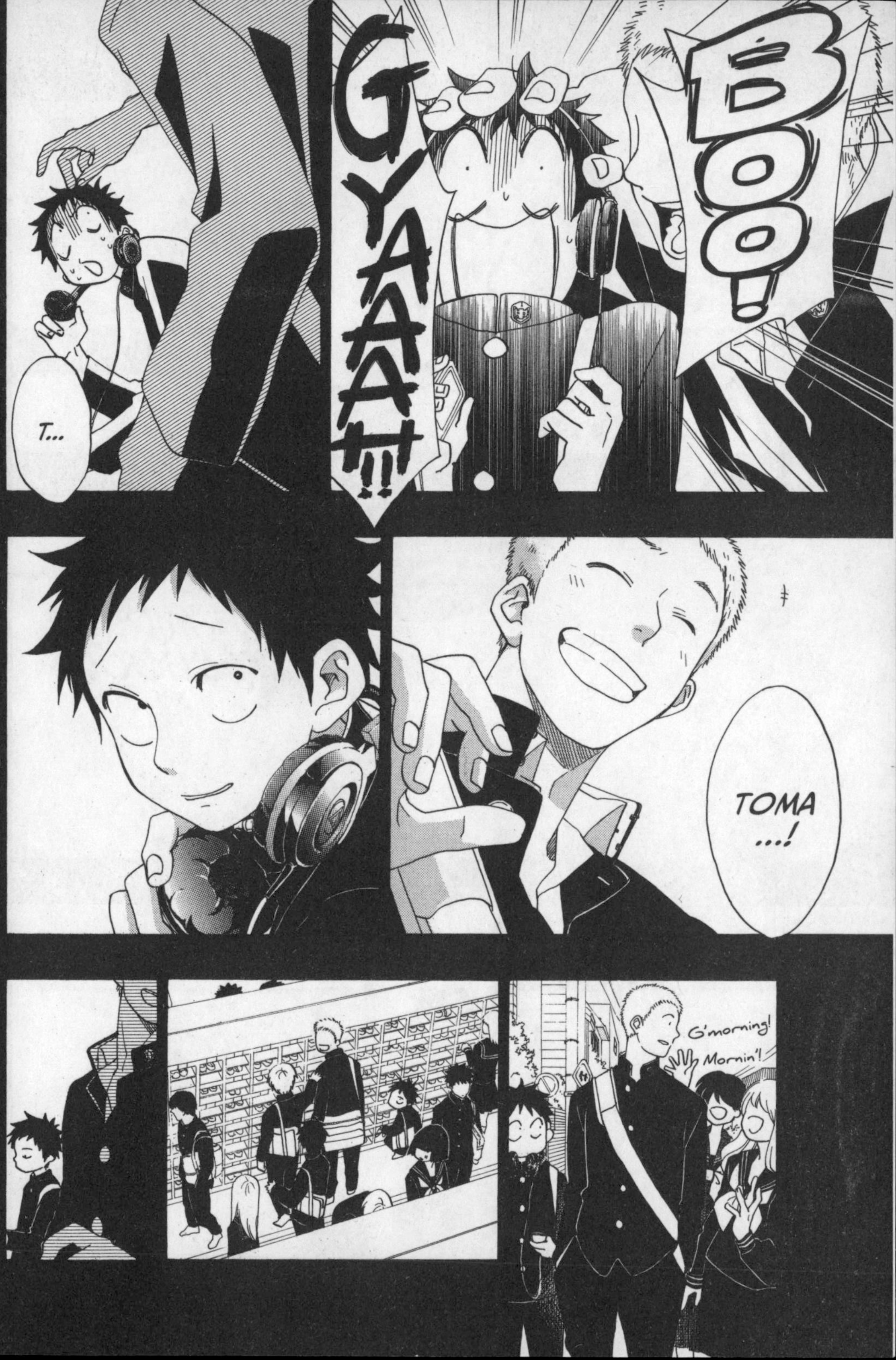

BOO!
GYAAAH!!
T...
TOMA ...!
G'morning!
Mornin'!

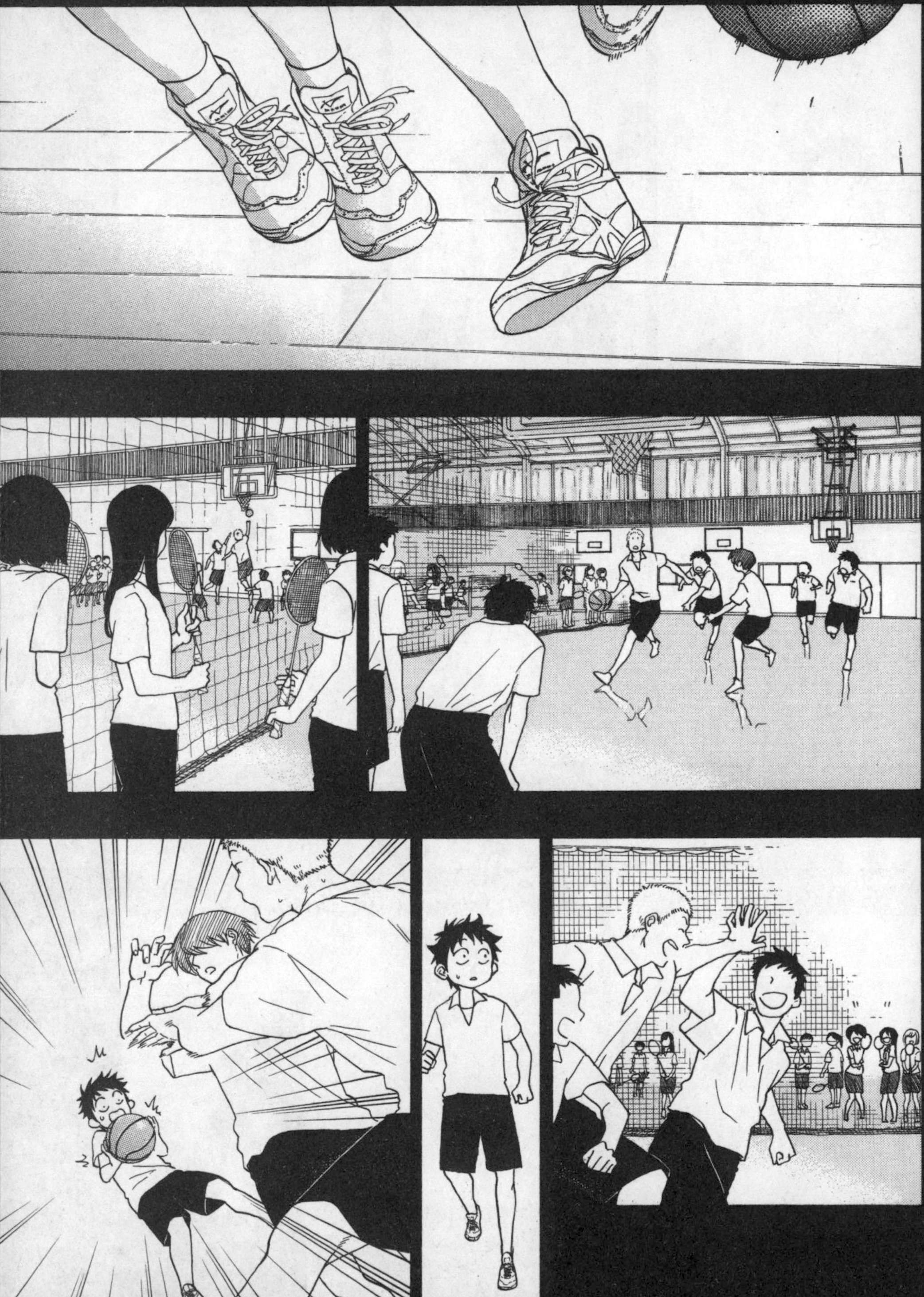

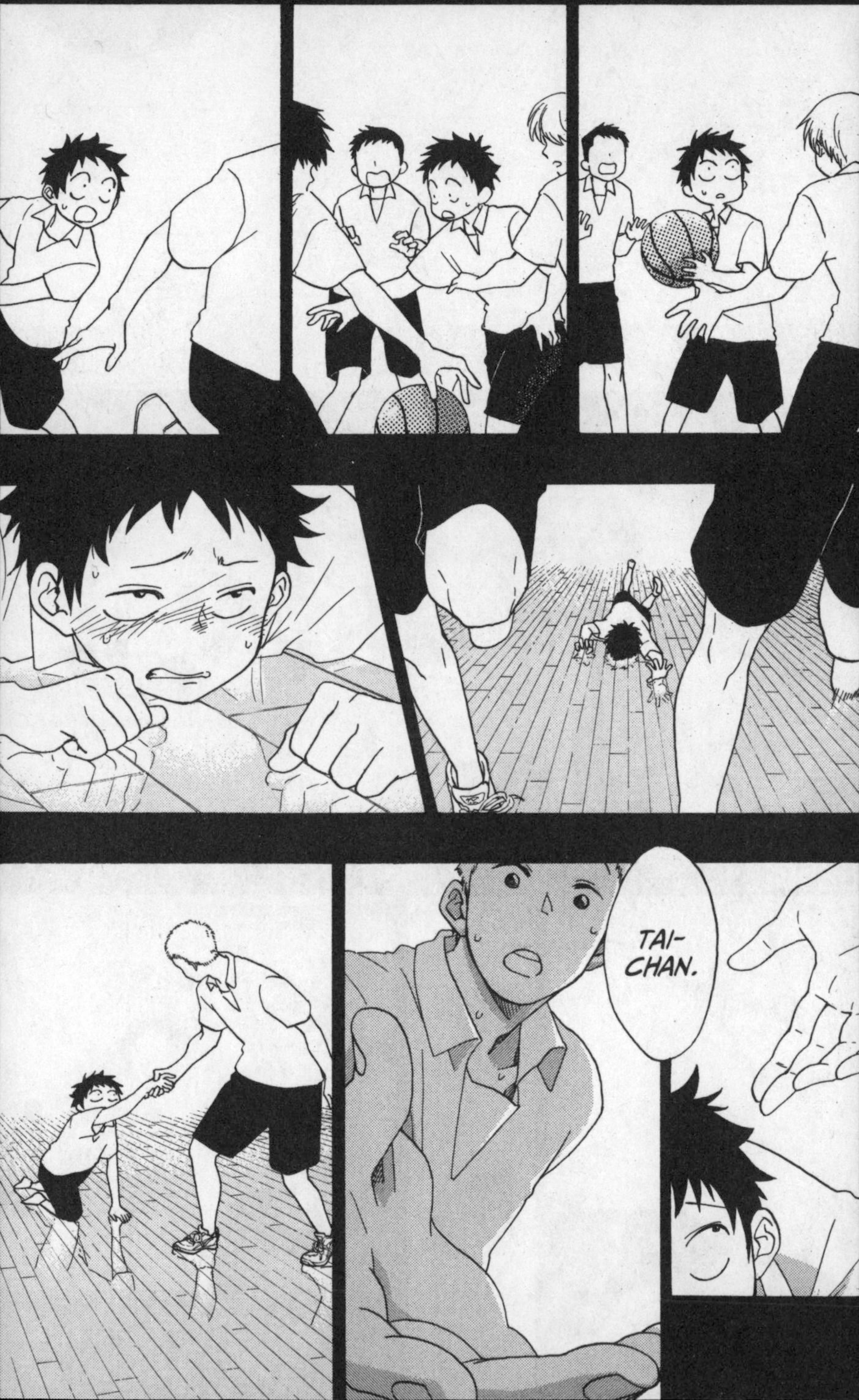
TAI-
CHAN.

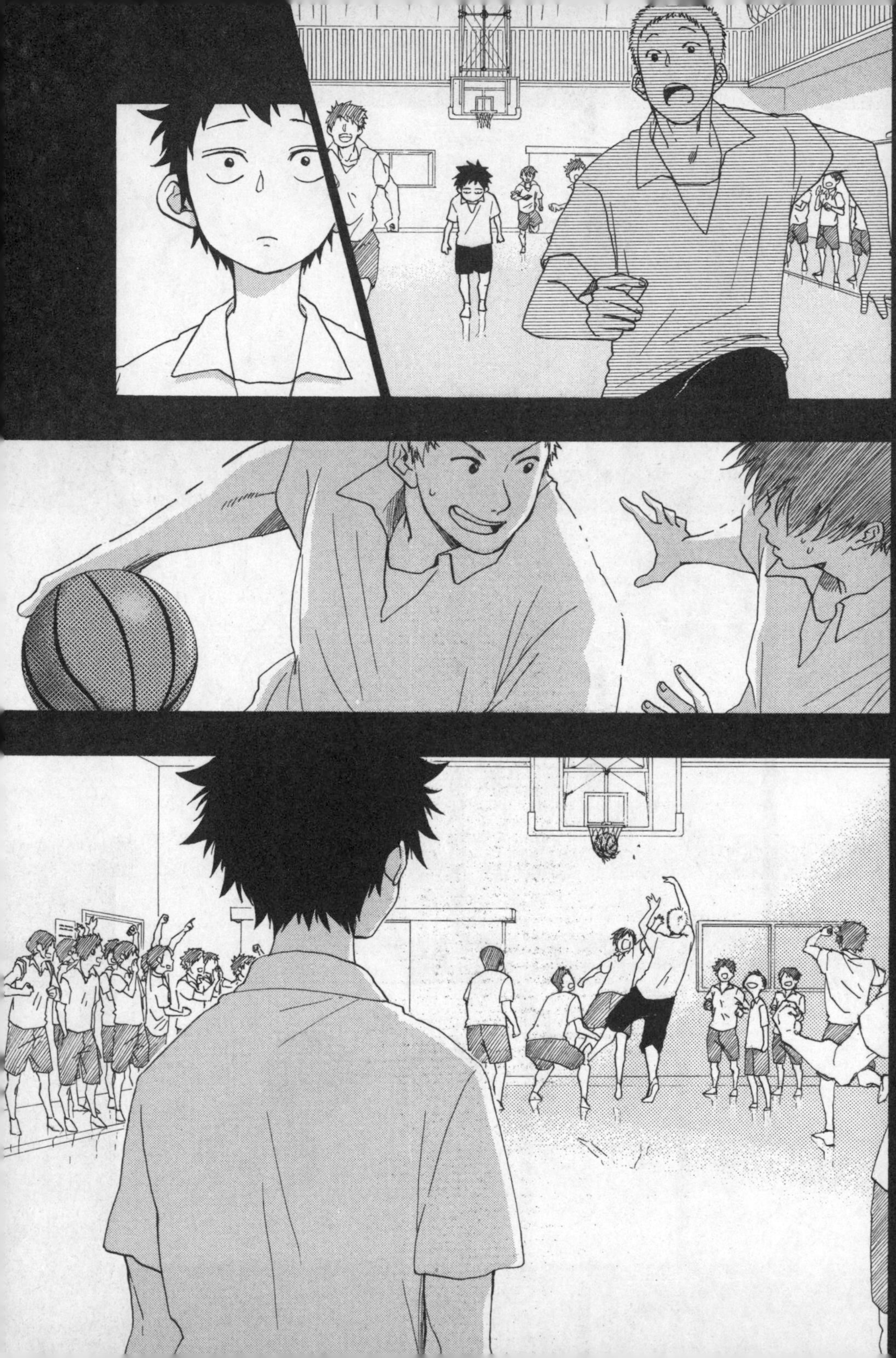

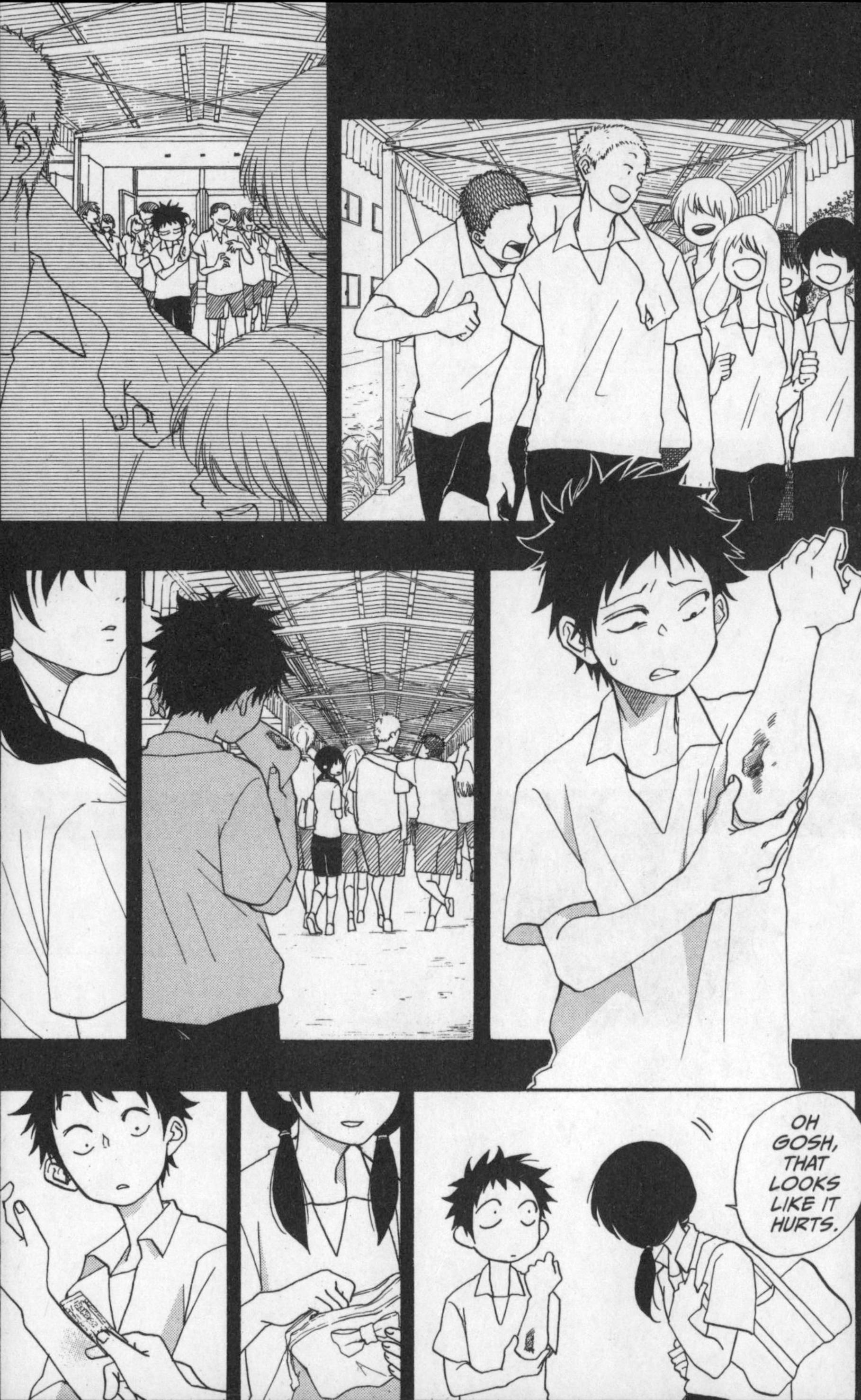
OH GOSH, THAT LOOKS LIKE IT HURTS.

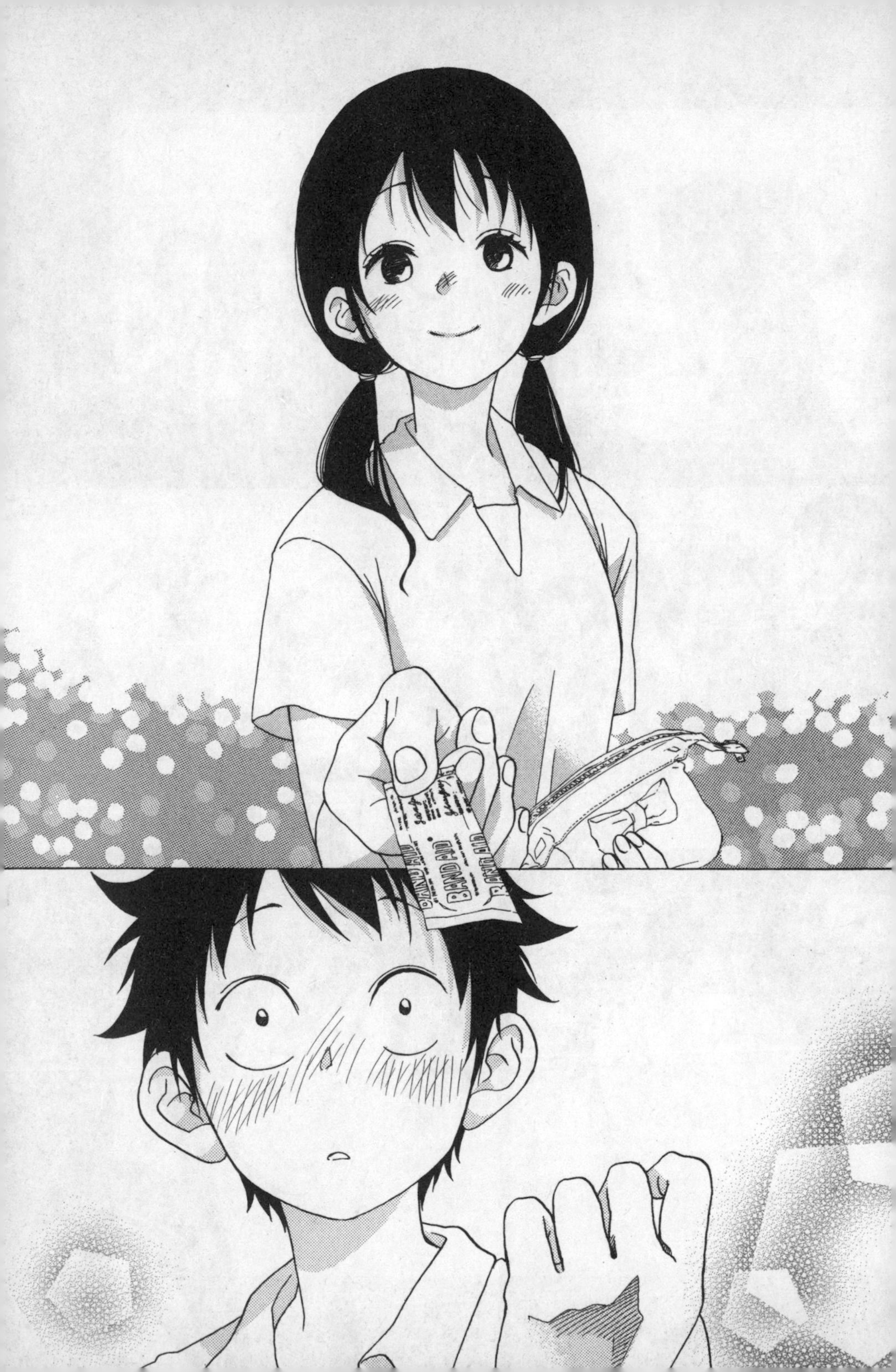
BAND AID

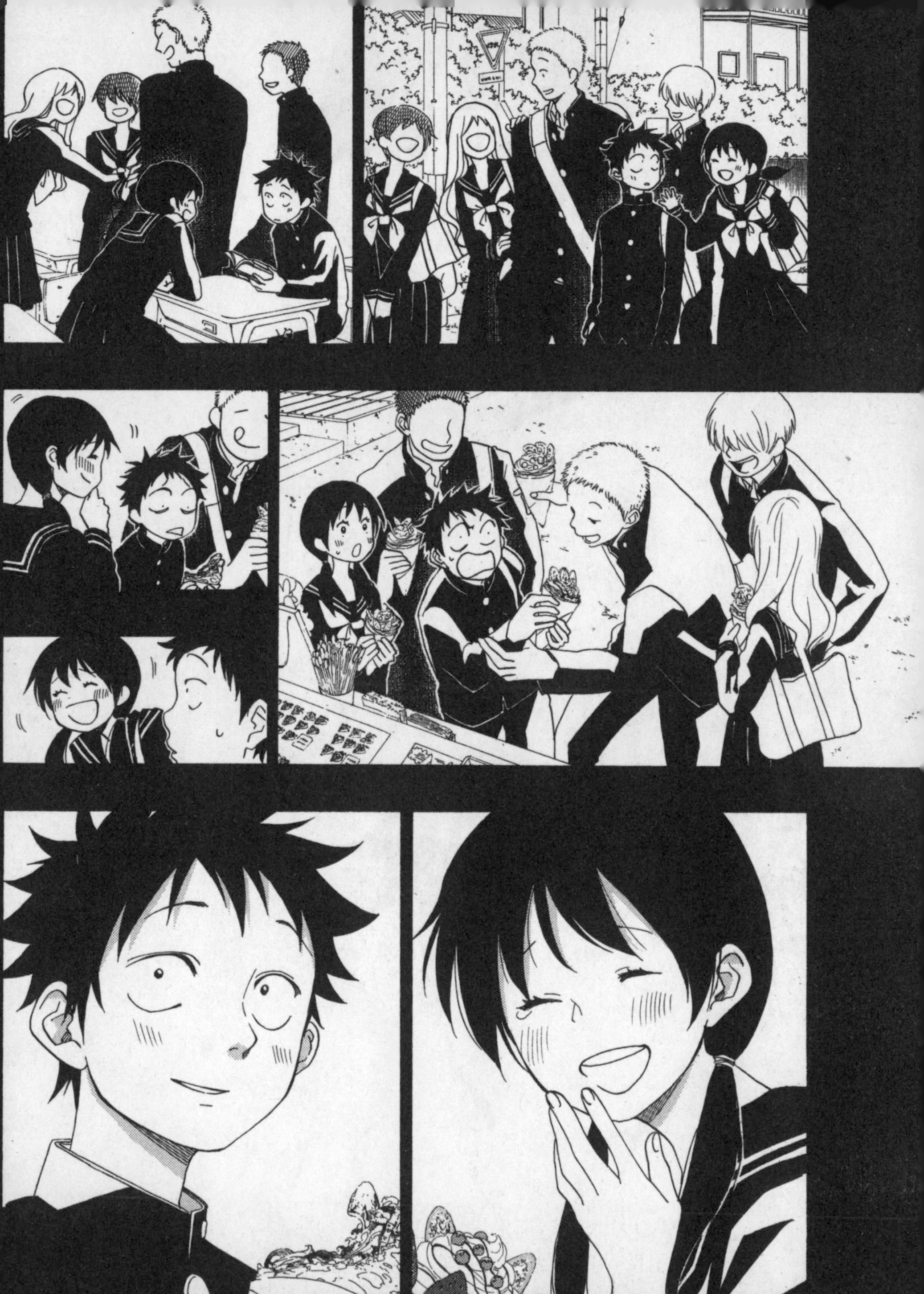

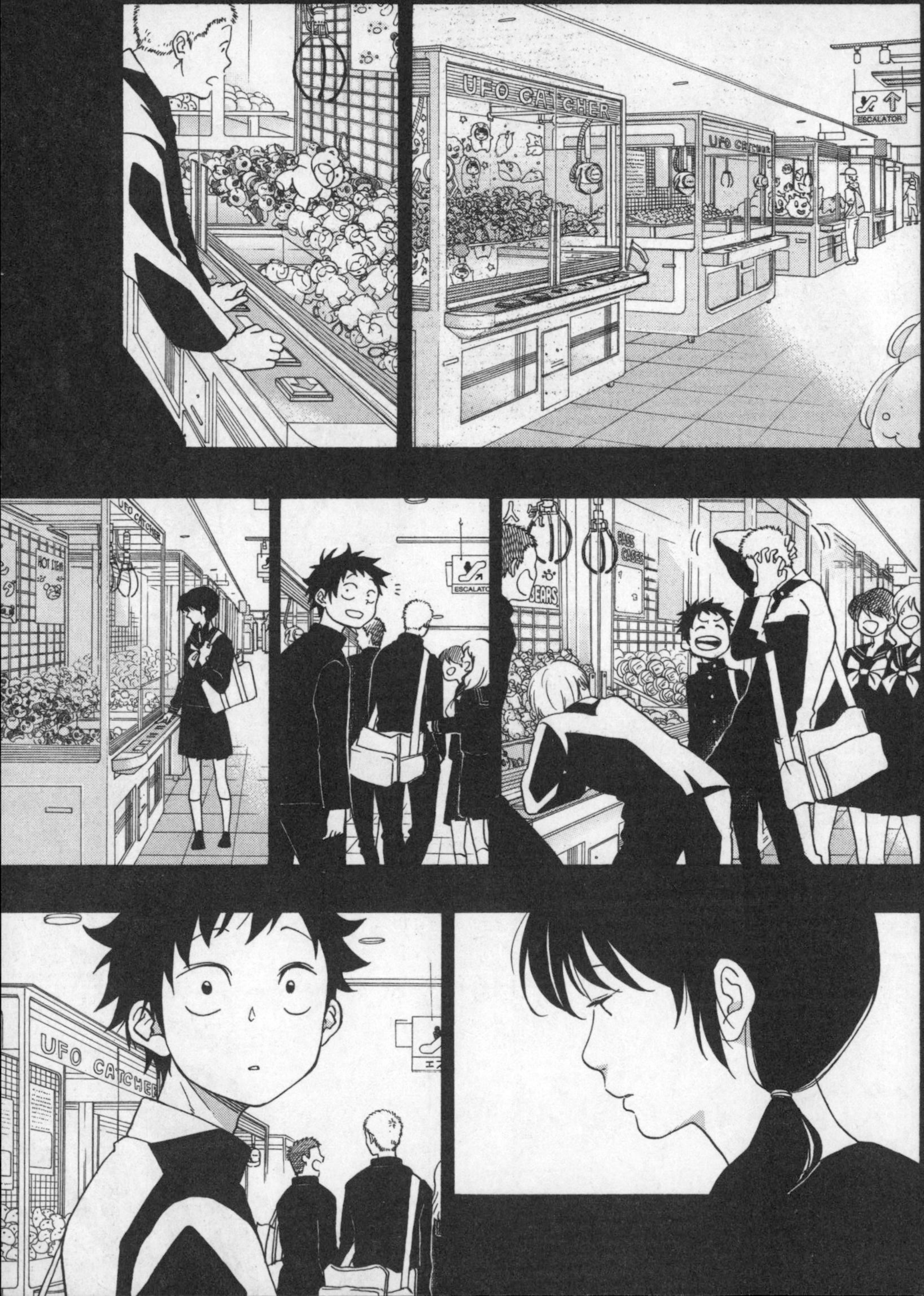
UFO CATCHER
ESCALATOR
UFO CATCHER
UFO CATCHER
ESCALATOR
BAGS CASES
BEARS
UFO CATCHER

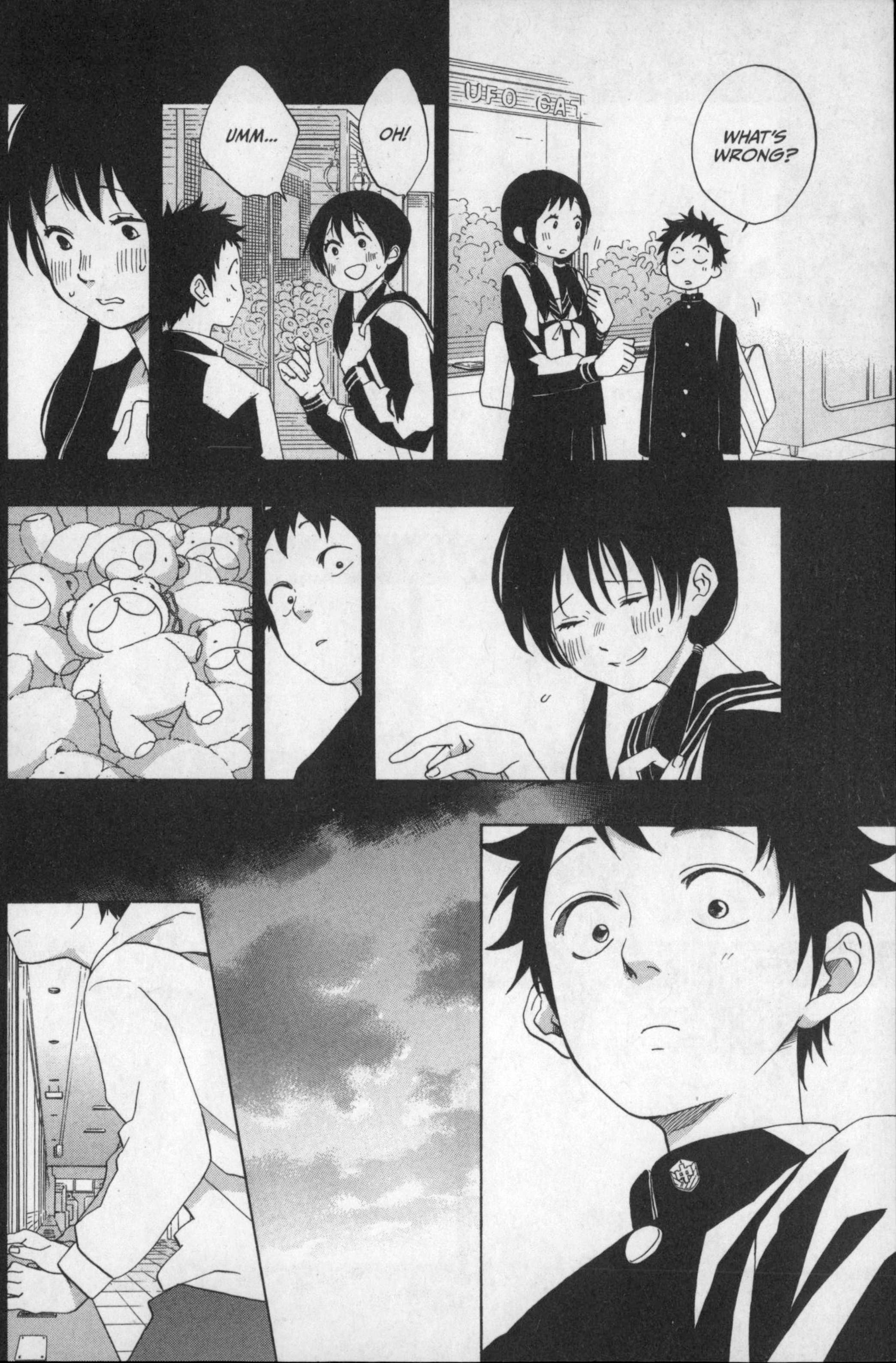
UFO CAT
WHAT'S WRONG?
OH!
UMM...

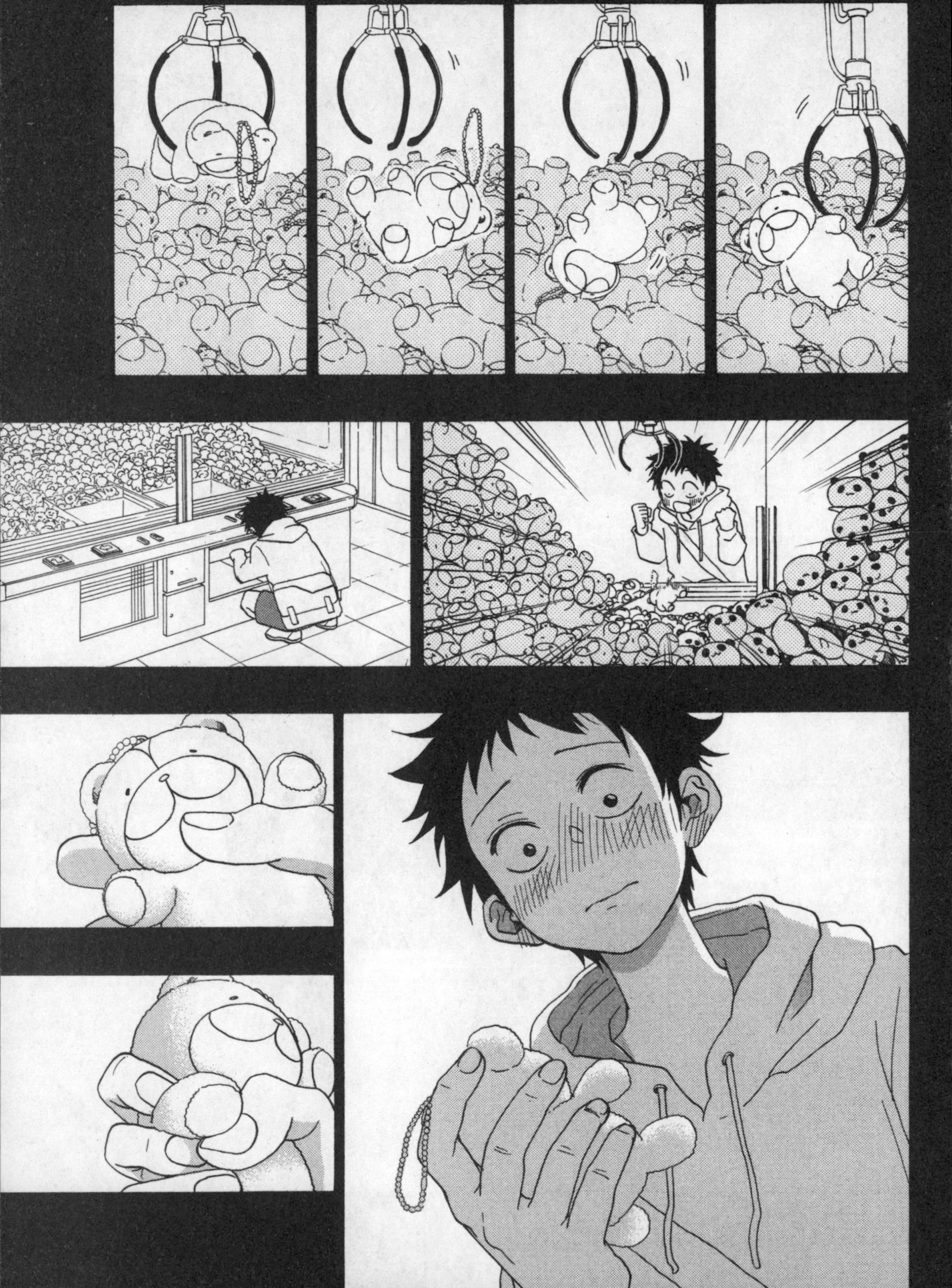

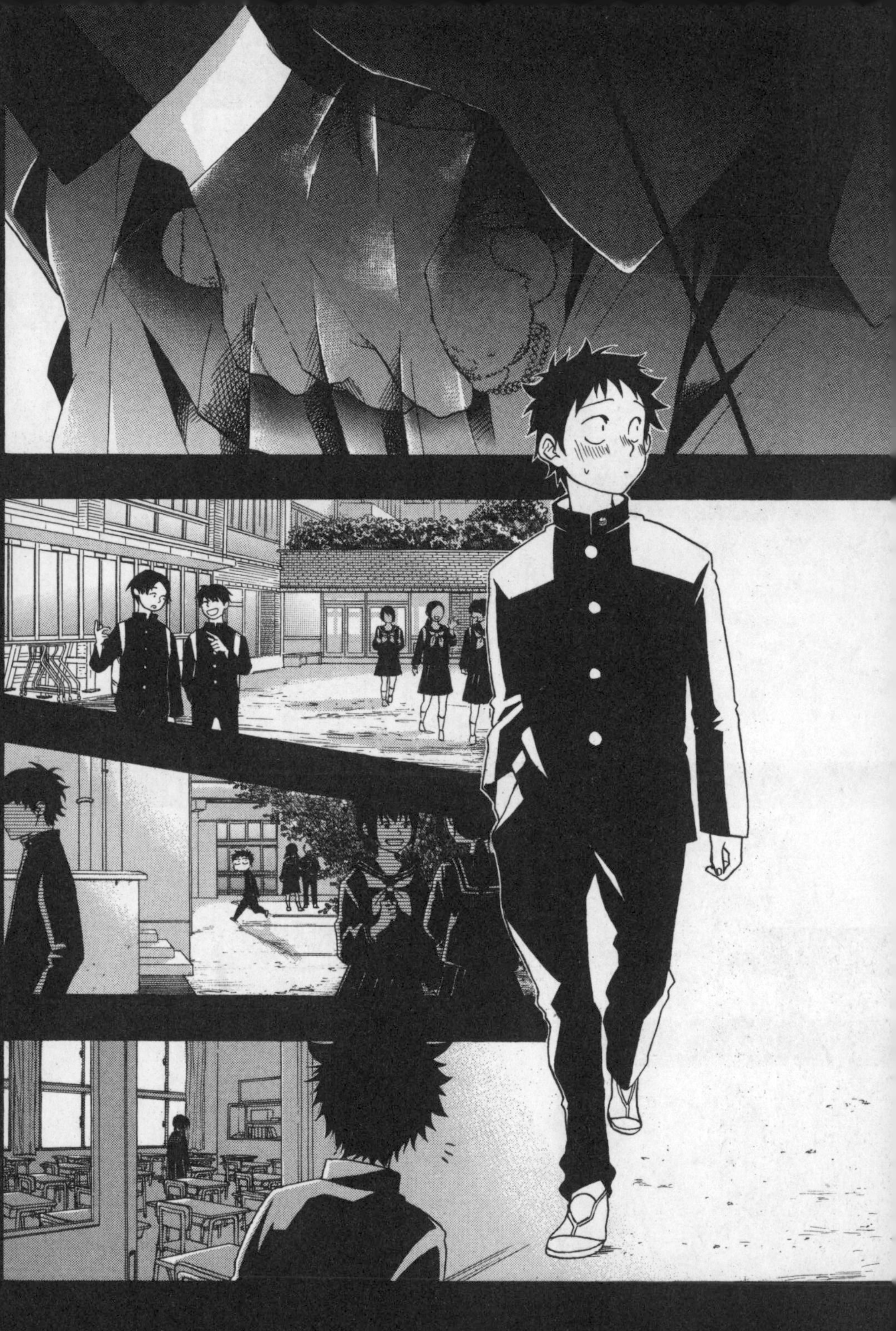

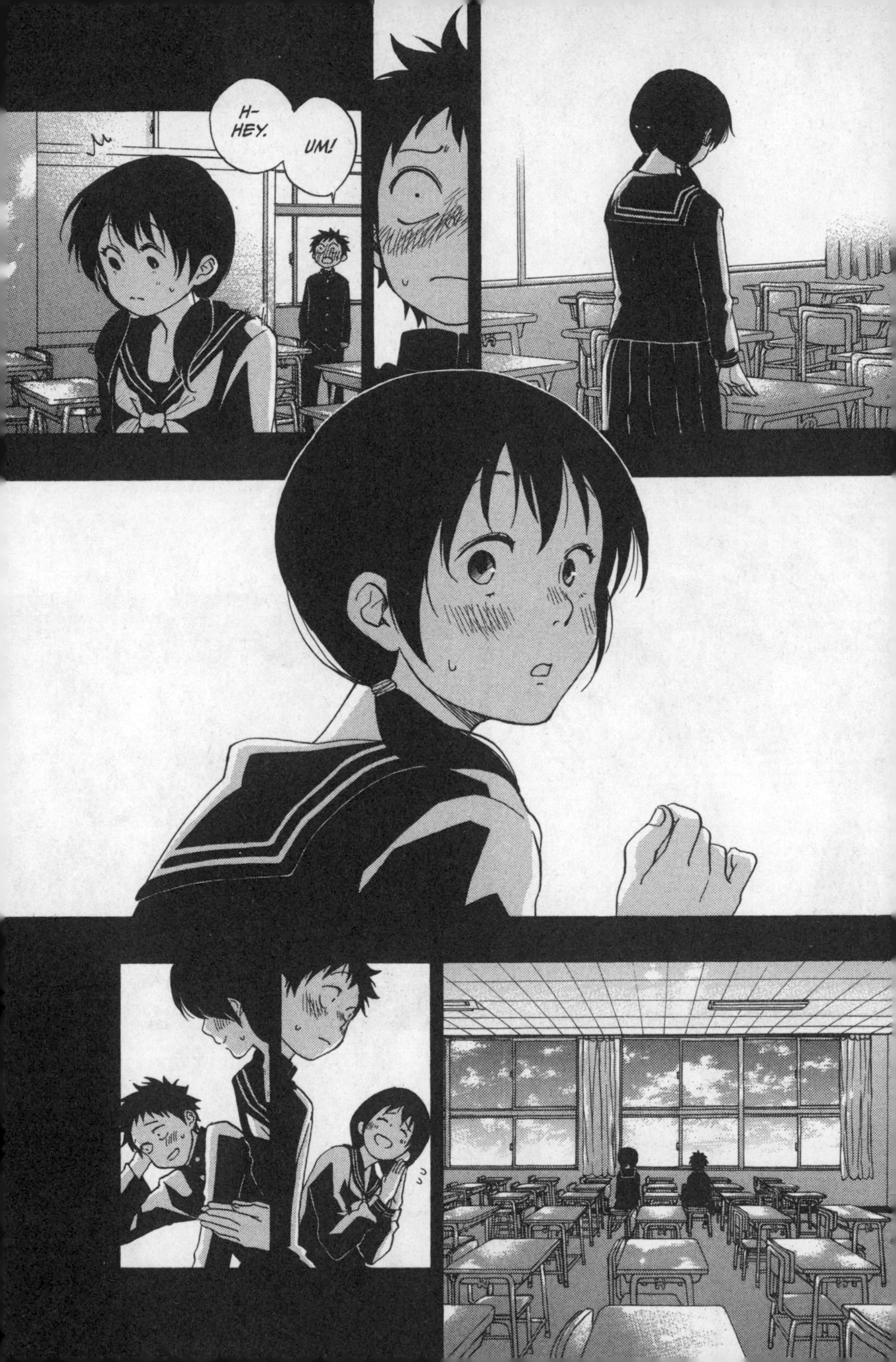

H-HEY.
UM!

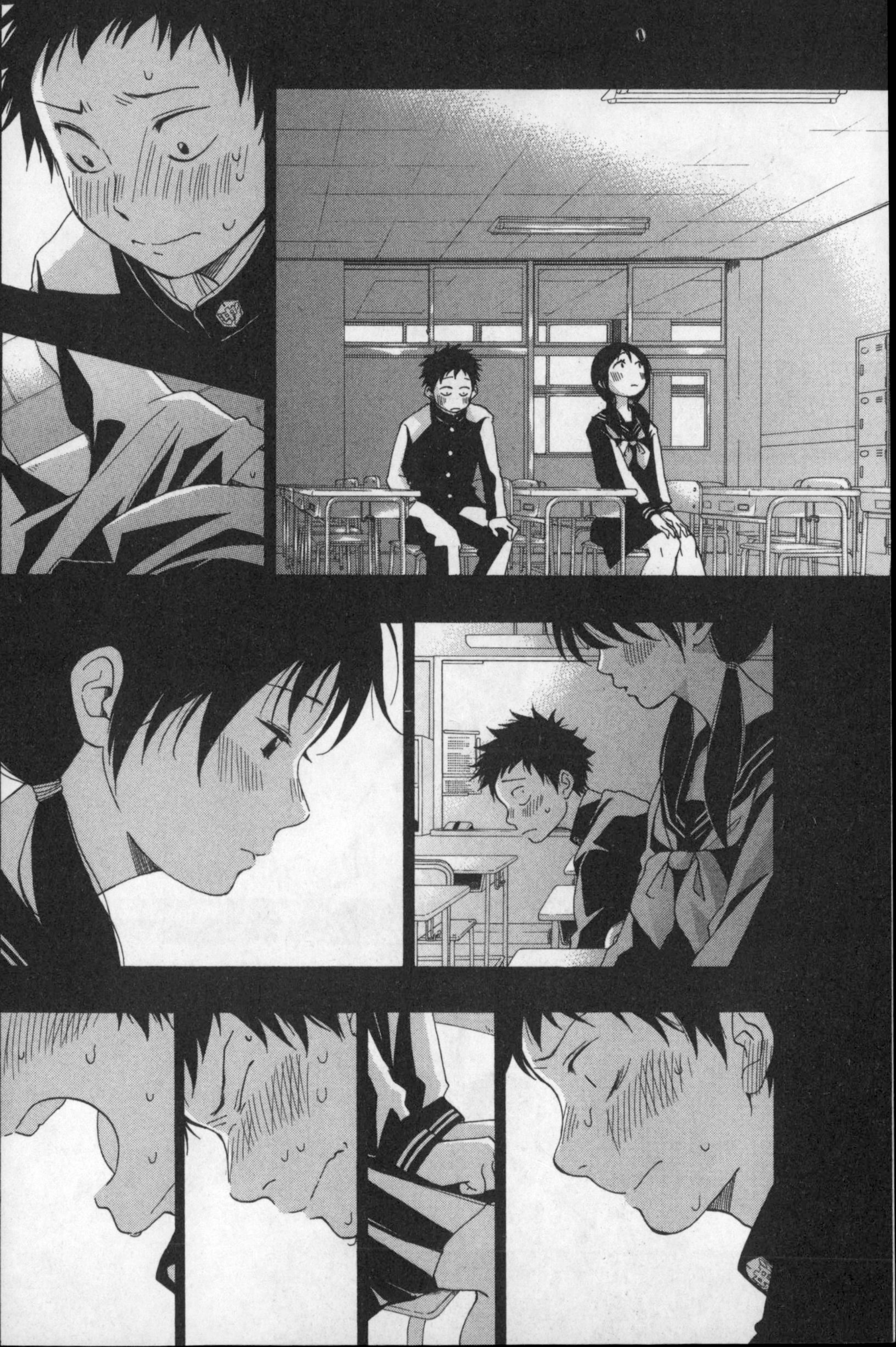

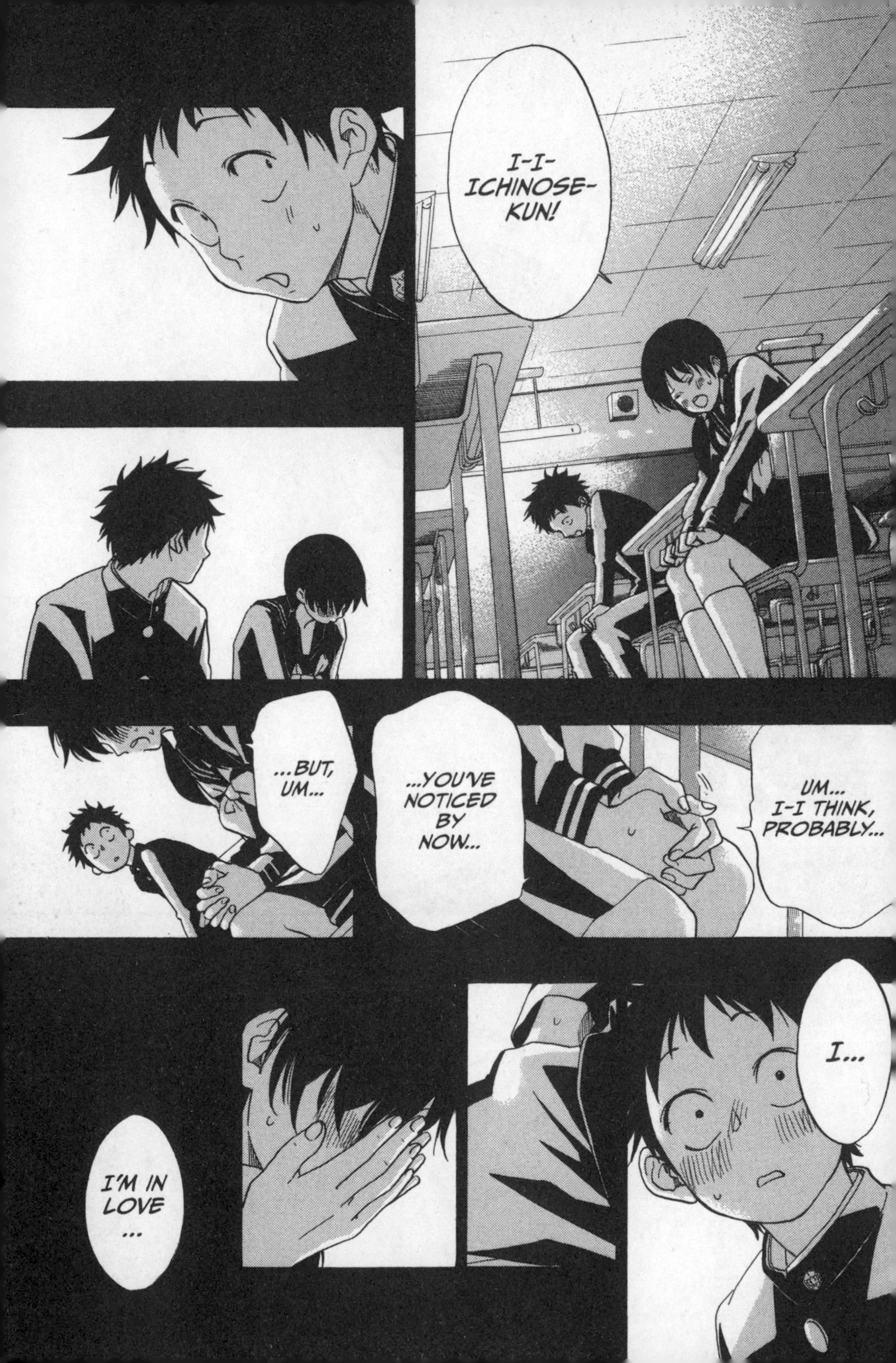

I-I-
ICHINOSE-
KUN!
UM...
I-I THINK,
PROBABLY...
...YOU'VE
NOTICED
BY
NOW...
...BUT,
UM...
I...
I'M IN
LOVE
...

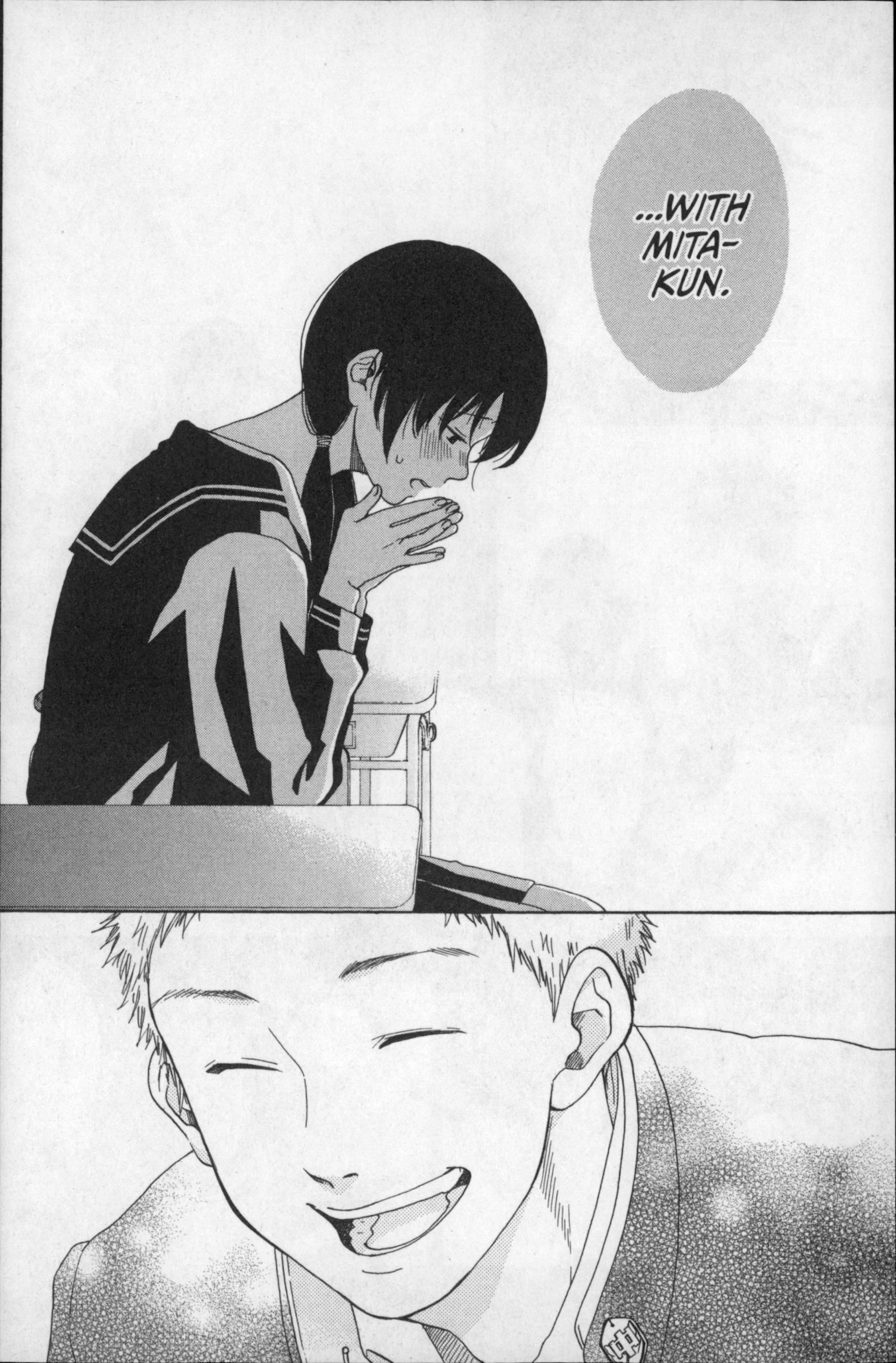
...WITH MITA-KUN.

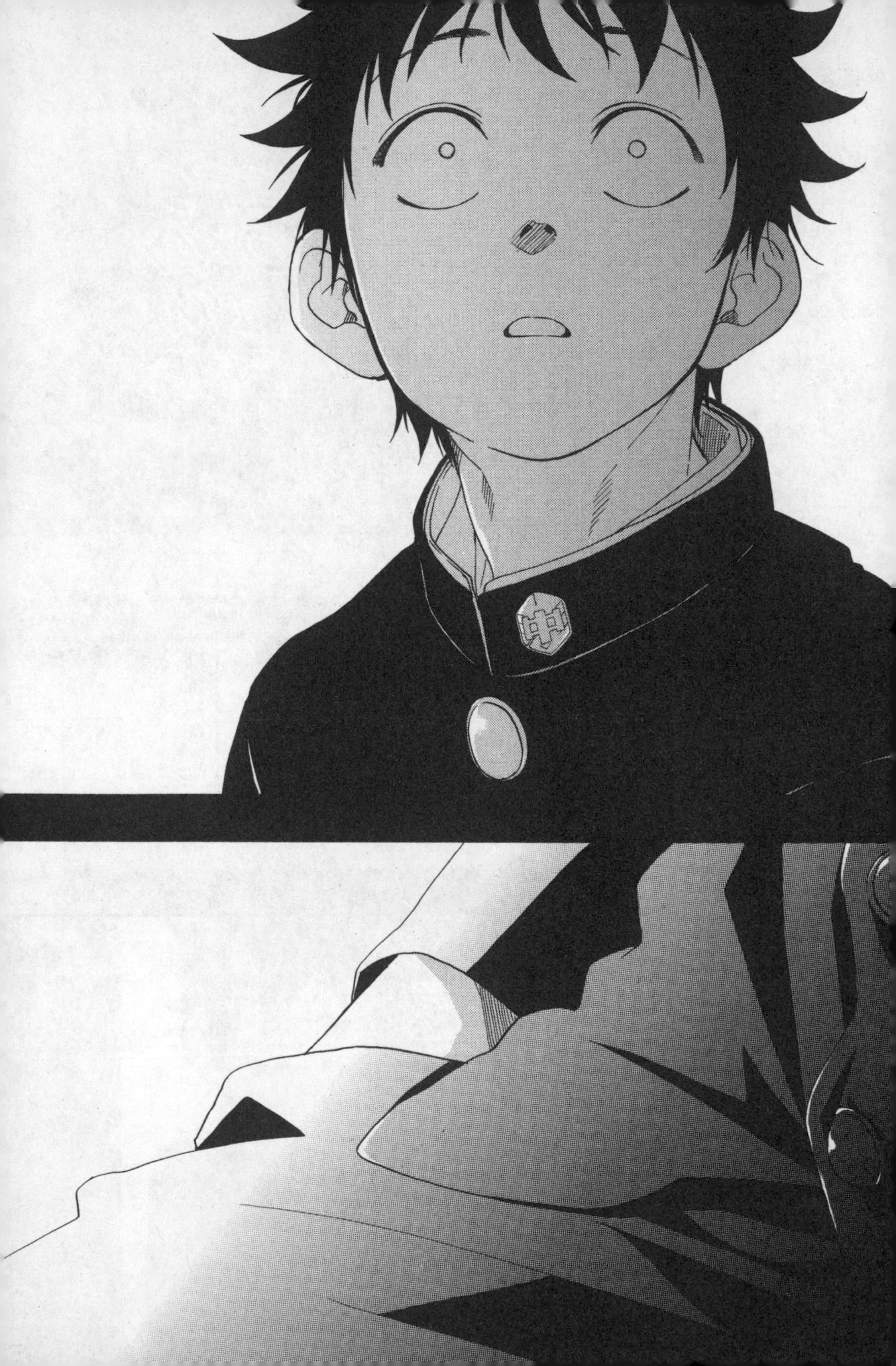

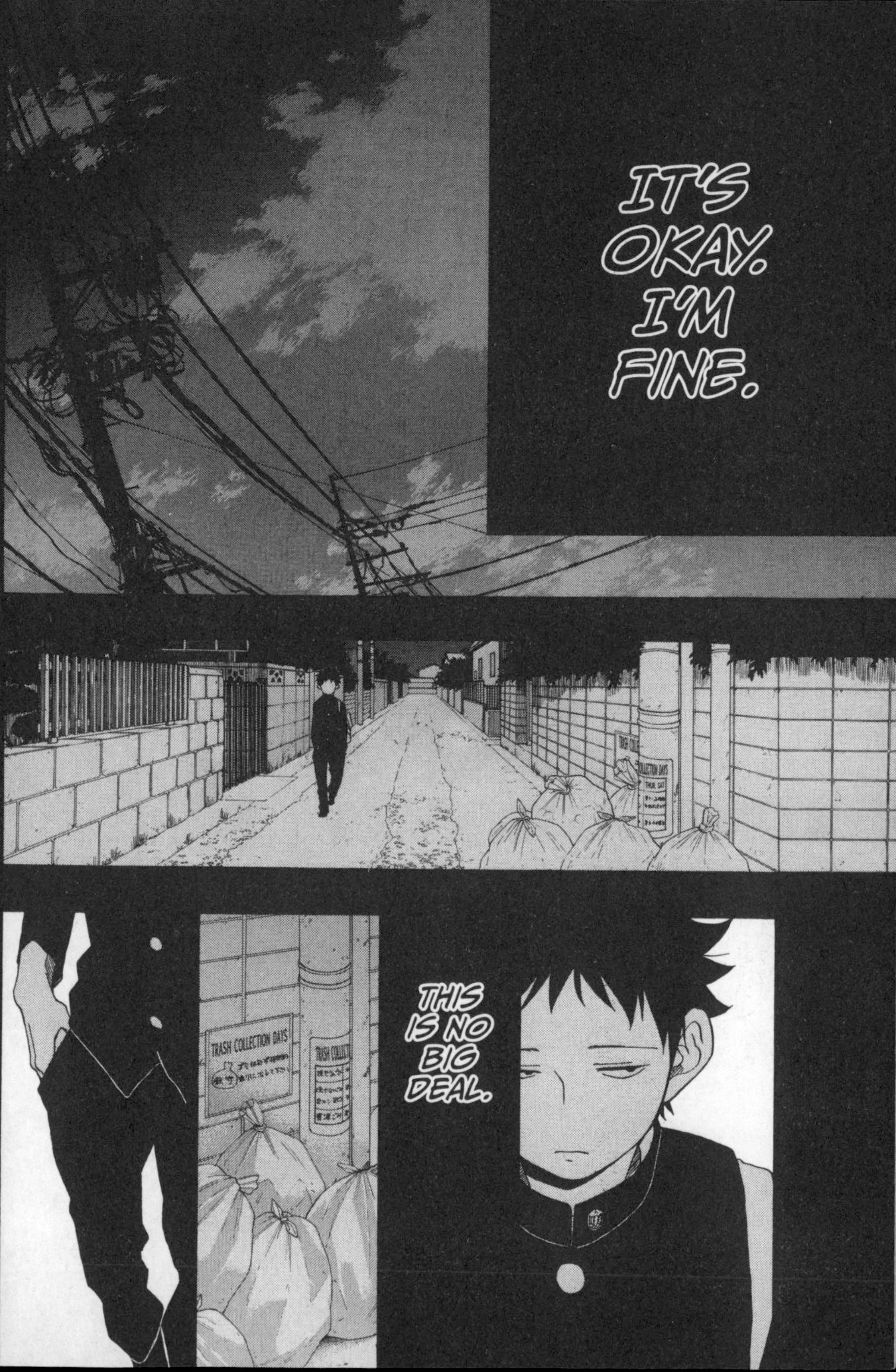
IT'S OKAY. I'M FINE.
TRASH COLLECTION DAYS
THIS IS NO BIG DEAL.
TRASH COLLECTION DAYS

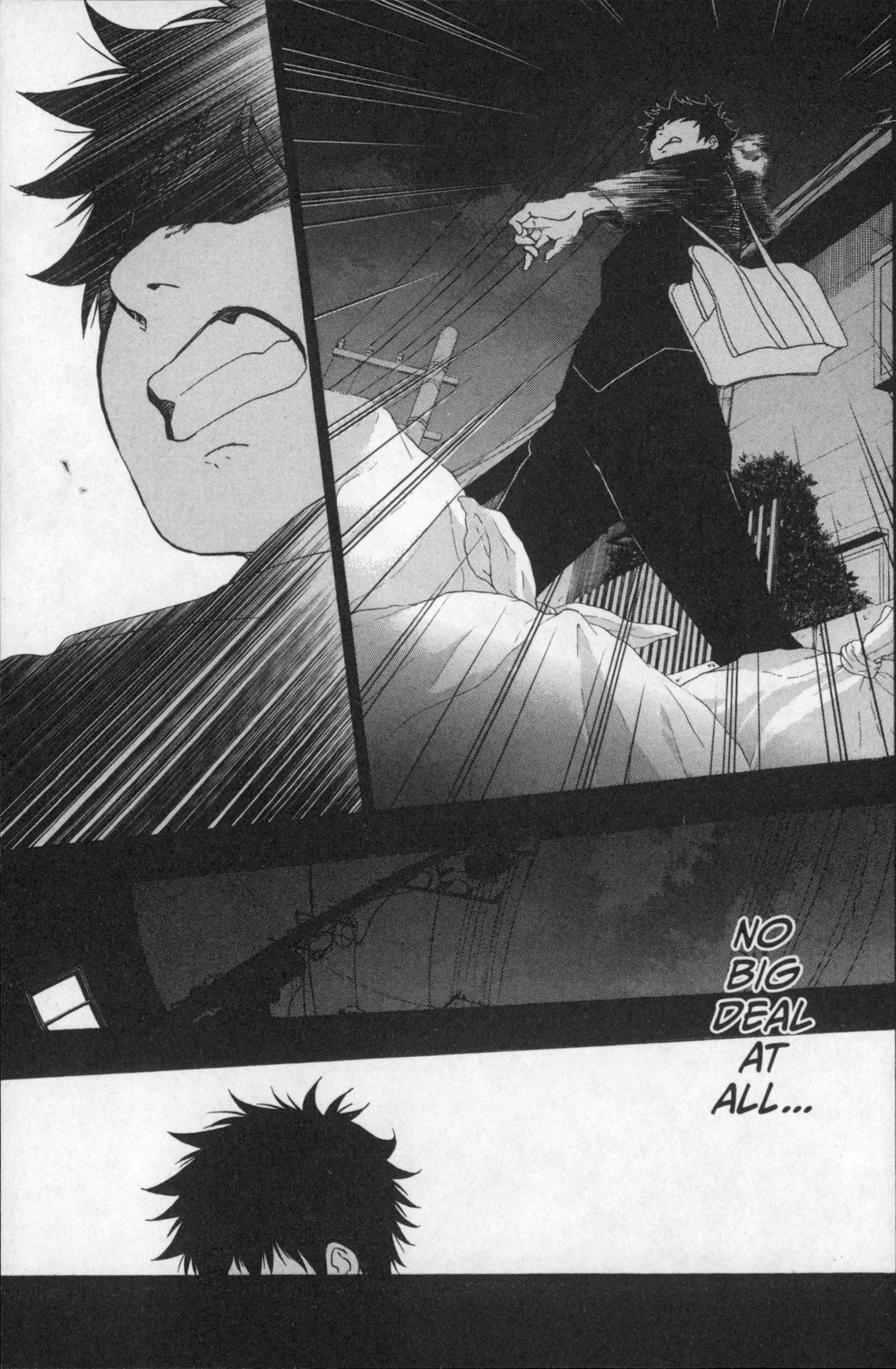
NO BIG DEAL AT ALL...

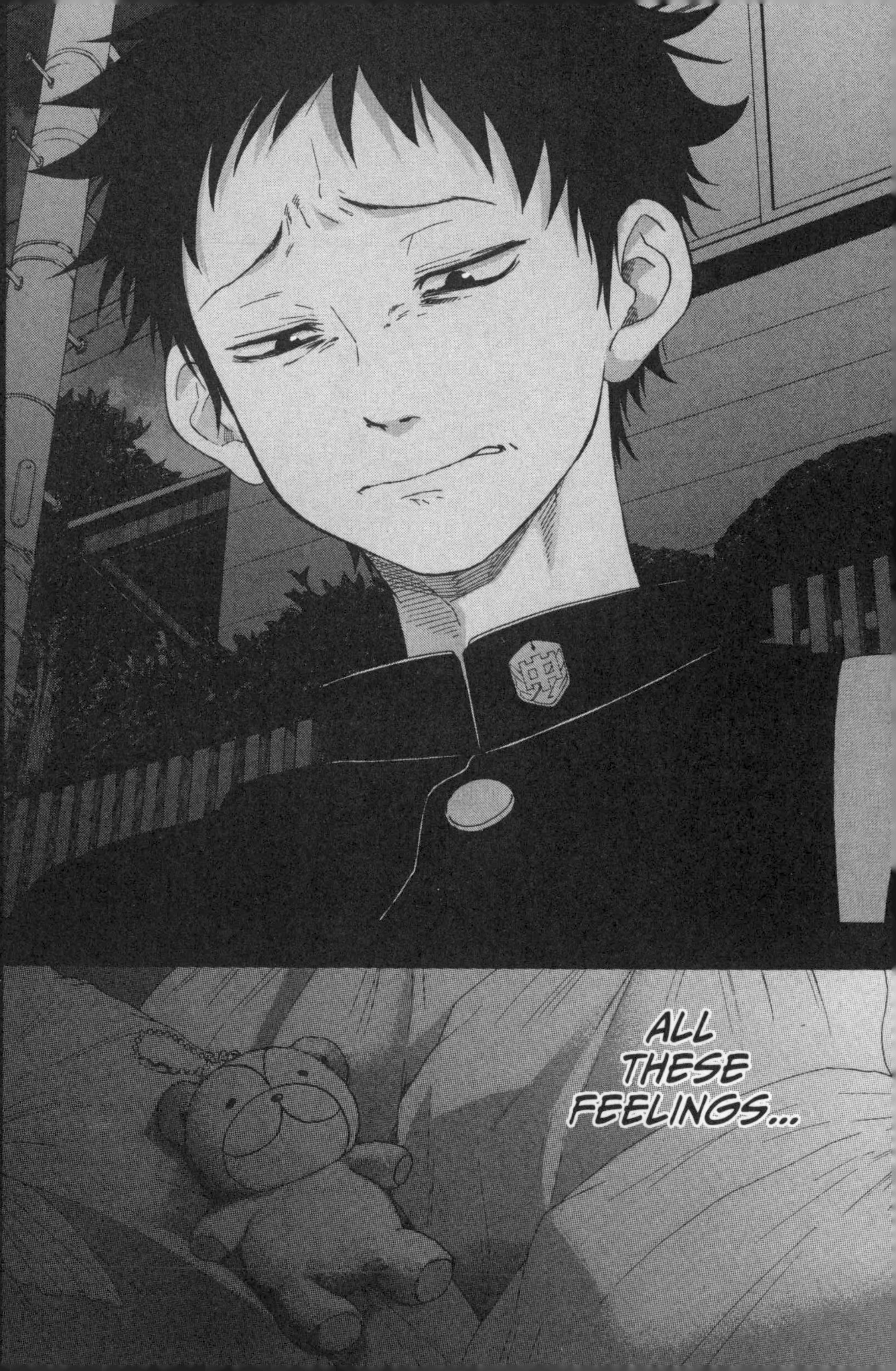
ALL THESE FEELINGS...

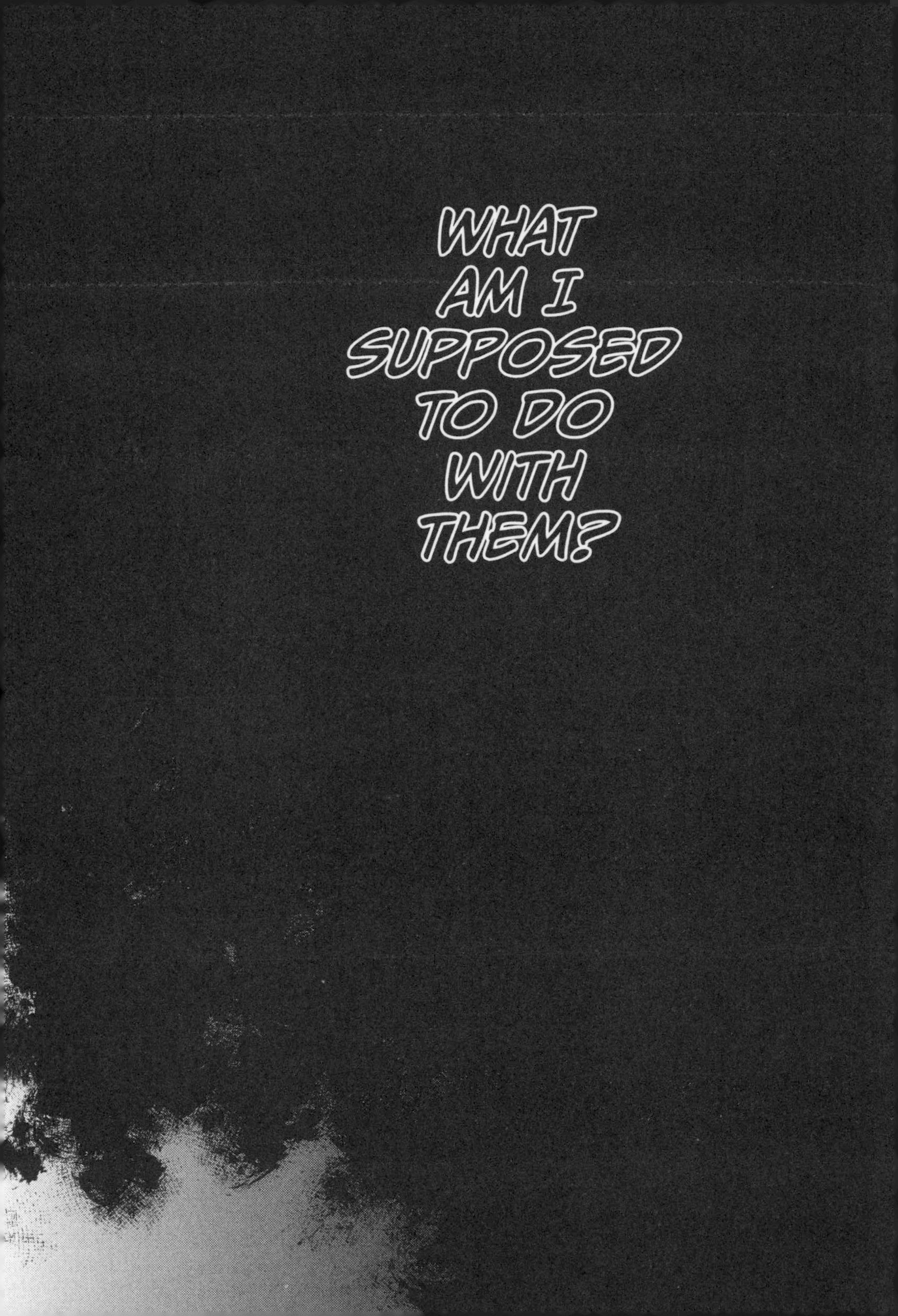
WHAT AM I SUPPOSED TO DO WITH THEM?

CHAPTER 17

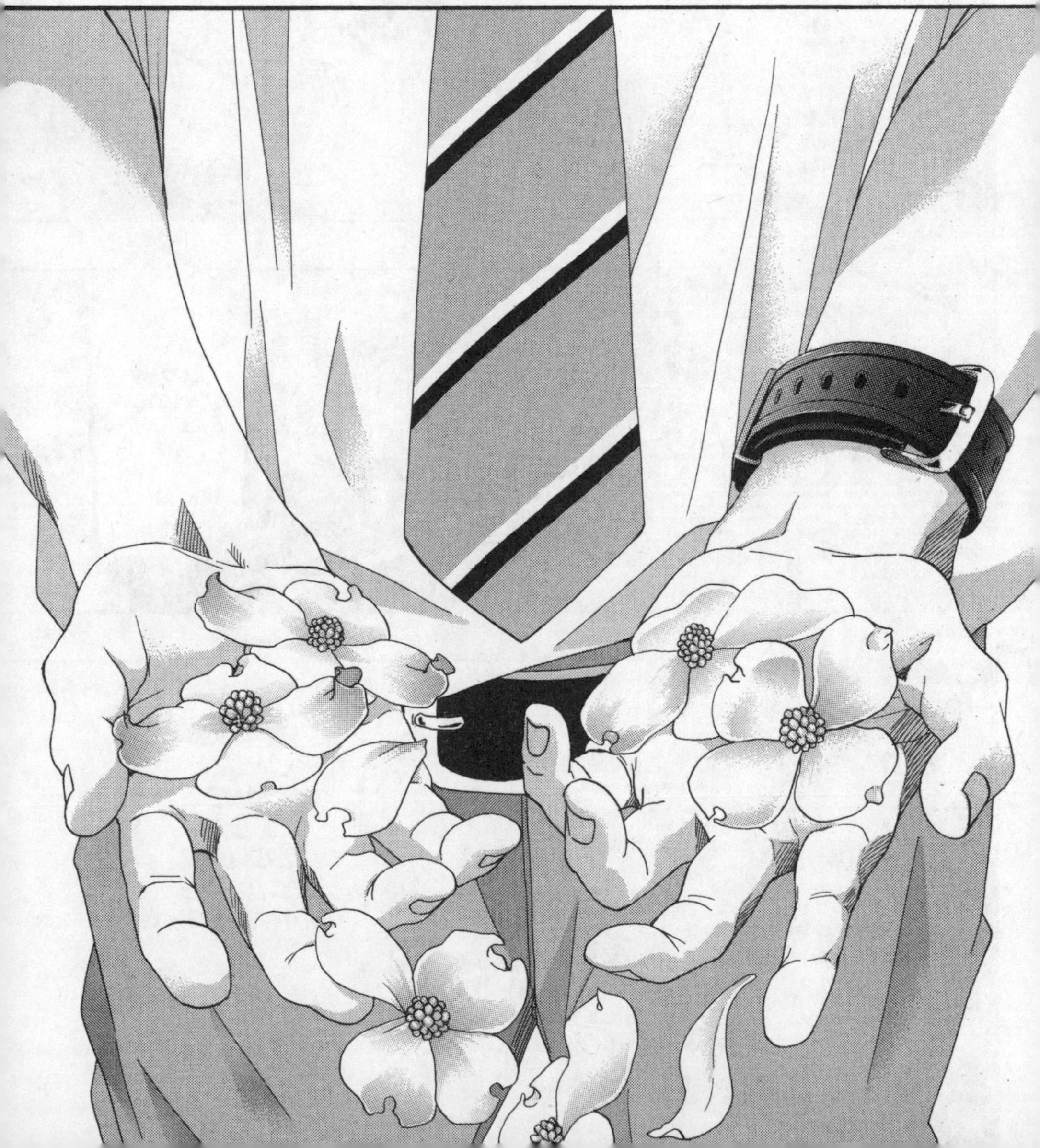

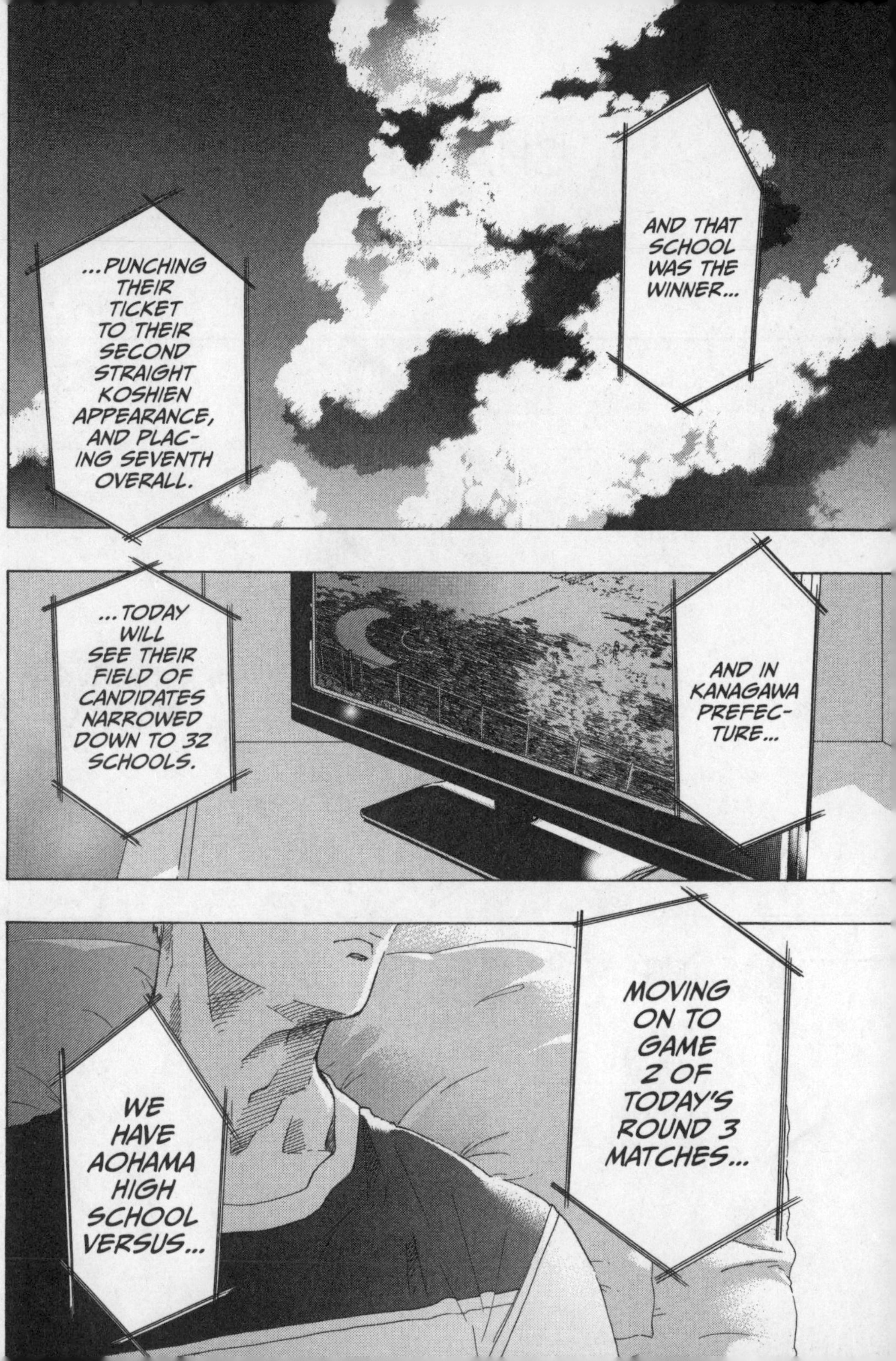
AND THAT SCHOOL WAS THE WINNER...
...PUNCHING THEIR TICKET TO THEIR SECOND STRAIGHT KOSHIEN APPEARANCE, AND PLAC-ING SEVENTH OVERALL.
AND IN KANAGAWA PREFEC-TURE...
...TODAY WILL SEE THEIR FIELD OF CANDIDATES NARROWED DOWN TO 32 SCHOOLS.
MOVING ON TO GAME 2 OF TODAY'S ROUND 3 MATCHES...
WE HAVE AOHAMA HIGH SCHOOL VERSUS...

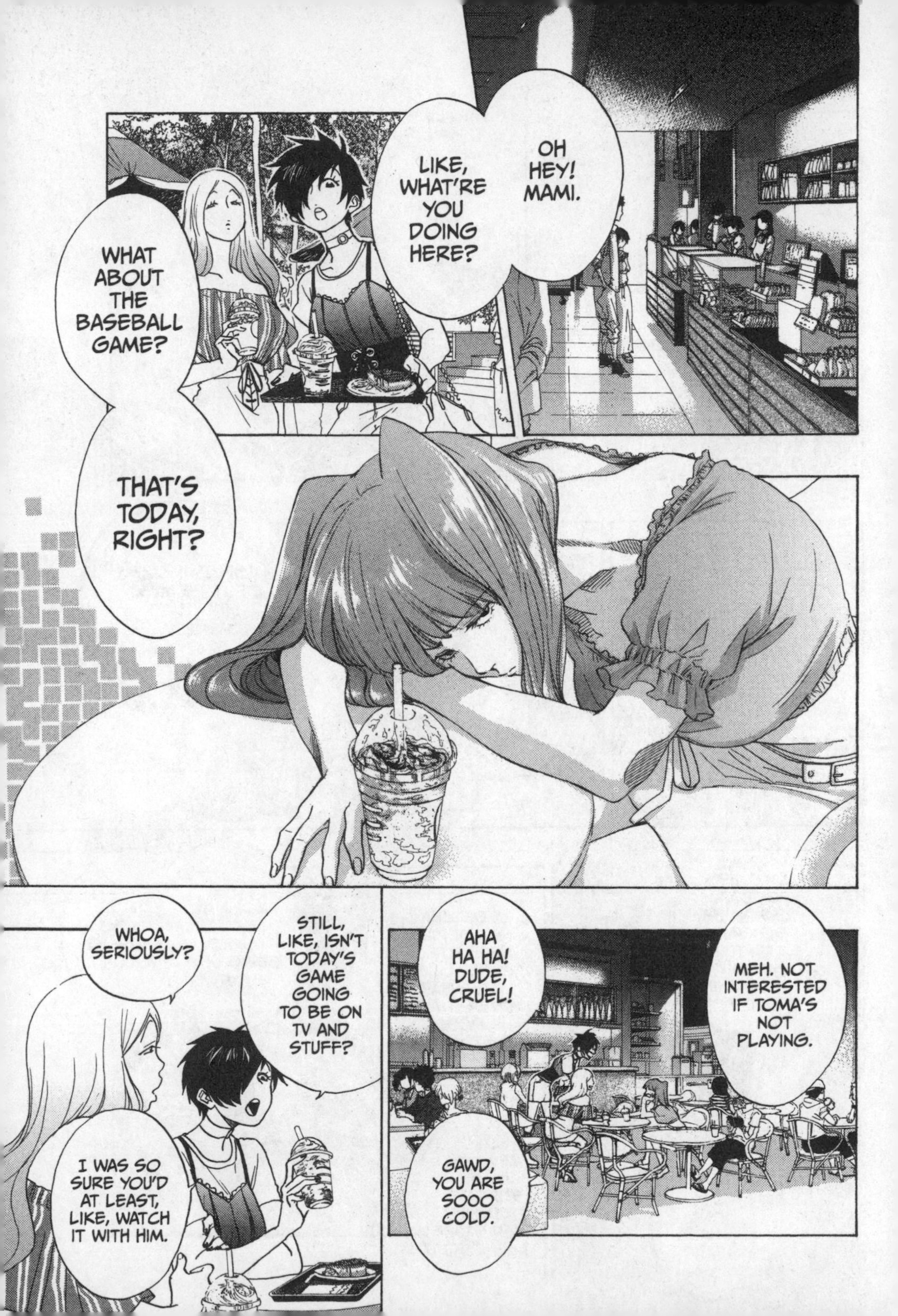
OH HEY! MAMI.
LIKE, WHAT'RE YOU DOING HERE?
WHAT ABOUT THE BASEBALL GAME?
THAT'S TODAY, RIGHT?
MEH. NOT INTERESTED IF TOMA'S NOT PLAYING.
AHA HA HA! DUDE, CRUEL!
GAWD, YOU ARE SOOO COLD.
STILL, LIKE, ISN'T TODAY'S GAME GOING TO BE ON TV AND STUFF?
WHOA, SERIOUSLY?
I WAS SO SURE YOU'D AT LEAST, LIKE, WATCH IT WITH HIM.

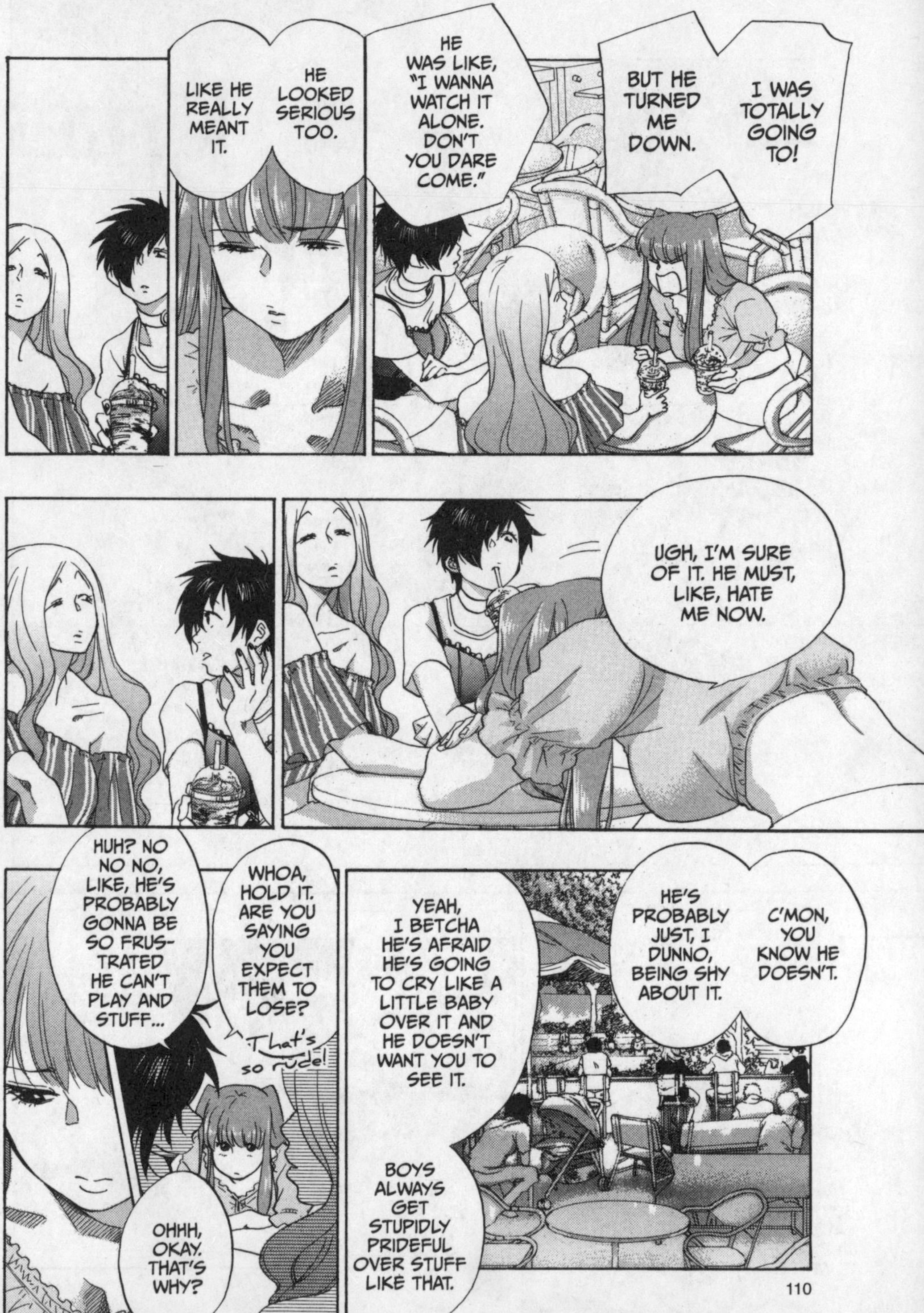

I WAS TOTALLY GOING TO!
BUT HE TURNED ME DOWN.
HE WAS LIKE, "I WANNA WATCH IT ALONE. DON'T YOU DARE COME."
HE LOOKED SERIOUS TOO.
LIKE HE REALLY MEANT IT.
UGH, I'M SURE OF IT. HE MUST, LIKE, HATE ME NOW.
C'MON, YOU KNOW HE DOESN'T.
HE'S PROBABLY JUST, I DUNNO, BEING SHY ABOUT IT.
YEAH, I BETCHA HE'S AFRAID HE'S GOING TO CRY LIKE A LITTLE BABY OVER IT AND HE DOESN'T WANT YOU TO SEE IT.
BOYS ALWAYS GET STUPIDLY PRIDEFUL OVER STUFF LIKE THAT.
WHOA, HOLD IT. ARE YOU SAYING YOU EXPECT THEM TO LOSE?
That's so rude!
HUH? NO NO NO, LIKE, HE'S PROBABLY GONNA BE SO FRUS-TRATED HE CAN'T PLAY AND STUFF...
OHHH, OKAY. THAT'S WHY?

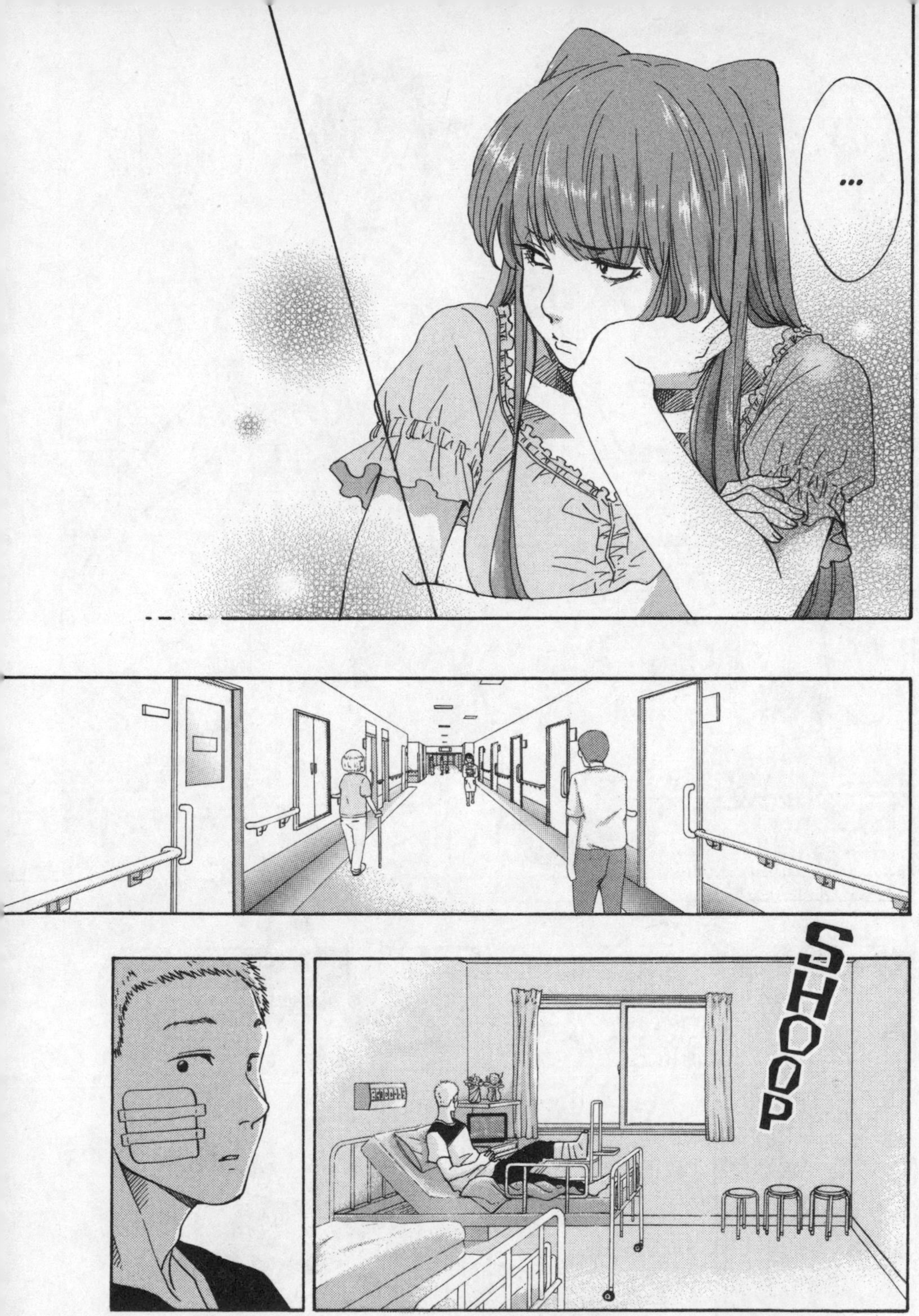

...
SHOOP

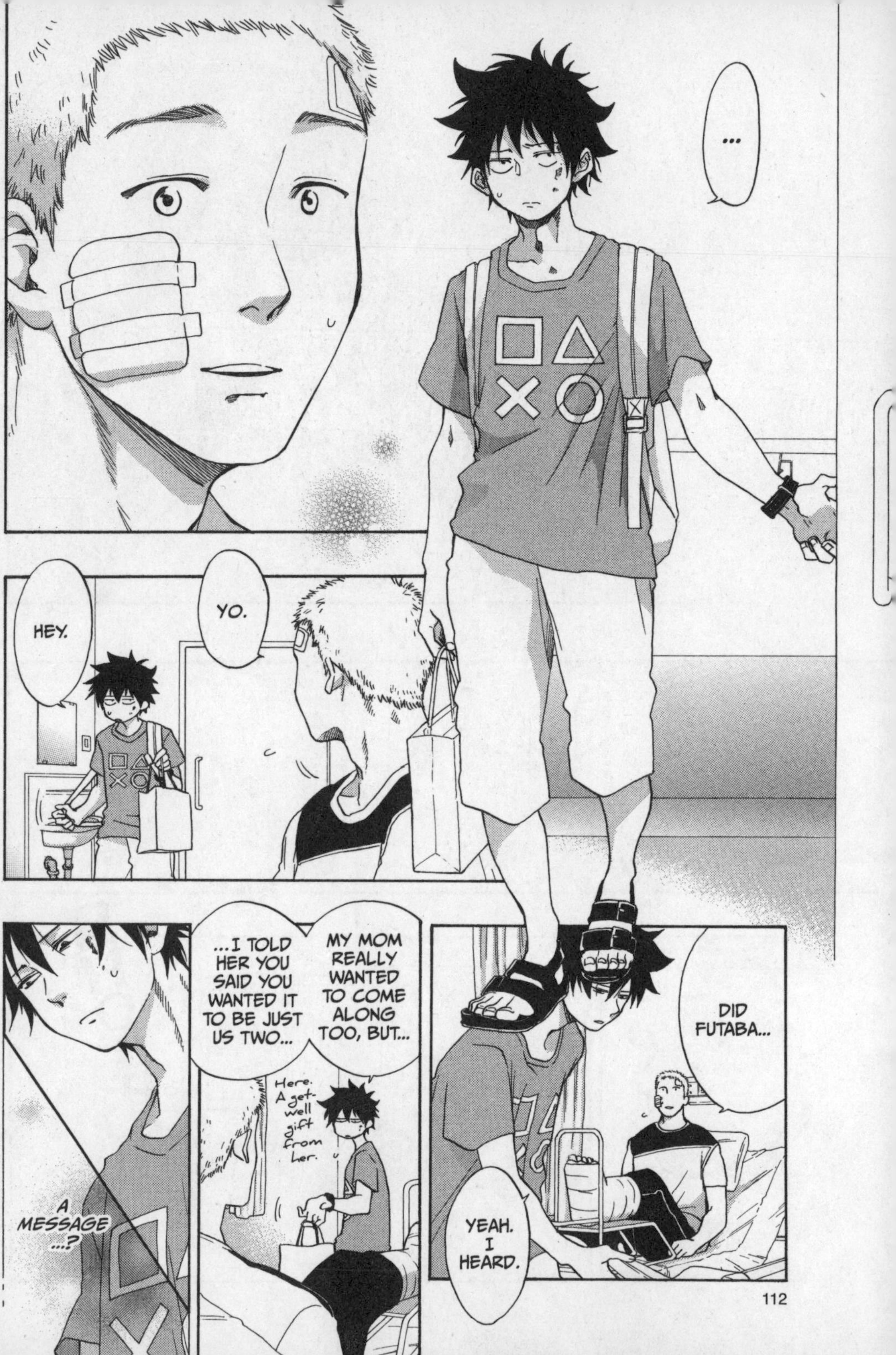
...
YO.
HEY.
DID FUTABA...
YEAH. I HEARD.
MY MOM REALLY WANTED TO COME ALONG TOO, BUT...
...I TOLD HER YOU SAID YOU WANTED IT TO BE JUST US TWO...
Here. A get-well gift from her.
A MESSAGE ...?

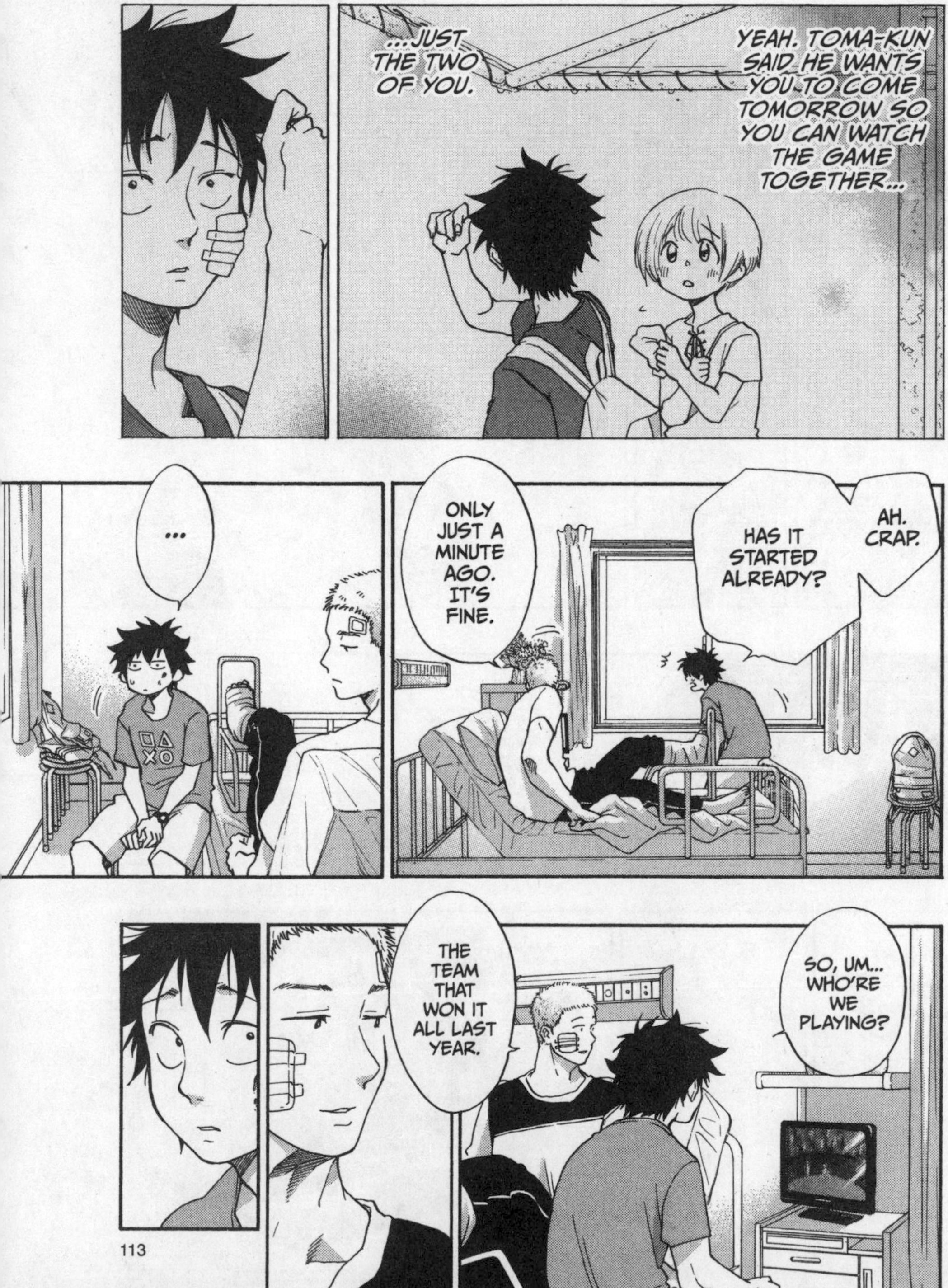
YEAH. TOMA-KUN SAID HE WANTS YOU TO COME TOMORROW SO YOU CAN WATCH THE GAME TOGETHER...
...JUST THE TWO OF YOU.
AH. CRAP.
HAS IT STARTED ALREADY?
ONLY JUST A MINUTE AGO. IT'S FINE.
...
SO, UM... WHO'RE WE PLAYING?
THE TEAM THAT WON IT ALL LAST YEAR.

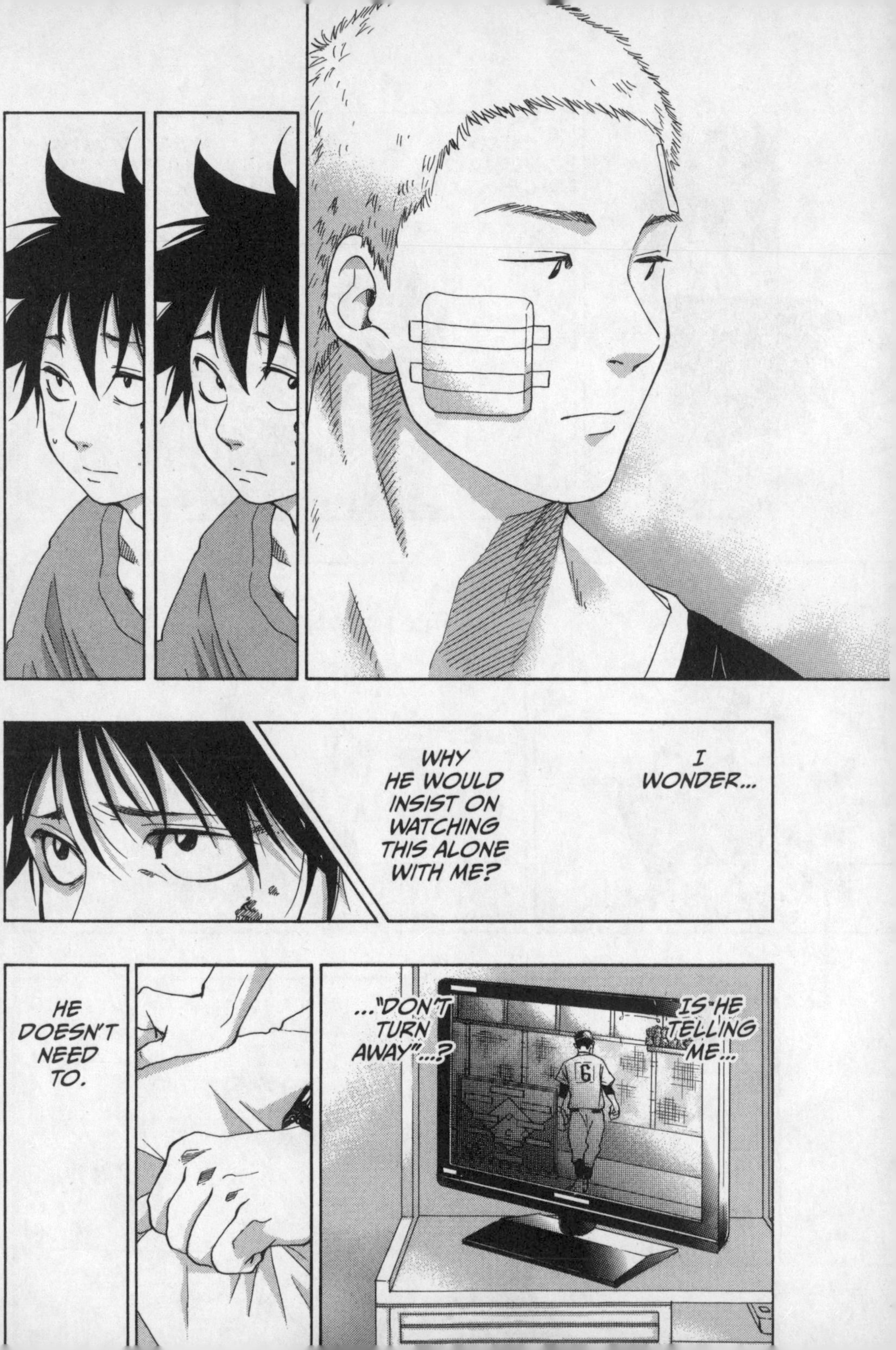
I WONDER...
WHY HE WOULD INSIST ON WATCHING THIS ALONE WITH ME?
IS HE TELLING ME...
..."DON'T TURN AWAY"...?
HE DOESN'T NEED TO.

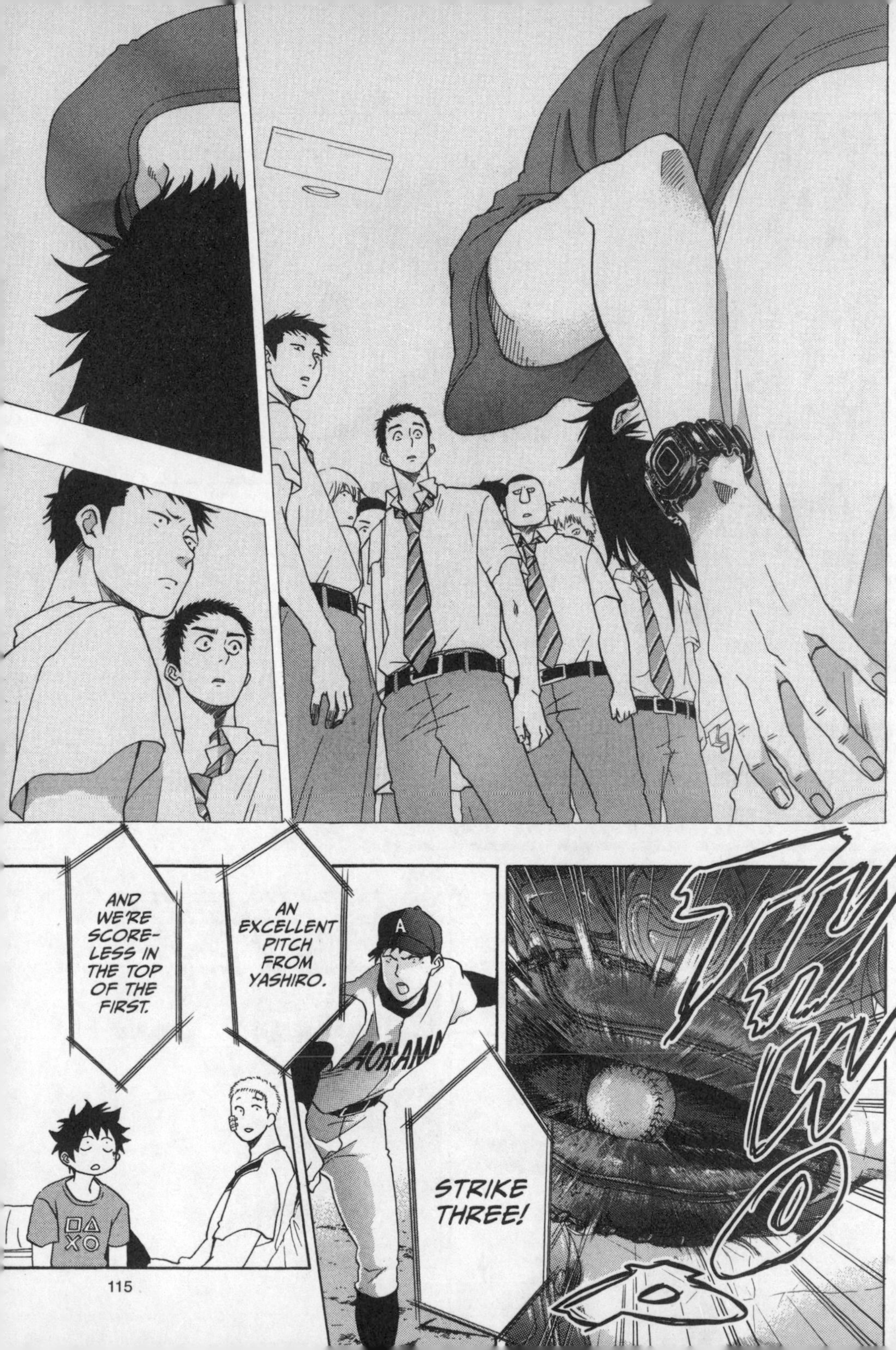
STRIKE THREE!
AN EXCELLENT PITCH FROM YASHIRO.
AND WE'RE SCORELESS IN THE TOP OF THE FIRST.
AOHAMA

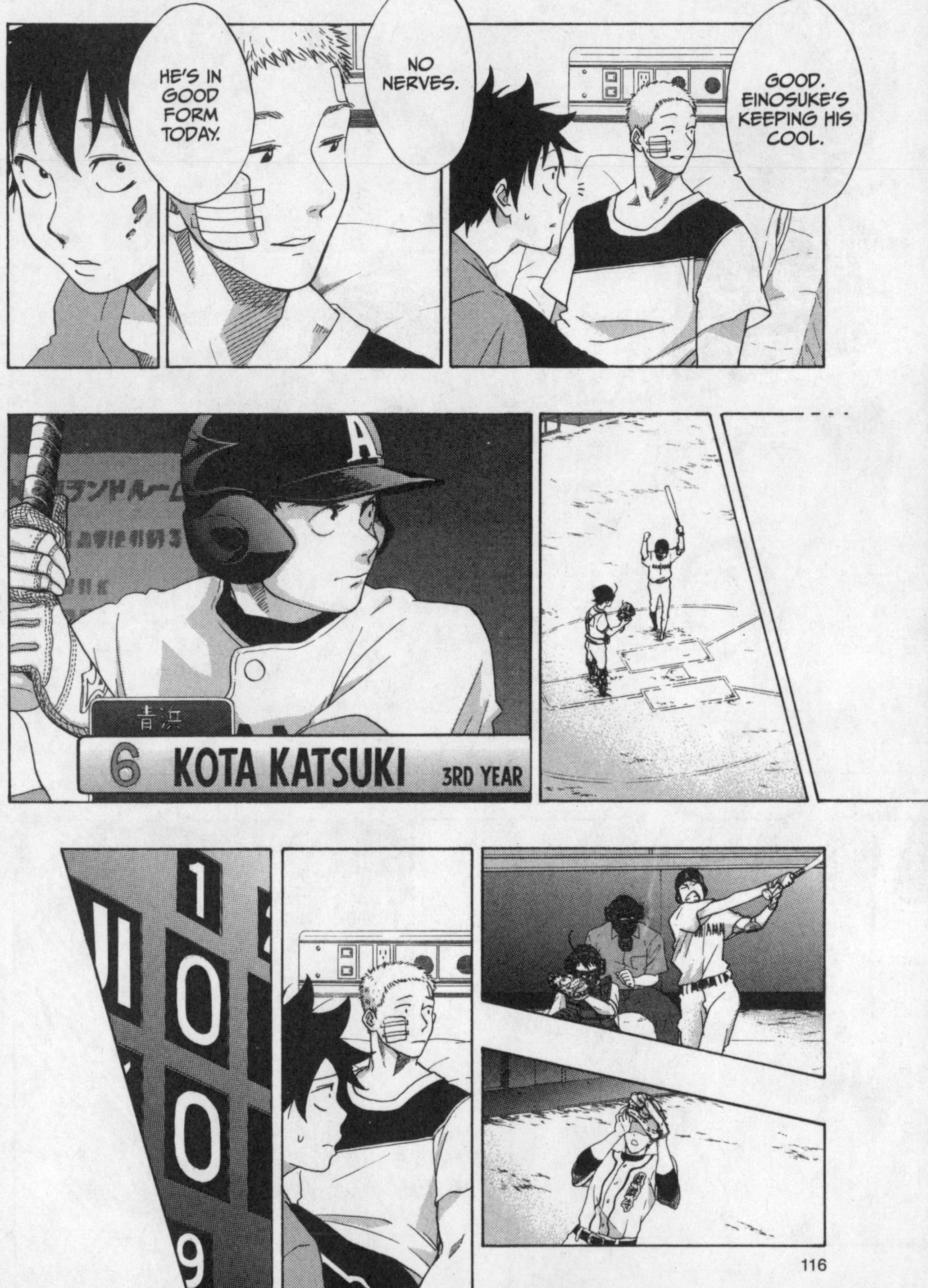
GOOD. EINOSUKE'S KEEPING HIS COOL.
NO NERVES.
HE'S IN GOOD FORM TODAY.
青浜
6 KOTA KATSUKI 3RD YEAR

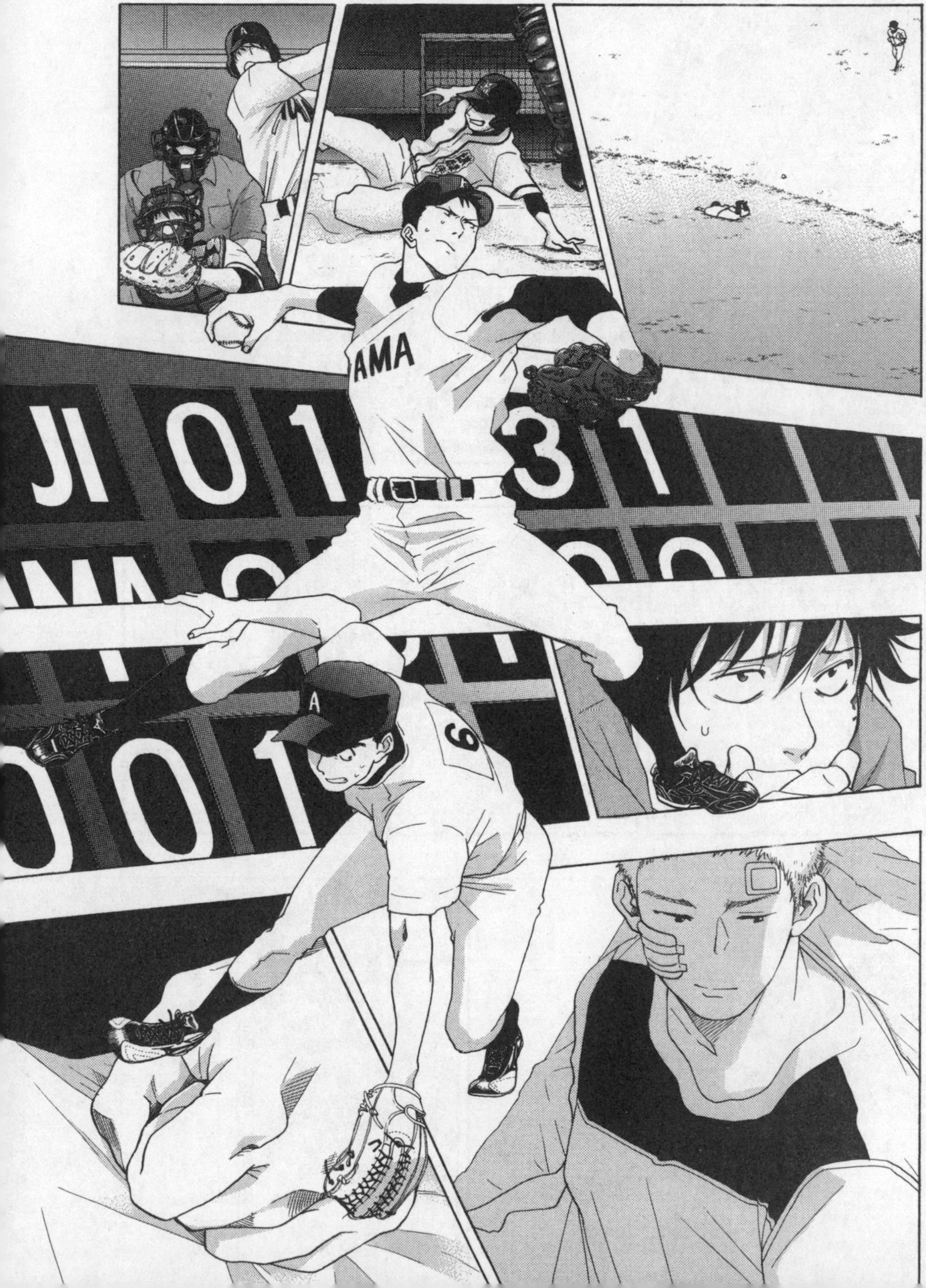

VWEEN
VWEEN VWEEN VWEEN

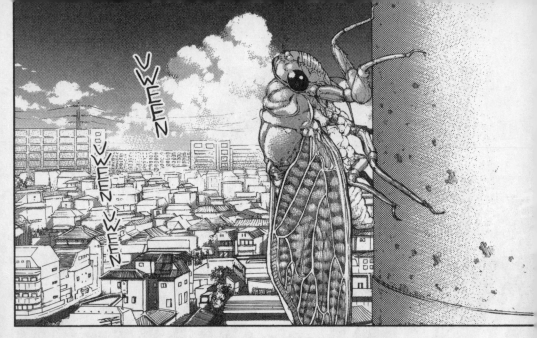

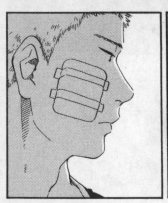

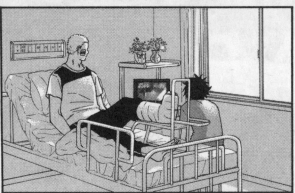

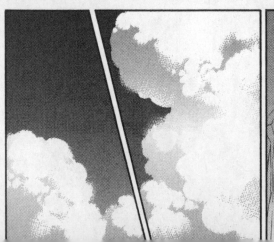

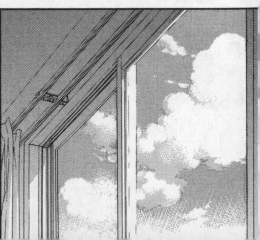

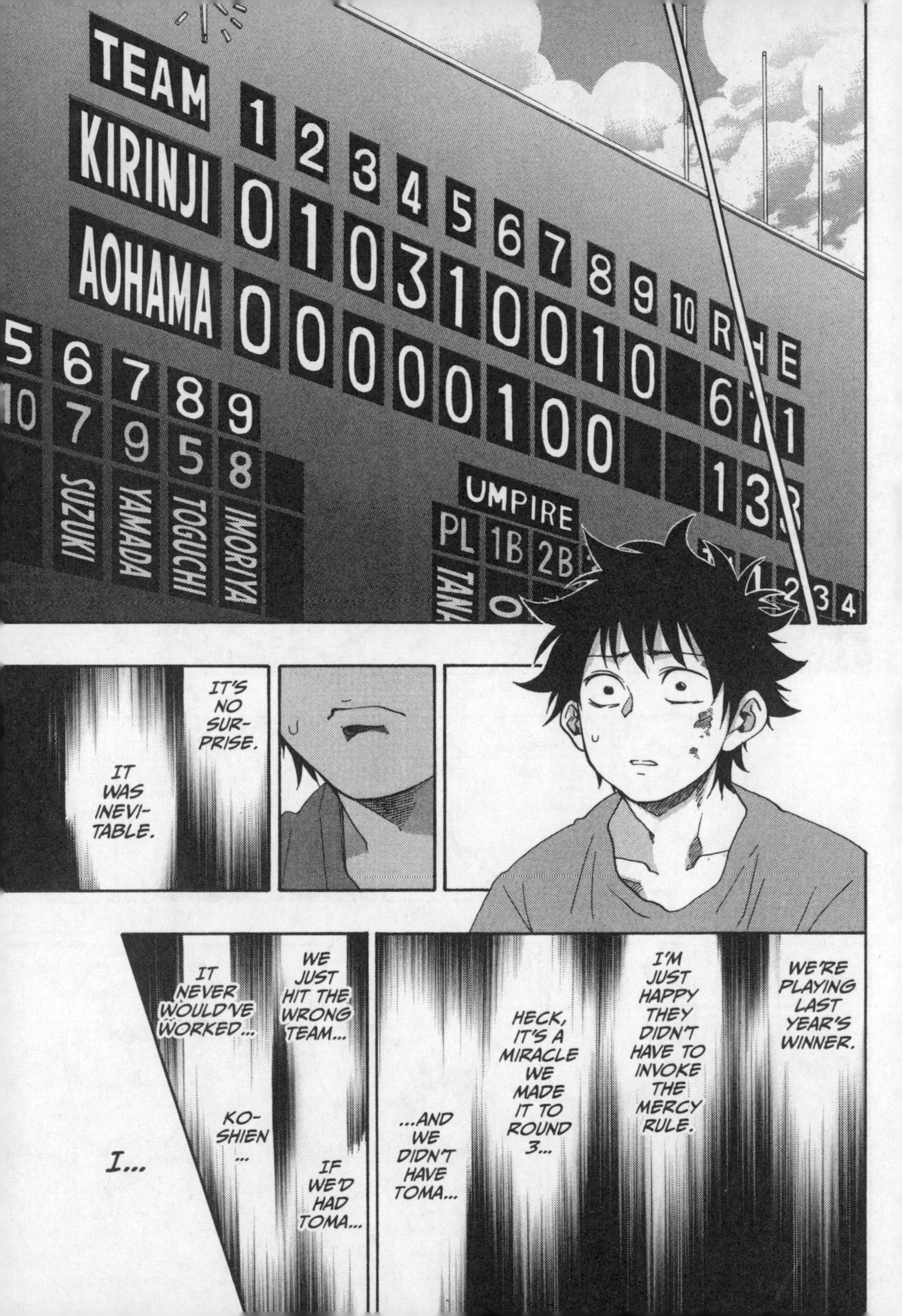
TEAM
KIRINJI
AOHAMA
SUZUKI
YAMADA
TOGUCHI
IMORIYA
UMPIRE
PL 1B 2B
IT'S NO SURPRISE.
IT WAS INEVITABLE.
WE'RE PLAYING LAST YEAR'S WINNER.
I'M JUST HAPPY THEY DIDN'T HAVE TO INVOKE THE MERCY RULE.
HECK, IT'S A MIRACLE WE MADE IT TO ROUND 3...
...AND WE DIDN'T HAVE TOMA...
IF WE'D HAD TOMA...
WE JUST HIT THE WRONG TEAM...
KOSHIEN...
IT NEVER WOULD'VE WORKED...
I...

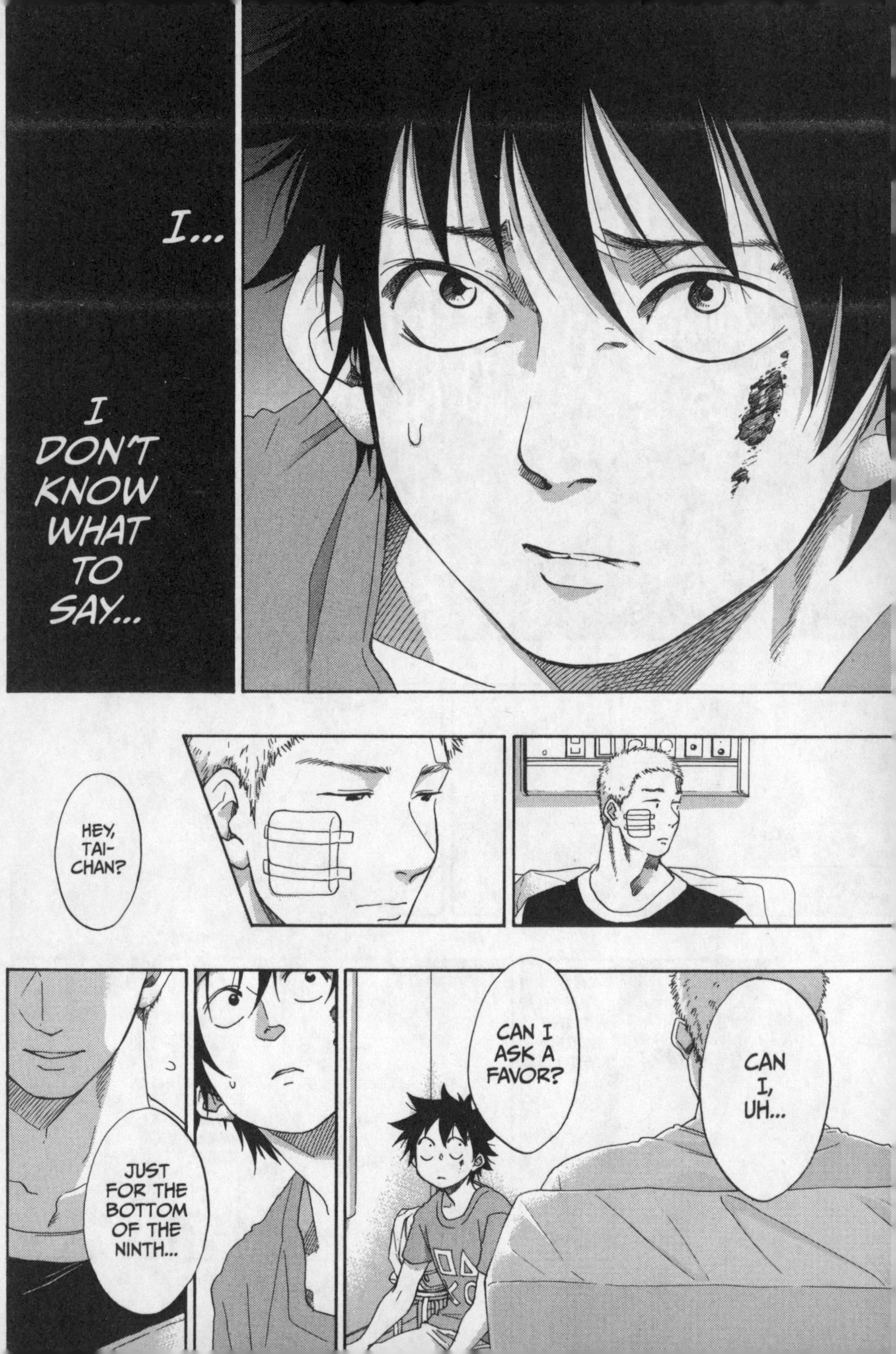
I...
I DON'T KNOW WHAT TO SAY...
HEY, TAI-CHAN?
CAN I, UH...
CAN I ASK A FAVOR?
JUST FOR THE BOTTOM OF THE NINTH...

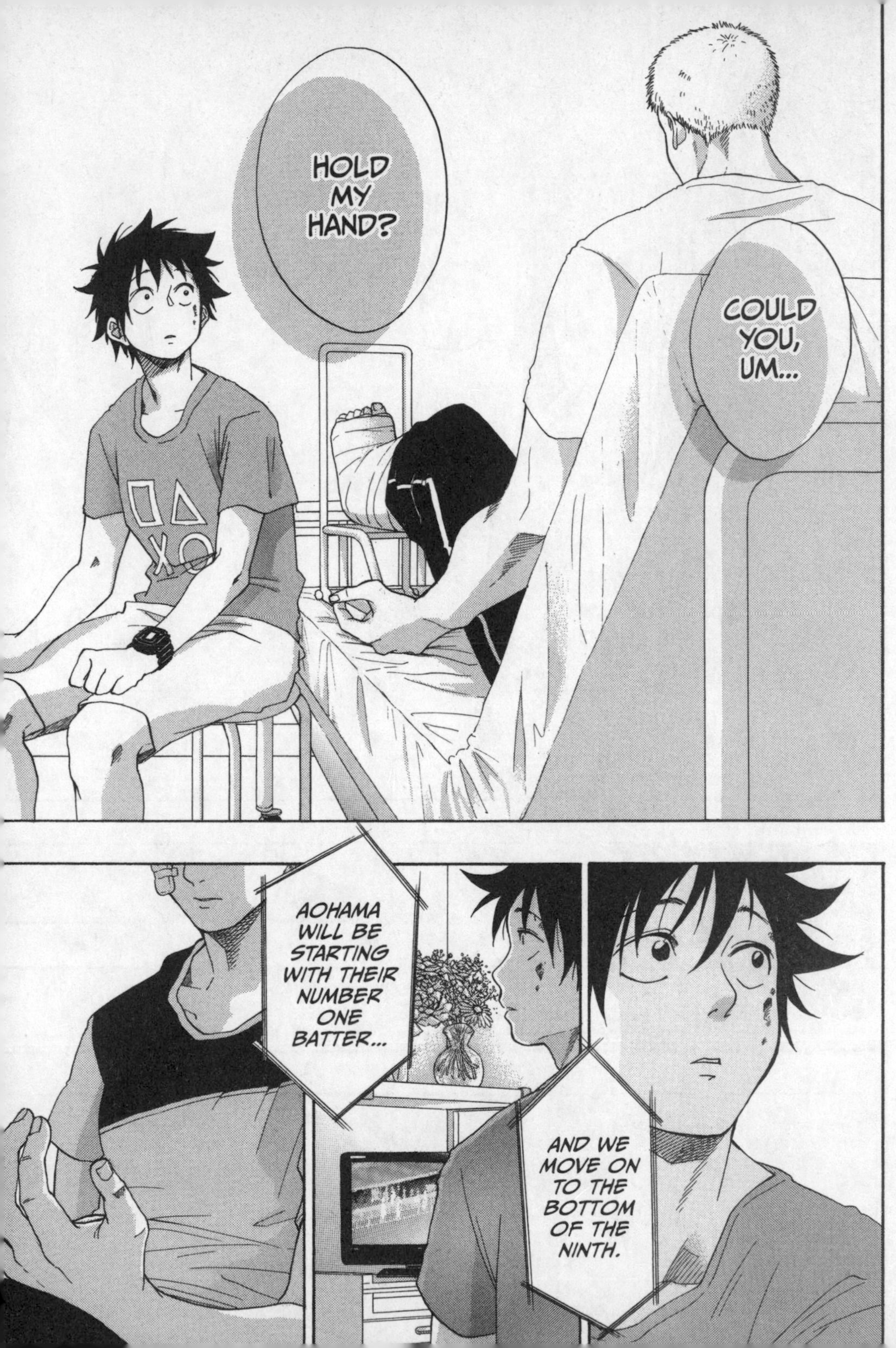
COULD YOU, UM...
HOLD MY HAND?
AOHAMA WILL BE STARTING WITH THEIR NUMBER ONE BATTER...
AND WE MOVE ON TO THE BOTTOM OF THE NINTH.

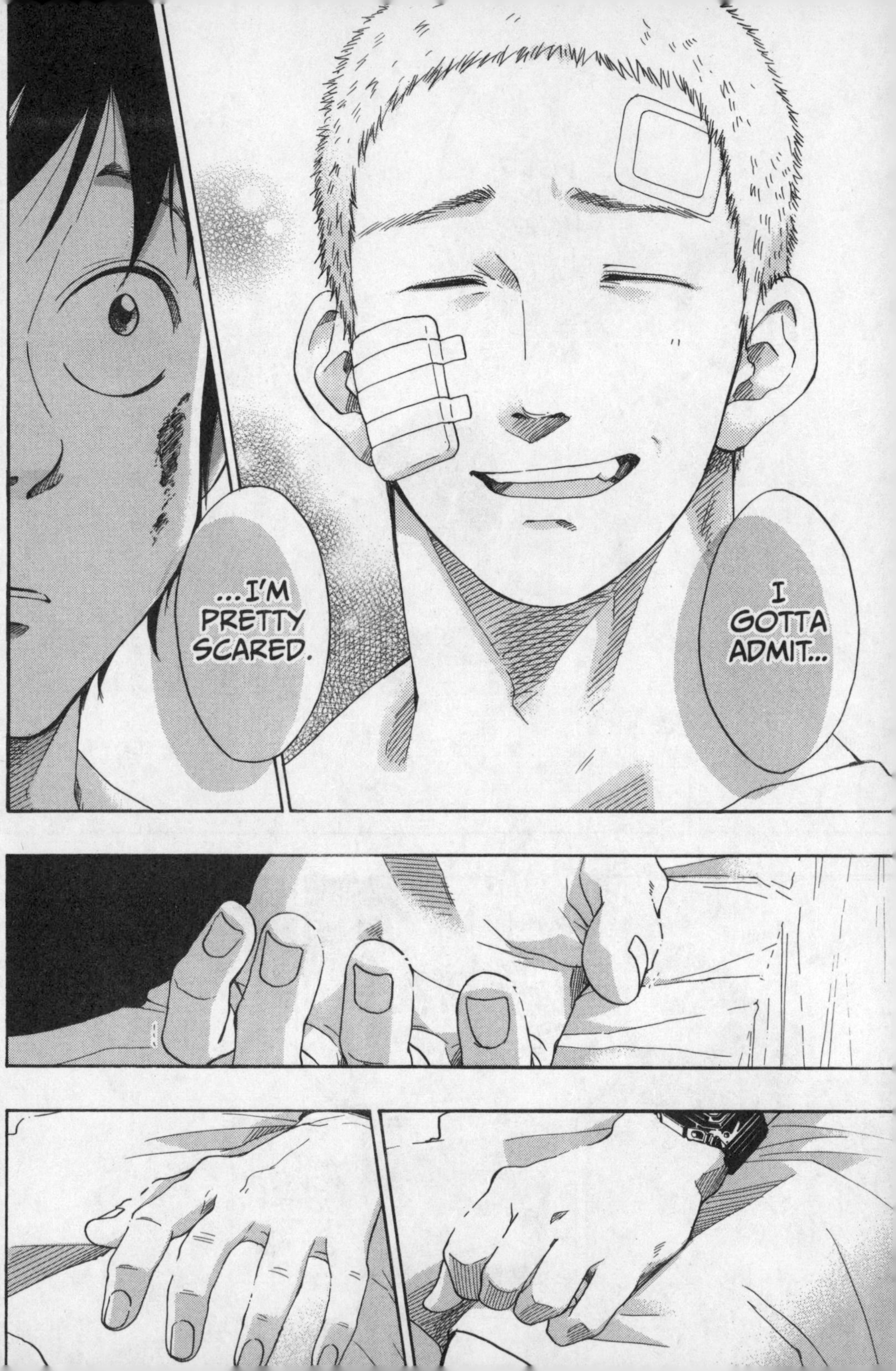
I GOTTA ADMIT...
...I'M PRETTY SCARED.

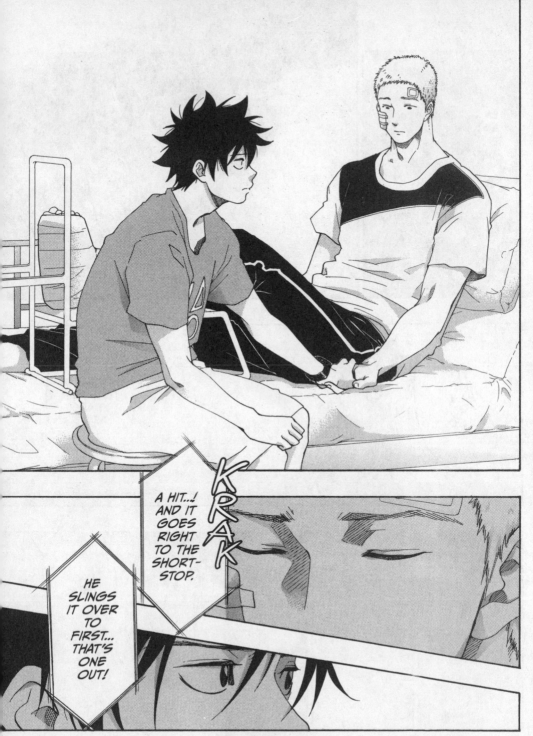

A HIT...! AND IT GOES RIGHT TO THE SHORT-STOP.

KRAK

HE SLINGS IT OVER TO FIRST... THAT'S ONE OUT!

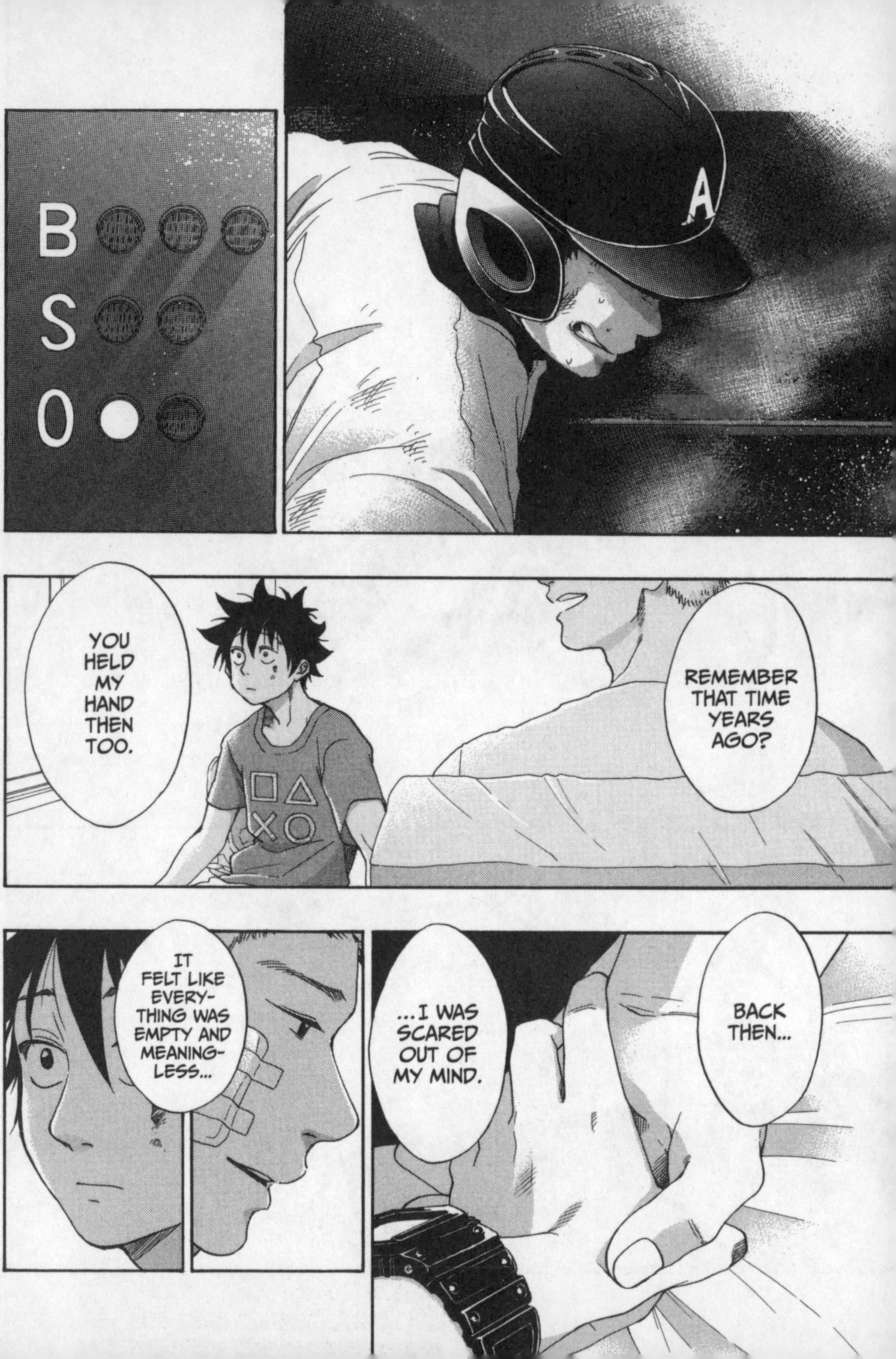
B
S
O
REMEMBER THAT TIME YEARS AGO?
YOU HELD MY HAND THEN TOO.
BACK THEN...
...I WAS SCARED OUT OF MY MIND.
IT FELT LIKE EVERY-THING WAS EMPTY AND MEANING-LESS...

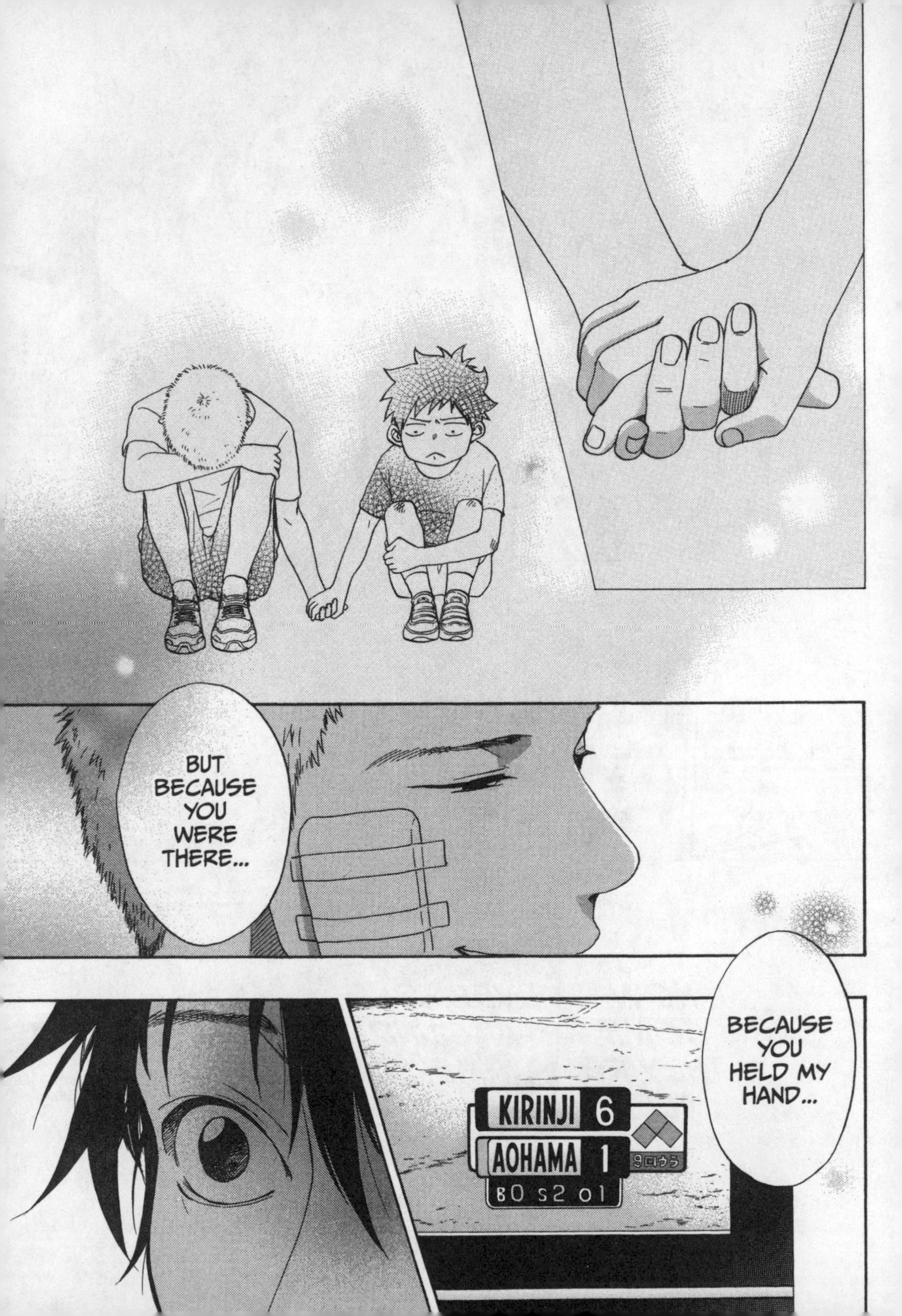
BUT BECAUSE YOU WERE THERE...
BECAUSE YOU HELD MY HAND...
KIRINJI 6
AOHAMA 1
9回ウラ
B0 S2 O1

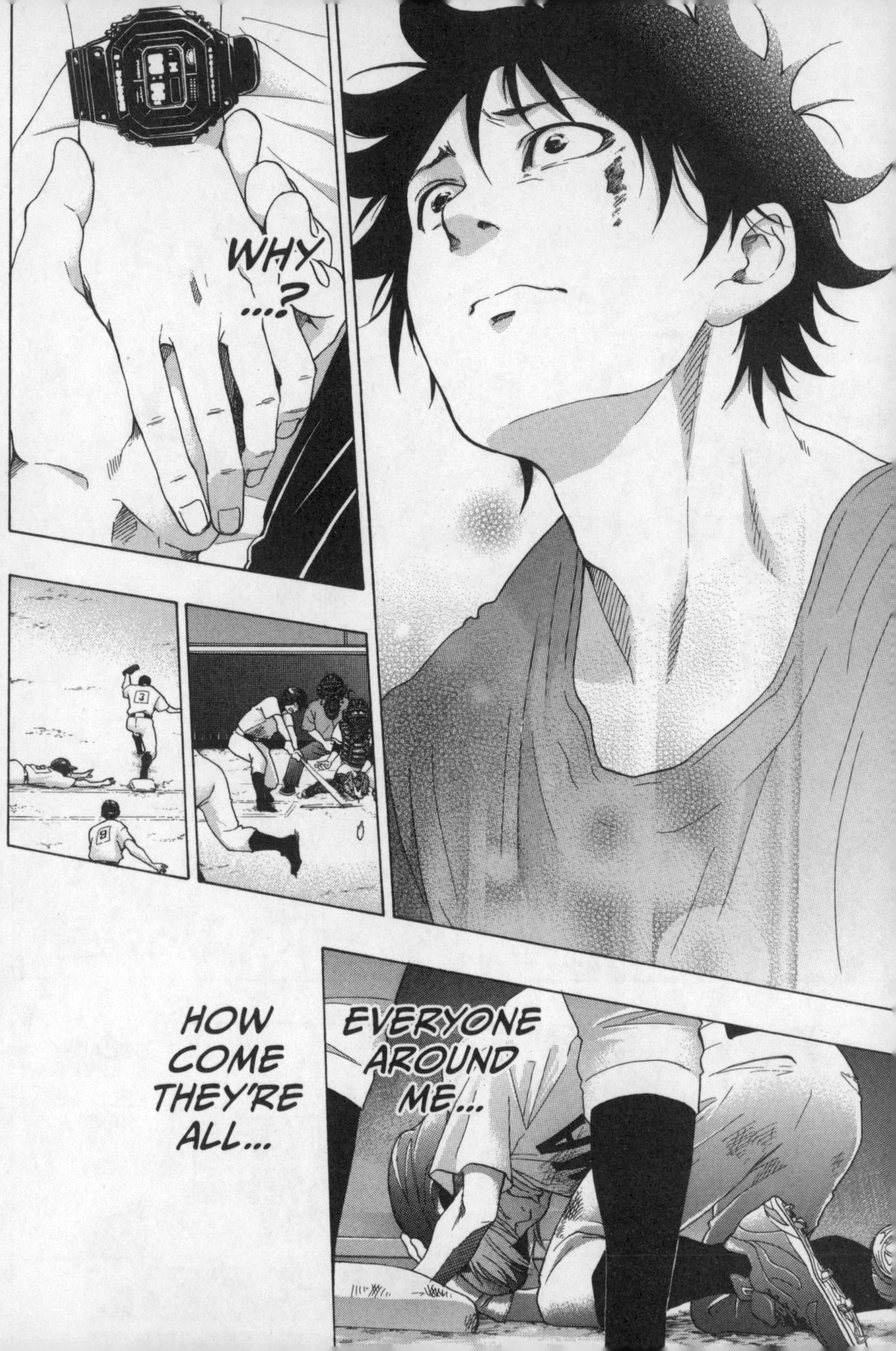
WHY ...?
EVERYONE AROUND ME...
HOW COME THEY'RE ALL...

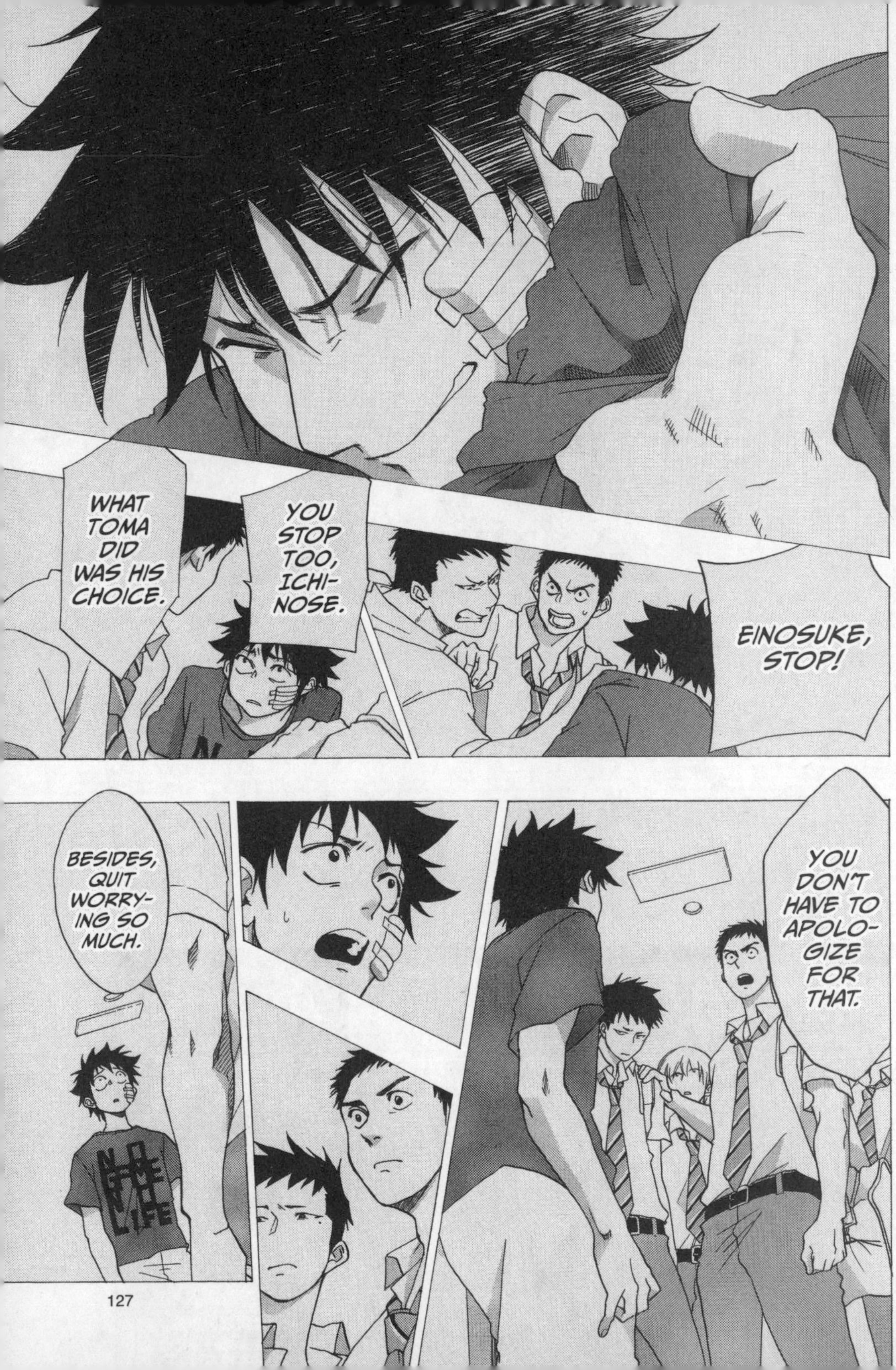
EINOSUKE, STOP!
YOU STOP TOO, ICHI-NOSE.
WHAT TOMA DID WAS HIS CHOICE.
YOU DON'T HAVE TO APOLO-GIZE FOR THAT.
BESIDES, QUIT WORRY-ING SO MUCH.
NO GIVE NO LIFE

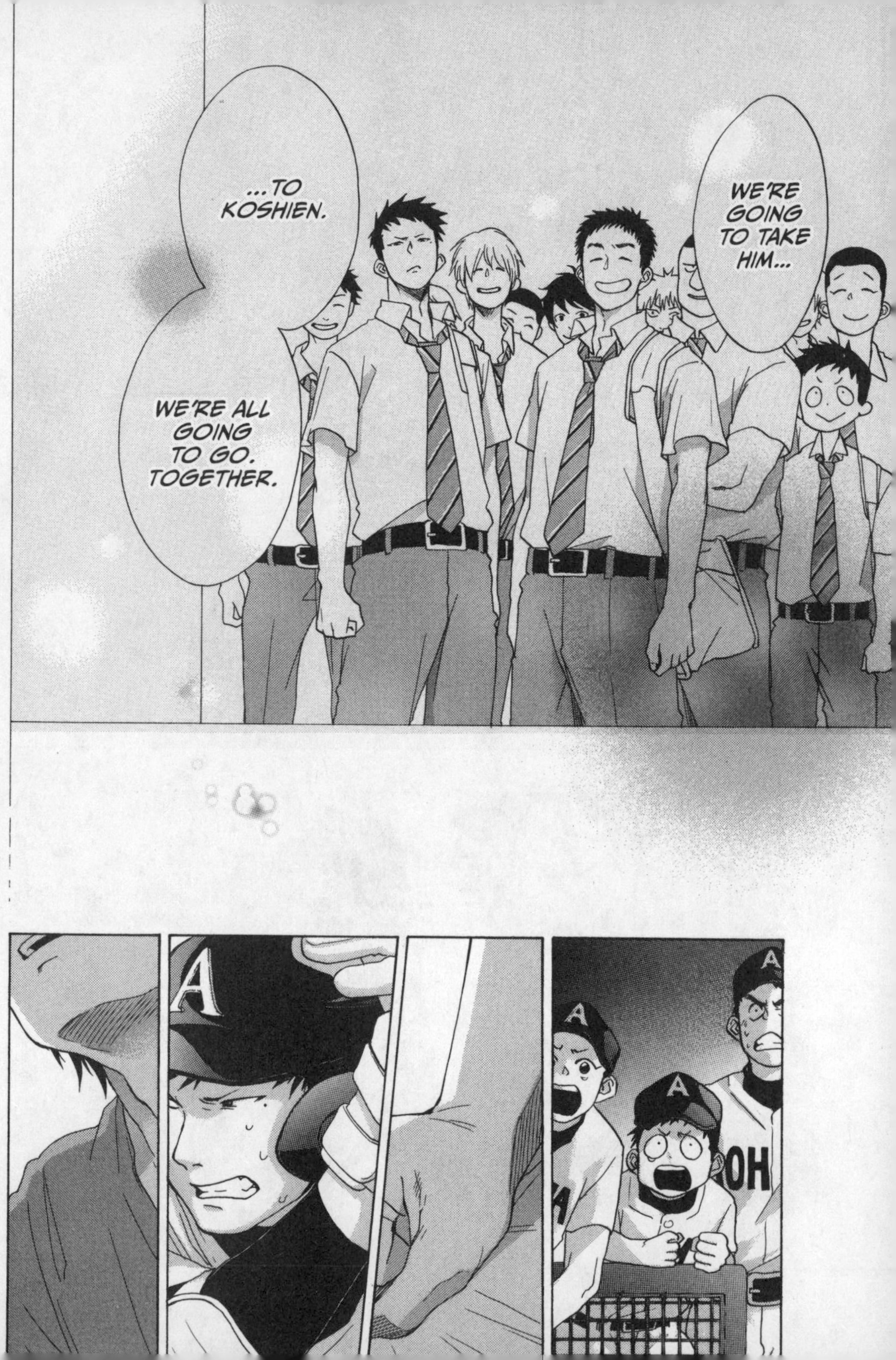
WE'RE GOING TO TAKE HIM...
...TO KOSHIEN.
WE'RE ALL GOING TO GO. TOGETHER.

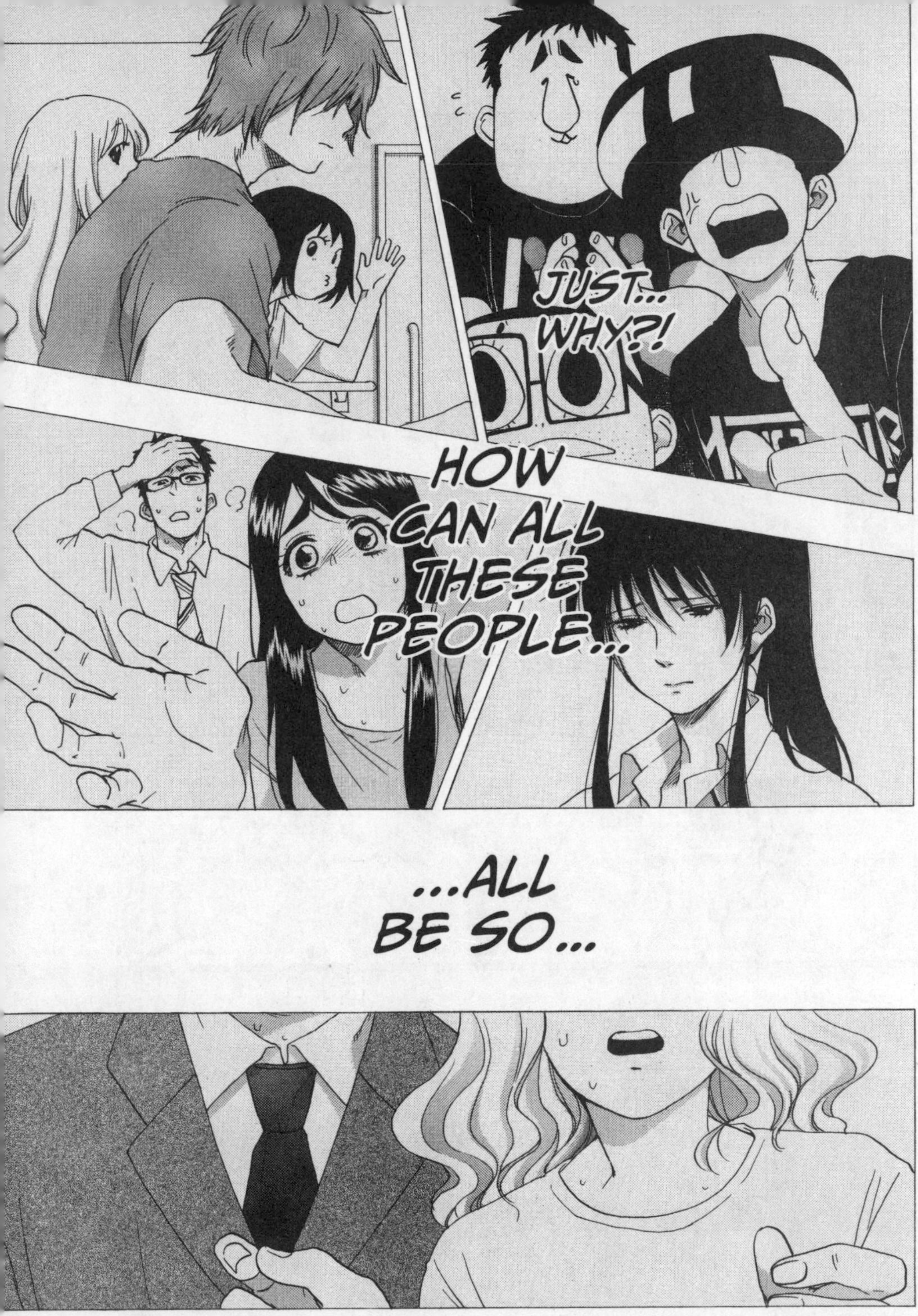
JUST... WHY?!
HOW CAN ALL THESE PEOPLE...
...ALL BE SO...

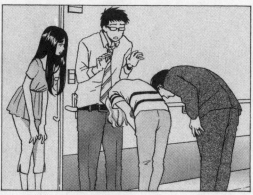

TAICHI.

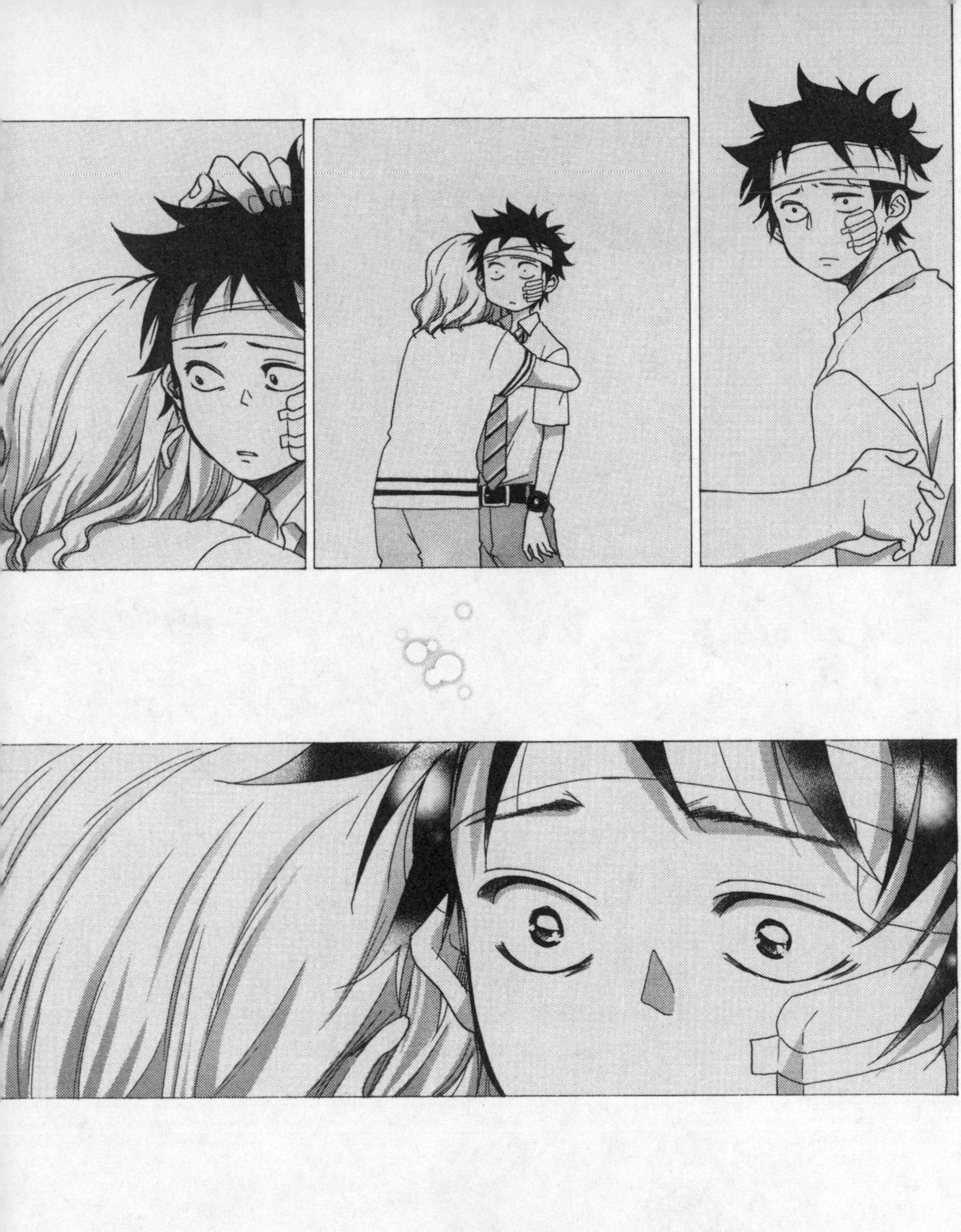
SO...

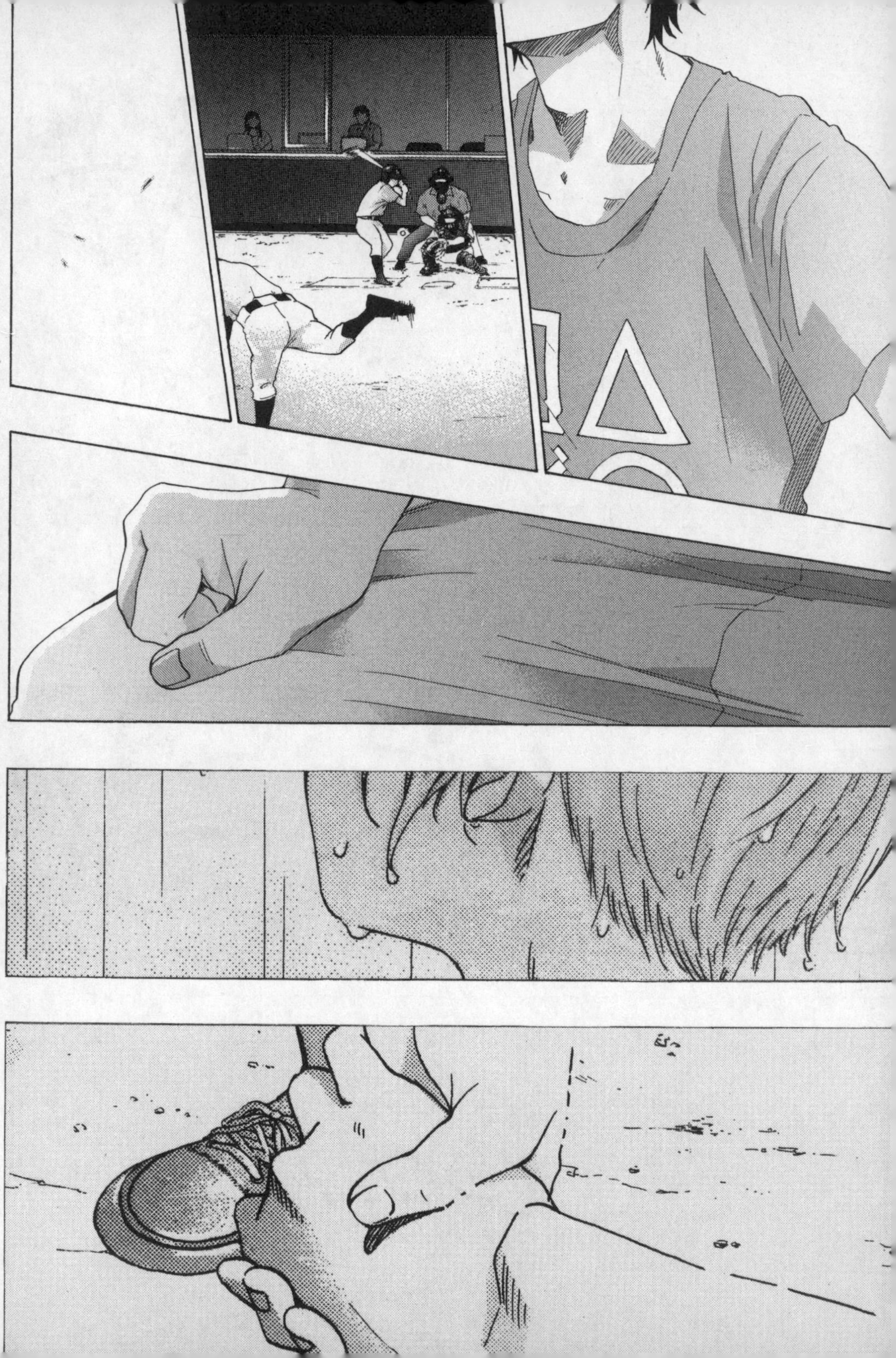

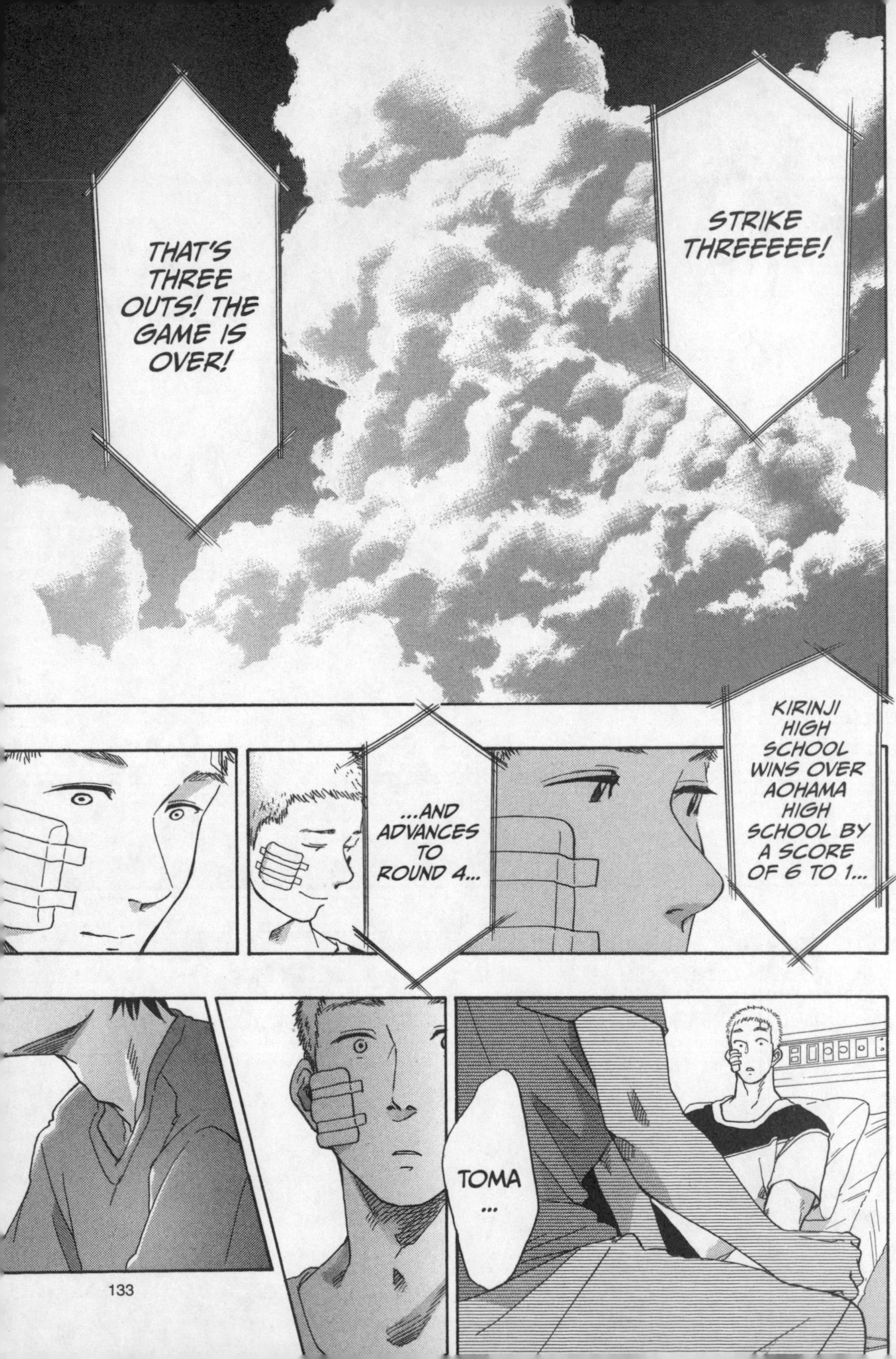
STRIKE THREEEEEE!
THAT'S THREE OUTS! THE GAME IS OVER!
KIRINJI HIGH SCHOOL WINS OVER AOHAMA HIGH SCHOOL BY A SCORE OF 6 TO 1...
...AND ADVANCES TO ROUND 4...
TOMA ...

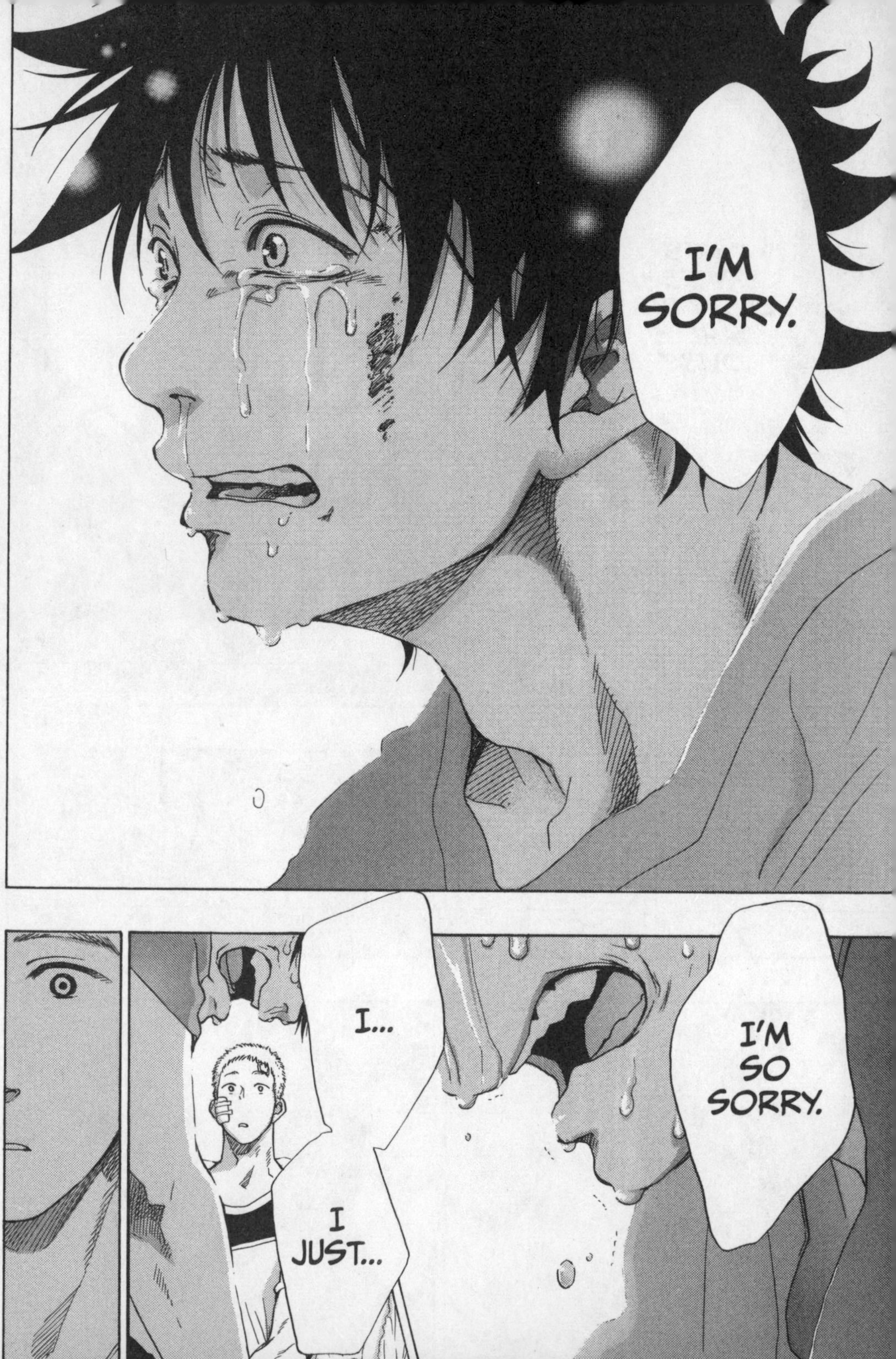
I'M SORRY.
I'M SO SORRY.
I...
I JUST...

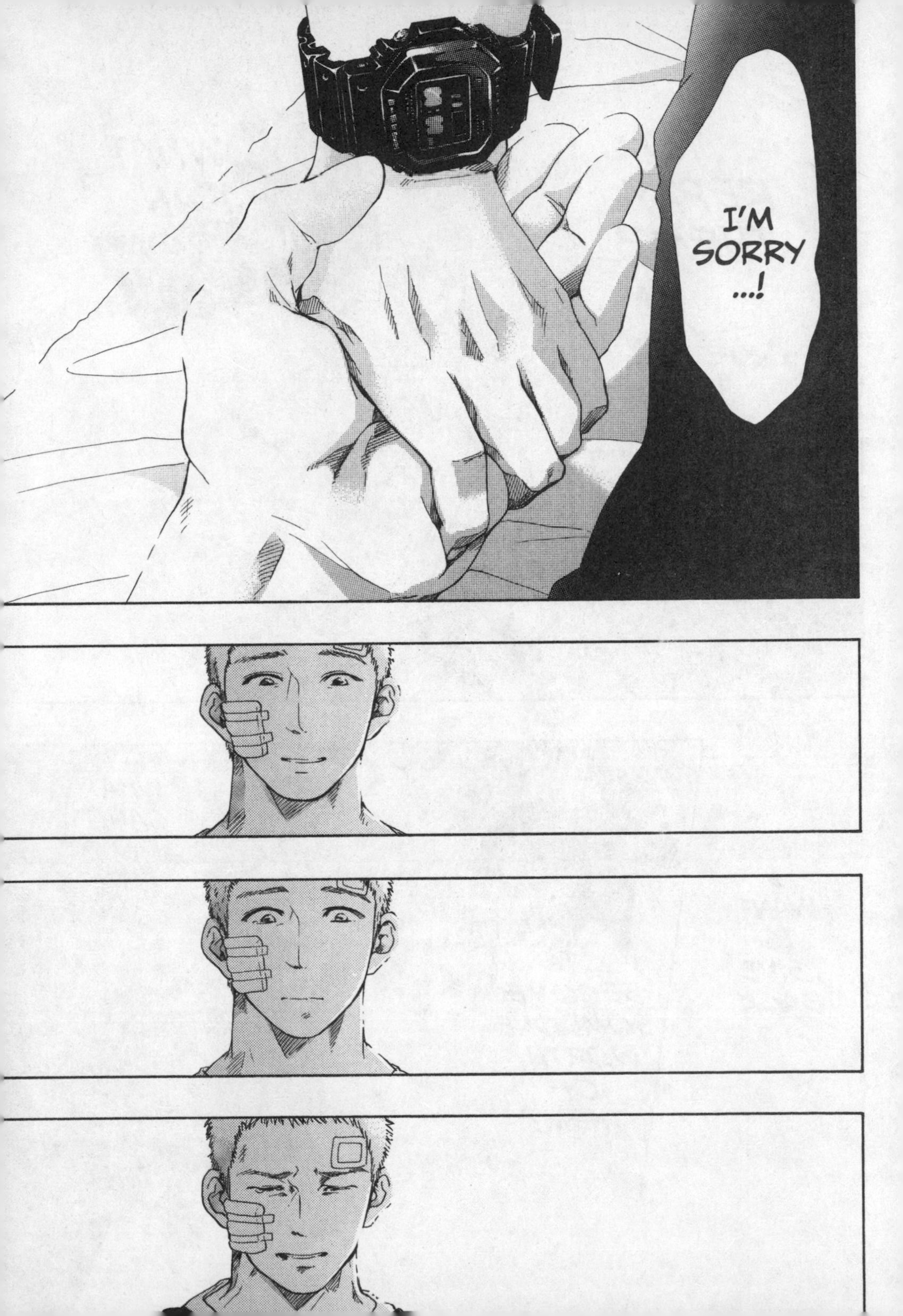
I'M SORRY ...!

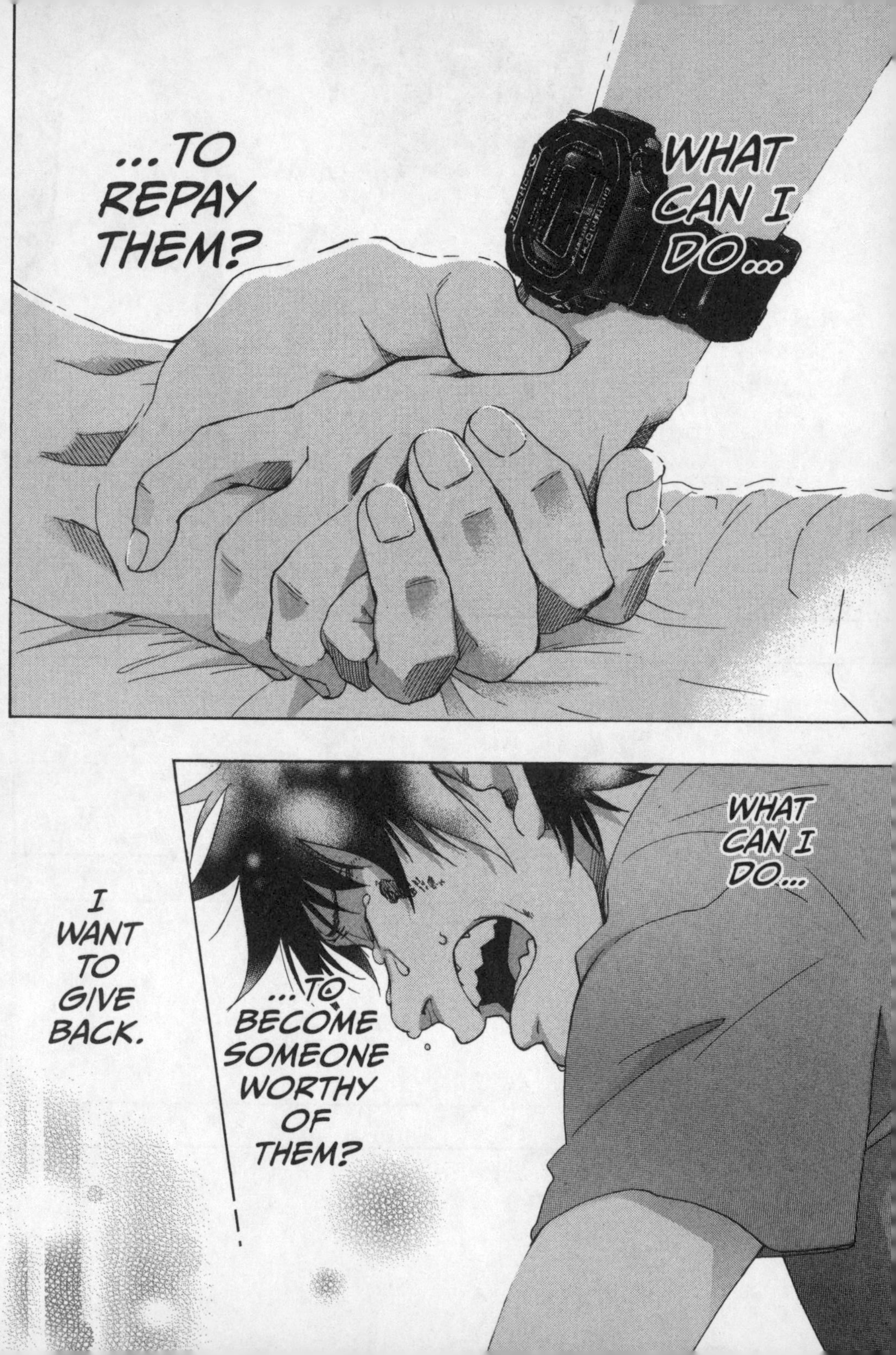
WHAT CAN I DO...
...TO REPAY THEM?
WHAT CAN I DO...
...TO BECOME SOMEONE WORTHY OF THEM?
I WANT TO GIVE BACK.

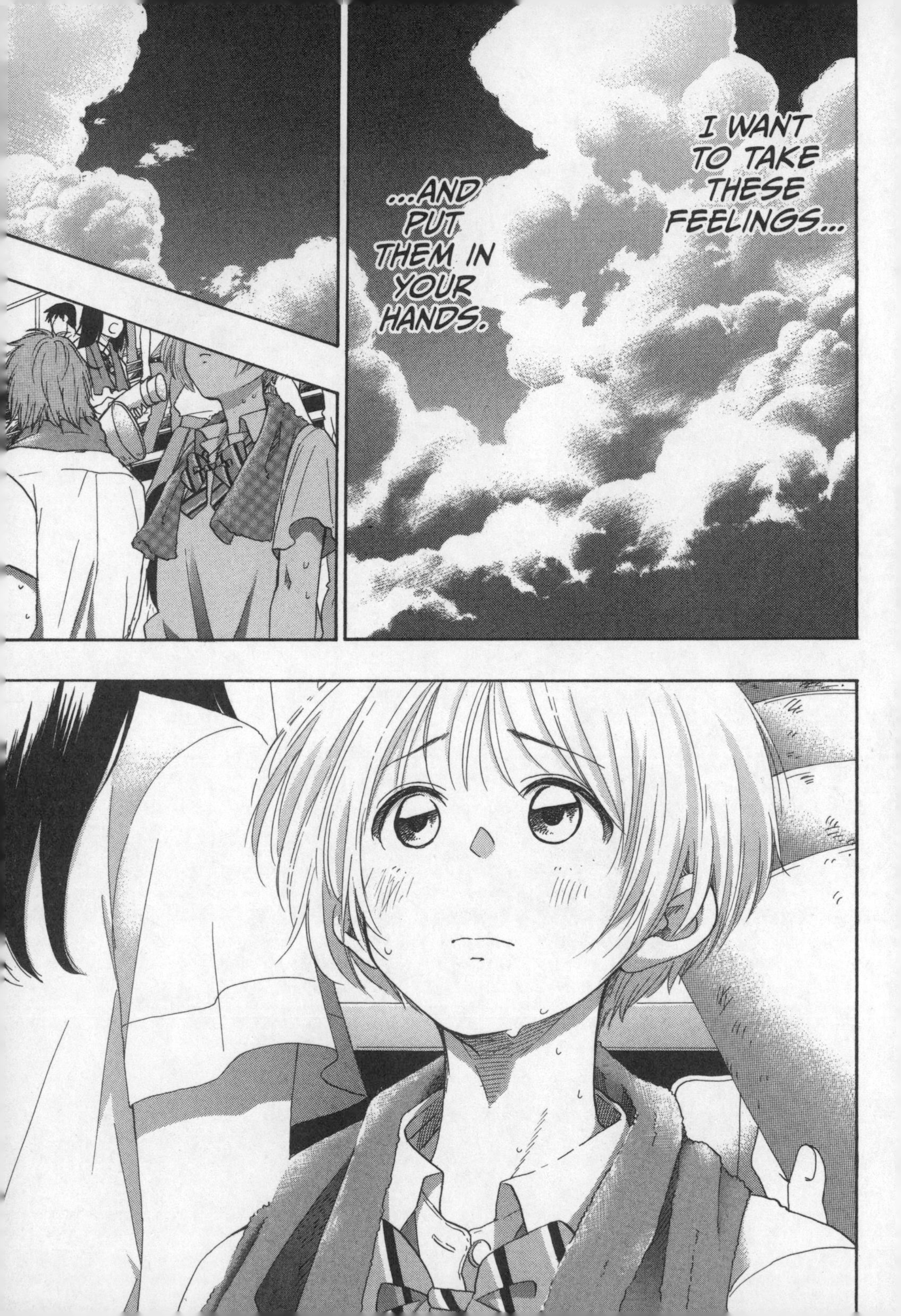
I WANT TO TAKE THESE FEELINGS...
...AND PUT THEM IN YOUR HANDS.

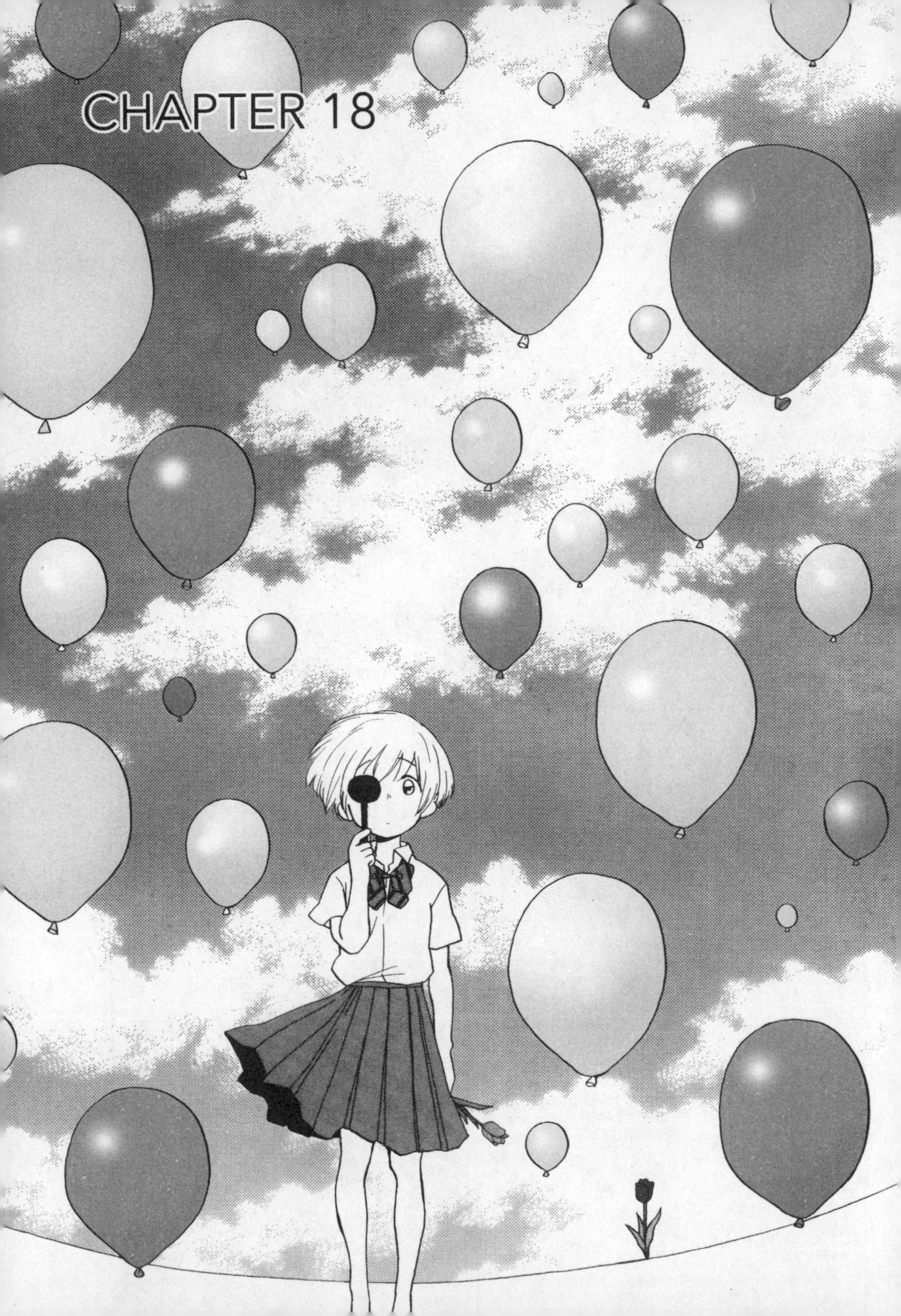
CHAPTER 18

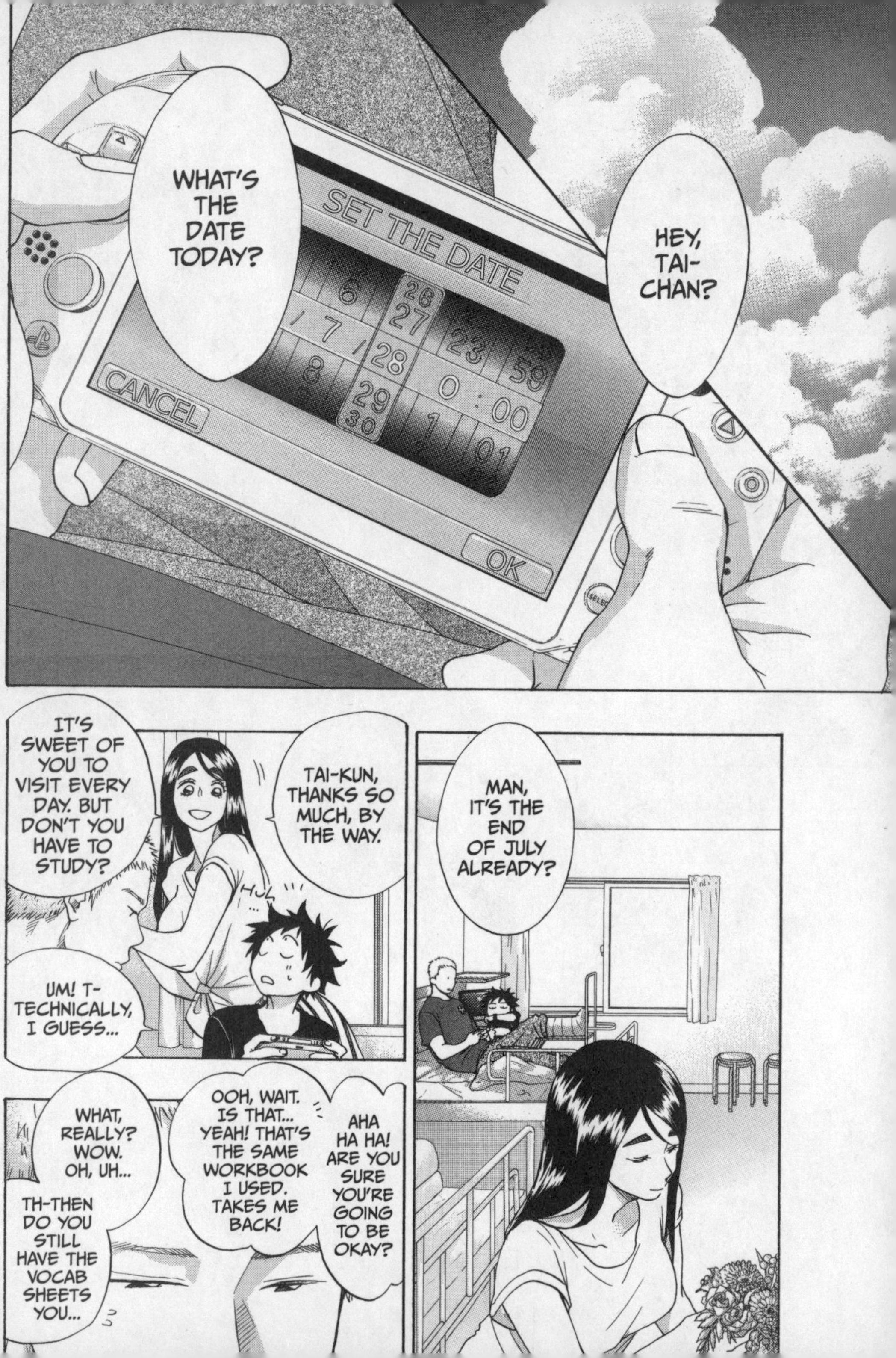
HEY, TAI-CHAN?
WHAT'S THE DATE TODAY?
SET THE DATE
CANCEL
OK
MAN, IT'S THE END OF JULY ALREADY?
TAI-KUN, THANKS SO MUCH, BY THE WAY.
IT'S SWEET OF YOU TO VISIT EVERY DAY. BUT DON'T YOU HAVE TO STUDY?
HUH...
UM! T-TECHNICALLY, I GUESS...
AHA HA HA! ARE YOU SURE YOU'RE GOING TO BE OKAY?
OOH, WAIT. IS THAT... YEAH! THAT'S THE SAME WORKBOOK I USED. TAKES ME BACK!
WHAT, REALLY? WOW. OH, UH...
TH-THEN DO YOU STILL HAVE THE VOCAB SHEETS YOU...

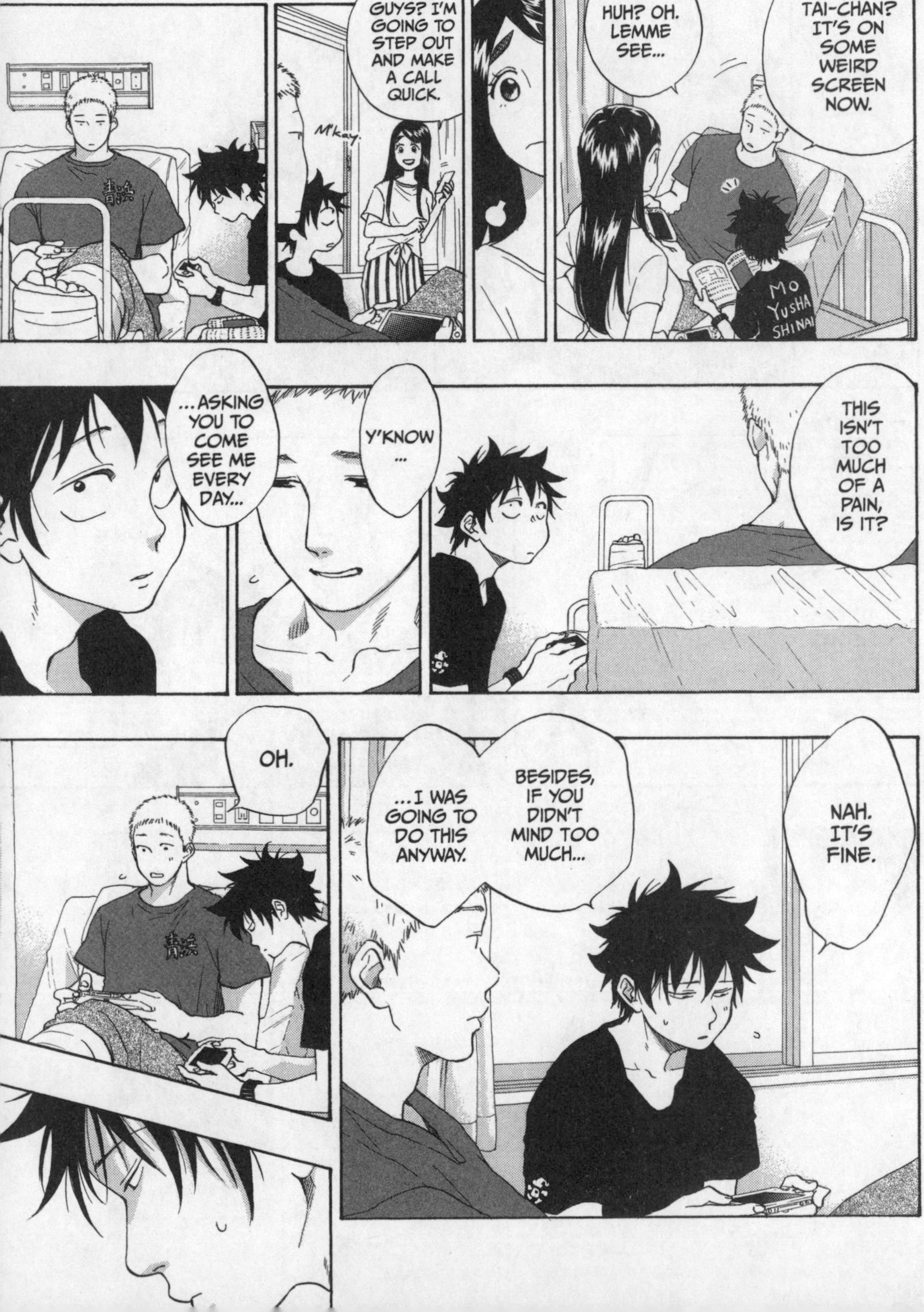
TAI-CHAN? IT'S ON SOME WEIRD SCREEN NOW.
HUH? OH. LEMME SEE...
Mo YUSHA SHINAI
HEY, GUYS? I'M GOING TO STEP OUT AND MAKE A CALL QUICK.
M'kay.
青浜
THIS ISN'T TOO MUCH OF A PAIN, IS IT?
Y'KNOW ...
...ASKING YOU TO COME SEE ME EVERY DAY...
NAH. IT'S FINE.
BESIDES, IF YOU DIDN'T MIND TOO MUCH...
...I WAS GOING TO DO THIS ANYWAY.
OH.
青浜

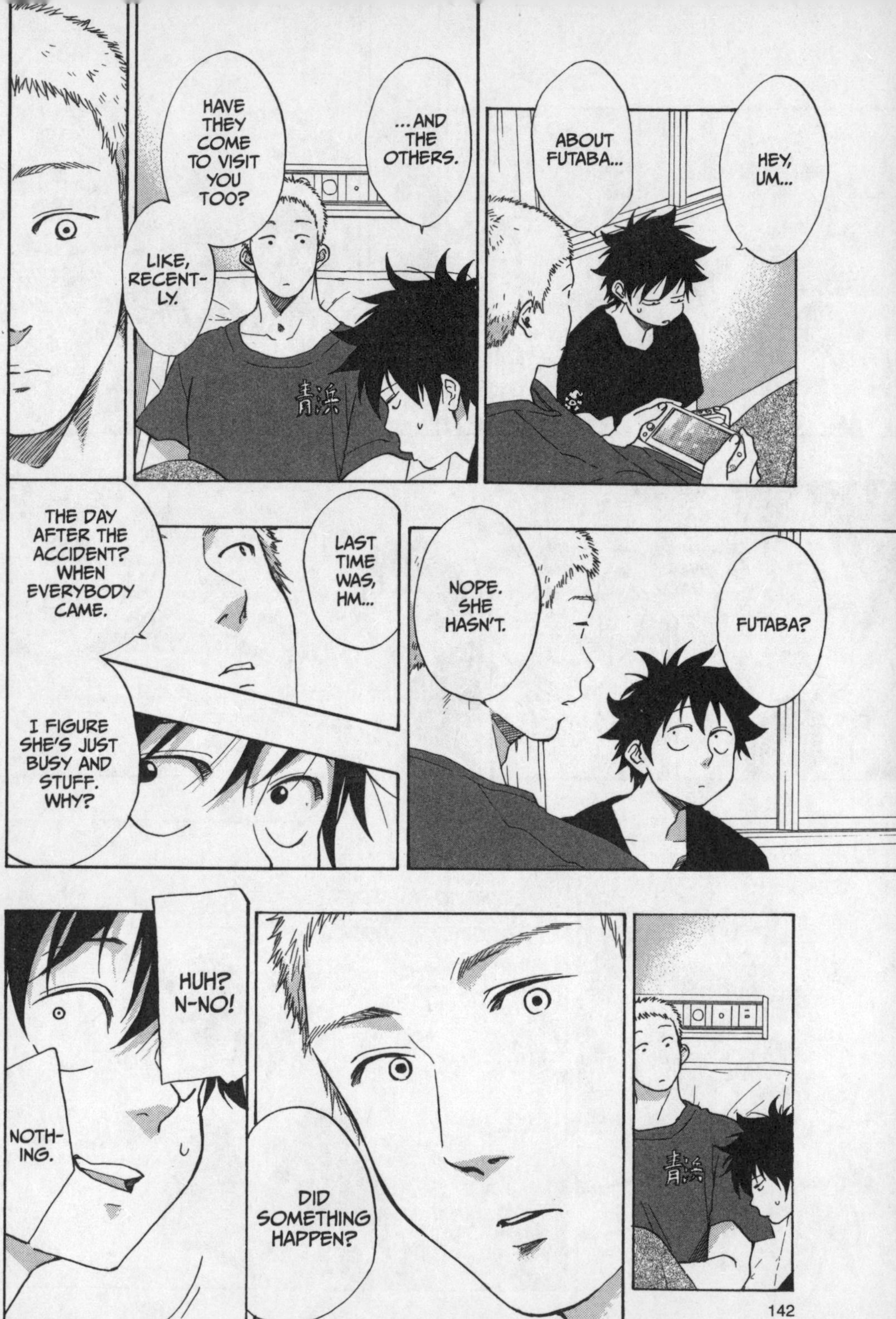

HEY, UM...
ABOUT FUTABA...
...AND THE OTHERS.
HAVE THEY COME TO VISIT YOU TOO?
LIKE, RECENTLY.
FUTABA?
NOPE. SHE HASN'T.
LAST TIME WAS, HM...
THE DAY AFTER THE ACCIDENT? WHEN EVERYBODY CAME.
I FIGURE SHE'S JUST BUSY AND STUFF. WHY?
DID SOMETHING HAPPEN?
HUH? N-NO!
NOTH-ING.

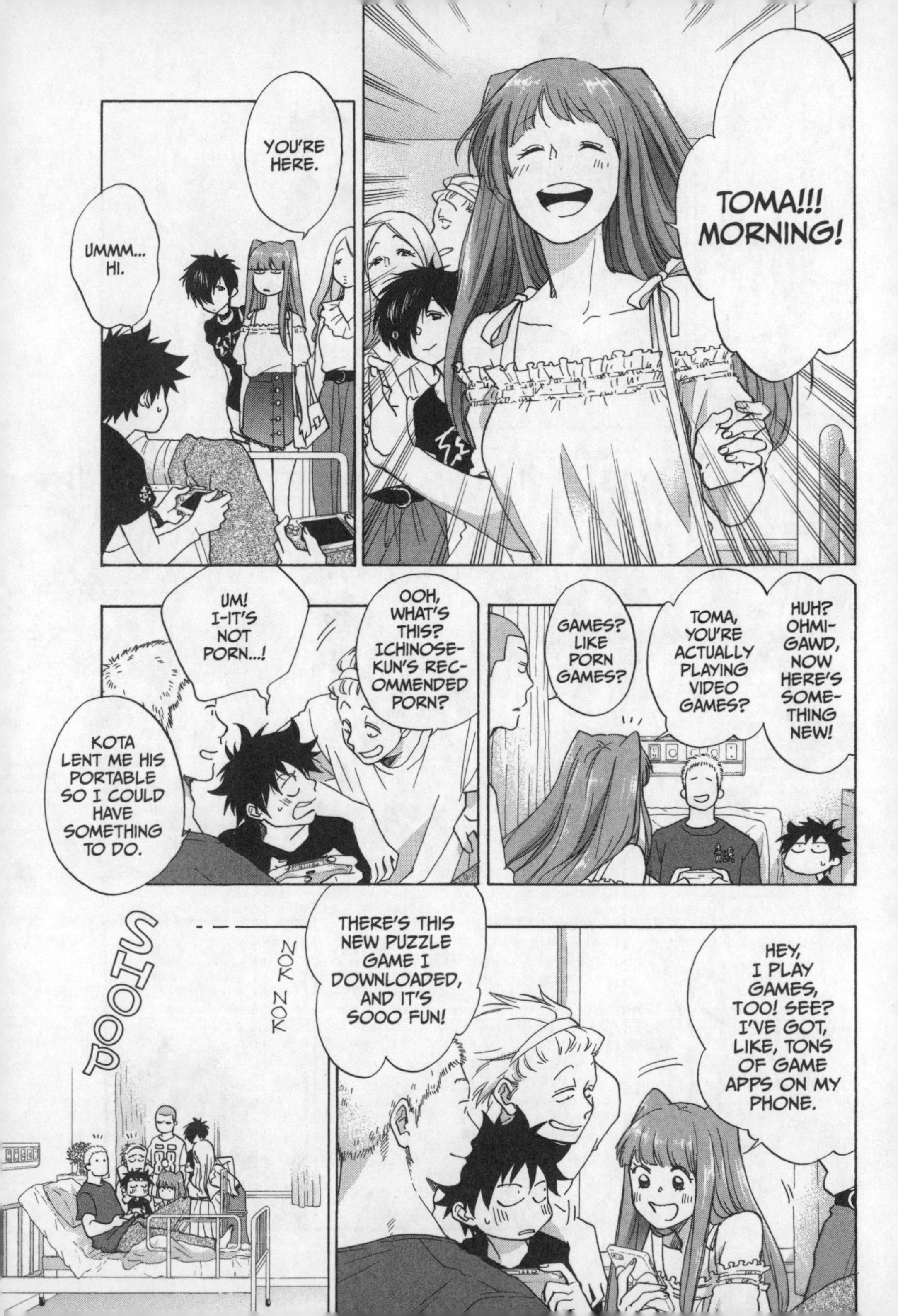

TOMA!!! MORNING!
YOU'RE HERE.
UMMM... HI.
HUH? OHMIGAWD, NOW HERE'S SOMETHING NEW!
TOMA, YOU'RE ACTUALLY PLAYING VIDEO GAMES?
GAMES? LIKE PORN GAMES?
OOH, WHAT'S THIS? ICHINOSE-KUN'S RECOMMENDED PORN?
UM! I-IT'S NOT PORN...!
KOTA LENT ME HIS PORTABLE SO I COULD HAVE SOMETHING TO DO.
HEY, I PLAY GAMES, TOO! SEE? I'VE GOT, LIKE, TONS OF GAME APPS ON MY PHONE.
THERE'S THIS NEW PUZZLE GAME I DOWNLOADED, AND IT'S SOOO FUN!
NOK NOK
SHOOP

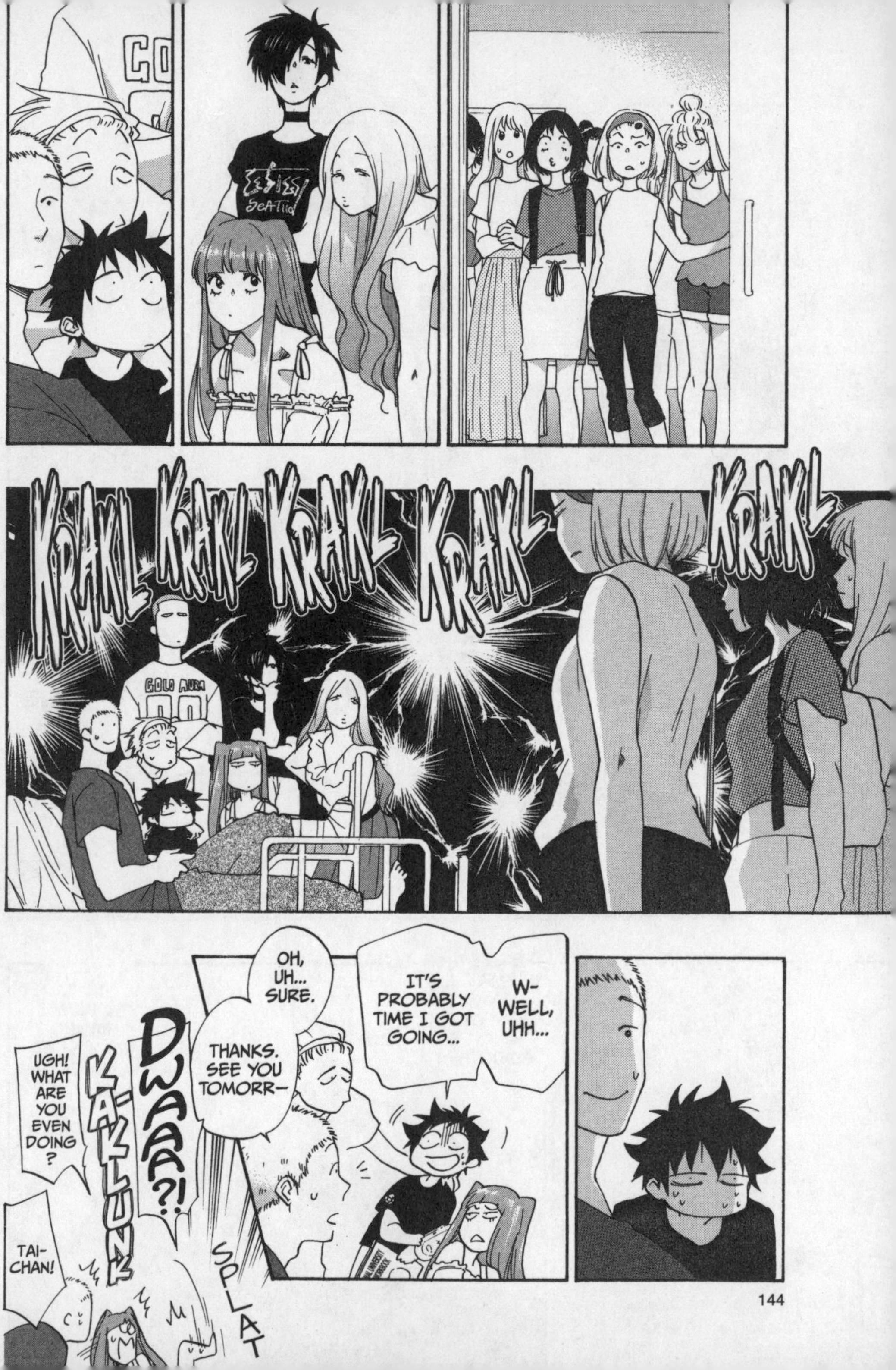
KRAKL
KRAKL
KRAKL
KRAKL
KRAKL
W-WELL, UHH...
IT'S PROBABLY TIME I GOT GOING...
OH, UH... SURE.
THANKS. SEE YOU TOMORR—
DWAAAA?!
KA-KLUNK
UGH! WHAT ARE YOU EVEN DOING?
TAI-CHAN!
SPLAT

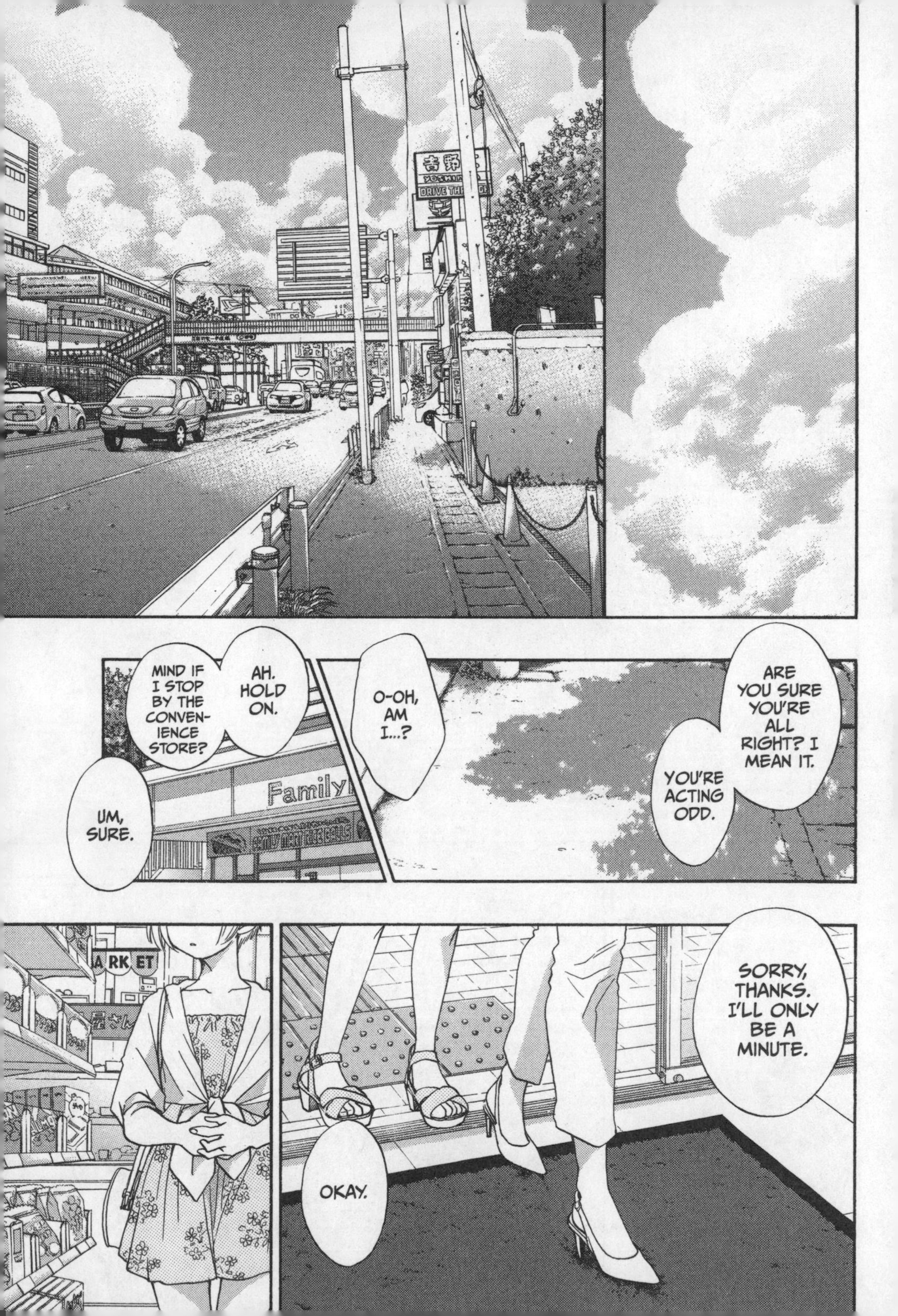
ARE YOU SURE YOU'RE ALL RIGHT? I MEAN IT.
YOU'RE ACTING ODD.
O-OH, AM I...?
AH. HOLD ON.
MIND IF I STOP BY THE CONVEN-IENCE STORE?
UM, SURE.
Family
SORRY, THANKS. I'LL ONLY BE A MINUTE.
OKAY.

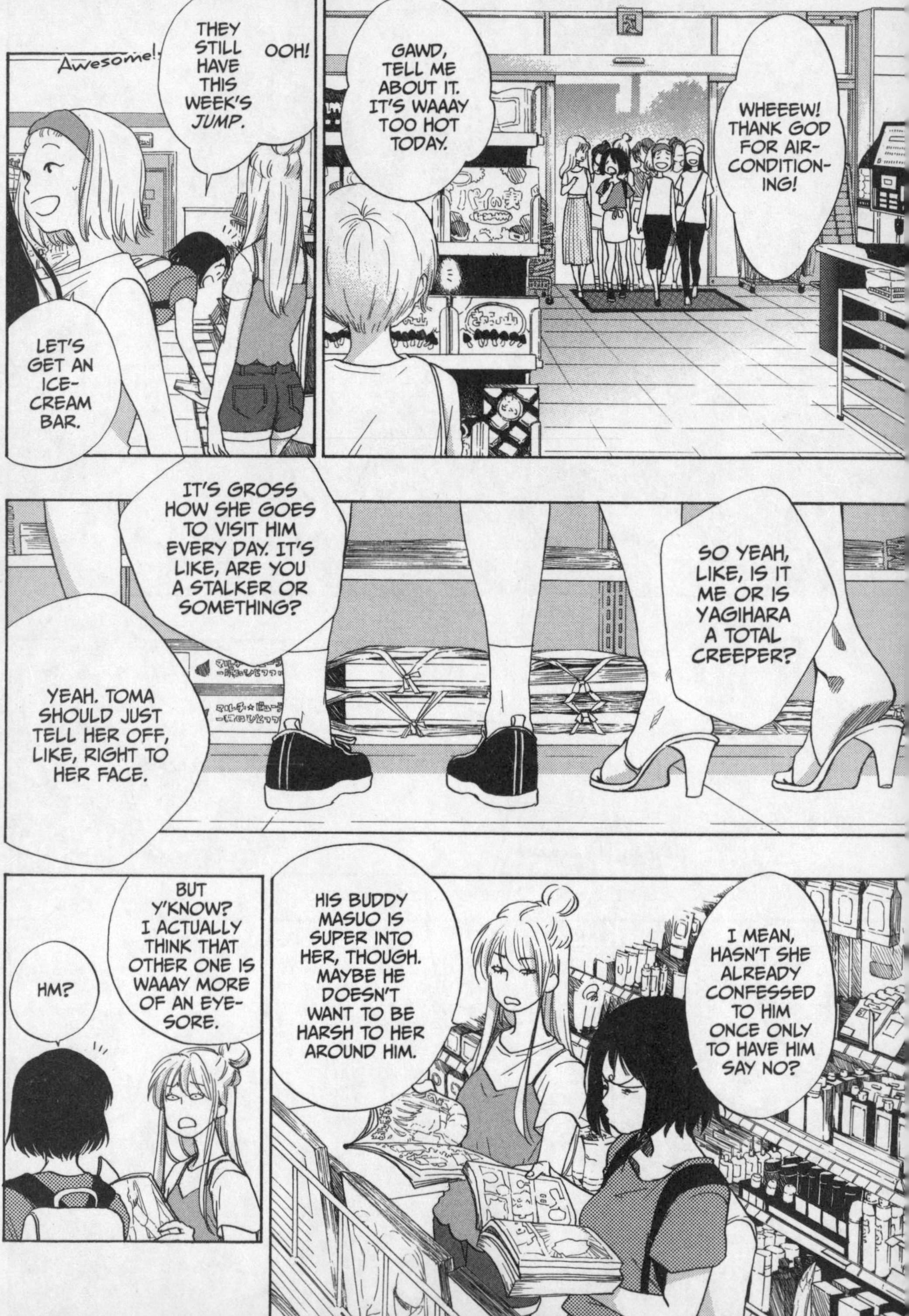
WHEEEW! THANK GOD FOR AIR-CONDITIONING!
GAWD, TELL ME ABOUT IT. IT'S WAAAY TOO HOT TODAY.
OOH!
THEY STILL HAVE THIS WEEK'S *JUMP*.
Awesome!
LET'S GET AN ICE-CREAM BAR.
SO YEAH, LIKE, IS IT ME OR IS YAGIHARA A TOTAL CREEPER?
IT'S GROSS HOW SHE GOES TO VISIT HIM EVERY DAY. IT'S LIKE, ARE YOU A STALKER OR SOMETHING?
YEAH. TOMA SHOULD JUST TELL HER OFF, LIKE, RIGHT TO HER FACE.
I MEAN, HASN'T SHE ALREADY CONFESSED TO HIM ONCE ONLY TO HAVE HIM SAY NO?
HIS BUDDY MASUO IS SUPER INTO HER, THOUGH. MAYBE HE DOESN'T WANT TO BE HARSH TO HER AROUND HIM.
BUT Y'KNOW? I ACTUALLY THINK THAT OTHER ONE IS WAAAY MORE OF AN EYE-SORE.
HM?

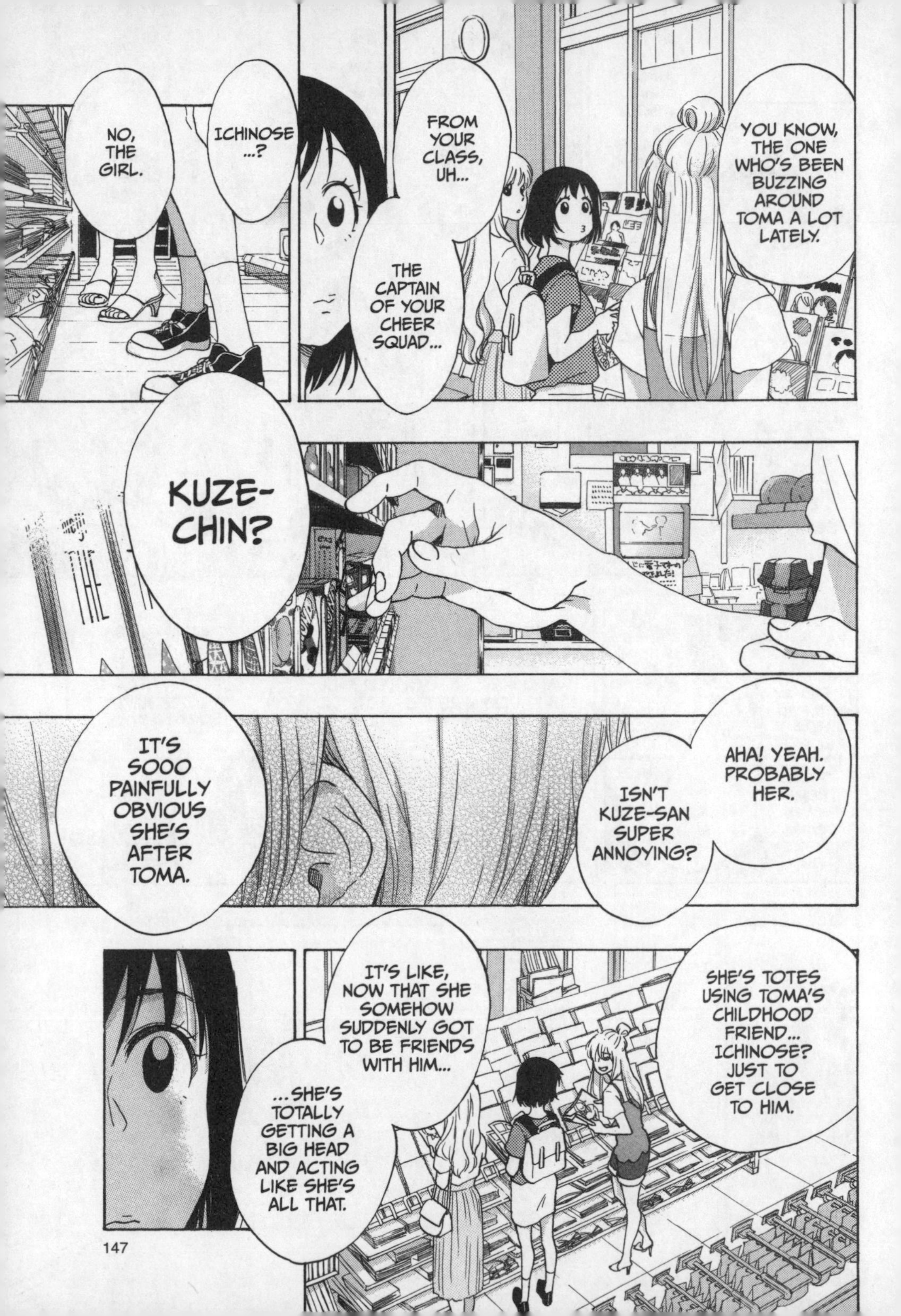
YOU KNOW, THE ONE WHO'S BEEN BUZZING AROUND TOMA A LOT LATELY.
FROM YOUR CLASS, UH...
THE CAPTAIN OF YOUR CHEER SQUAD...
ICHINOSE ...?
NO, THE GIRL.
KUZE-CHIN?
AHA! YEAH. PROBABLY HER.
ISN'T KUZE-SAN SUPER ANNOYING?
IT'S SOOO PAINFULLY OBVIOUS SHE'S AFTER TOMA.
SHE'S TOTES USING TOMA'S CHILDHOOD FRIEND... ICHINOSE? JUST TO GET CLOSE TO HIM.
IT'S LIKE, NOW THAT SHE SOMEHOW SUDDENLY GOT TO BE FRIENDS WITH HIM...
...SHE'S TOTALLY GETTING A BIG HEAD AND ACTING LIKE SHE'S ALL THAT.

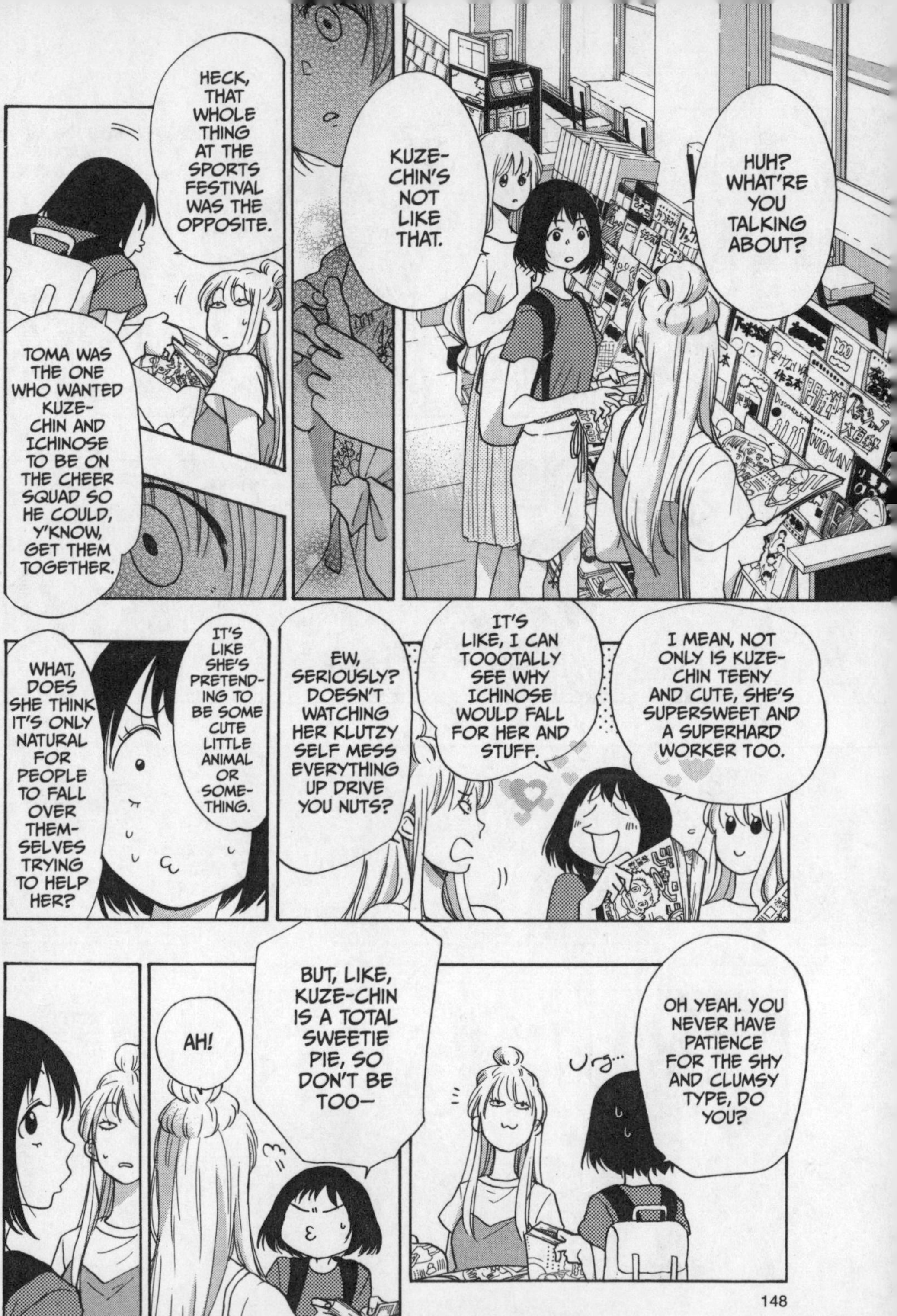
HUH? WHAT'RE YOU TALKING ABOUT?
KUZE-CHIN'S NOT LIKE THAT.
HECK, THAT WHOLE THING AT THE SPORTS FESTIVAL WAS THE OPPOSITE.
TOMA WAS THE ONE WHO WANTED KUZE-CHIN AND ICHINOSE TO BE ON THE CHEER SQUAD SO HE COULD, Y'KNOW, GET THEM TOGETHER.
I MEAN, NOT ONLY IS KUZE-CHIN TEENY AND CUTE, SHE'S SUPERSWEET AND A SUPERHARD WORKER TOO.
IT'S LIKE, I CAN TOOOTALLY SEE WHY ICHINOSE WOULD FALL FOR HER AND STUFF.
EW, SERIOUSLY? DOESN'T WATCHING HER KLUTZY SELF MESS EVERYTHING UP DRIVE YOU NUTS?
IT'S LIKE SHE'S PRETENDING TO BE SOME CUTE LITTLE ANIMAL OR SOMETHING.
WHAT, DOES SHE THINK IT'S ONLY NATURAL FOR PEOPLE TO FALL OVER THEMSELVES TRYING TO HELP HER?
OH YEAH. YOU NEVER HAVE PATIENCE FOR THE SHY AND CLUMSY TYPE, DO YOU?
Urg...
BUT, LIKE, KUZE-CHIN IS A TOTAL SWEETIE PIE, SO DON'T BE TOO—
AH!

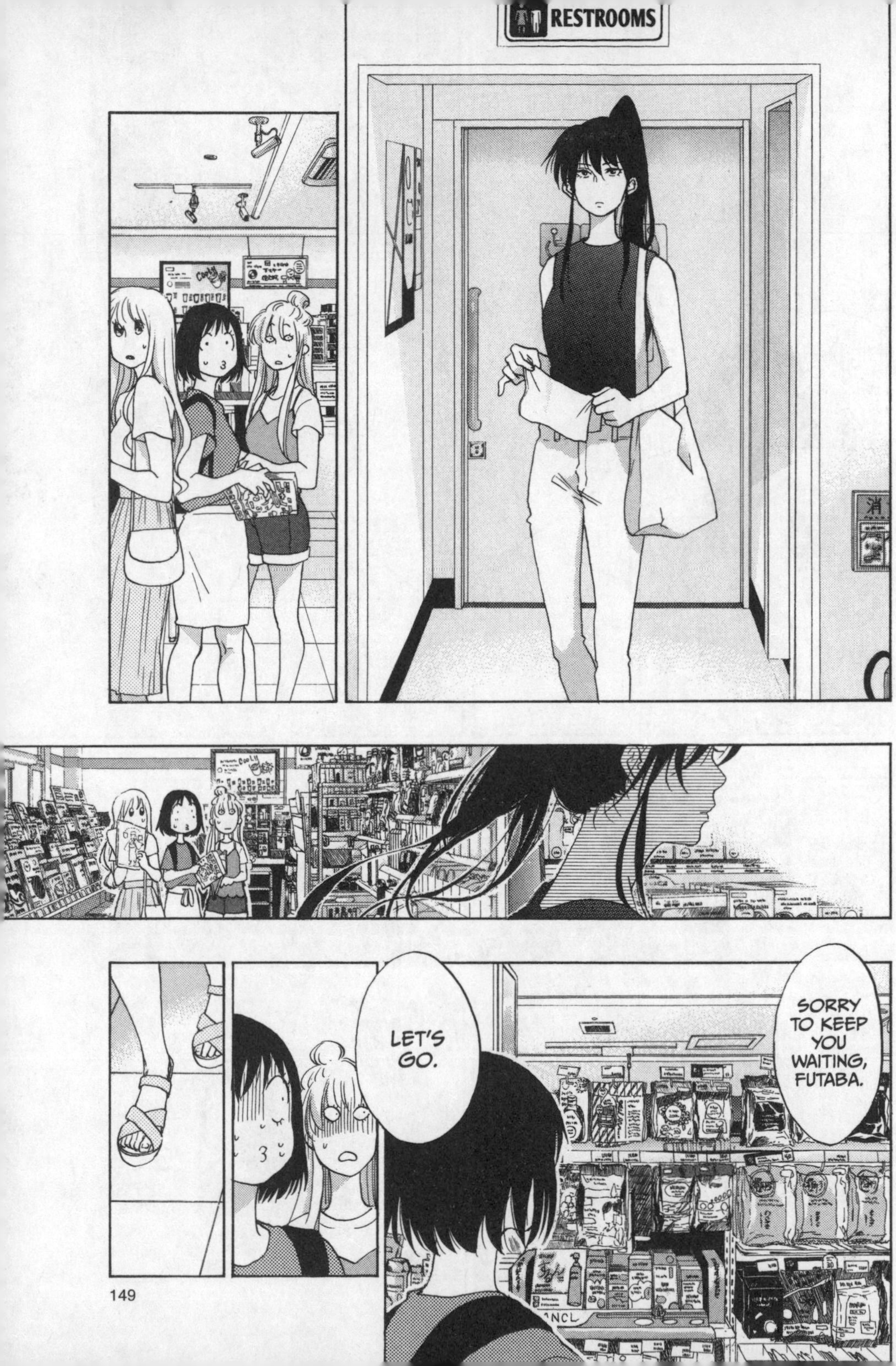
RESTROOMS
SORRY TO KEEP YOU WAITING, FUTABA.
LET'S GO.

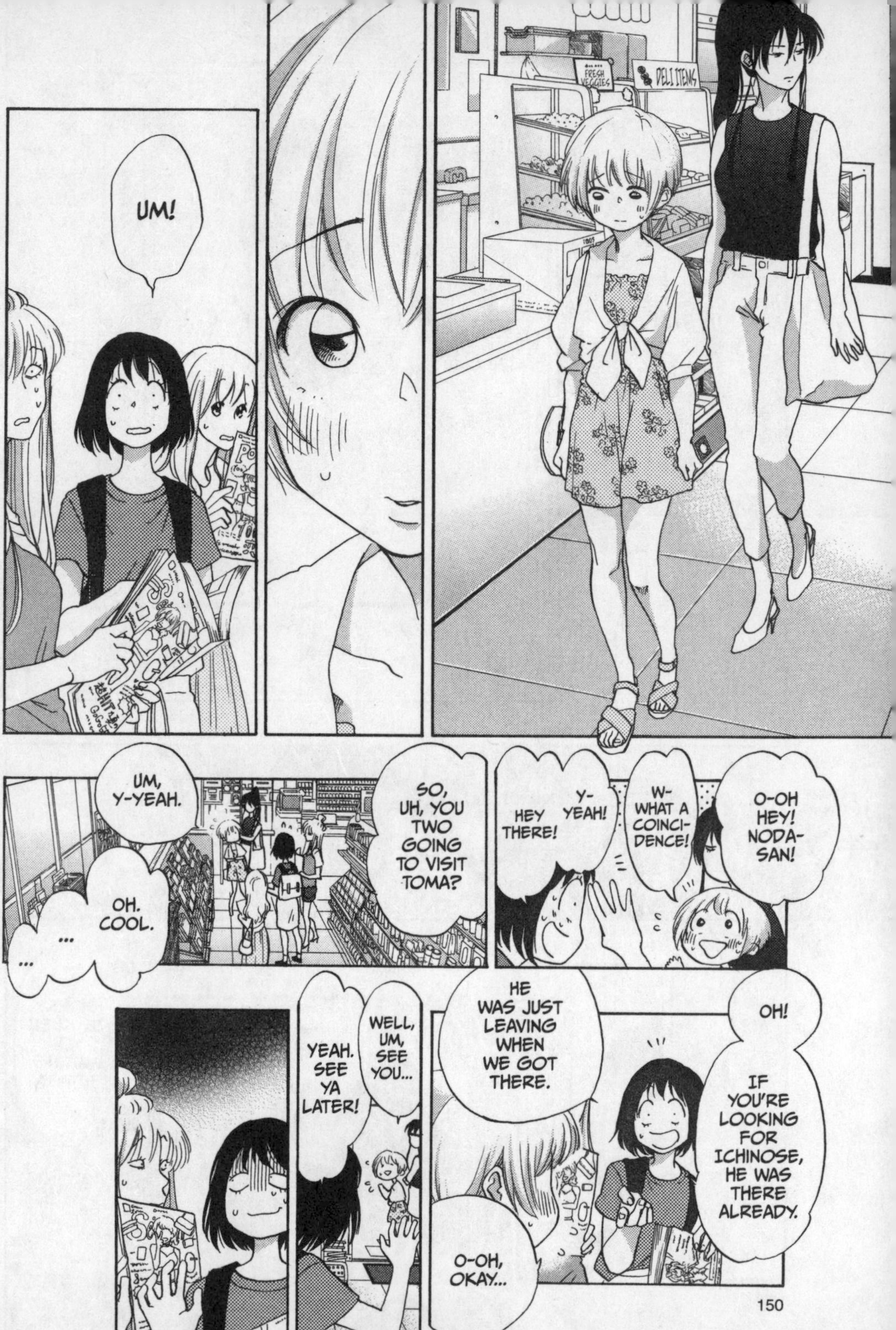
FRESH VEGGIES
DELI ITEMS
UM!
O-OH HEY! NODA-SAN!
W-WHAT A COINCIDENCE!
Y-YEAH!
HEY THERE!
SO, UH, YOU TWO GOING TO VISIT TOMA?
UM, Y-YEAH.
OH. COOL.
...
...
OH!
IF YOU'RE LOOKING FOR ICHINOSE, HE WAS THERE ALREADY.
HE WAS JUST LEAVING WHEN WE GOT THERE.
O-OH, OKAY...
WELL, UM, SEE YOU...
YEAH. SEE YA LATER!

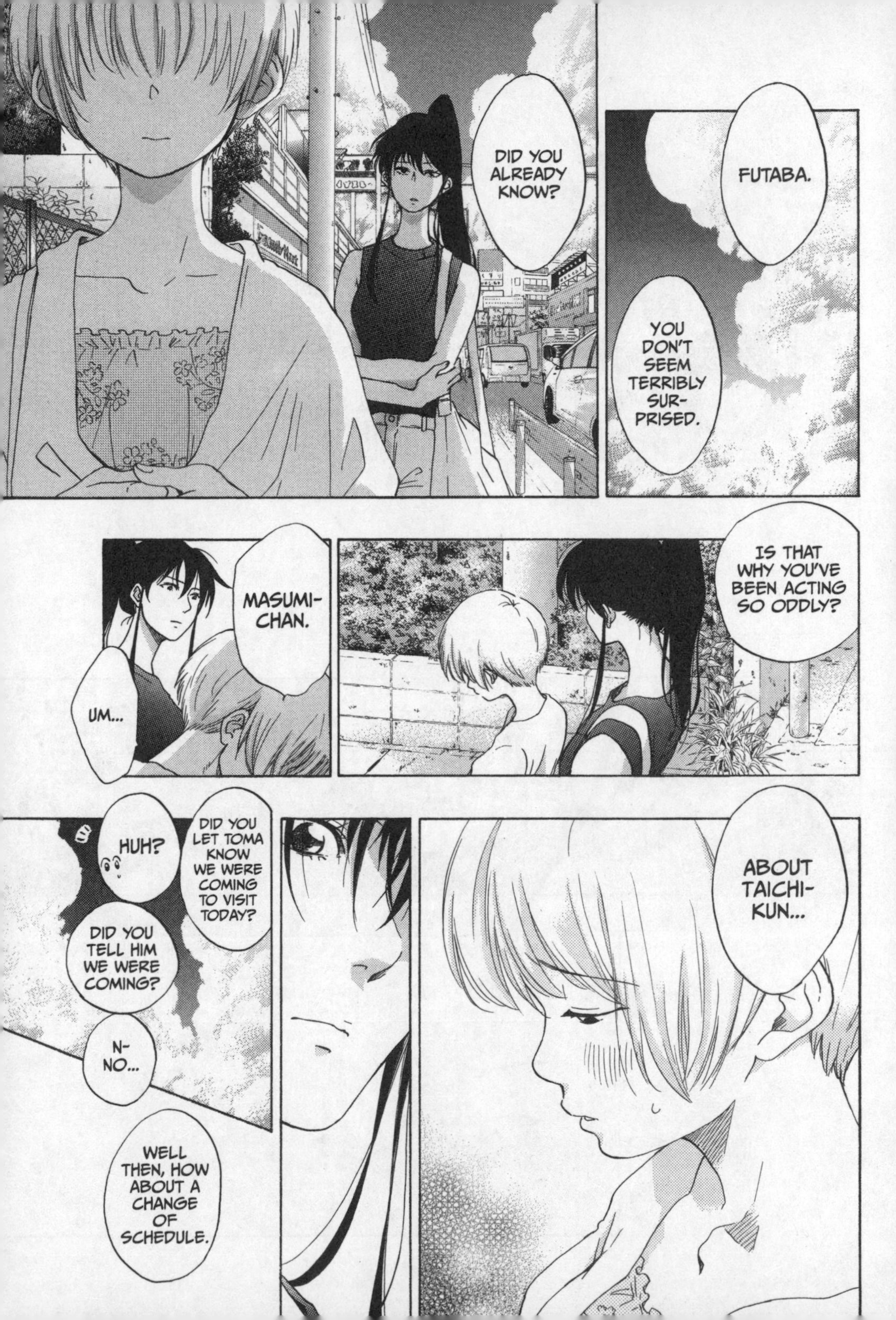
FUTABA.
YOU DON'T SEEM TERRIBLY SUR-PRISED.
DID YOU ALREADY KNOW?
IS THAT WHY YOU'VE BEEN ACTING SO ODDLY?
MASUMI-CHAN.
UM...
ABOUT TAICHI-KUN...
DID YOU LET TOMA KNOW WE WERE COMING TO VISIT TODAY?
HUH?
DID YOU TELL HIM WE WERE COMING?
N-NO...
WELL THEN, HOW ABOUT A CHANGE OF SCHEDULE.

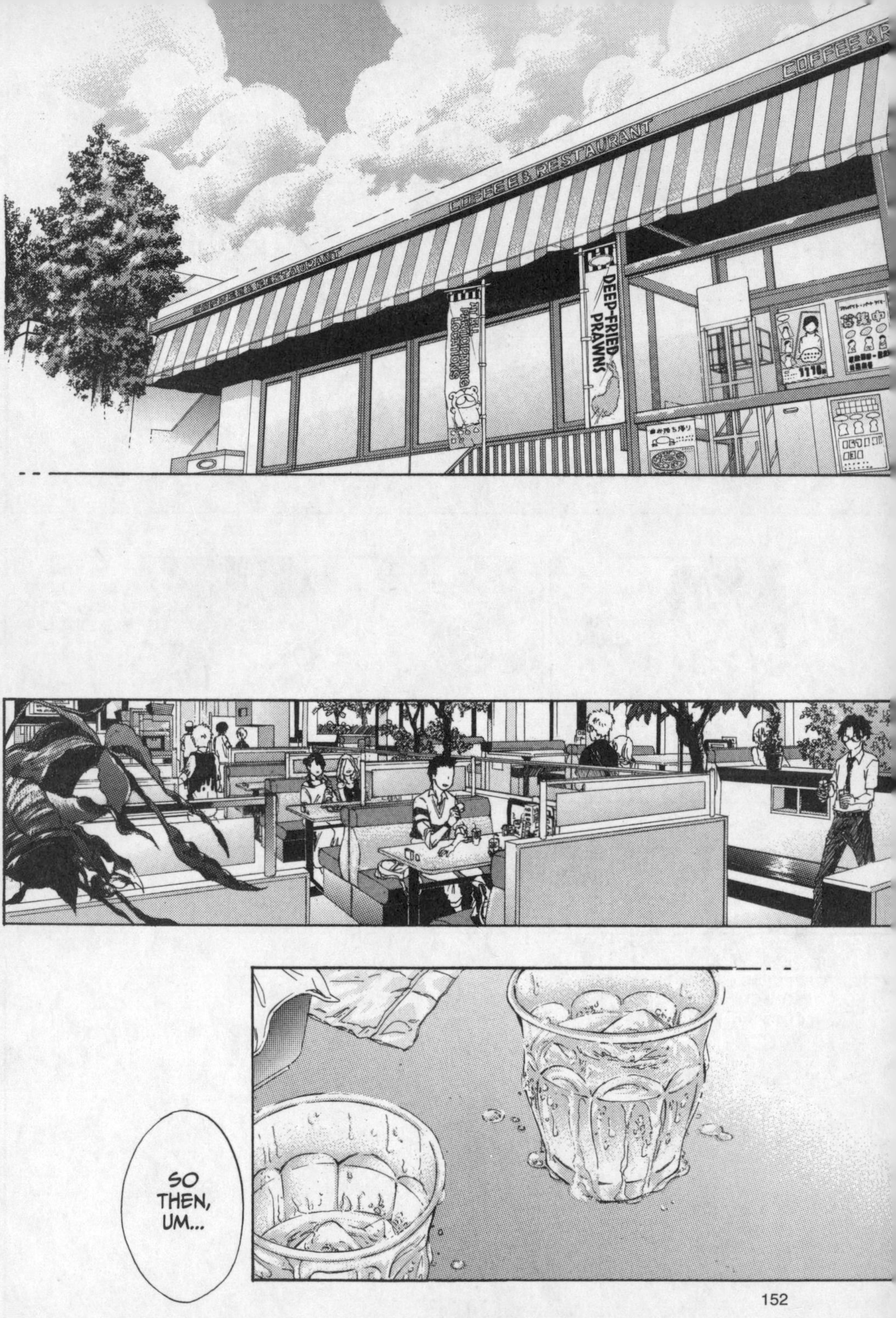
COFFEE & RESTAURANT
DEEP-FRIED PRAWNS
AT ALL PARTICIPATING LOCATIONS
SO THEN, UM...

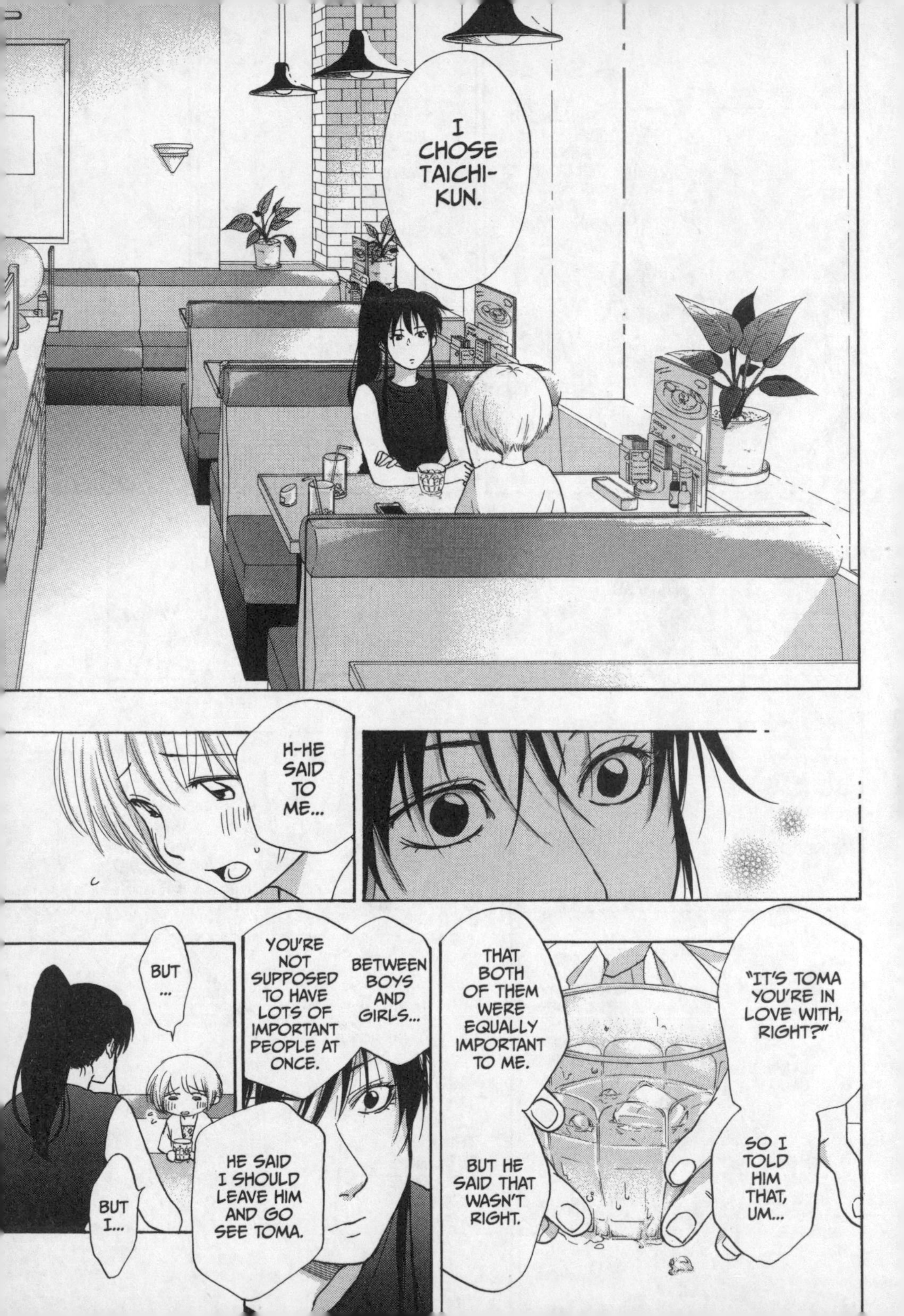
I CHOSE TAICHI-KUN.
H-HE SAID TO ME...
"IT'S TOMA YOU'RE IN LOVE WITH, RIGHT?"
SO I TOLD HIM THAT, UM...
THAT BOTH OF THEM WERE EQUALLY IMPORTANT TO ME.
BUT HE SAID THAT WASN'T RIGHT.
BETWEEN BOYS AND GIRLS...
YOU'RE NOT SUPPOSED TO HAVE LOTS OF IMPORTANT PEOPLE AT ONCE.
HE SAID I SHOULD LEAVE HIM AND GO SEE TOMA.
BUT ...
BUT I...

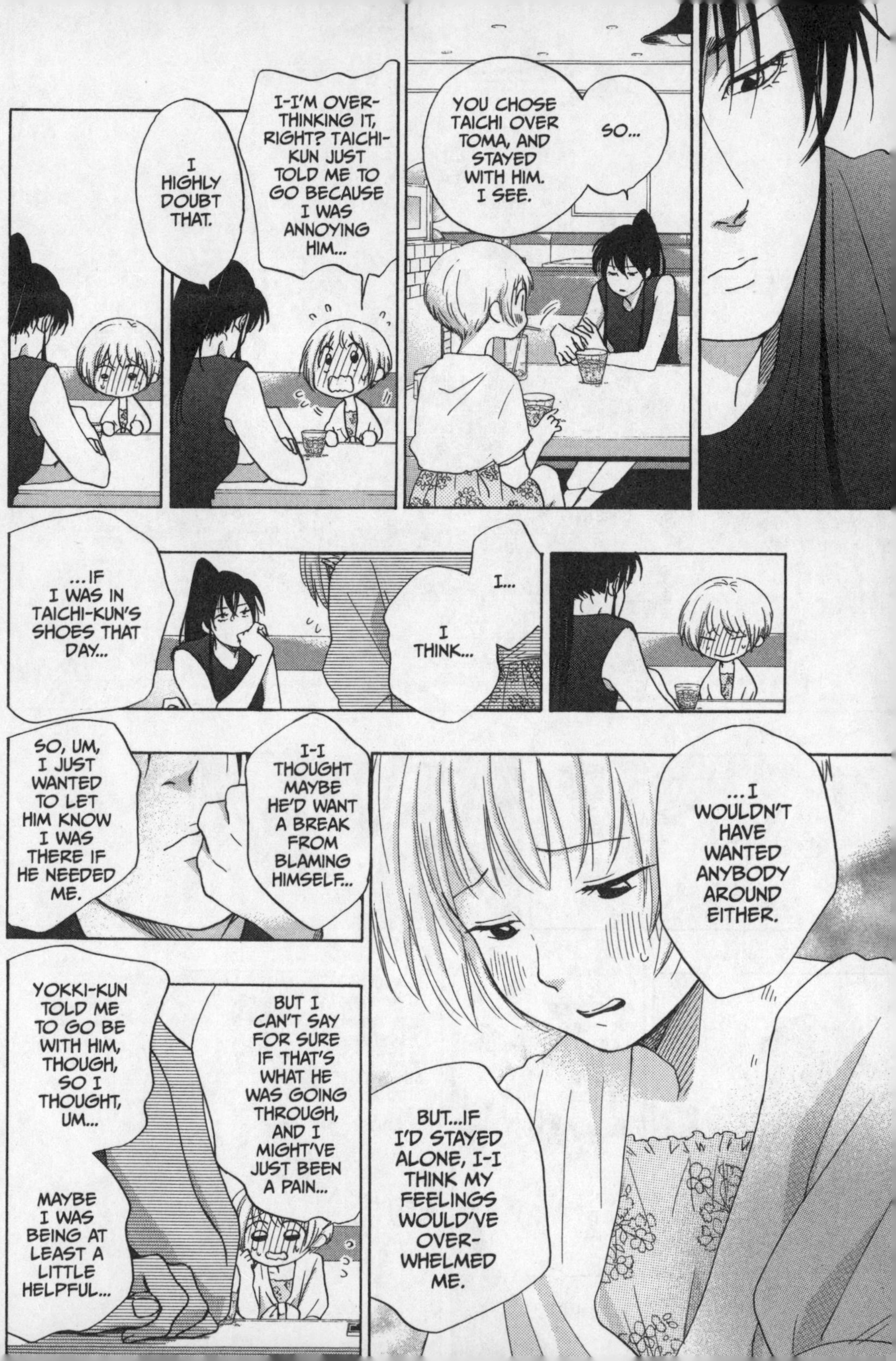
SO...
YOU CHOSE TAICHI OVER TOMA, AND STAYED WITH HIM. I SEE.
I-I'M OVER-THINKING IT, RIGHT? TAICHI-KUN JUST TOLD ME TO GO BECAUSE I WAS ANNOYING HIM...
I HIGHLY DOUBT THAT.
I...
I THINK...
...IF I WAS IN TAICHI-KUN'S SHOES THAT DAY...
...I WOULDN'T HAVE WANTED ANYBODY AROUND EITHER.
BUT...IF I'D STAYED ALONE, I-I THINK MY FEELINGS WOULD'VE OVER-WHELMED ME.
I-I THOUGHT MAYBE HE'D WANT A BREAK FROM BLAMING HIMSELF...
SO, UM, I JUST WANTED TO LET HIM KNOW I WAS THERE IF HE NEEDED ME.
BUT I CAN'T SAY FOR SURE IF THAT'S WHAT HE WAS GOING THROUGH, AND I MIGHT'VE JUST BEEN A PAIN...
YOKKI-KUN TOLD ME TO GO BE WITH HIM, THOUGH, SO I THOUGHT, UM...
MAYBE I WAS BEING AT LEAST A LITTLE HELPFUL...

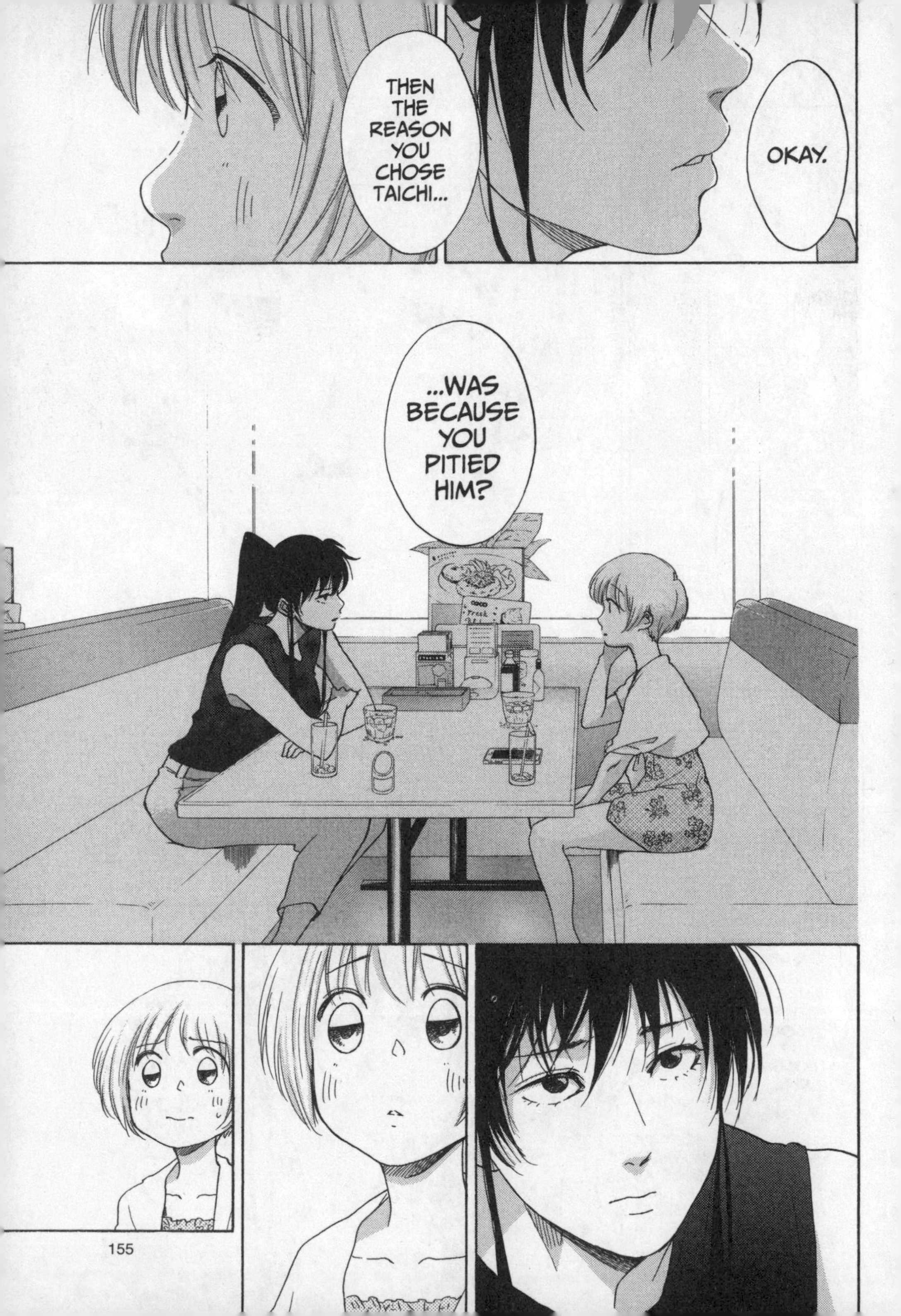
OKAY.
THEN THE REASON YOU CHOSE TAICHI...
...WAS BECAUSE YOU PITIED HIM?

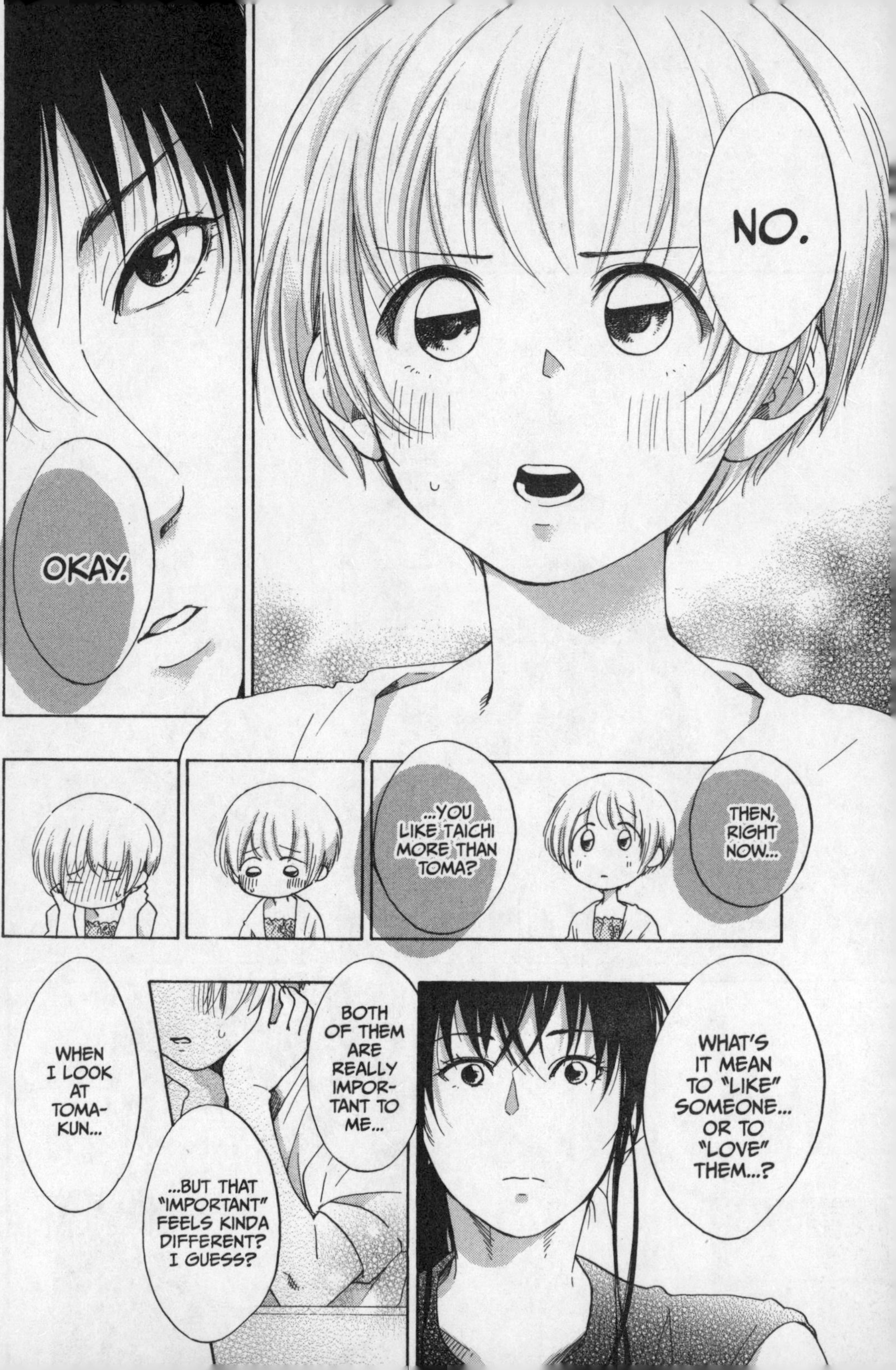
NO.
OKAY.
THEN, RIGHT NOW...
...YOU LIKE TAICHI MORE THAN TOMA?
WHAT'S IT MEAN TO "LIKE" SOMEONE... OR TO "LOVE" THEM...?
BOTH OF THEM ARE REALLY IMPOR-TANT TO ME...
...BUT THAT "IMPORTANT" FEELS KINDA DIFFERENT? I GUESS?
WHEN I LOOK AT TOMA-KUN...

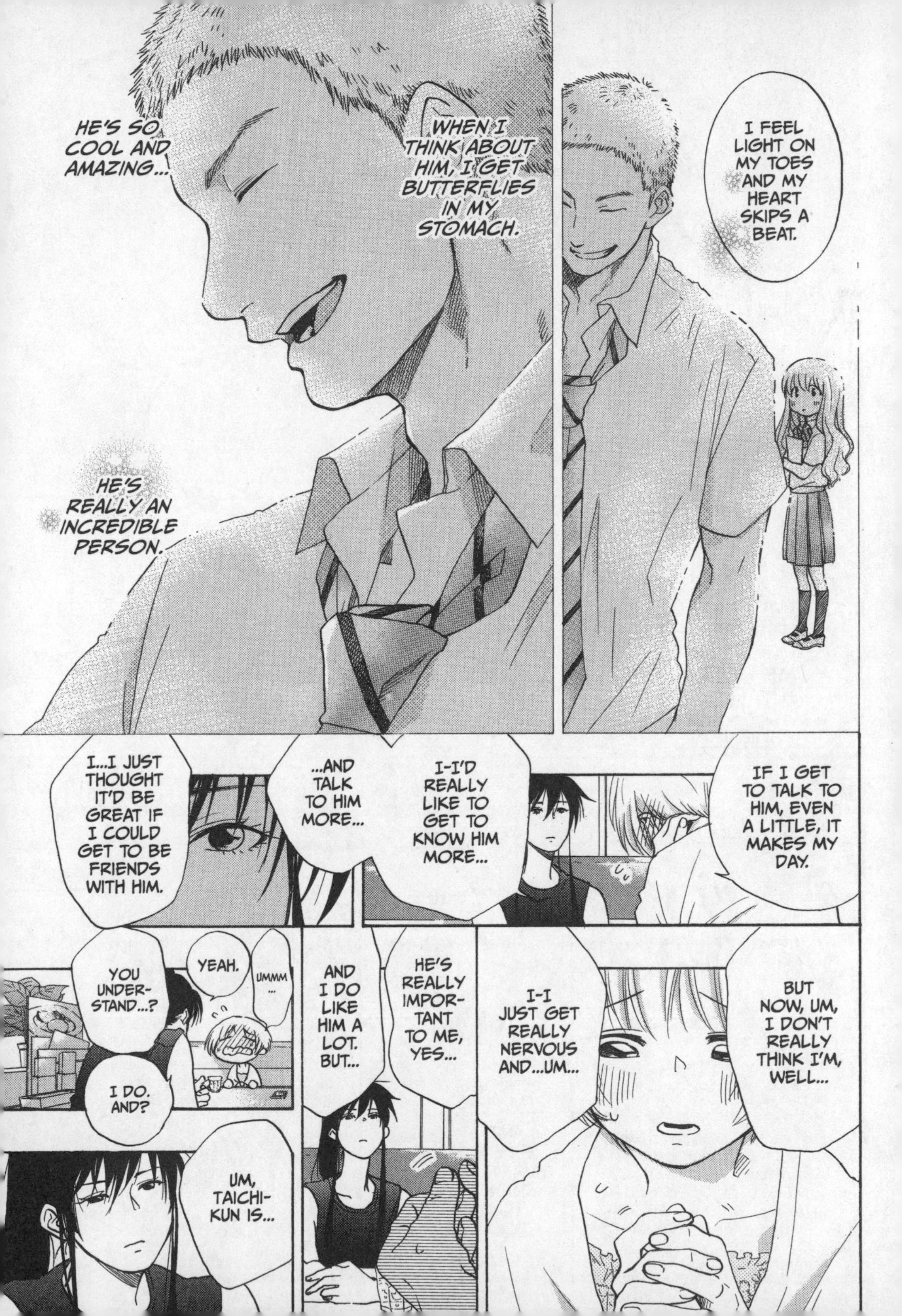

I FEEL LIGHT ON MY TOES AND MY HEART SKIPS A BEAT.
WHEN I THINK ABOUT HIM, I GET BUTTERFLIES IN MY STOMACH.
HE'S SO COOL AND AMAZING...
HE'S REALLY AN INCREDIBLE PERSON.
IF I GET TO TALK TO HIM, EVEN A LITTLE, IT MAKES MY DAY.
I-I'D REALLY LIKE TO GET TO KNOW HIM MORE...
...AND TALK TO HIM MORE...
I...I JUST THOUGHT IT'D BE GREAT IF I COULD GET TO BE FRIENDS WITH HIM.
BUT NOW, UM, I DON'T REALLY THINK I'M, WELL...
I-I JUST GET REALLY NERVOUS AND...UM...
HE'S REALLY IMPOR-TANT TO ME, YES...
AND I DO LIKE HIM A LOT. BUT...
UM, TAICHI-KUN IS...
UMMM...
YEAH.
YOU UNDER-STAND...?
I DO. AND?

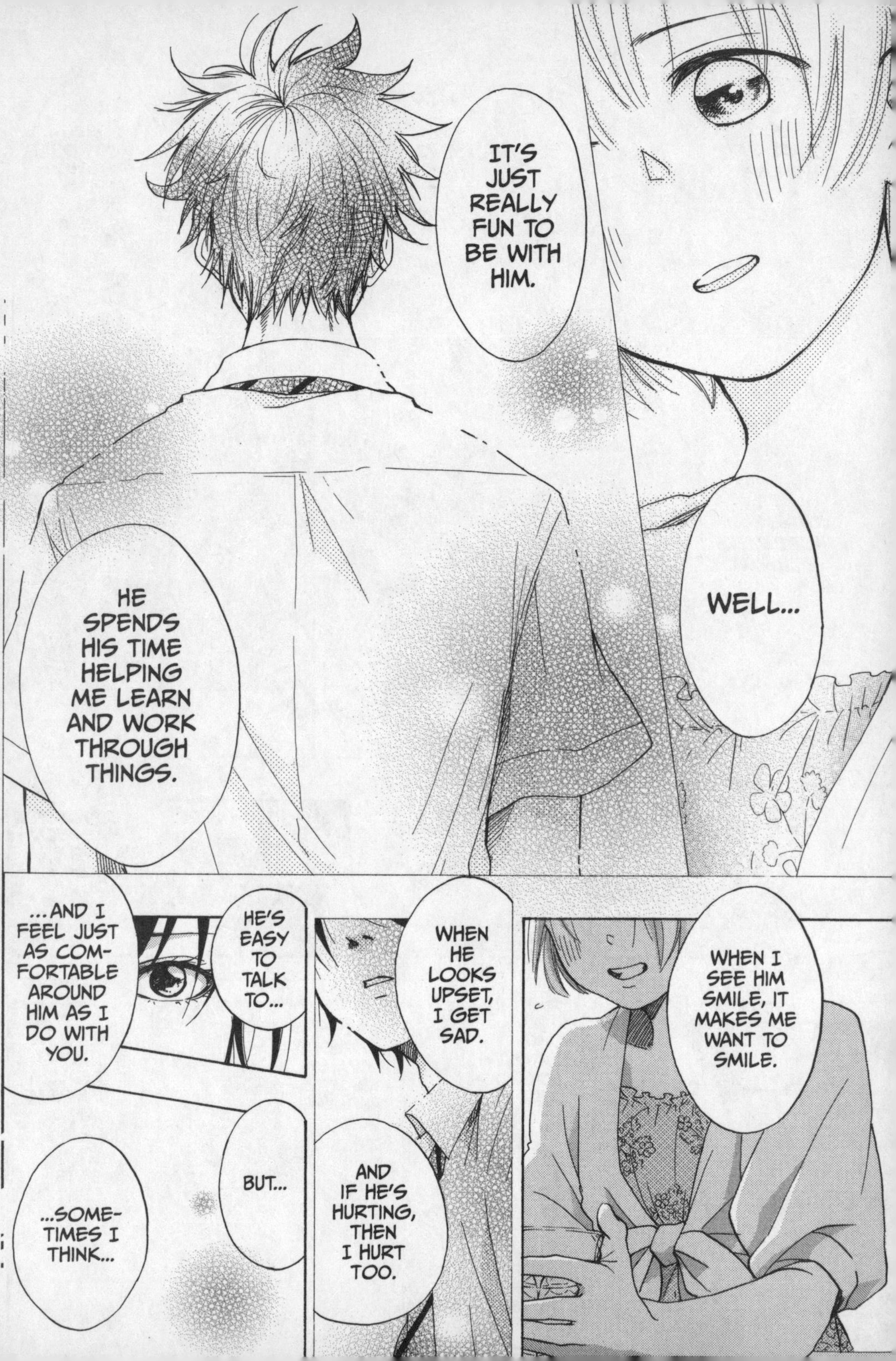
IT'S JUST REALLY FUN TO BE WITH HIM.
WELL...
HE SPENDS HIS TIME HELPING ME LEARN AND WORK THROUGH THINGS.
WHEN I SEE HIM SMILE, IT MAKES ME WANT TO SMILE.
WHEN HE LOOKS UPSET, I GET SAD.
AND IF HE'S HURTING, THEN I HURT TOO.
HE'S EASY TO TALK TO...
...AND I FEEL JUST AS COM-FORTABLE AROUND HIM AS I DO WITH YOU.
BUT...
...SOME-TIMES I THINK...

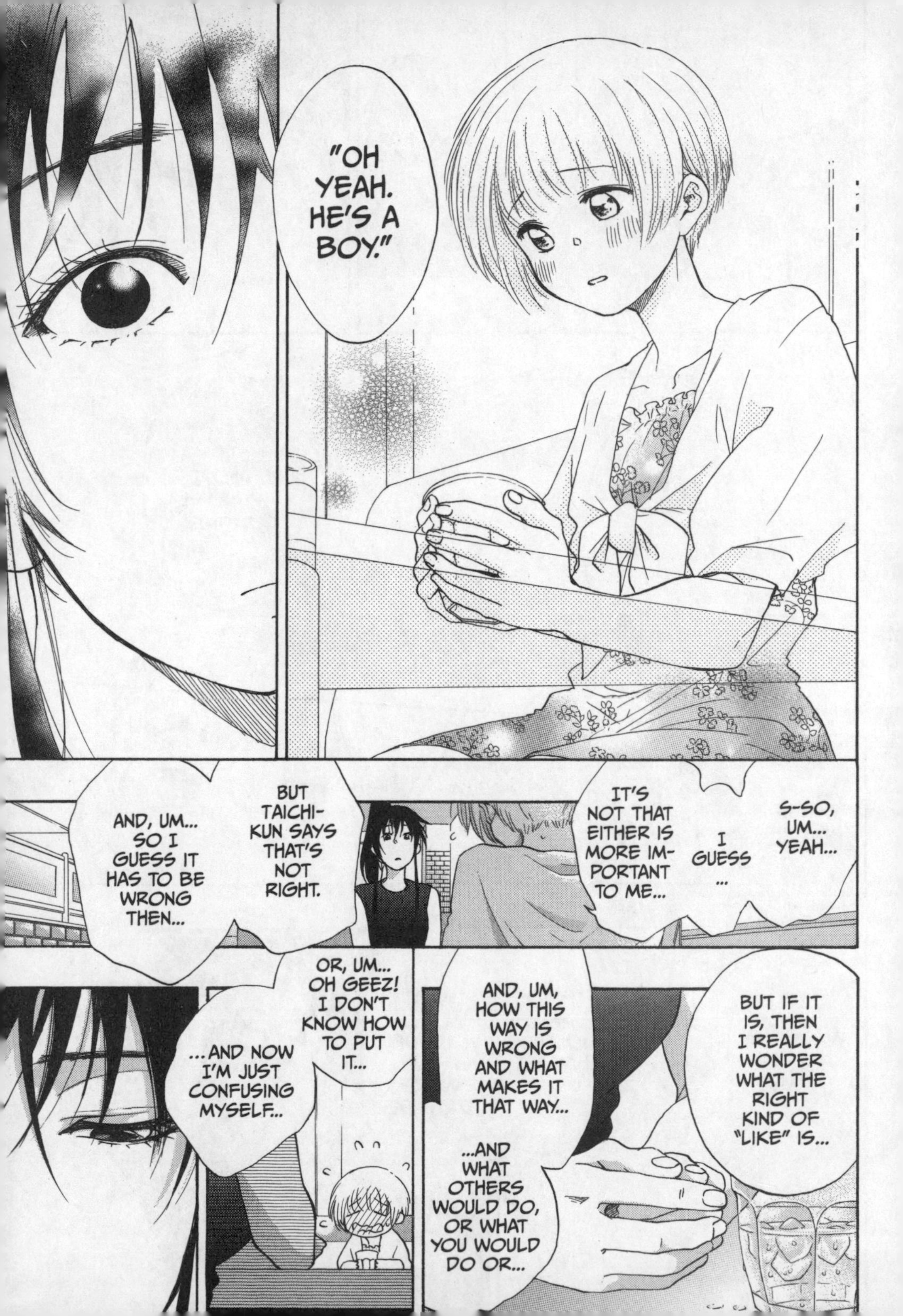
"OH YEAH. HE'S A BOY."
S-SO, UM... YEAH...
I GUESS ...
IT'S NOT THAT EITHER IS MORE IM-PORTANT TO ME...
BUT TAICHI-KUN SAYS THAT'S NOT RIGHT.
AND, UM... SO I GUESS IT HAS TO BE WRONG THEN...
BUT IF IT IS, THEN I REALLY WONDER WHAT THE RIGHT KIND OF "LIKE" IS...
AND, UM, HOW THIS WAY IS WRONG AND WHAT MAKES IT THAT WAY...
...AND WHAT OTHERS WOULD DO, OR WHAT YOU WOULD DO OR...
OR, UM... OH GEEZ! I DON'T KNOW HOW TO PUT IT...
...AND NOW I'M JUST CONFUSING MYSELF...

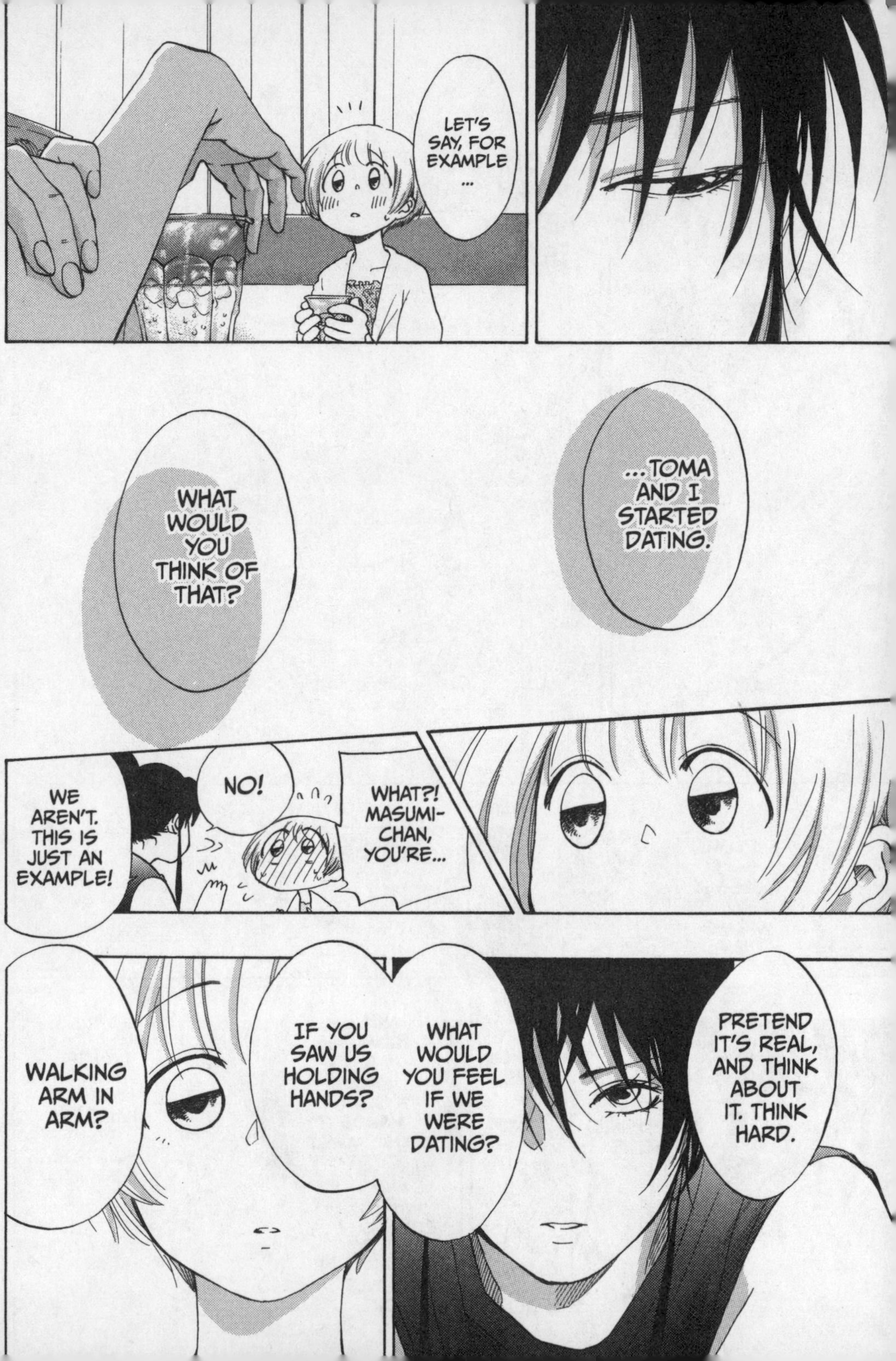
LET'S SAY, FOR EXAMPLE ...
...TOMA AND I STARTED DATING.
WHAT WOULD YOU THINK OF THAT?
WHAT?! MASUMI-CHAN, YOU'RE...
NO!
WE AREN'T. THIS IS JUST AN EXAMPLE!
PRETEND IT'S REAL, AND THINK ABOUT IT. THINK HARD.
WHAT WOULD YOU FEEL IF WE WERE DATING?
IF YOU SAW US HOLDING HANDS?
WALKING ARM IN ARM?

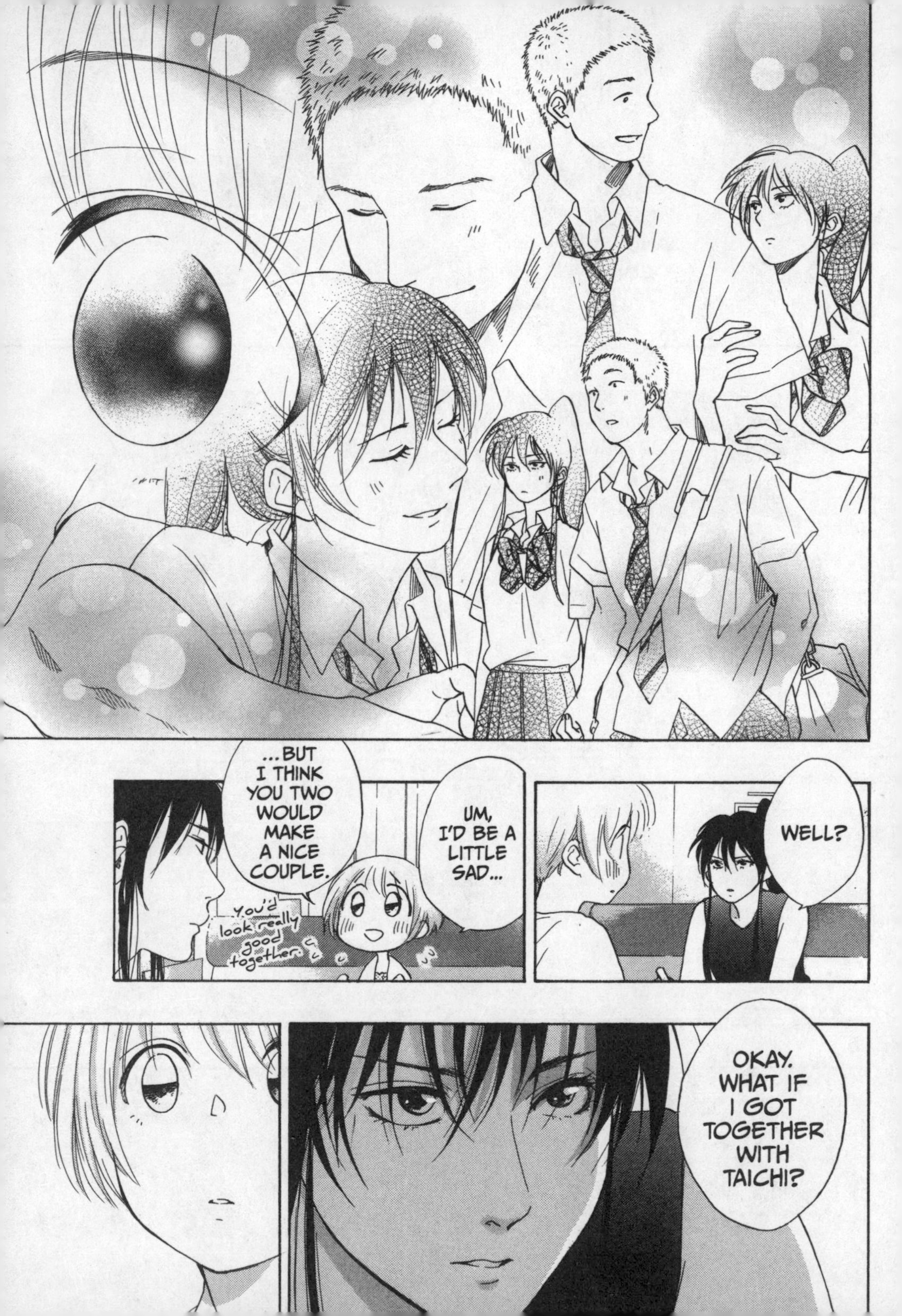
WELL?
UM, I'D BE A LITTLE SAD...
...BUT I THINK YOU TWO WOULD MAKE A NICE COUPLE.
You'd look really good together.
OKAY. WHAT IF I GOT TOGETHER WITH TAICHI?

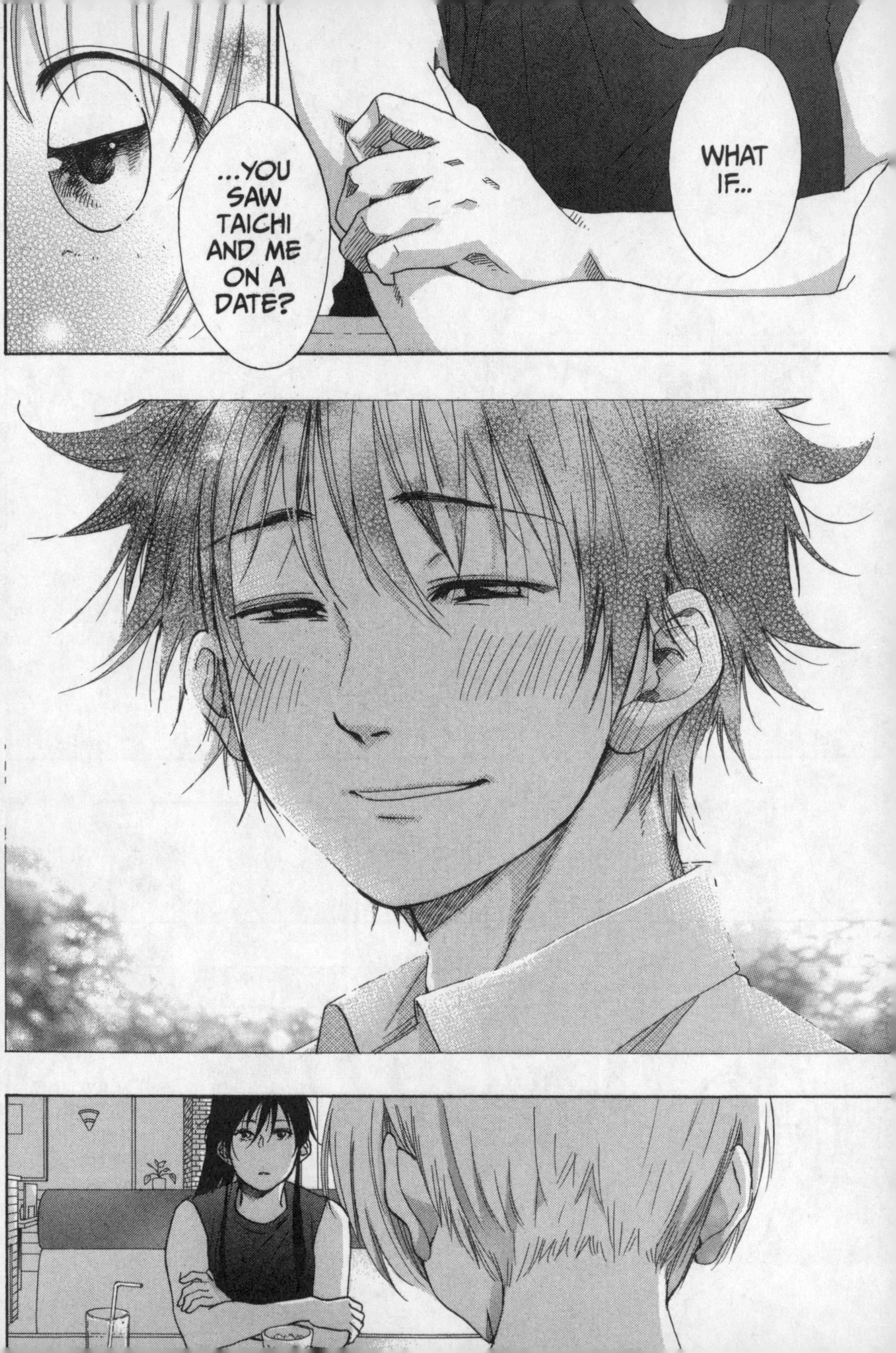
WHAT IF...
...YOU SAW TAICHI AND ME ON A DATE?

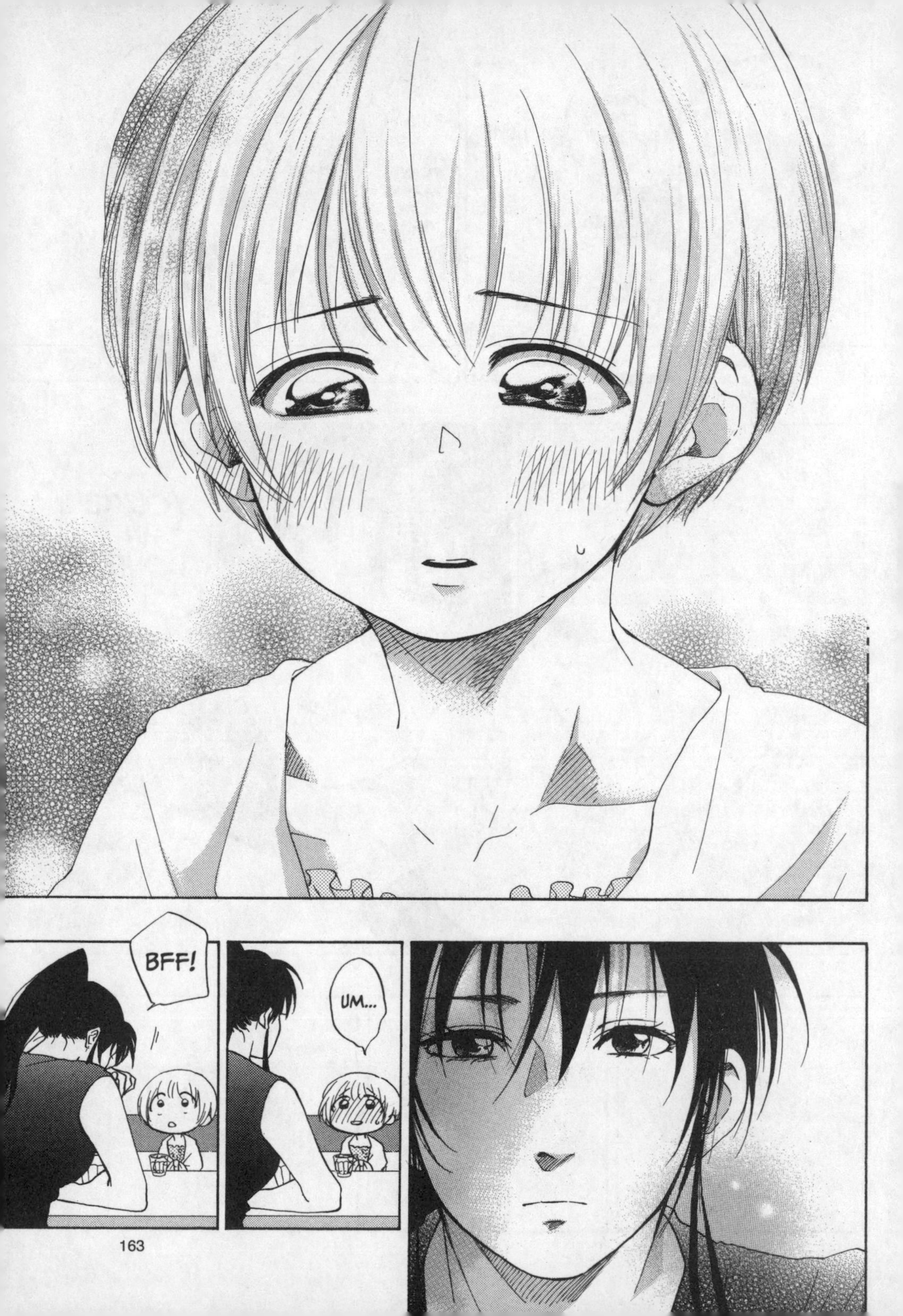
UM...
BFF!

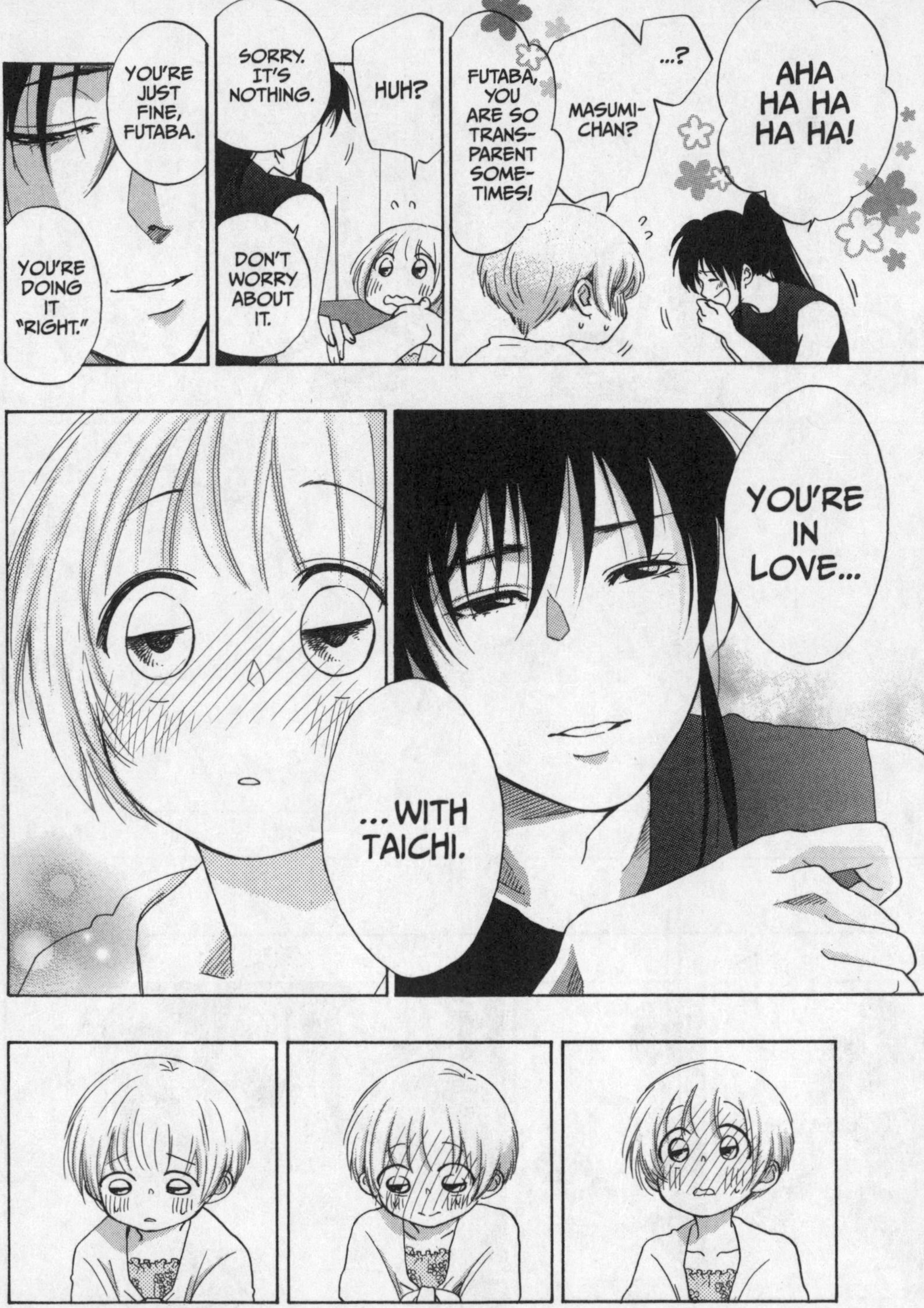
AHA HA HA HA HA!
...?
MASUMI-CHAN?
FUTABA, YOU ARE SO TRANSPARENT SOMETIMES!
HUH?
SORRY. IT'S NOTHING.
DON'T WORRY ABOUT IT.
YOU'RE JUST FINE, FUTABA.
YOU'RE DOING IT "RIGHT."
YOU'RE IN LOVE...
...WITH TAICHI.

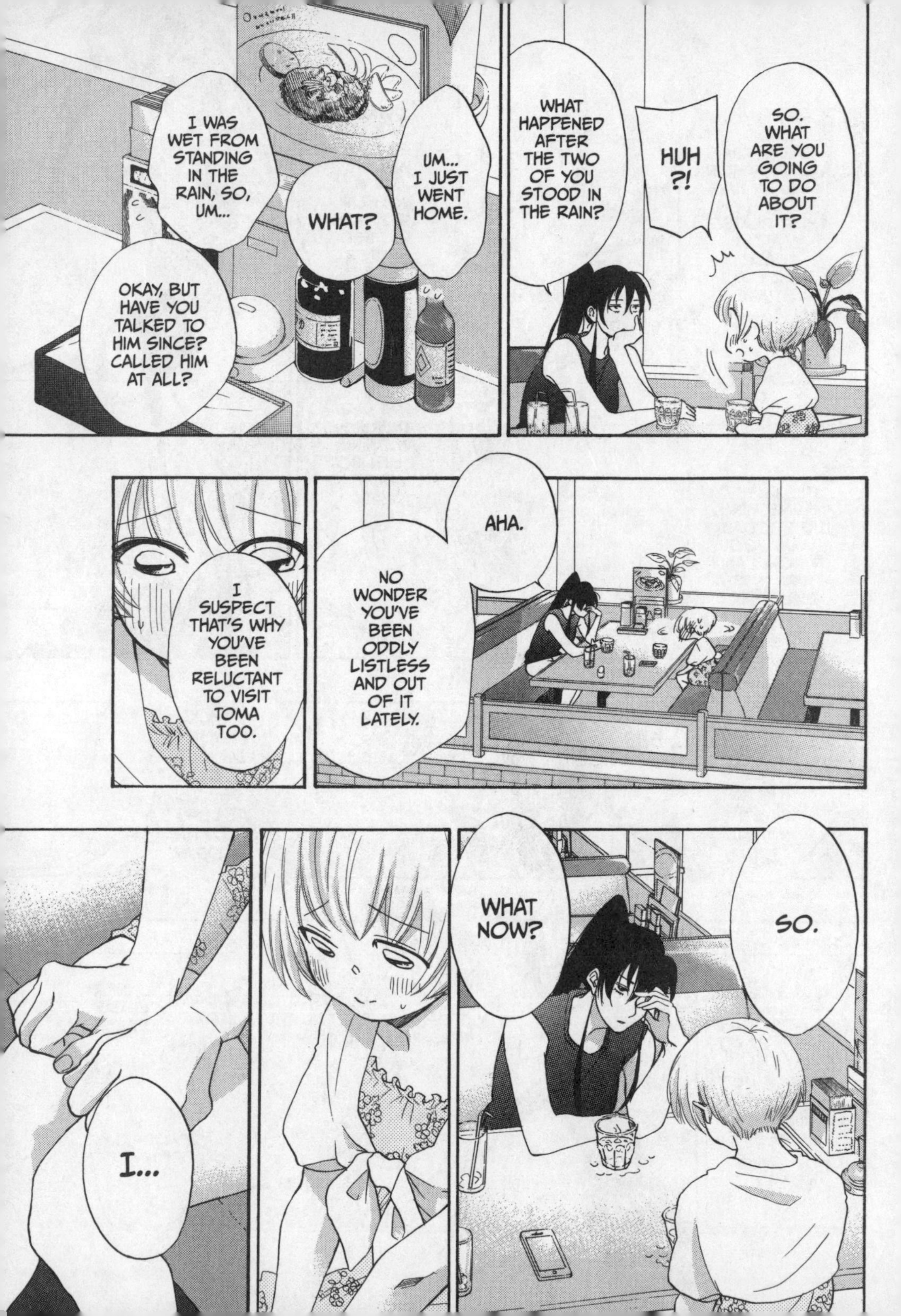
SO. WHAT ARE YOU GOING TO DO ABOUT IT?
HUH?!
WHAT HAPPENED AFTER THE TWO OF YOU STOOD IN THE RAIN?
UM... I JUST WENT HOME.
WHAT?
I WAS WET FROM STANDING IN THE RAIN, SO, UM...
OKAY, BUT HAVE YOU TALKED TO HIM SINCE? CALLED HIM AT ALL?
AHA.
NO WONDER YOU'VE BEEN ODDLY LISTLESS AND OUT OF IT LATELY.
I SUSPECT THAT'S WHY YOU'VE BEEN RELUCTANT TO VISIT TOMA TOO.
SO.
WHAT NOW?
I...

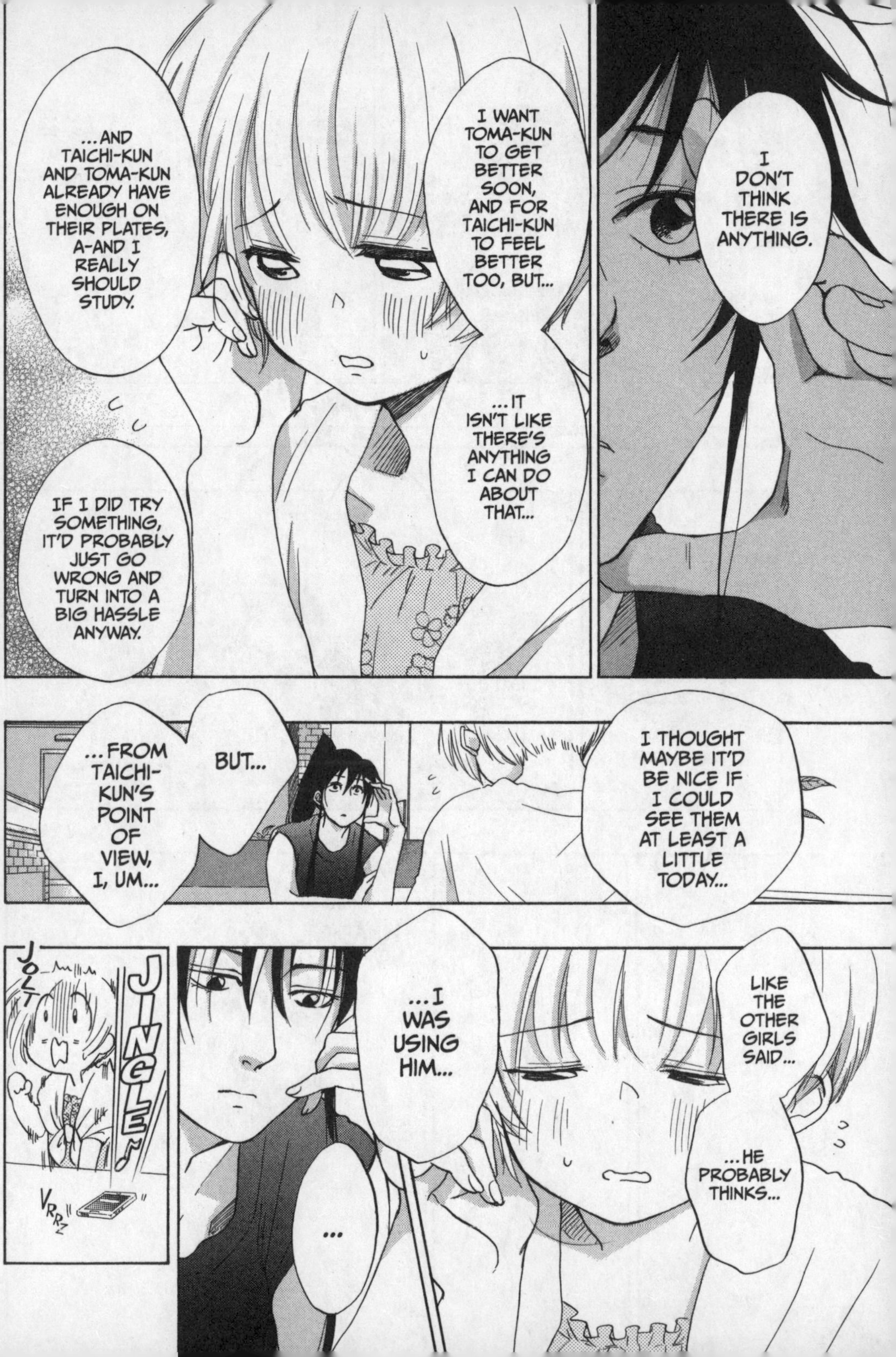

I DON'T THINK THERE IS ANYTHING.
I WANT TOMA-KUN TO GET BETTER SOON, AND FOR TAICHI-KUN TO FEEL BETTER TOO, BUT...
...IT ISN'T LIKE THERE'S ANYTHING I CAN DO ABOUT THAT...
...AND TAICHI-KUN AND TOMA-KUN ALREADY HAVE ENOUGH ON THEIR PLATES, A-AND I REALLY SHOULD STUDY.
IF I DID TRY SOMETHING, IT'D PROBABLY JUST GO WRONG AND TURN INTO A BIG HASSLE ANYWAY.
I THOUGHT MAYBE IT'D BE NICE IF I COULD SEE THEM AT LEAST A LITTLE TODAY...
BUT...
...FROM TAICHI-KUN'S POINT OF VIEW, I, UM...
LIKE THE OTHER GIRLS SAID...
...HE PROBABLY THINKS...
...I WAS USING HIM...
...
JINGLE
JOLT
VRRZ

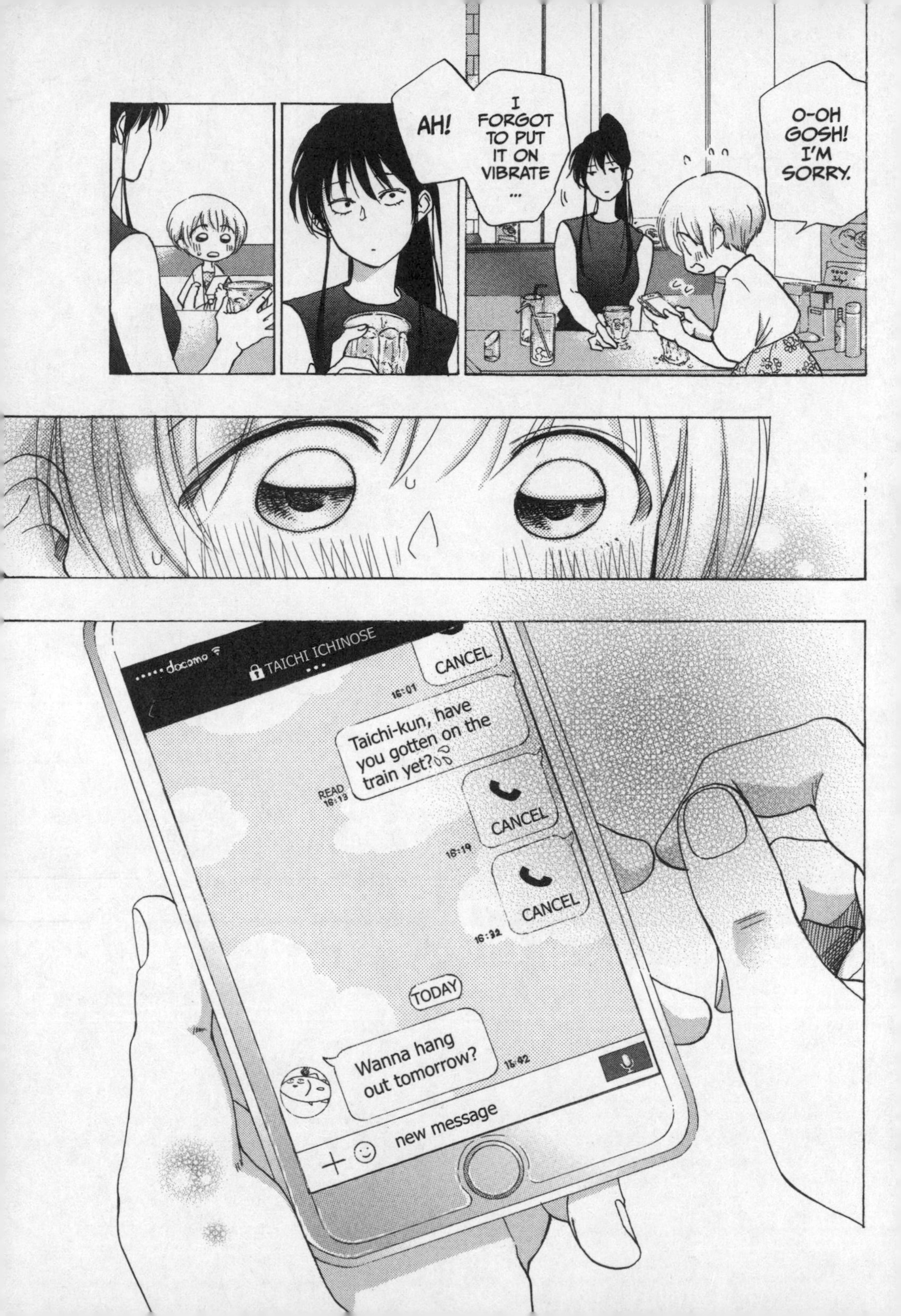

O-OH GOSH! I'M SORRY.
AH!
I FORGOT TO PUT IT ON VIBRATE ...
docomo
TAICHI ICHINOSE
CANCEL
16:01
Taichi-kun, have you gotten on the train yet?
READ 16:13
CANCEL
16:19
CANCEL
16:32
TODAY
Wanna hang out tomorrow?
16:42
new message

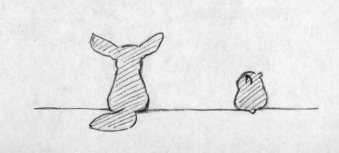

CHAPTER 19

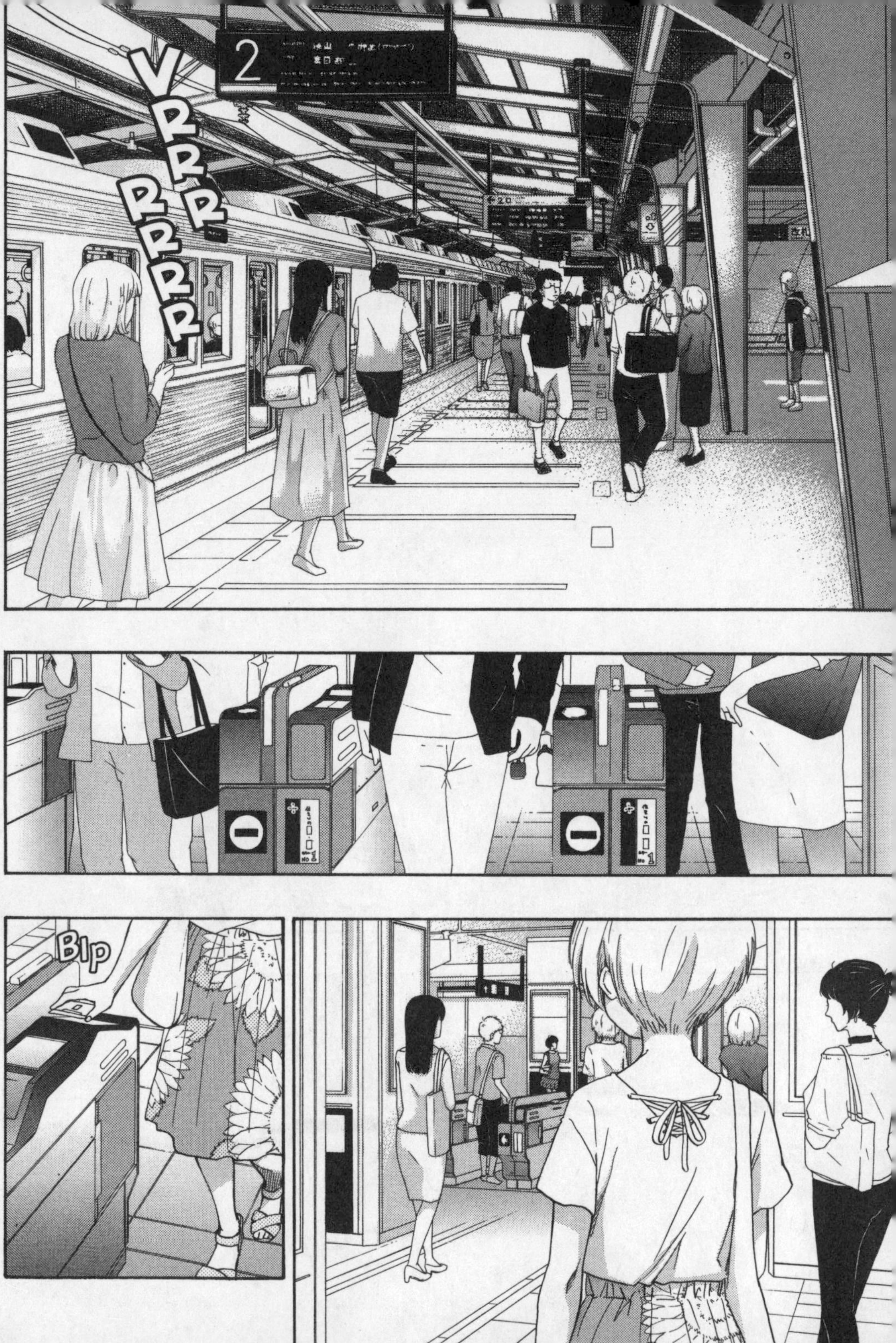
VRRR
RRRR
Bip

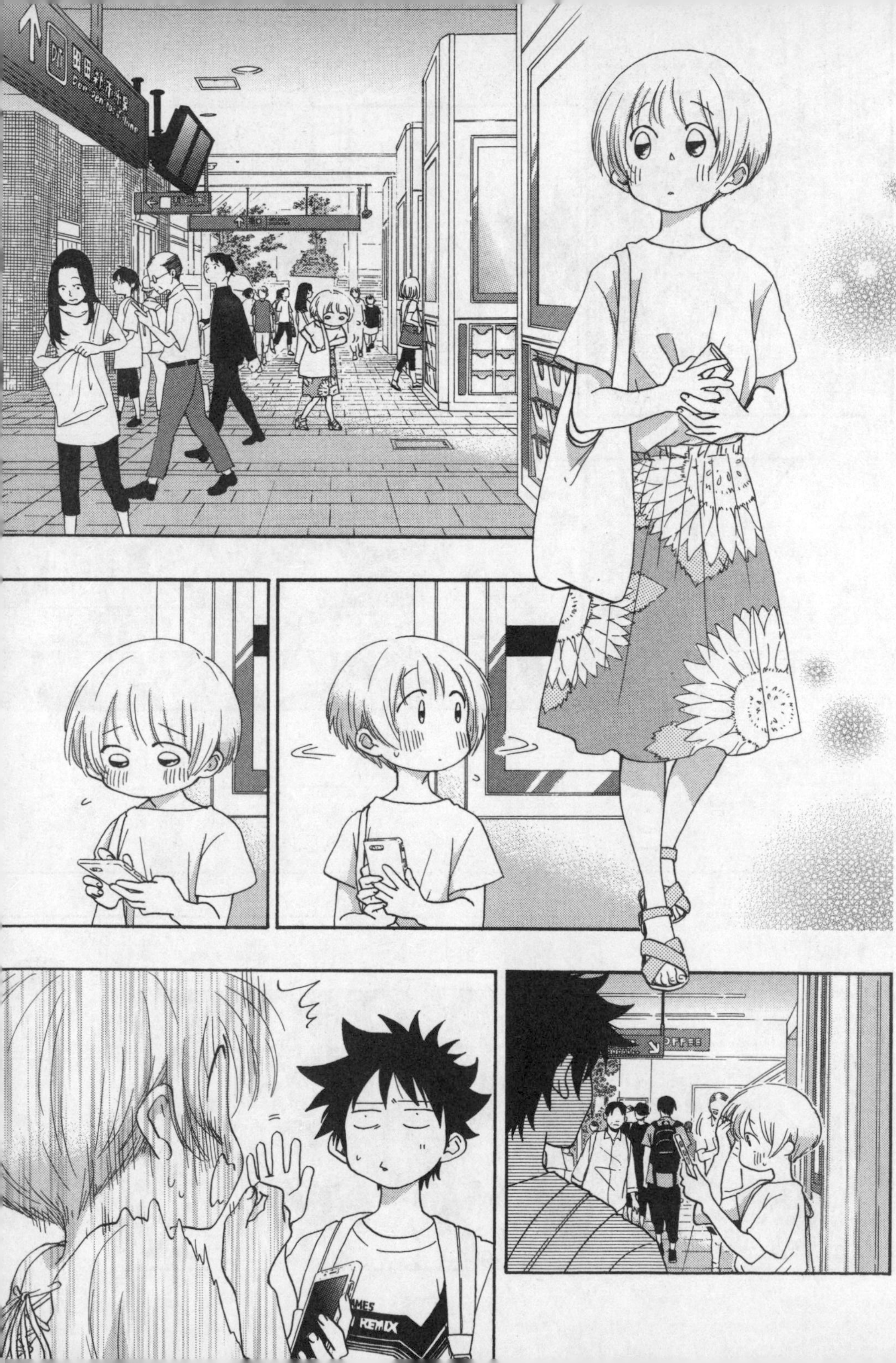

DT
REMIX

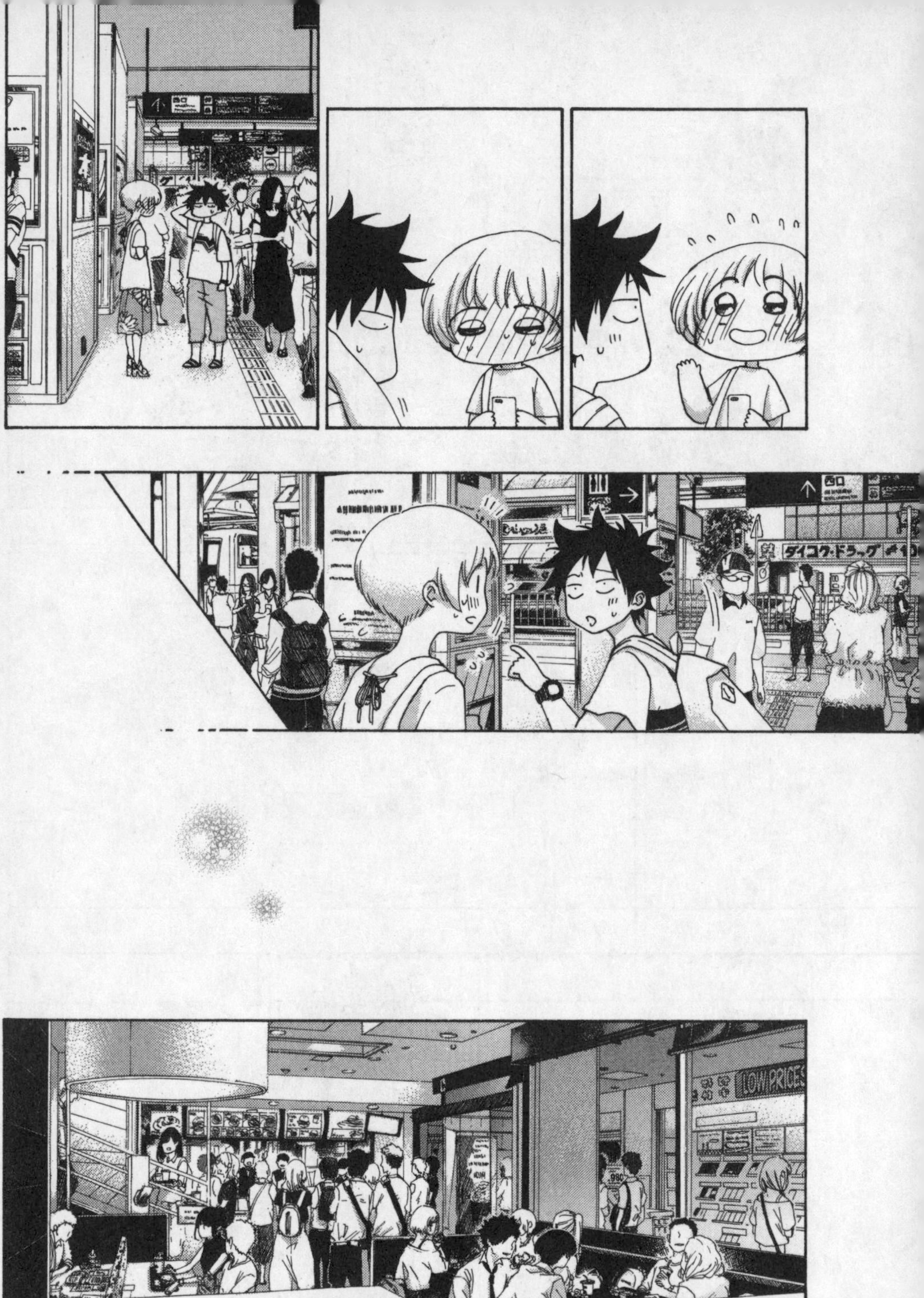
ダイコク・ドラッグ
LOW PRICES

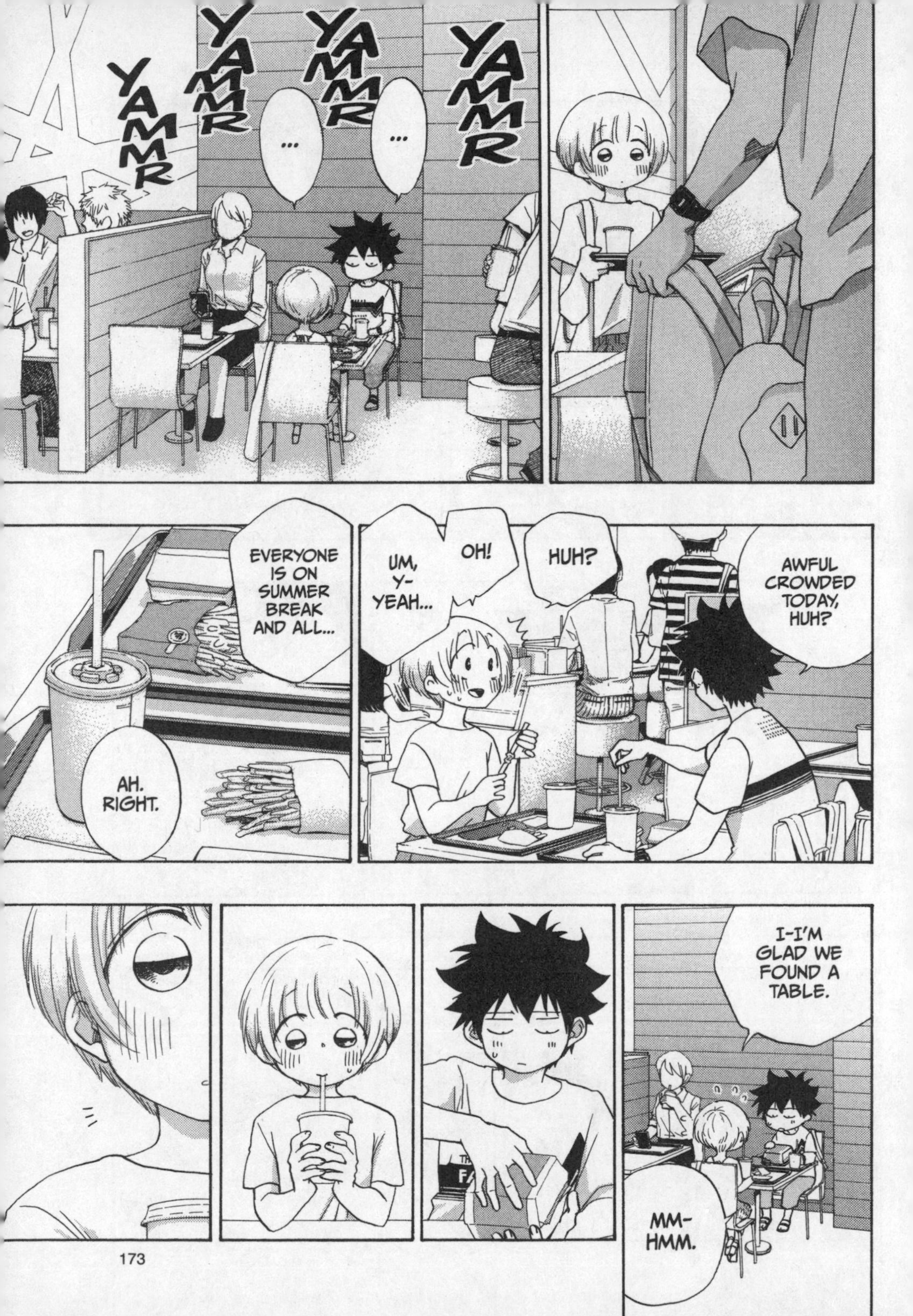
YAMMR
...
YAMMR
...
YAMMR
YAMMR
AWFUL CROWDED TODAY, HUH?
HUH?
OH!
UM, Y-YEAH...
EVERYONE IS ON SUMMER BREAK AND ALL...
AH. RIGHT.
I-I'M GLAD WE FOUND A TABLE.
MM-HMM.

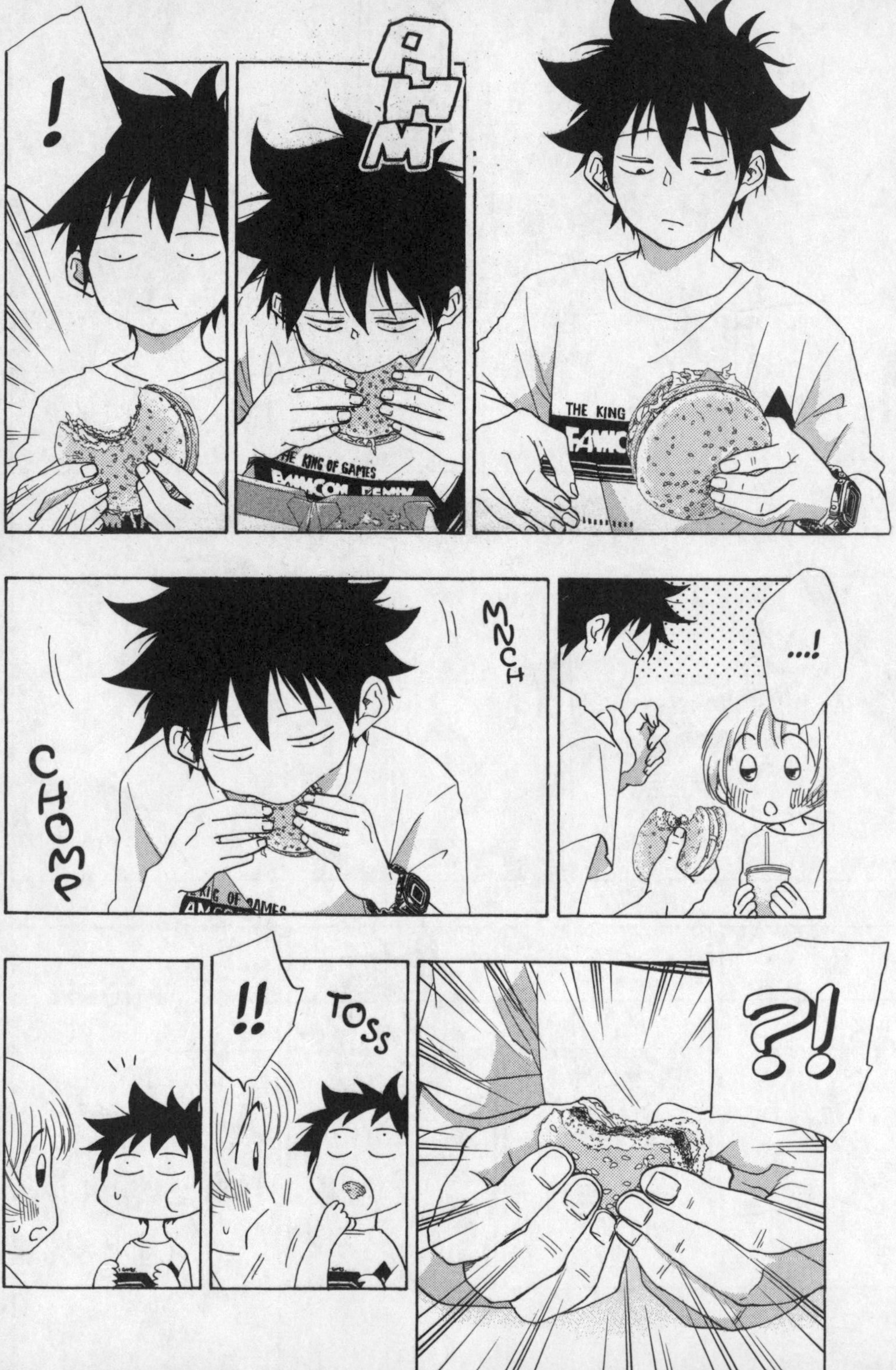

AHM
!
THE KING
THE KING OF GAMES
MNCH
CHOMP
...!
?!
TOSS
!!

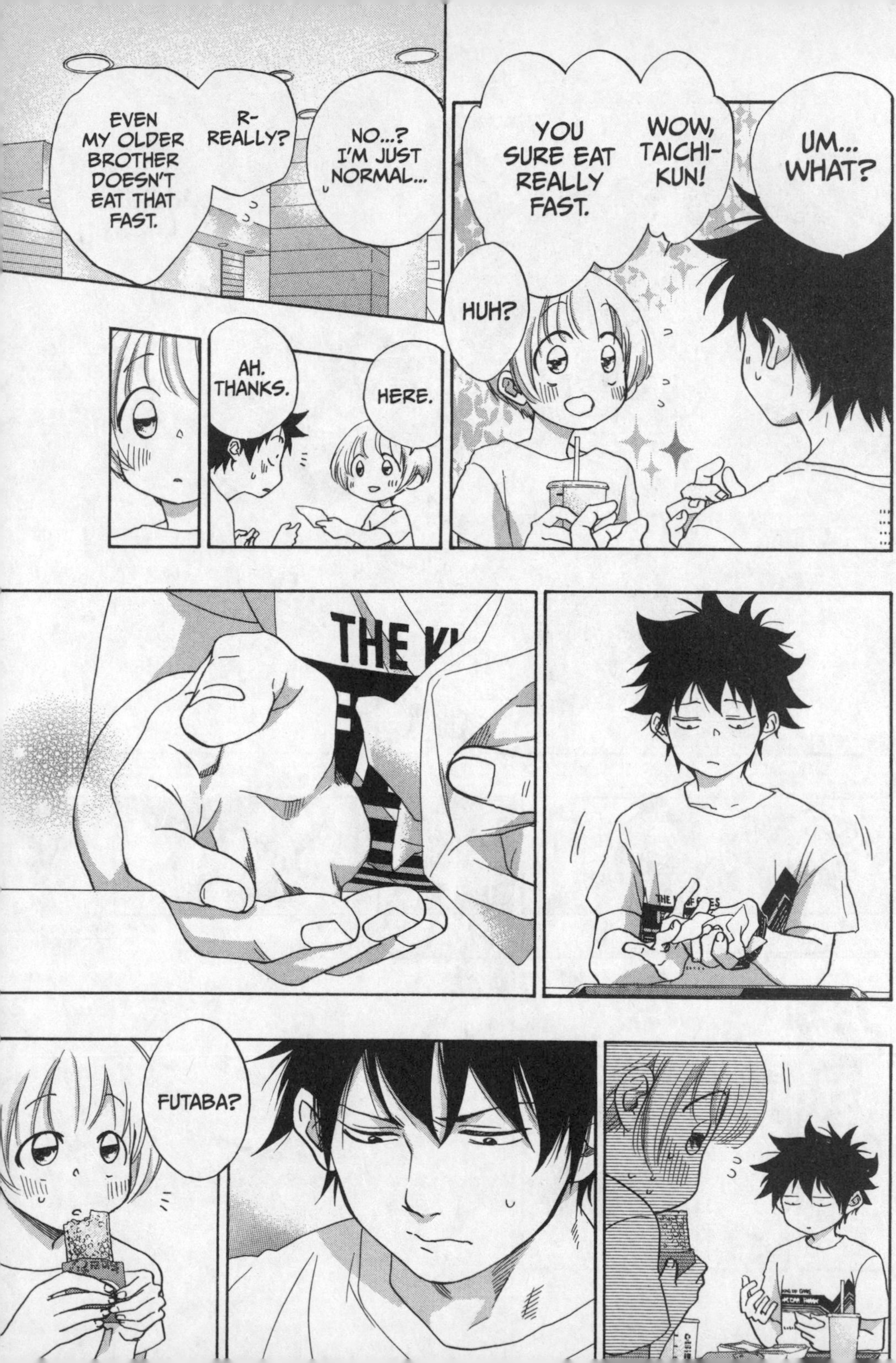
UM... WHAT?
WOW, TAICHI-KUN!
YOU SURE EAT REALLY FAST.
HUH?
NO...? I'M JUST NORMAL...
R- REALLY?
EVEN MY OLDER BROTHER DOESN'T EAT THAT FAST.
HERE.
AH. THANKS.
FUTABA?

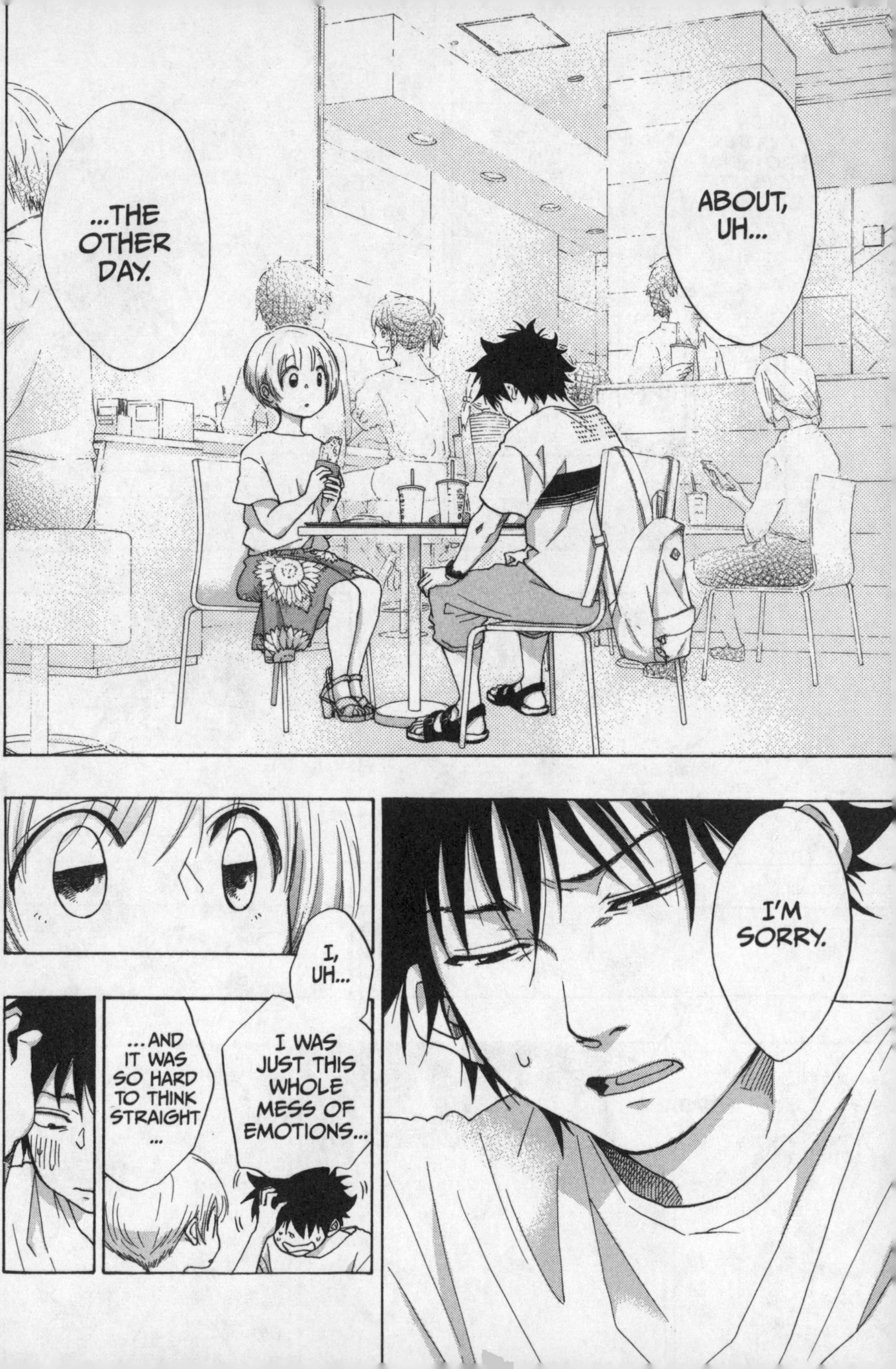
ABOUT, UH...
...THE OTHER DAY.
I'M SORRY.
I, UH...
I WAS JUST THIS WHOLE MESS OF EMOTIONS...
...AND IT WAS SO HARD TO THINK STRAIGHT ...

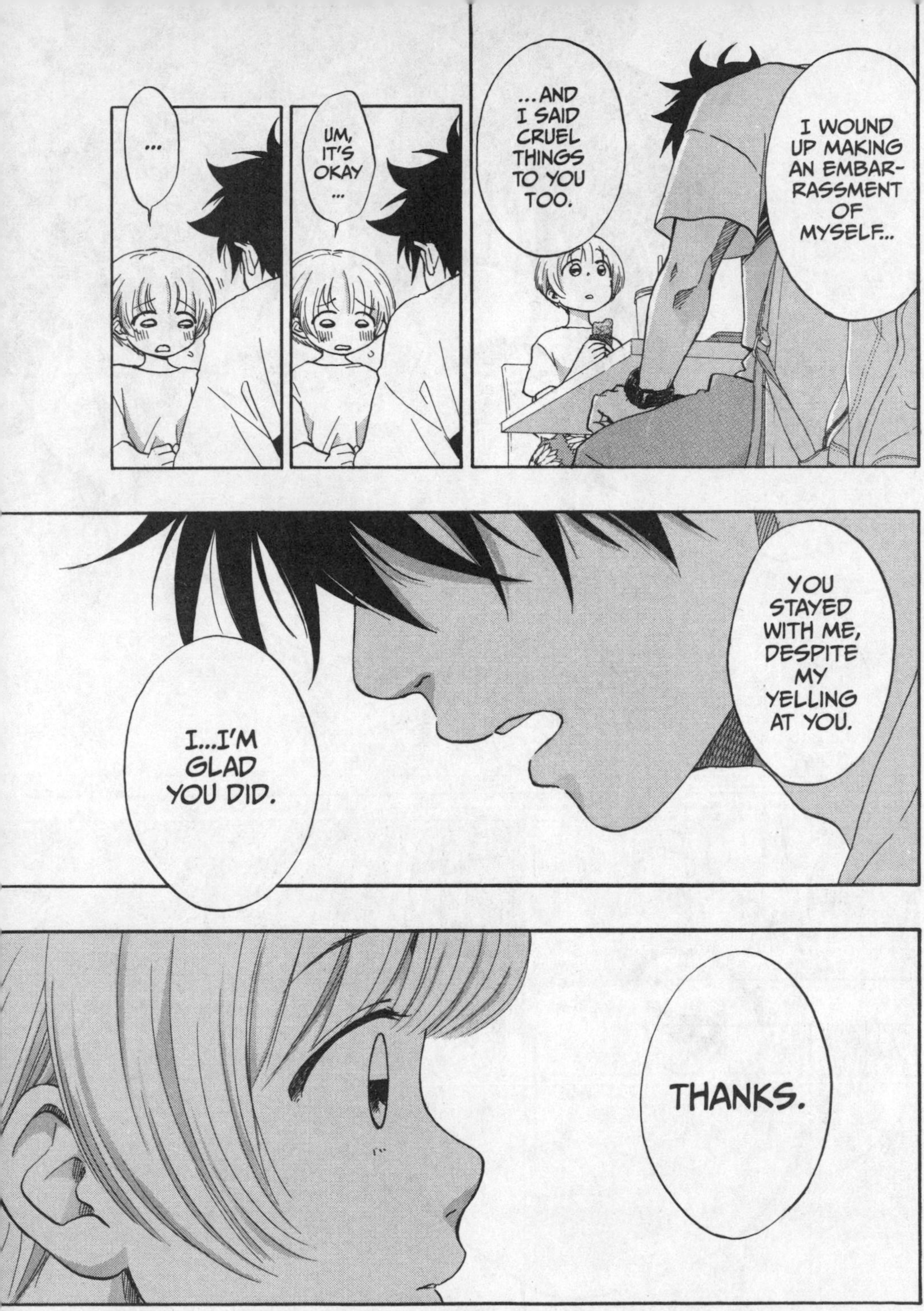
I WOUND UP MAKING AN EMBAR-RASSMENT OF MYSELF...
...AND I SAID CRUEL THINGS TO YOU TOO.
UM, IT'S OKAY ...
...
YOU STAYED WITH ME, DESPITE MY YELLING AT YOU.
I...I'M GLAD YOU DID.
THANKS.

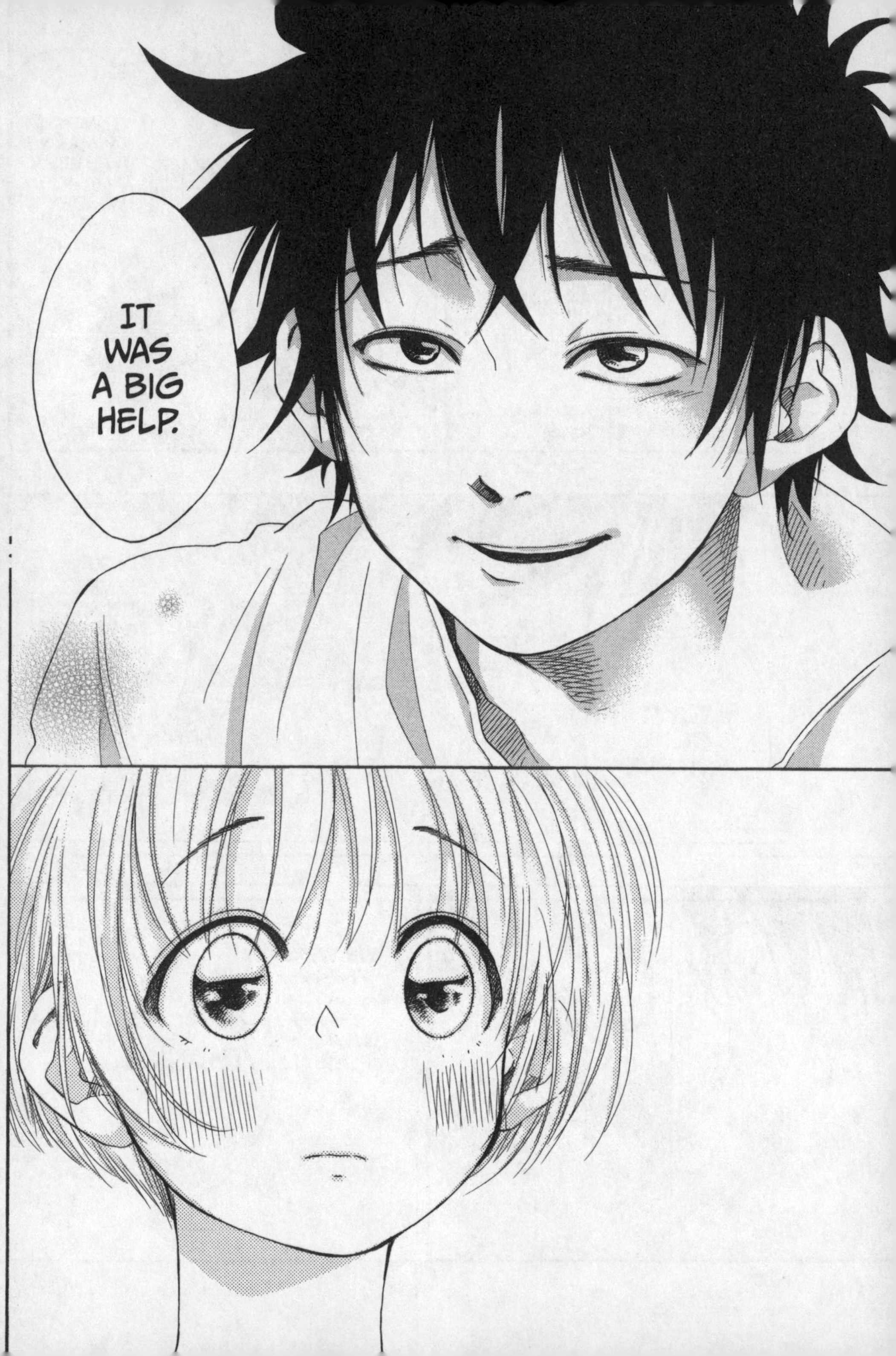
IT WAS A BIG HELP.

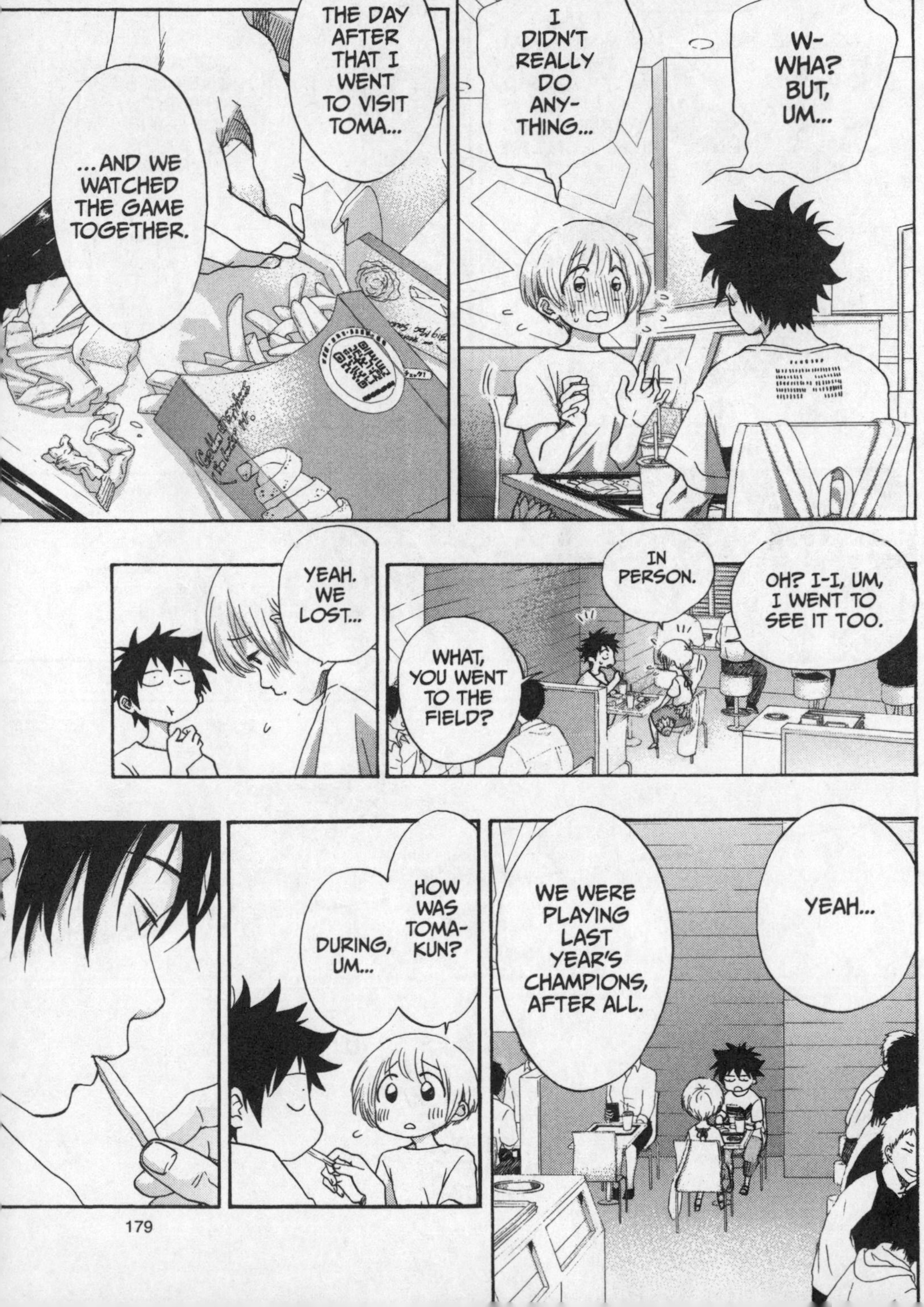
W-WHA? BUT, UM...
I DIDN'T REALLY DO ANYTHING...
THE DAY AFTER THAT I WENT TO VISIT TOMA...
...AND WE WATCHED THE GAME TOGETHER.
OH? I-I, UM, I WENT TO SEE IT TOO.
IN PERSON.
WHAT, YOU WENT TO THE FIELD?
YEAH. WE LOST...
YEAH...
WE WERE PLAYING LAST YEAR'S CHAMPIONS, AFTER ALL.
HOW WAS TOMA-KUN?
DURING, UM...

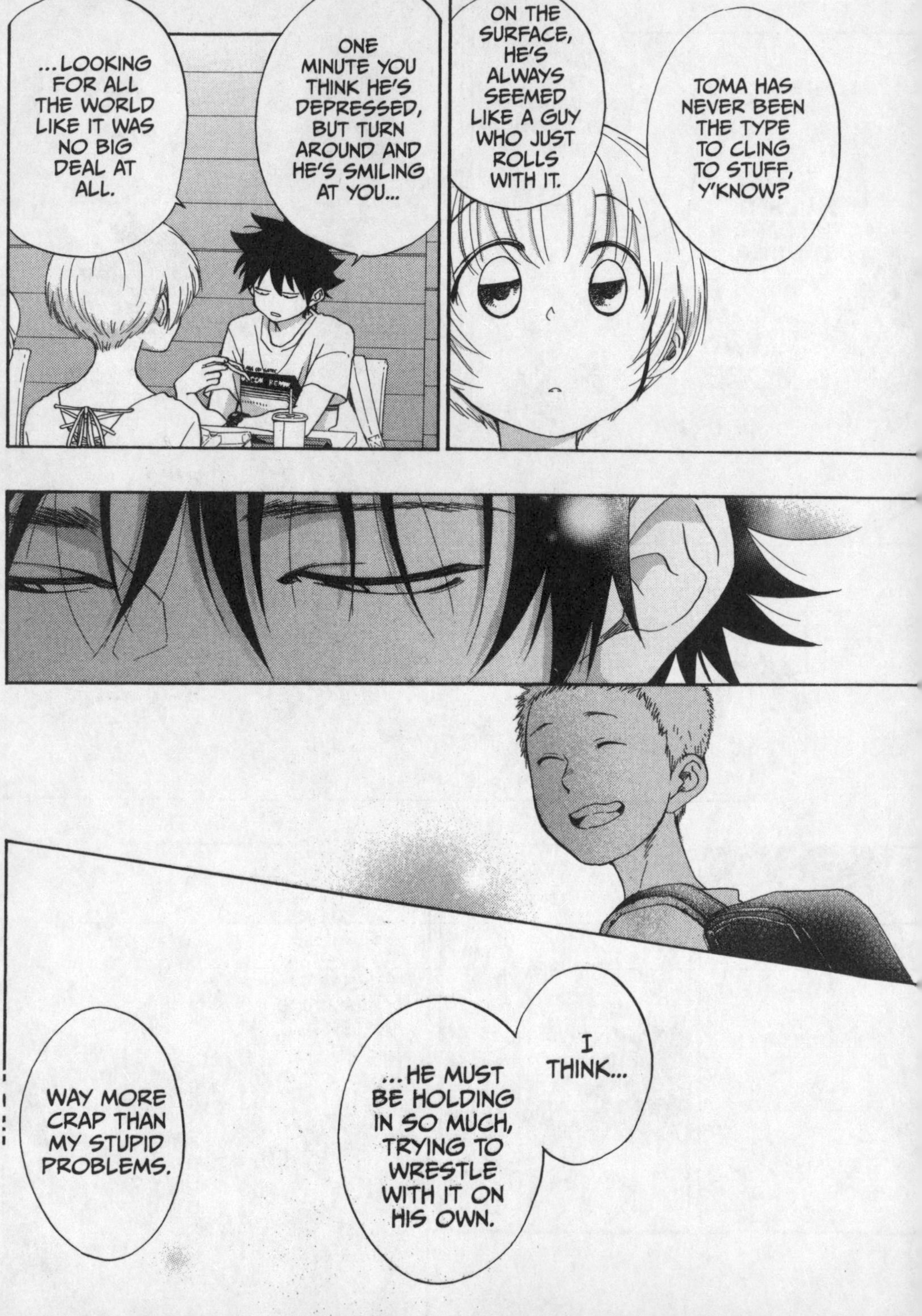
TOMA HAS NEVER BEEN THE TYPE TO CLING TO STUFF, Y'KNOW?
ON THE SURFACE, HE'S ALWAYS SEEMED LIKE A GUY WHO JUST ROLLS WITH IT.
ONE MINUTE YOU THINK HE'S DEPRESSED, BUT TURN AROUND AND HE'S SMILING AT YOU...
...LOOKING FOR ALL THE WORLD LIKE IT WAS NO BIG DEAL AT ALL.
I THINK...
...HE MUST BE HOLDING IN SO MUCH, TRYING TO WRESTLE WITH IT ON HIS OWN.
WAY MORE CRAP THAN MY STUPID PROBLEMS.

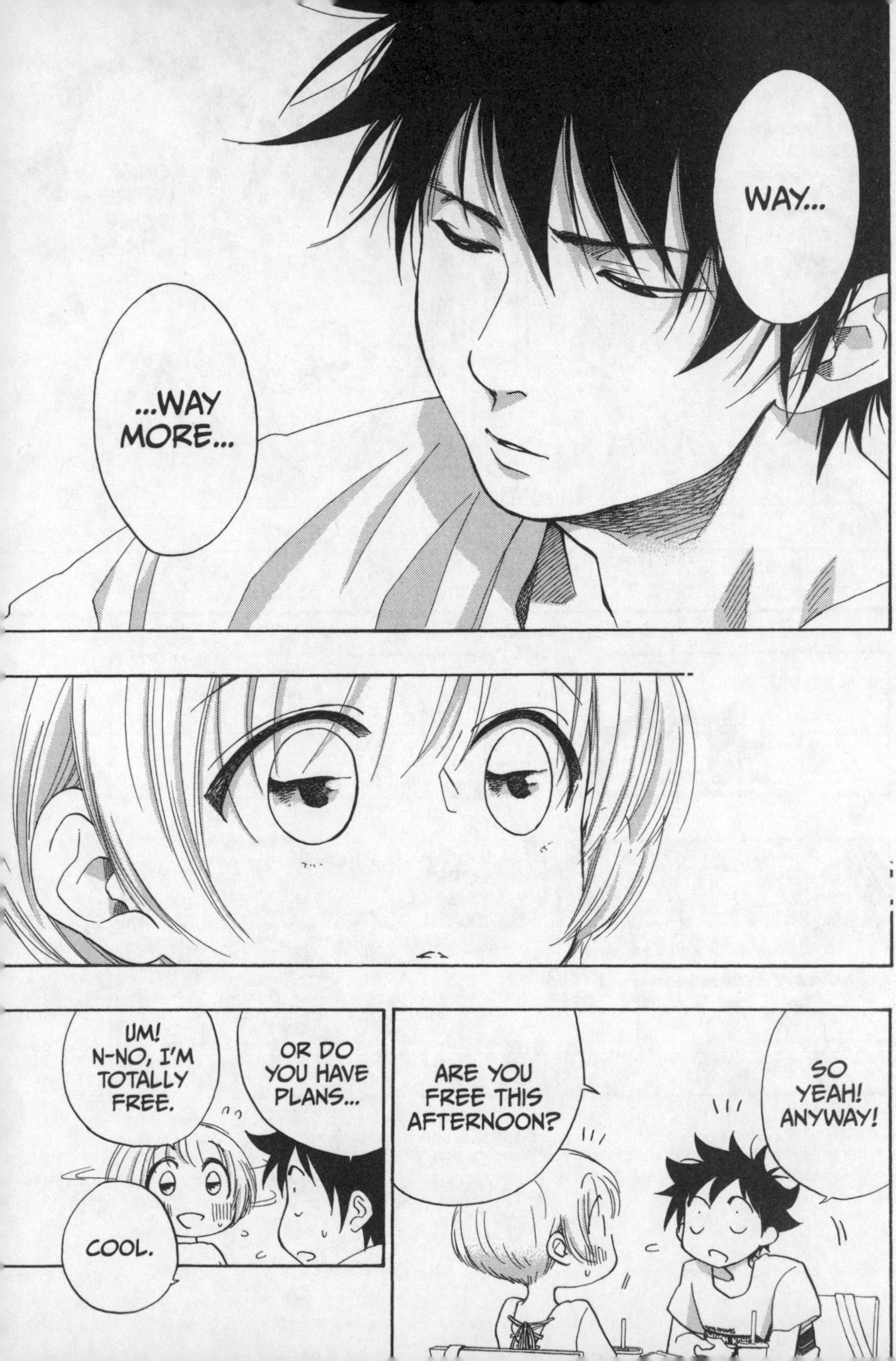
WAY...
...WAY MORE...
SO YEAH! ANYWAY!
ARE YOU FREE THIS AFTERNOON?
OR DO YOU HAVE PLANS...
UM! N-NO, I'M TOTALLY FREE.
COOL.

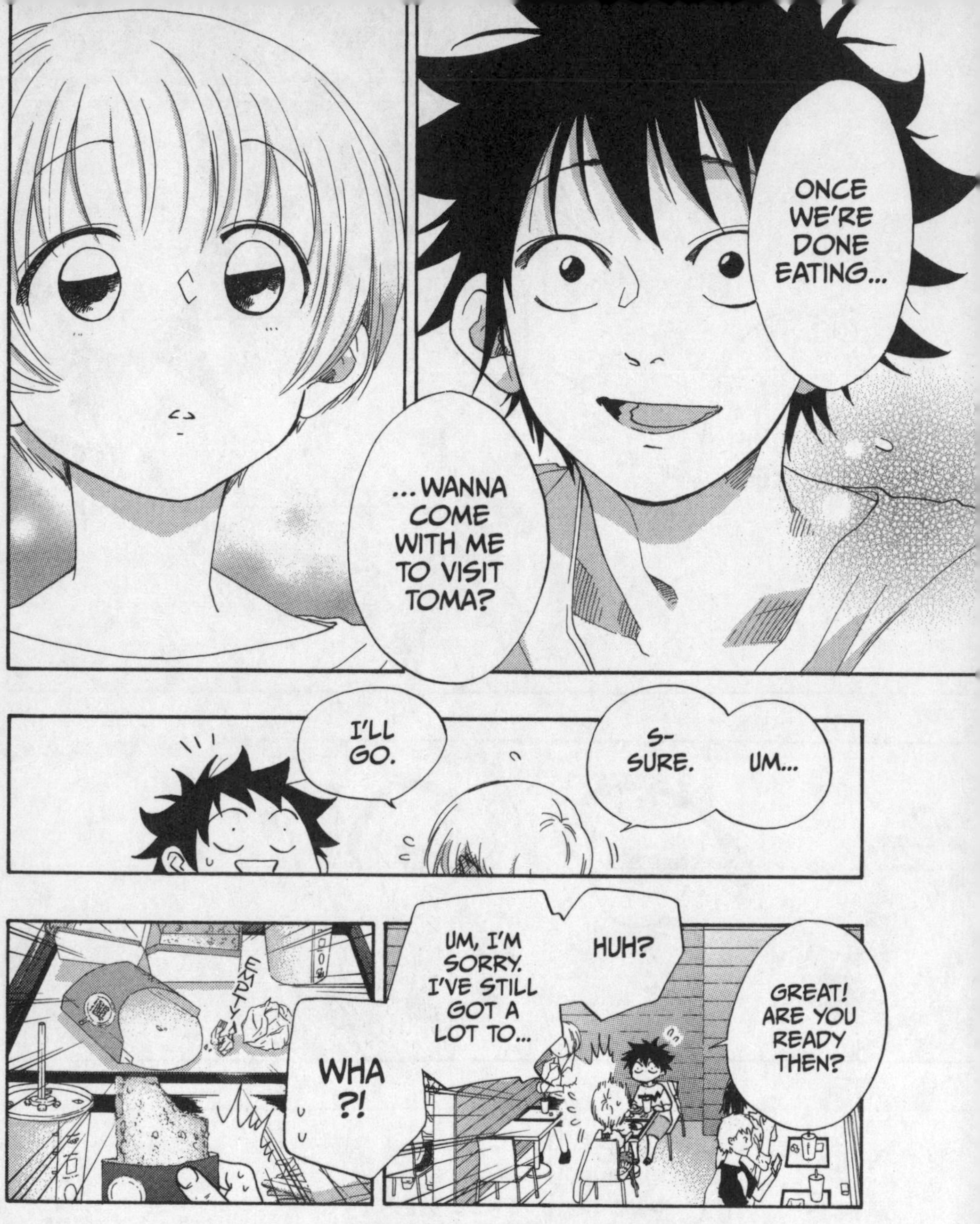
ONCE WE'RE DONE EATING...
...WANNA COME WITH ME TO VISIT TOMA?
S-SURE. UM...
I'LL GO.
GREAT! ARE YOU READY THEN?
HUH?
UM, I'M SORRY. I'VE STILL GOT A LOT TO...
EMPTY
WHA ?!
Gosh, Taichi-kun! When did you finish? That was fast!
Huh? No it wasn't. It was normal...
No, it was fast...!

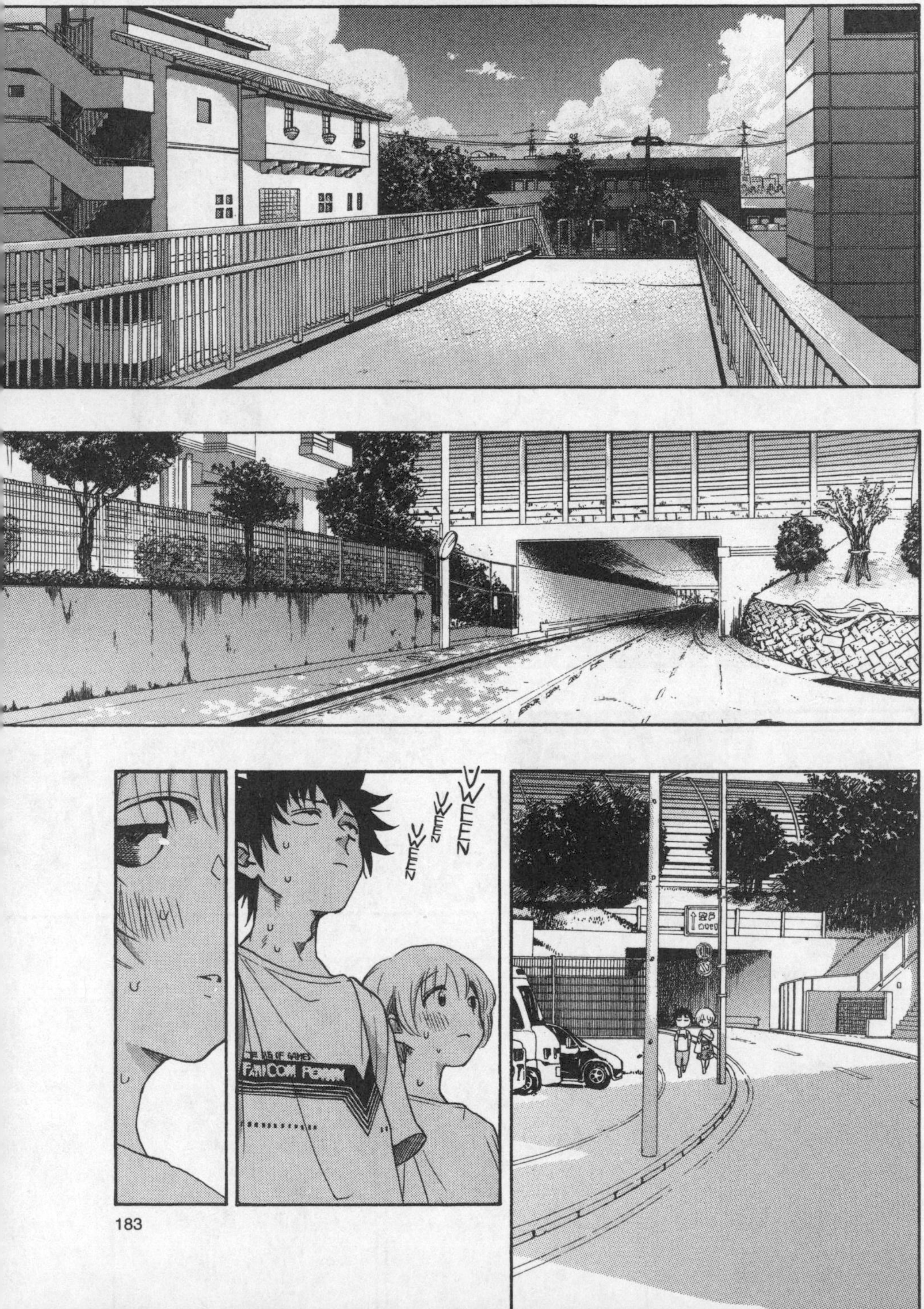
VWEEN
VWEEN
VWEEN

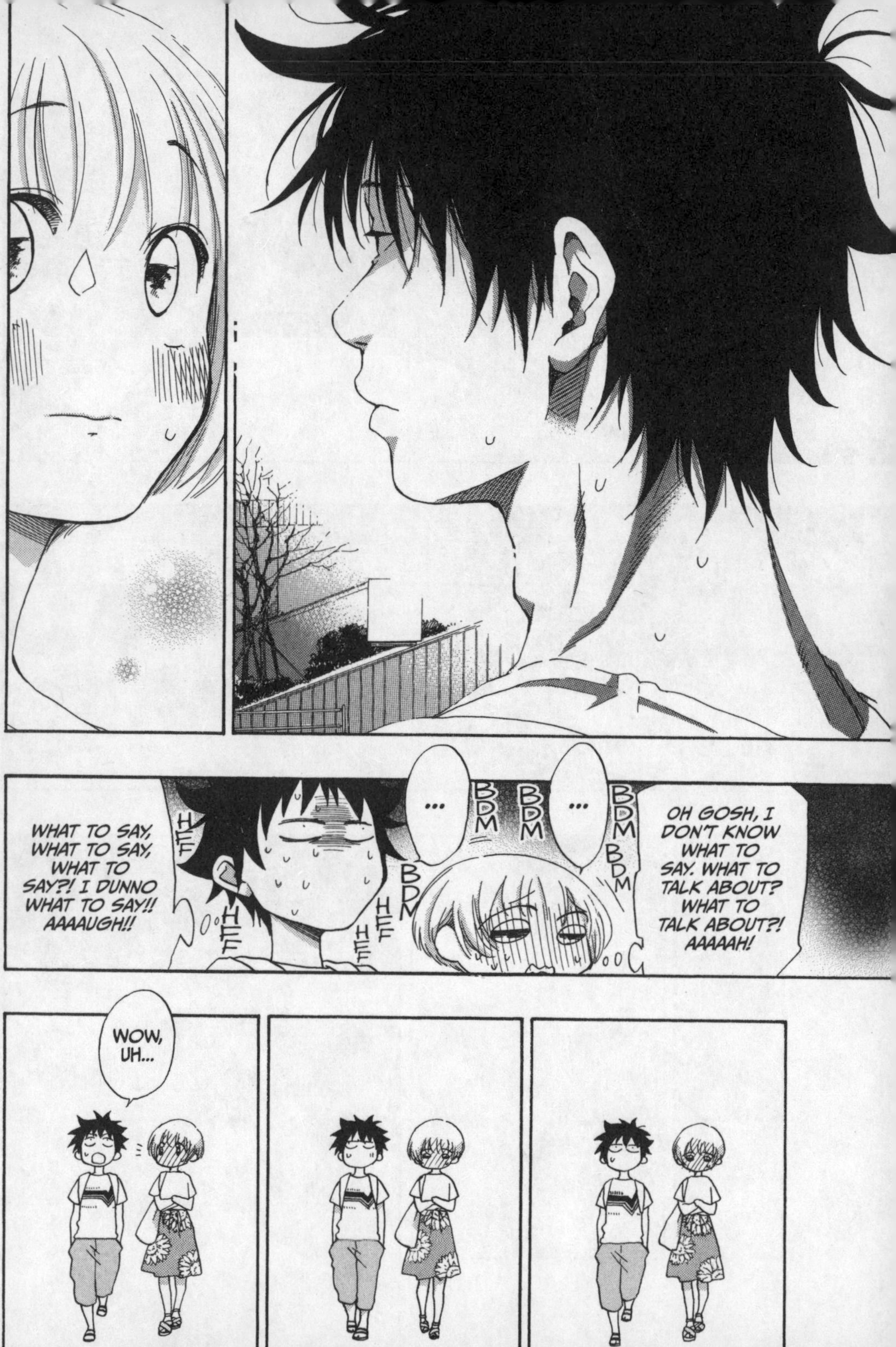

OH GOSH, I DON'T KNOW WHAT TO SAY. WHAT TO TALK ABOUT? WHAT TO TALK ABOUT?! AAAAAH!
BDM BDM BDM
...
BDM BDM
...
BDM BDM
HEF HEF
HEF HEF
WHAT TO SAY, WHAT TO SAY, WHAT TO SAY?! I DUNNO WHAT TO SAY!! AAAAUGH!!
WOW, UH...

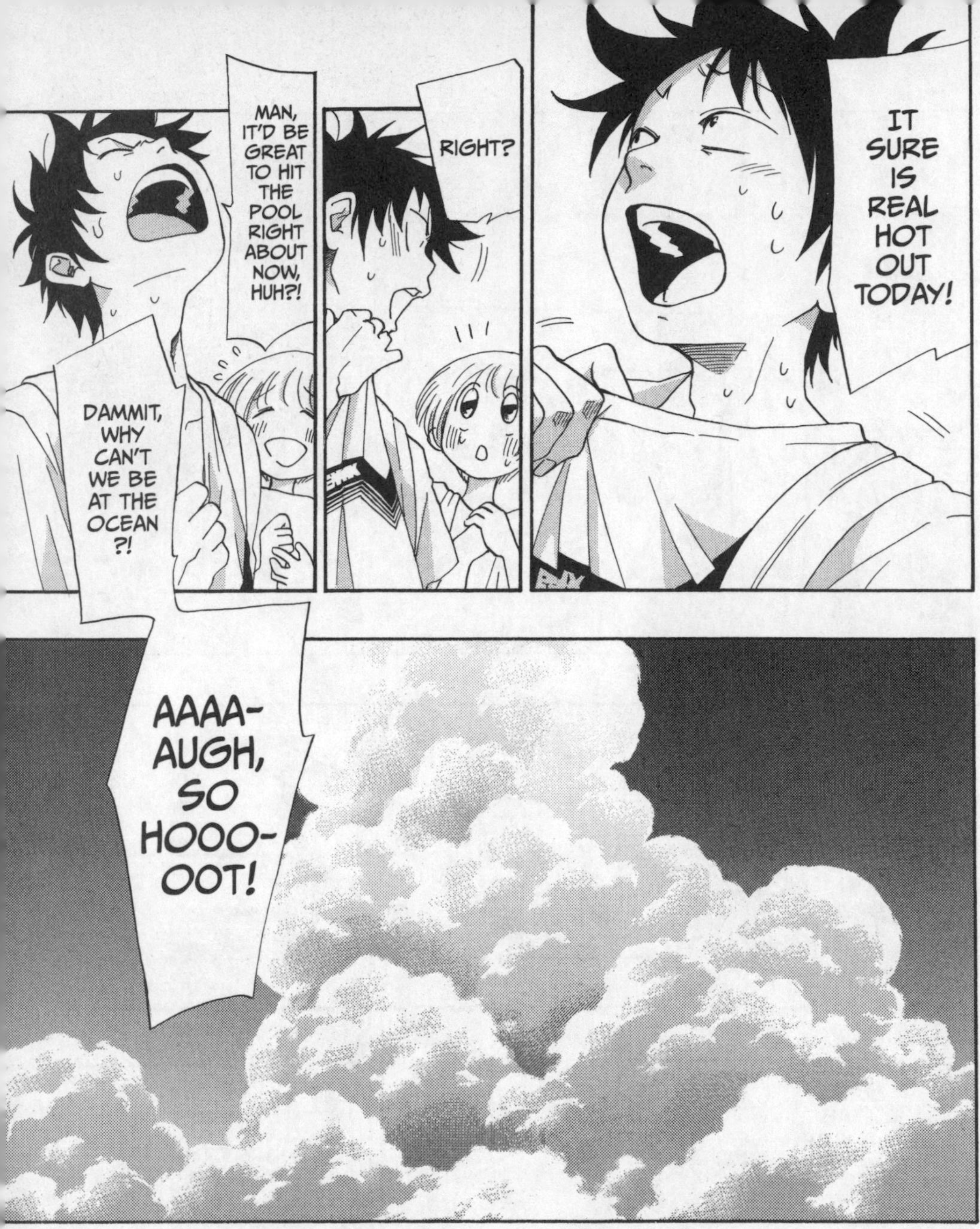
IT SURE IS REAL HOT OUT TODAY!
RIGHT?
MAN, IT'D BE GREAT TO HIT THE POOL RIGHT ABOUT NOW, HUH?!
DAMMIT, WHY CAN'T WE BE AT THE OCEAN?!
AAAA-AUGH, SO HOOOO-OOT!

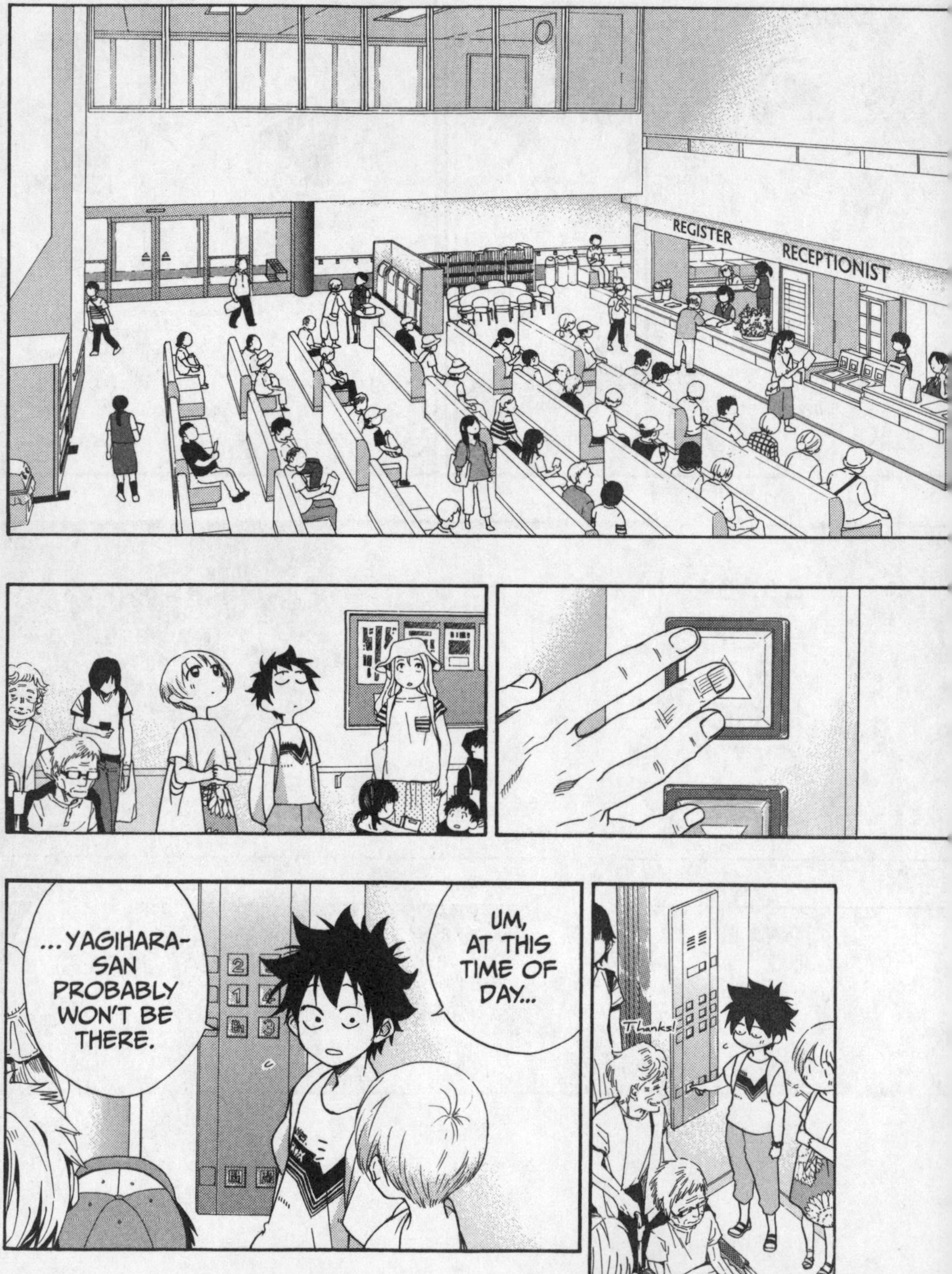
REGISTER
RECEPTIONIST
T-Thanks!
UM, AT THIS TIME OF DAY...
...YAGIHARA-SAN PROBABLY WON'T BE THERE.

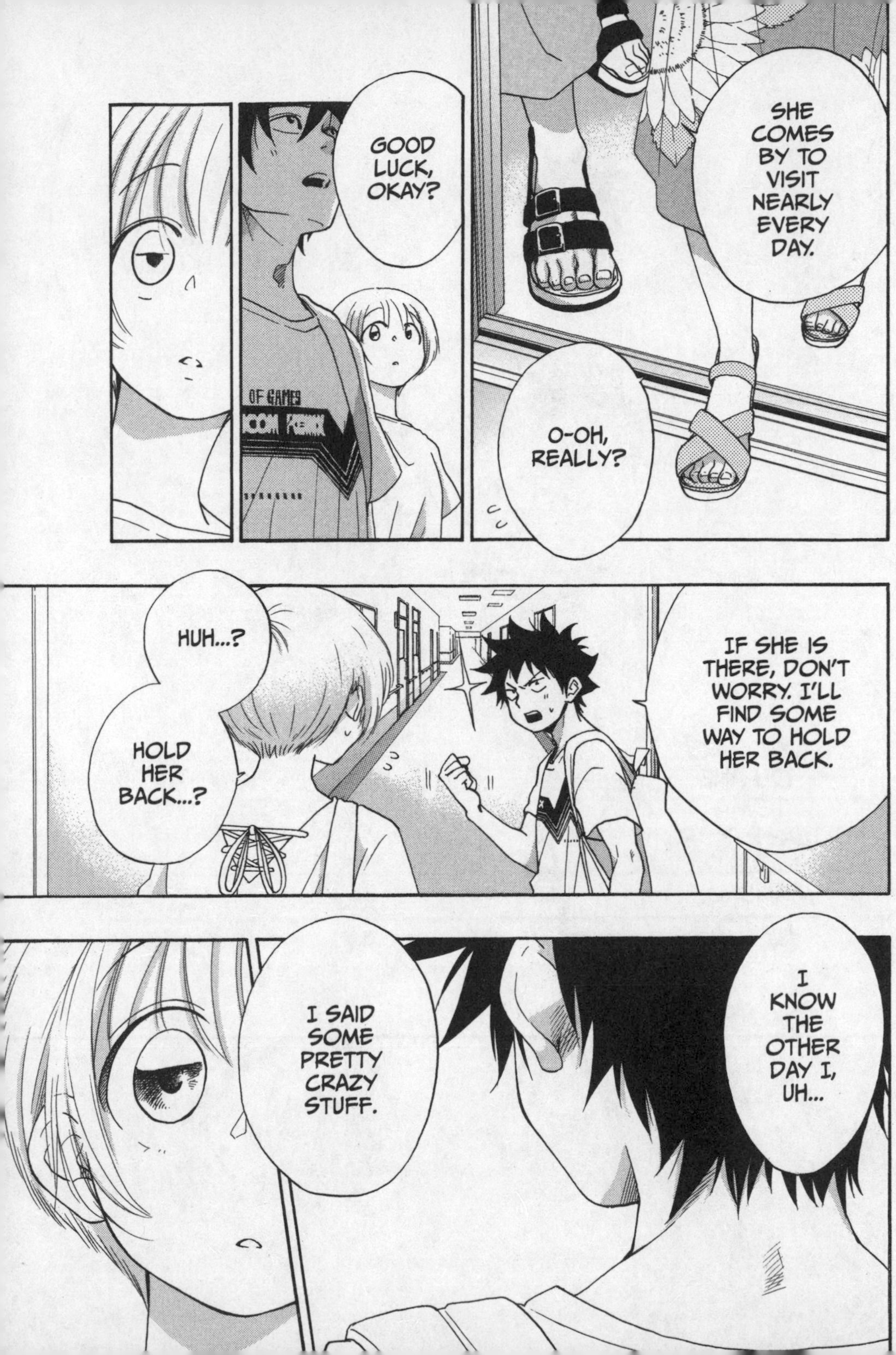
SHE COMES BY TO VISIT NEARLY EVERY DAY.
O-OH, REALLY?
GOOD LUCK, OKAY?
IF SHE IS THERE, DON'T WORRY. I'LL FIND SOME WAY TO HOLD HER BACK.
HUH...?
HOLD HER BACK...?
I KNOW THE OTHER DAY I, UH...
I SAID SOME PRETTY CRAZY STUFF.

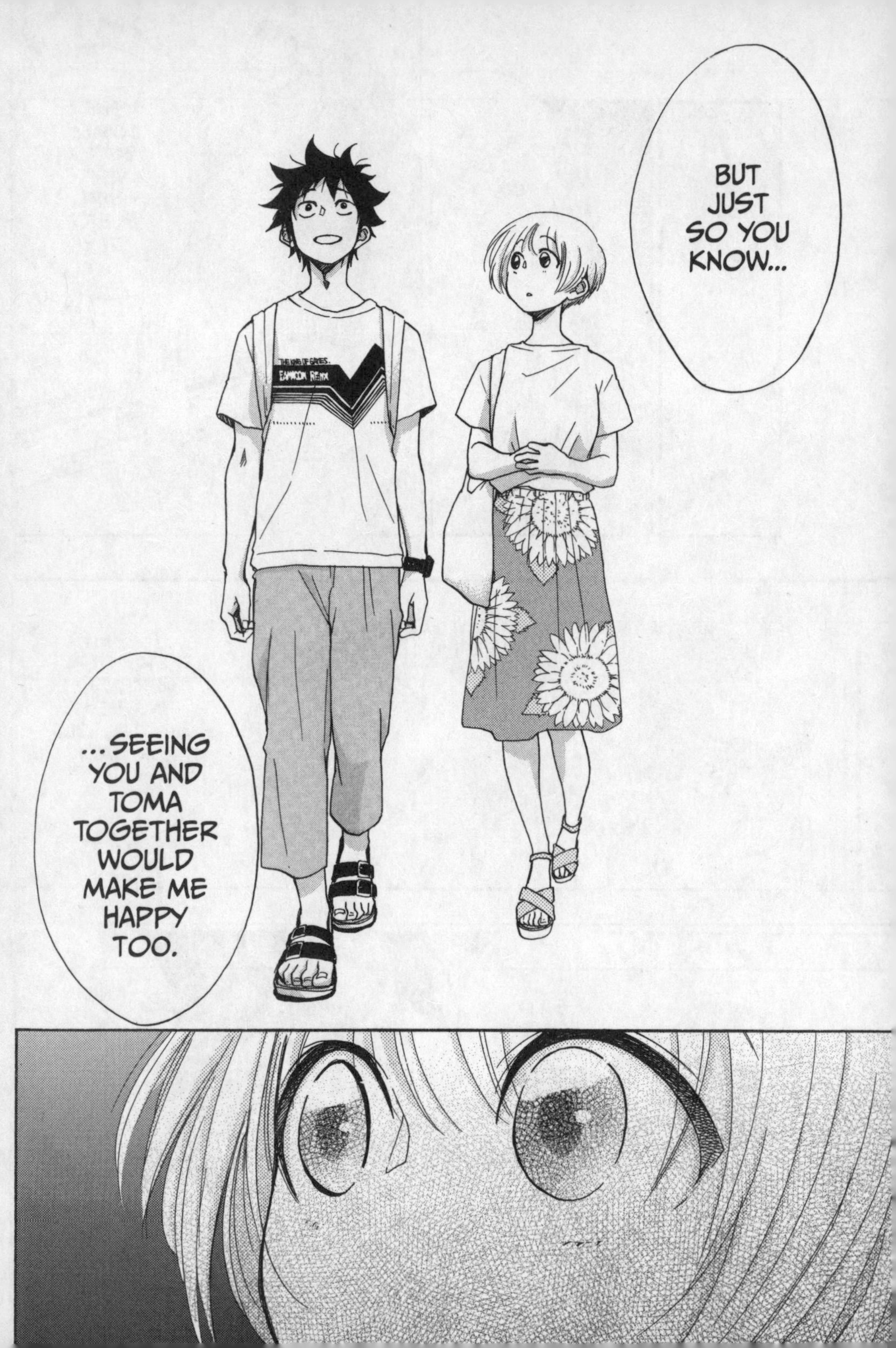
BUT JUST SO YOU KNOW...
...SEEING YOU AND TOMA TOGETHER WOULD MAKE ME HAPPY TOO.

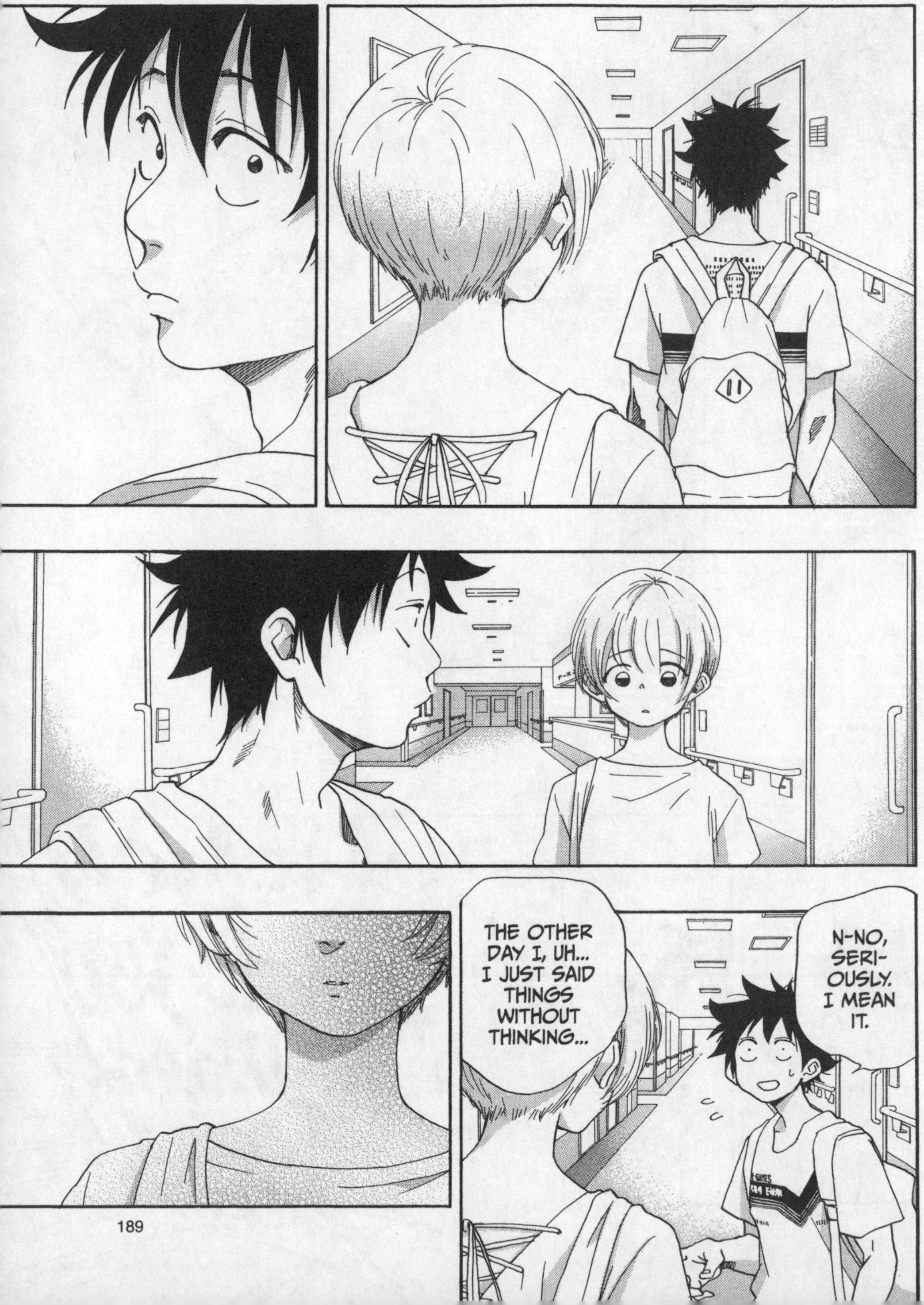
N-NO, SERI-OUSLY. I MEAN IT.
THE OTHER DAY I, UH... I JUST SAID THINGS WITHOUT THINKING...

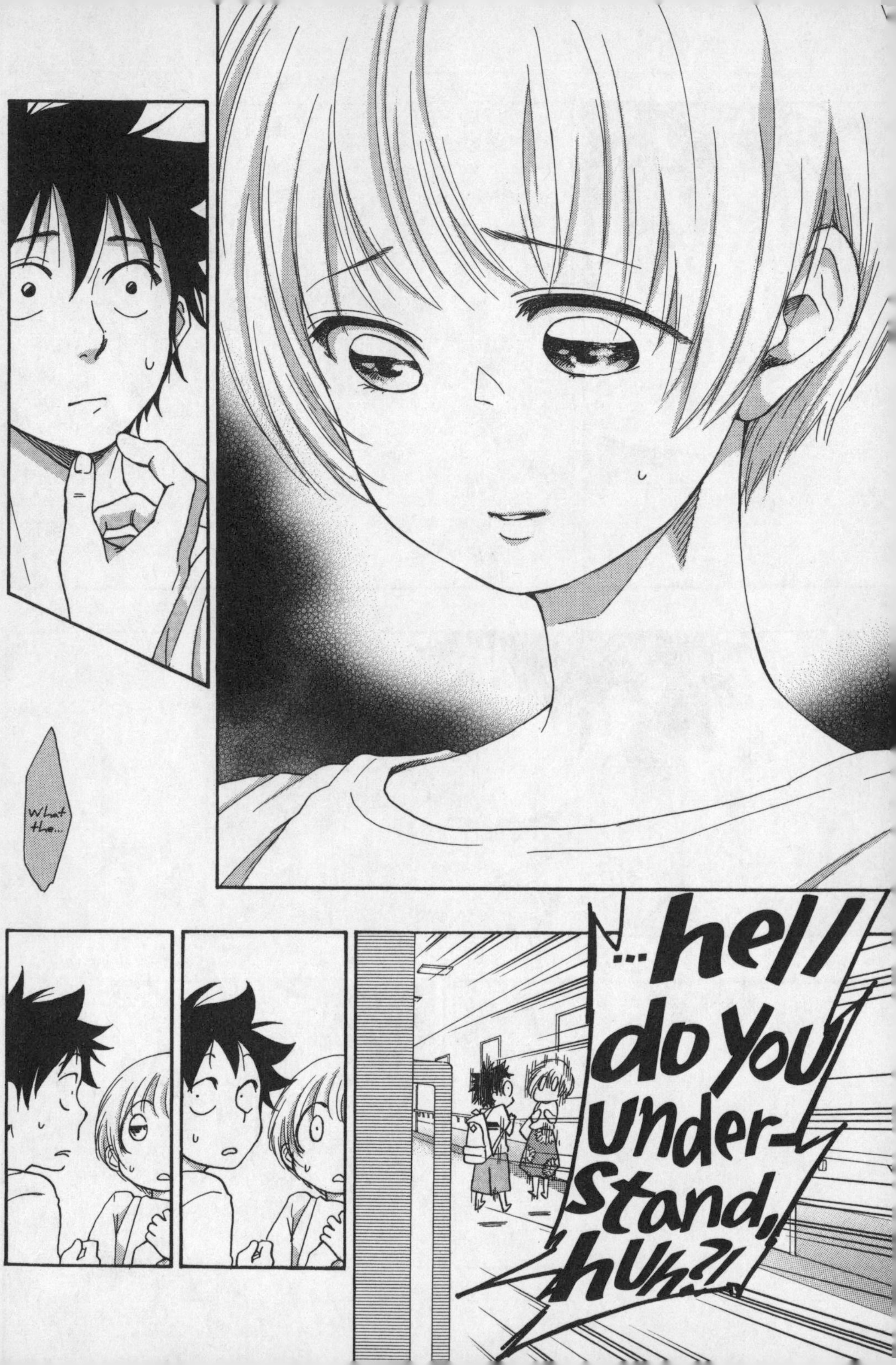

What the...
...hell do you under-stand, huh?!

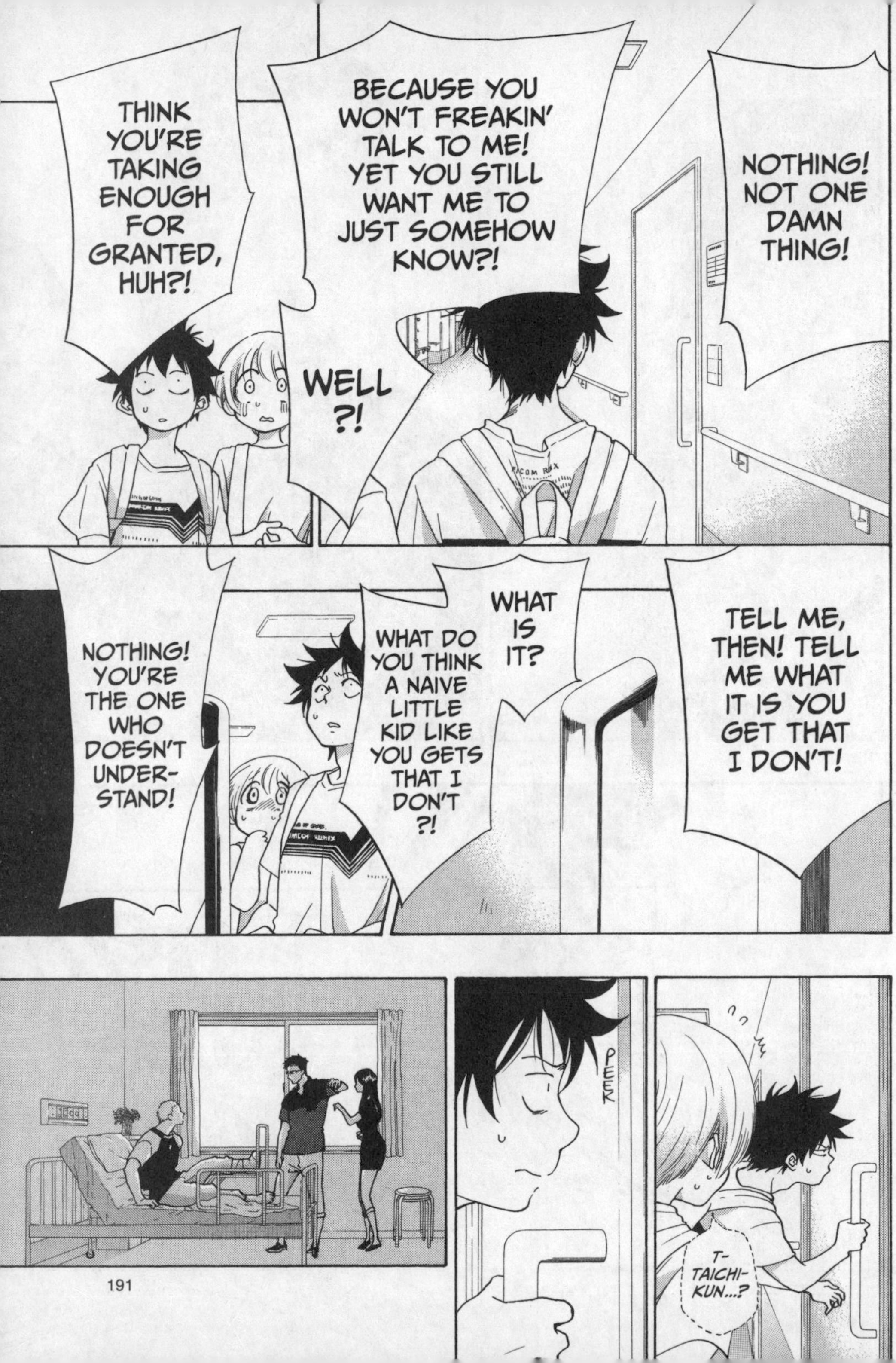
NOTHING! NOT ONE DAMN THING!
BECAUSE YOU WON'T FREAKIN' TALK TO ME! YET YOU STILL WANT ME TO JUST SOMEHOW KNOW?!
THINK YOU'RE TAKING ENOUGH FOR GRANTED, HUH?!
WELL?!
TELL ME, THEN! TELL ME WHAT IT IS YOU GET THAT I DON'T!
WHAT IS IT?
WHAT DO YOU THINK A NAIVE LITTLE KID LIKE YOU GETS THAT I DON'T?!
NOTHING! YOU'RE THE ONE WHO DOESN'T UNDER-STAND!
PEEK
T-TAICHI-KUN...?

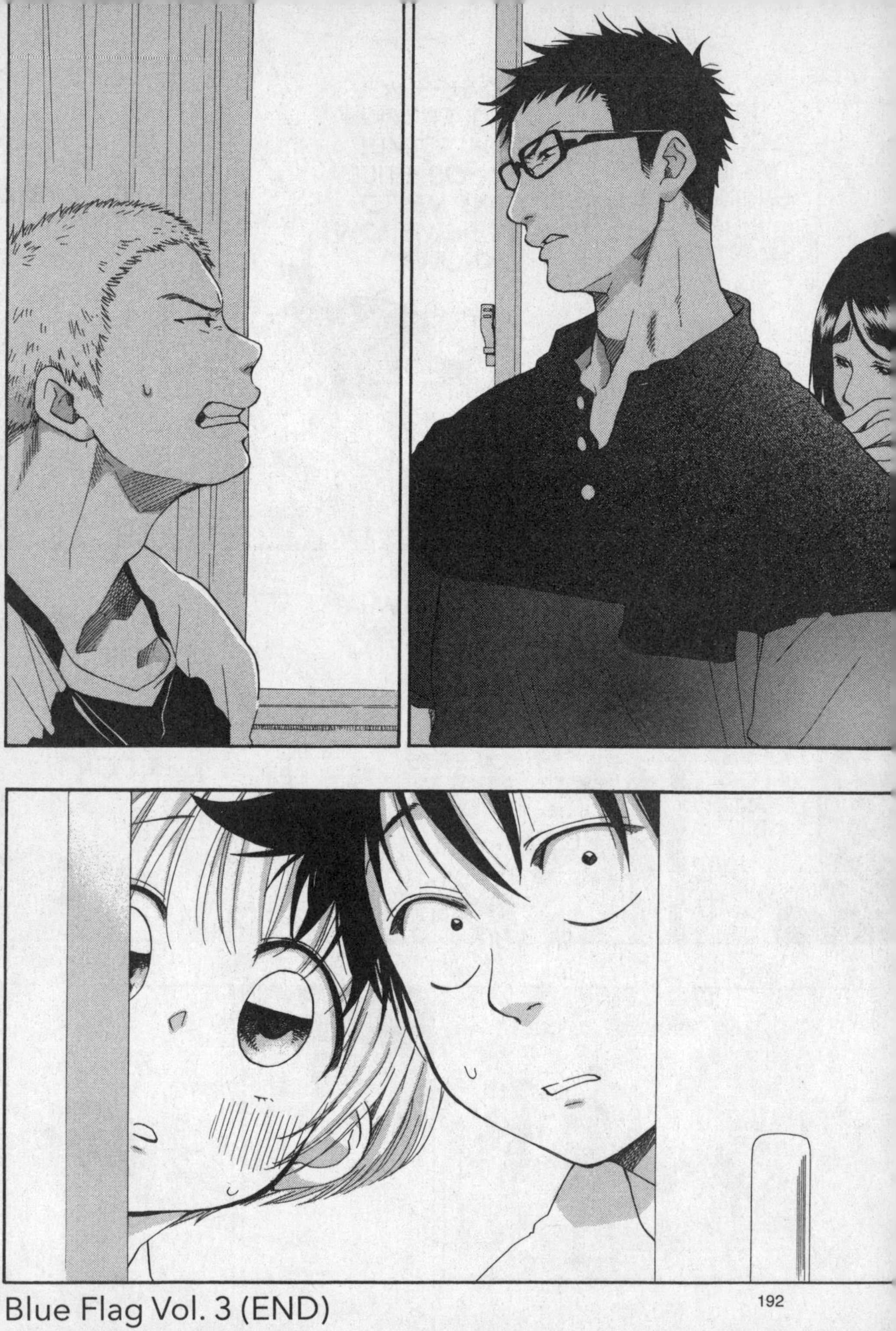

Blue Flag Vol. 3 (END)

Bonus Story
BLUE SKETCHES

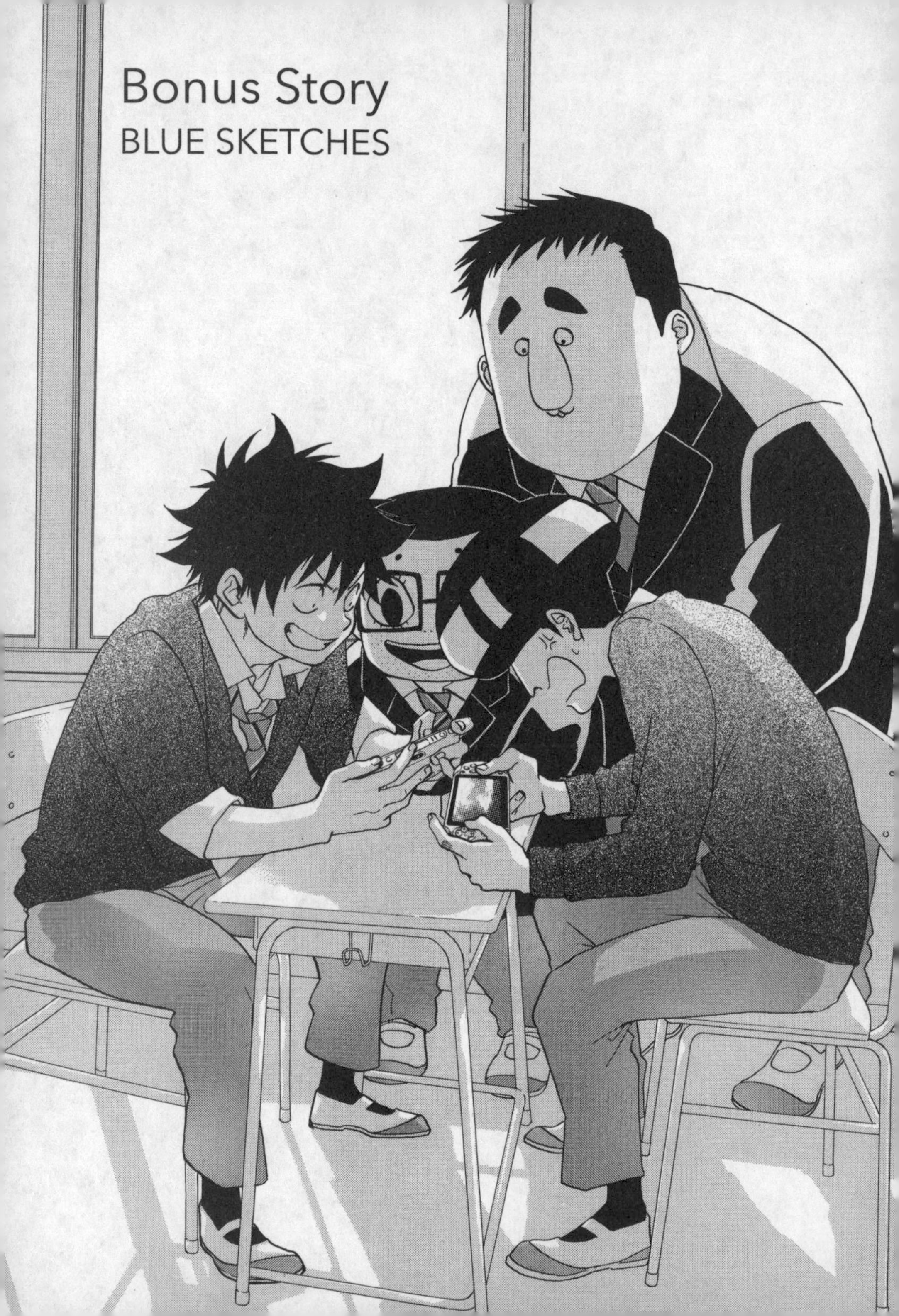

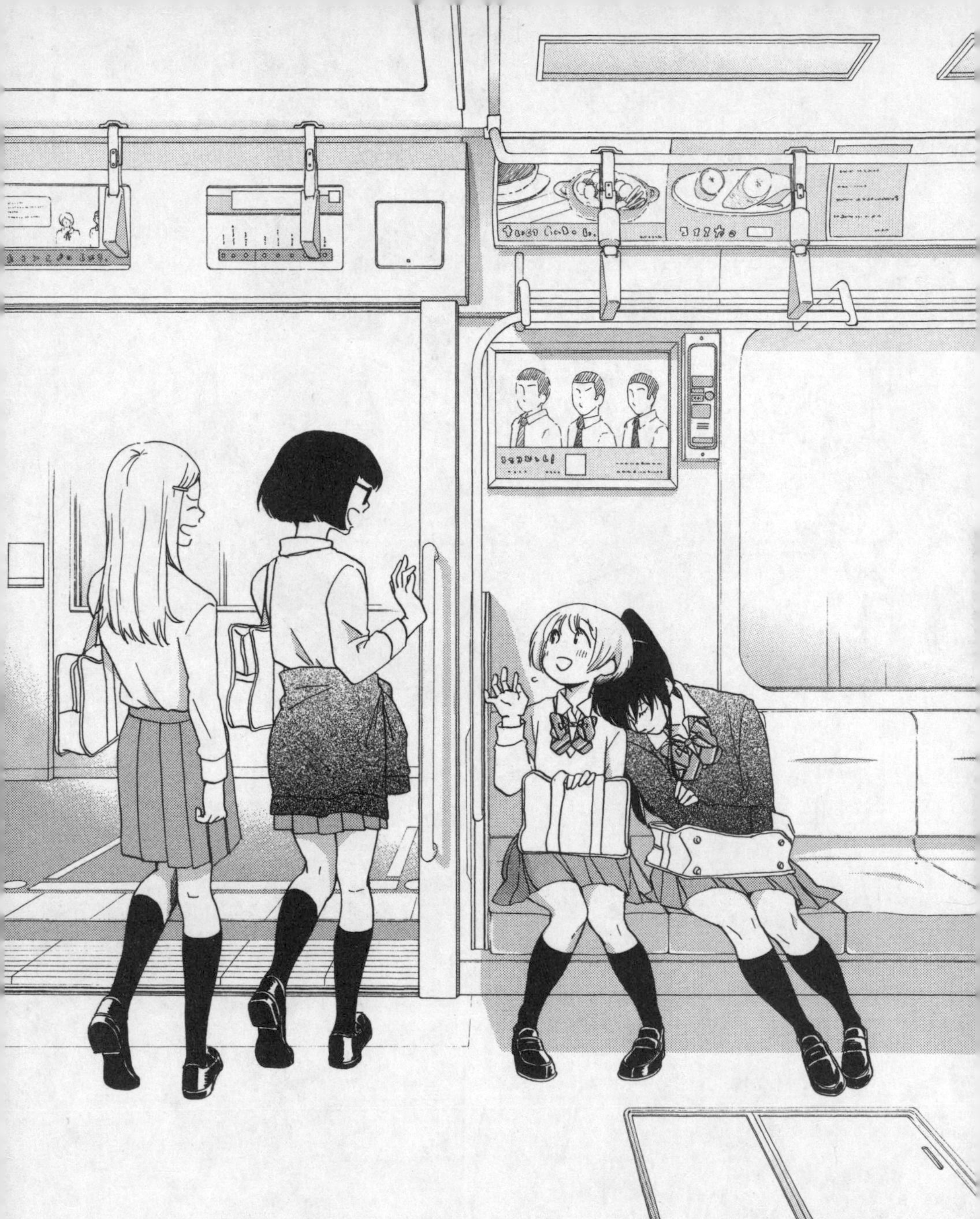

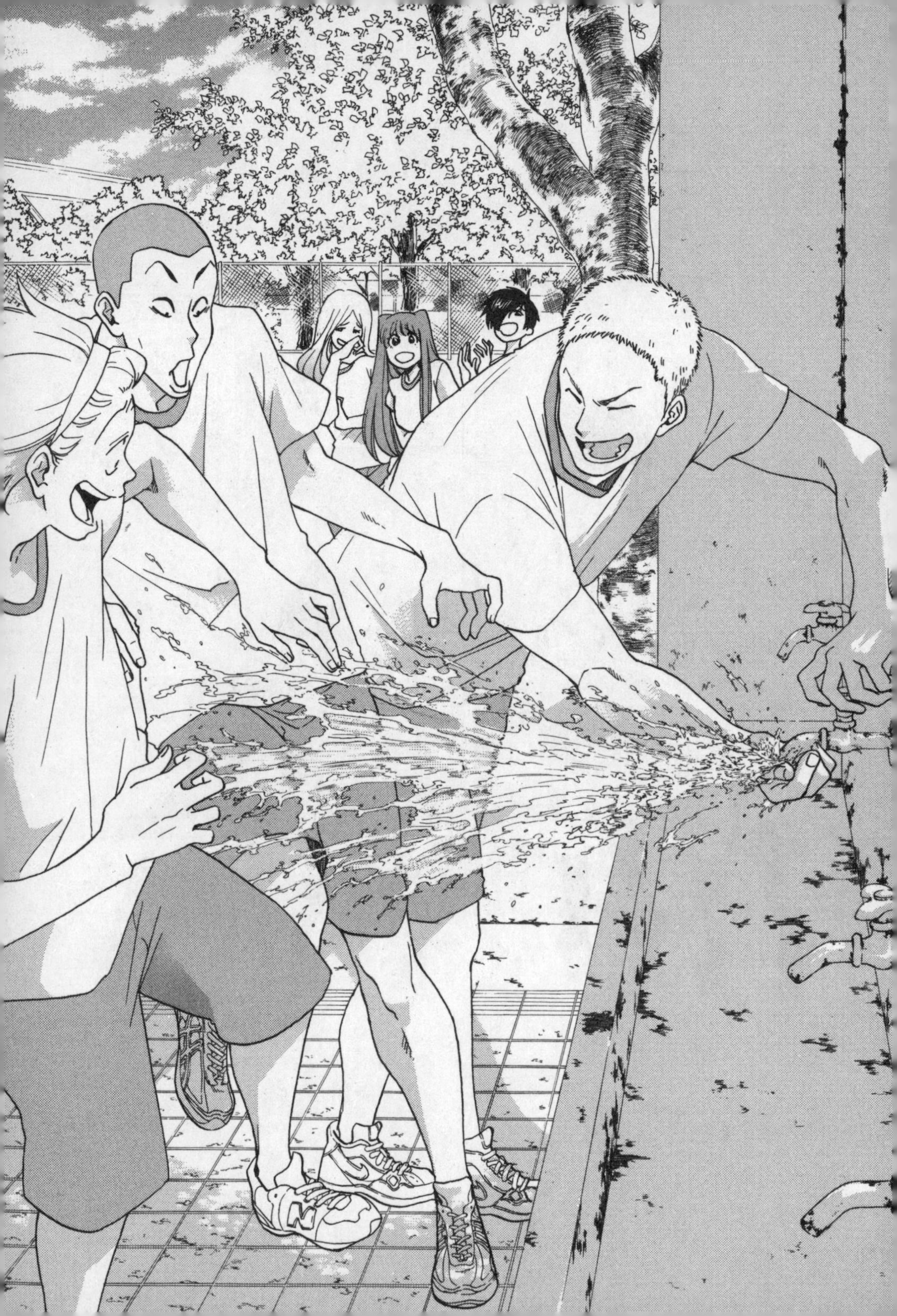

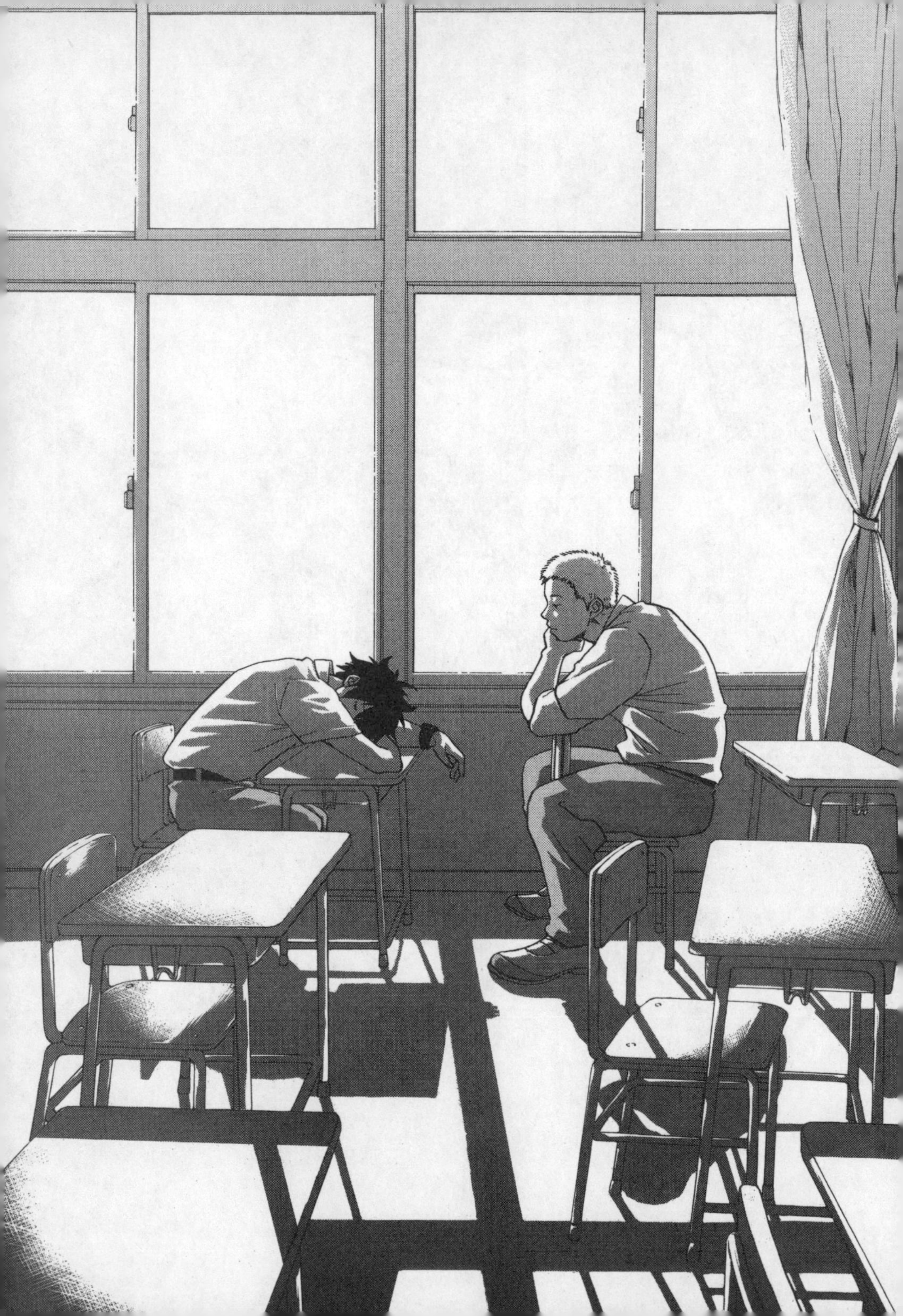

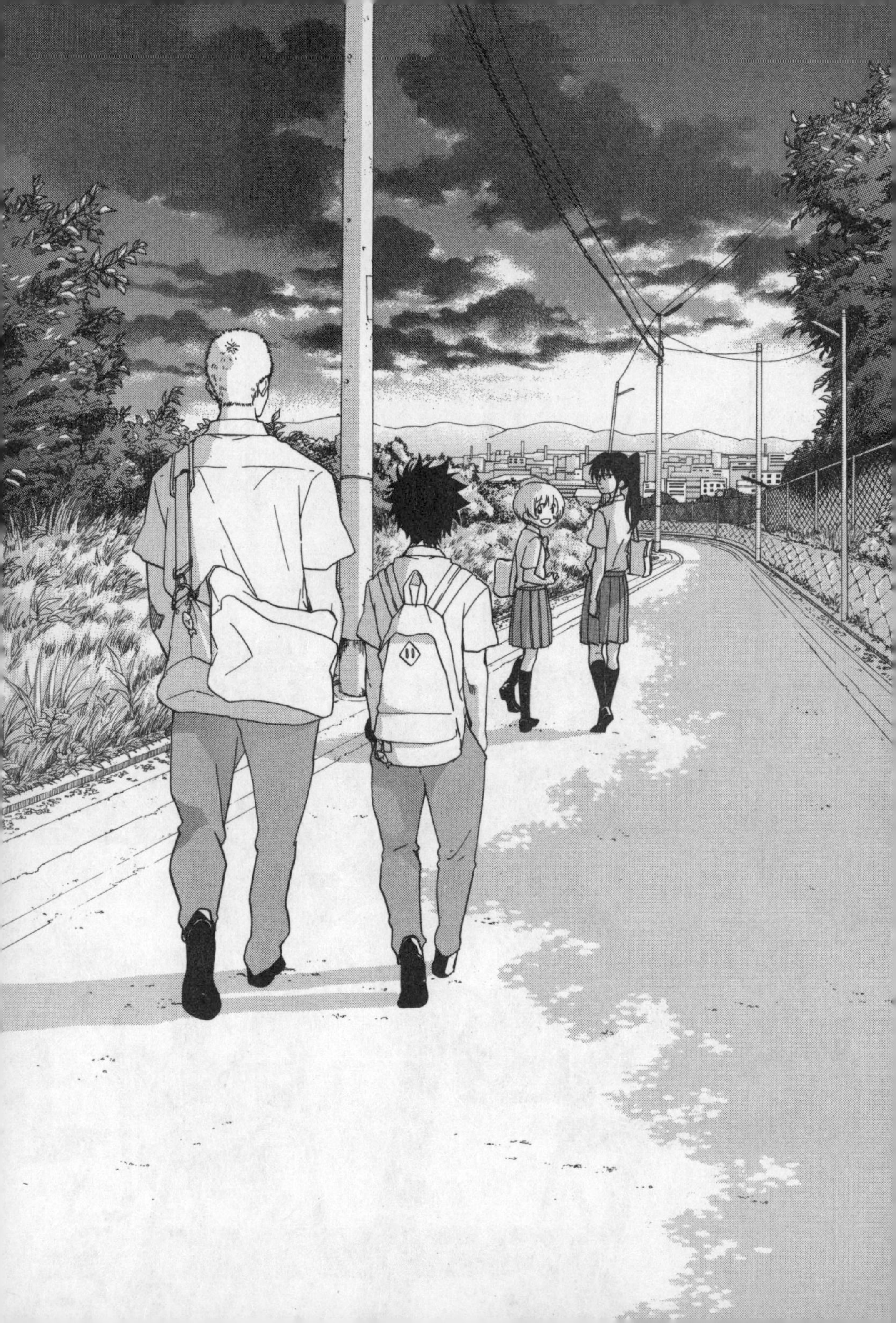

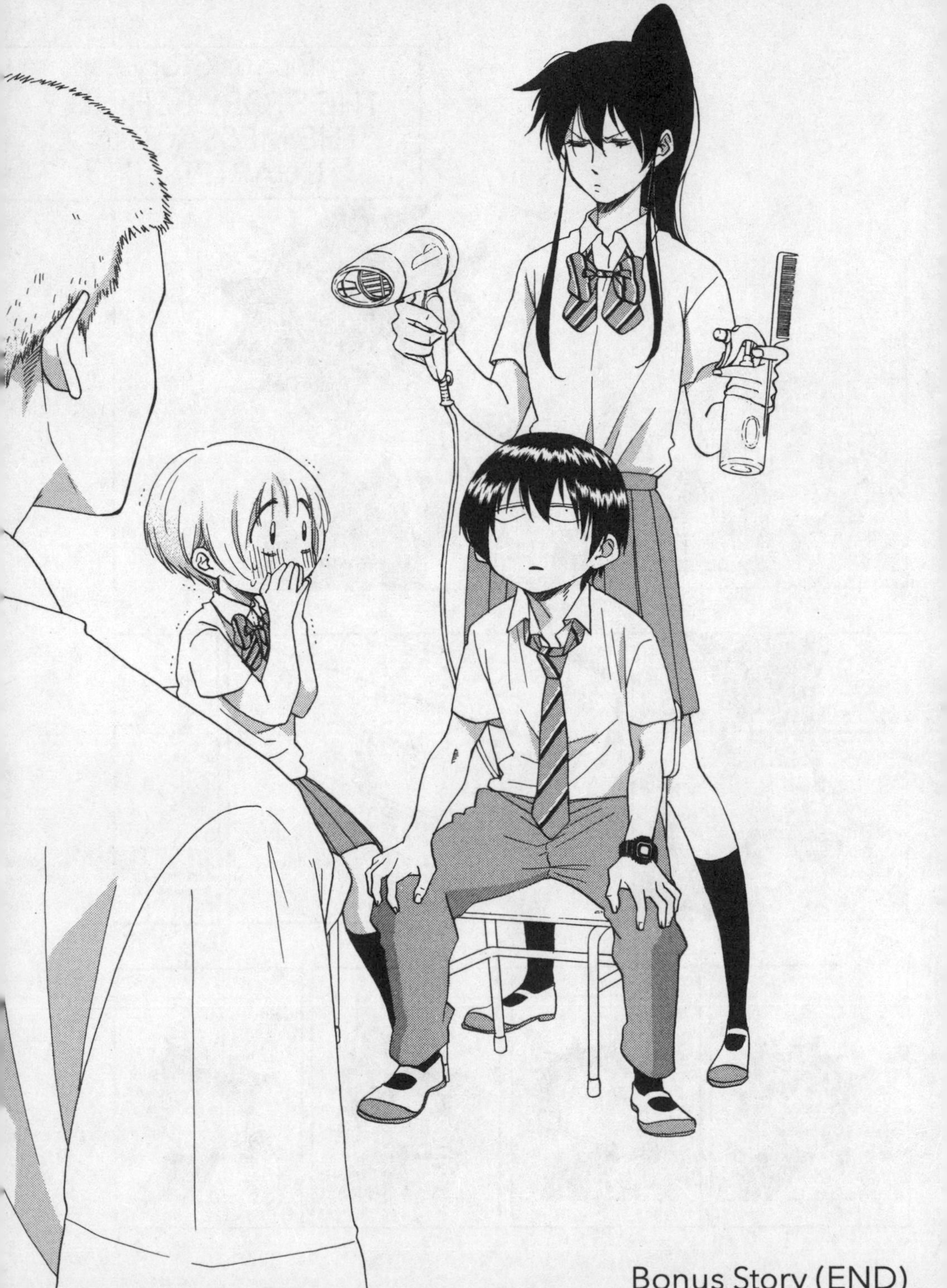

Bonus Story (END)

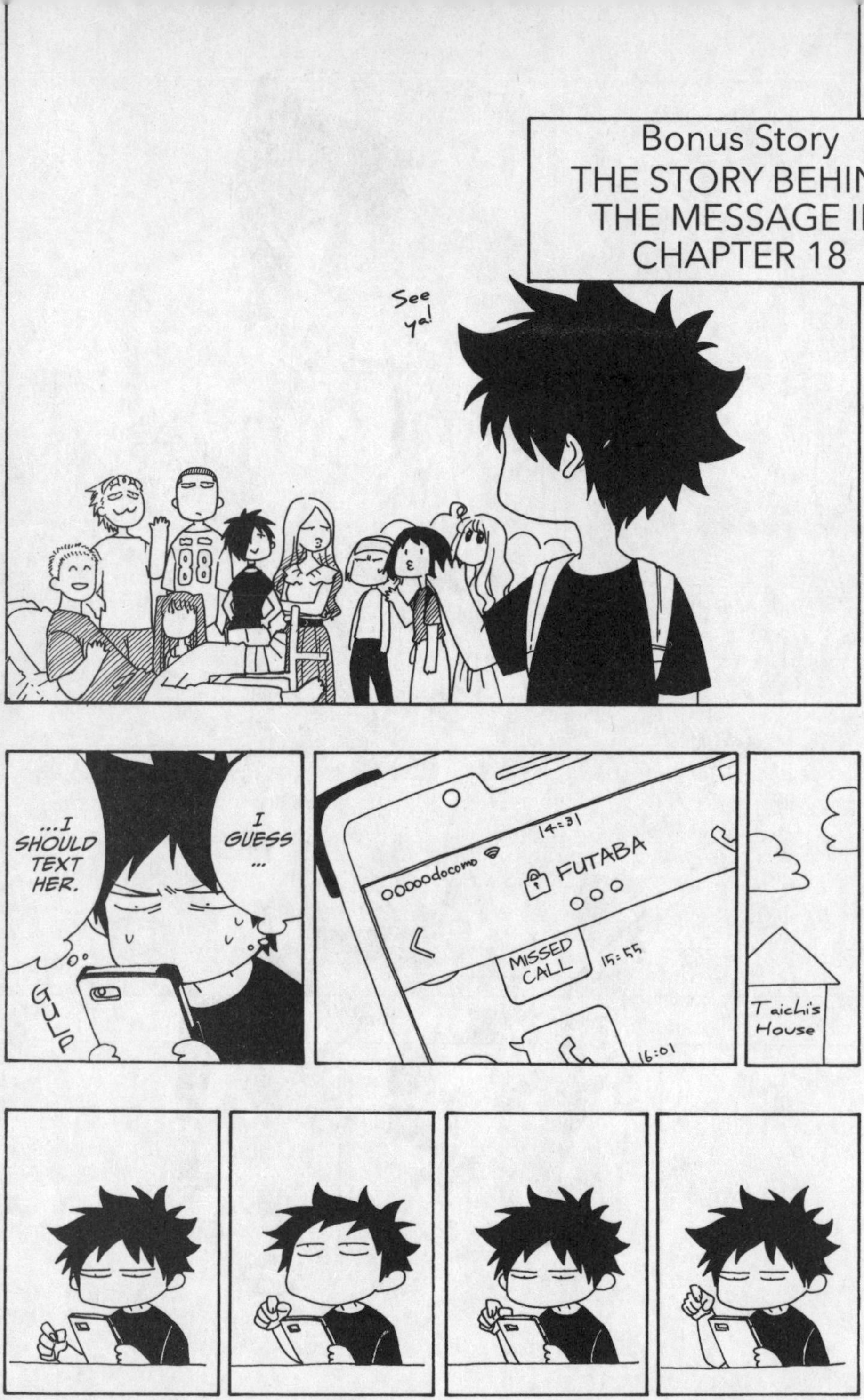
Bonus Story
THE STORY BEHIND THE MESSAGE IN CHAPTER 18
See ya!
Taichi's House
14:31
OOOOOdocomo
FUTABA
MISSED CALL
15:55
16:01
I GUESS...
...I SHOULD TEXT HER.
GULP

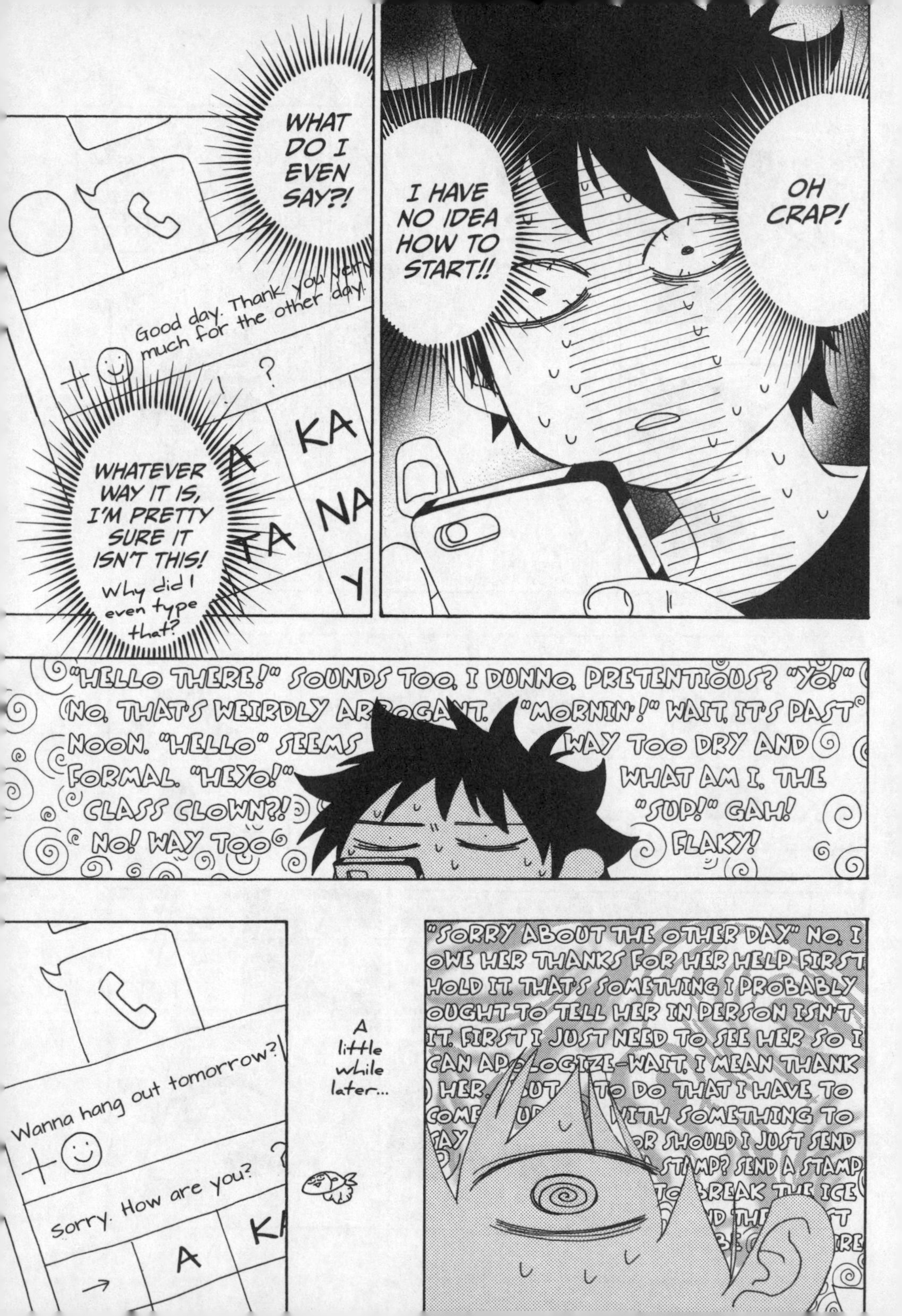
OH CRAP!
I HAVE NO IDEA HOW TO START!!
WHAT DO I EVEN SAY?!
Good day. Thank you very much for the other day.
KA
NA
TA
Y
WHATEVER WAY IT IS, I'M PRETTY SURE IT ISN'T THIS!
Why did I even type that?
"HELLO THERE!" SOUNDS TOO, I DUNNO, PRETENTIOUS? "YO!" NO, THAT'S WEIRDLY AR GANT. "MORNIN'!" WAIT, IT'S PAST NOON. "HELLO" SEEMS WAY TOO DRY AND FORMAL. "HEYO!" WHAT AM I, THE CLASS CLOWN?! "SUP!" GAH! NO! WAY TOO FLAKY!
"SORRY ABOUT THE OTHER DAY." NO, I OWE HER THANKS FOR HER HELP FIRST. HOLD IT. THAT'S SOMETHING I PROBABLY OUGHT TO TELL HER IN PERSON ISN'T IT. FIRST I JUST NEED TO SEE HER SO I CAN AP LOGIZE—WAIT, I MEAN THANK HER. UT TO DO THAT I HAVE TO COME WITH SOMETHING TO SAY OR SHOULD I JUST SEND STAMP? SEND A STAMP TO BREAK THE ICE
A little while later...
Wanna hang out tomorrow?
Sorry. How are you?
A
KA

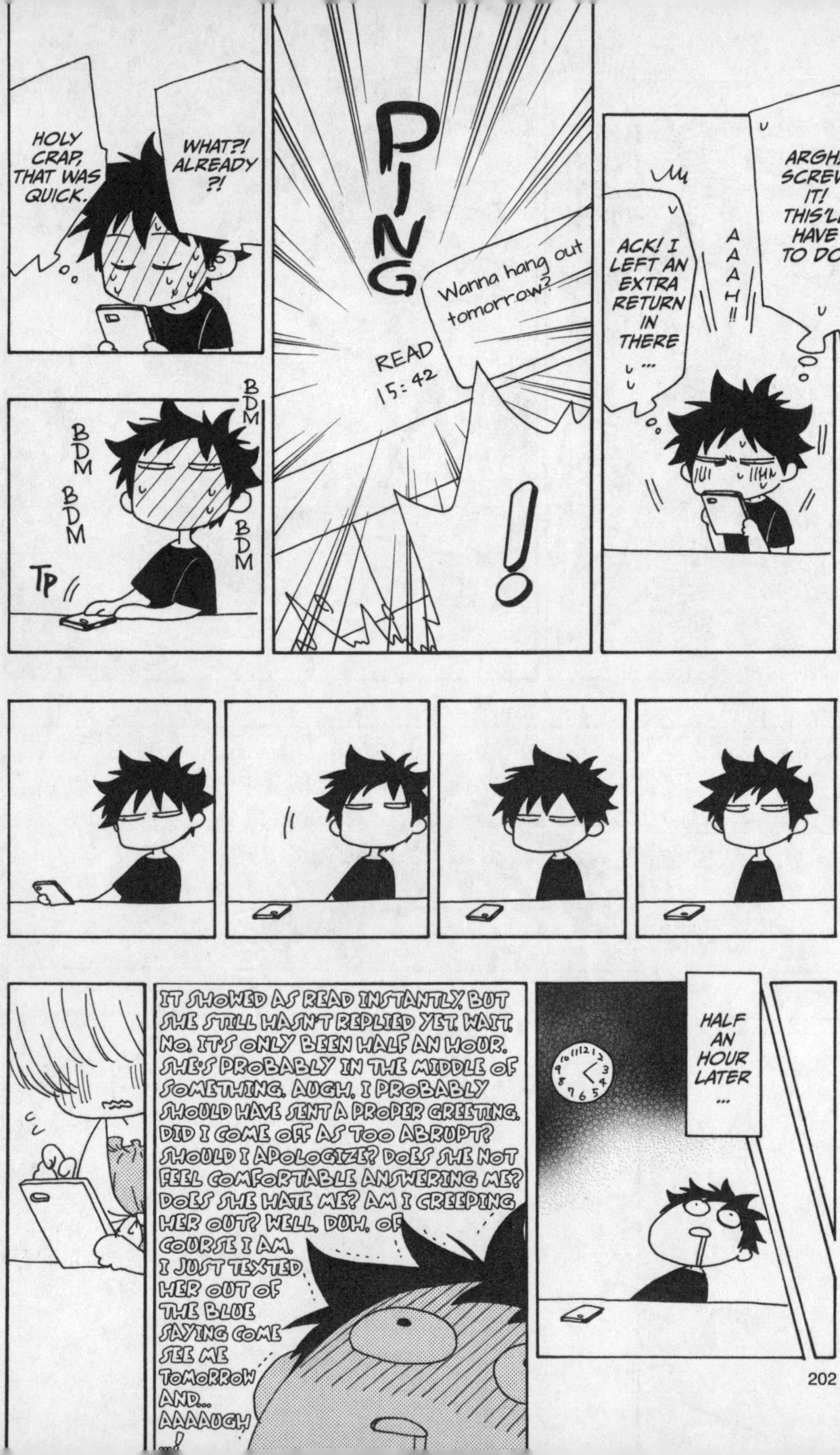
ARGH! SCREW IT! THIS'LL HAVE TO DO!
AAAAH!!
ACK! I LEFT AN EXTRA RETURN IN THERE...
PING
Wanna hang out tomorrow?
READ 15:42
!
WHAT?! ALREADY?!
HOLY CRAP, THAT WAS QUICK.
BDM BDM
BDM BDM
BDM BDM
TP
HALF AN HOUR LATER...
IT SHOWED AS READ INSTANTLY, BUT SHE STILL HASN'T REPLIED YET. WAIT, NO. IT'S ONLY BEEN HALF AN HOUR. SHE'S PROBABLY IN THE MIDDLE OF SOMETHING. AUGH, I PROBABLY SHOULD HAVE SENT A PROPER GREETING. DID I COME OFF AS TOO ABRUPT? SHOULD I APOLOGIZE? DOES SHE NOT FEEL COMFORTABLE ANSWERING ME? DOES SHE HATE ME? AM I CREEPING HER OUT? WELL, DUH, OF COURSE I AM. I JUST TEXTED HER OUT OF THE BLUE SAYING COME SEE ME TOMORROW AND... AAAAUGH!

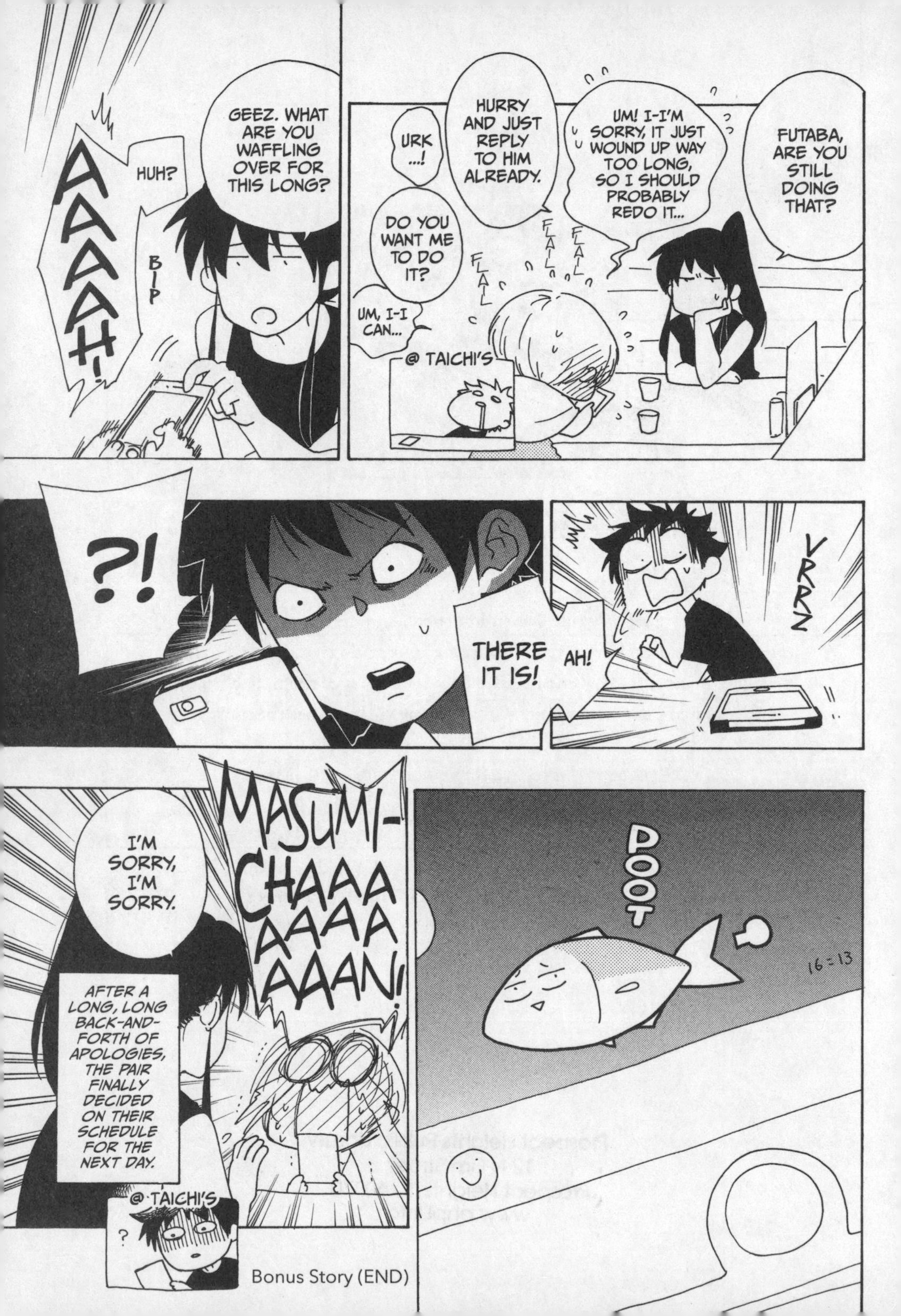
FUTABA, ARE YOU STILL DOING THAT?
UM! I-I'M SORRY, IT JUST WOUND UP WAY TOO LONG, SO I SHOULD PROBABLY REDO IT...
FLAIL
FLAIL
FLAIL
HURRY AND JUST REPLY TO HIM ALREADY.
URK ...!
DO YOU WANT ME TO DO IT?
UM, I-I CAN...
@ TAICHI'S
GEEZ. WHAT ARE YOU WAFFLING OVER FOR THIS LONG?
HUH?
BIP
AAAAH!
VRRZ
AH!
THERE IT IS!
?!
POOT
16:13
MASUMI-CHAAAAAAAAAAN!
I'M SORRY, I'M SORRY.
AFTER A LONG, LONG BACK-AND-FORTH OF APOLOGIES, THE PAIR FINALLY DECIDED ON THEIR SCHEDULE FOR THE NEXT DAY.
@ TAICHI'S
?

Bonus Story (END)

KAITO

I used to play games when I needed a break from work,
but lately I've been having trouble finding time to do that. I keep buying
new games, but I still haven't been able to open most of them. Right now,
my staff are the ones who are enjoying my video games the most.

*KAITO began his manga career at the age of 20, when
his one-shot "Happy Magi" debuted in* Weekly Shonen Jump.
He published the series Cross Manage *in 2012. In 2015,
he returned to* Weekly Shonen Jump *with* Buddy Strike.
KAITO started work on Blue Flag *in* Jump+ *in 2017.*

Prospect Heights Public Library
12 N Elm Street
Prospect Heights, IL 60070
www.phpl.info